PRESCHOOL AND EARLY CHILDHOOD TREATMENT DIRECTIONS

ADVANCES IN SCHOOL PSYCHOLOGY

Edited by
Maribeth Gettinger
Stephen N. Elliott
Thomas R. Kratochwill

Preschool and Early Childhood Treatment Directions

PRESCHOOL AND EARLY CHILDHOOD TREATMENT DIRECTIONS

Edited by
MARIBETH GETTINGER
STEPHEN N. ELLIOTT
THOMAS R. KRATOCHWILL
University of Wisconsin—Madison

LEA LAWRENCE ERLBAUM ASSOCIATES, PUBLISHERS
1992   Hillsdale, New Jersey   Hove and London

Lawrence Erlbaum Associates, Inc., Publishers
365 Broadway
Hillsdale, New Jersey 07642

Library of Congress Cataloging-in-Publication Data

Preschool and early childhood treatment directions / [edited by]
    Maribeth Gettinger, Stephen N. Elliott, Thomas R. Kratochwill.
       p. cm. — (Advances in school psychology)
    Includes bibliographical references and index.
    ISBN 0-8058-0757-8
    1. Early childhood education—United States. 2. School
psychology. I. Gettinger, Maribeth. II. Elliott, Stephen N.
III. Kratochwill, Thomas R. IV. Series: Advances in school
psychology (Unnumbered)
LB1139.25.P75   1992
372.21′0973—dc20
                                                 91-47582
                                                     CIP

Printed in the United States of America
10 9 8 7 6 5 4 3 2 1

This series is dedicated to improved services to children
and to schools, and especially to Tyler Thomas.
Thomas R. Kratochwill

Dedicated to my sons, Dustin Rhodes and Andrew Taylor,
and to my loving wife, Anita.
Stephen N. Elliott

To my boys, Brad, Trevor, and Grady.
Maribeth Gettinger

Contributors

(Numbers in parentheses indicate the pages on which the author's contribution begins.)

Douglas H. Clements (187)
State University of New York at
   Buffalo
Buffalo, NY

Kristin Droege (113)
University of California, Los Angeles
Los Angeles, CA

Joan L. Ershler (7)
University of Wisconsin-Madison
Madison, WI

Carollee Howes (113)
University of California, Los Angeles
Los Angeles, CA

Bonnie Nastasi (187)
Illinois State University
Normal, IL

Sheri L. Nimetz (151)
University of Virginia
Charlottesville, VA

Kathleen D. Paget (89)
University of South Carolina
Columbia, SC

Leslie Phillipsen (113)
University of California, Los Angeles
Los Angeles, CA

Robert C. Pianta (151)
University of Virginia
Charlottesville, VA

Cathy F. Telzrow (55)
Cuyahoga Special Education Service
   Center
Cleveland, OH

Advisory Board

Contents

Preface

In Volumes I through VIII, the *Advances in School Psychology* has taken a broad-based focus to account for the diversity in school psychology research, theory, and practice. Each of these previous volumes included original reviews of diverse literature which dealt with recent developments relevant to the field of school psychology. With the publication of this volume, the focus of the *Advances* will change. Each volume will now adopt a specific thematic focus and include reviews directly related to a common theme. For the first volume in this thematic series, we have focused on the topic of early childhood education and treatment directions. The chapters in this volume address a range of specific topics and research that represent advances in the field of early childhood services for school psychology.

Appreciation is extended to the advisory board members and the contributing authors. We also thank Karen Kraemer for her assistance in the preparation of this volume.

Thomas R. Kratochwill
Stephen N. Elliott
Maribeth Gettinger

Overview

Maribeth Gettinger
Stephen N. Elliott
Thomas R. Kratochwill
University of Wisconsin-Madison

The provision of early childhood educational and psychological services has been an area of considerable growth over the past 25 years. The field of school psychology has been affected by the burgeoning interest in preschool and early childhood services. The passage of Public Law 99-457, in particular, offered a strong impetus for expanding research, practice, and training in school psychology to incorporate early childhood services. In effect, PL 99-457 mandates the provision of free, appropriate public education to children with handicaps between the ages of 3 and 5 and has initiated the development of service delivery models for young children. As a result of trends in both public policy and clinical practices, school psychologists increasingly are being faced with issues surrounding the provision of comprehensive services to preschool-age children and their families.

Professionals in psychology, education, and medicine have long been aware of the importance of assessment and intervention during children's preschool years. According to Guralnick and Bennett (1987), developmental research supports the notion that preschool years represent a critical period in children's lives. Early childhood is a time during which environmental events can substantially affect children's long-term development. For example, researchers have learned that parental characteristics during the early years, such as the quality and quantity of verbal interactions, are strongly associated with a child's development (Ludlow, 1981). Psychologists have also established connections between adverse environmental situations experienced during the preschool years, such as parental divorce or child abuse, and later social or personality development (Rutter, 1981). Furthermore, educational research, beginning with the classic studies of Kirk (1958) and Skeels (1966), has documented significant positive

1

effects of early intervention programs on children's social and cognitive development. More recent research has provided further support for the effectiveness of early intervention efforts, documenting that young children are susceptible to appropriate behavioral change and that early intervention may foster the acquisition of prerequisites for later learning (Casto & Mastropieri, 1986). In sum, research findings from both developmental psychology and educational research have served to initiate our current interest in and commitment to early childhood intervention.

A consequence of the recent trend toward preschool services is a growing need for professionals who are appropriately trained to address the assessment and intervention issues involved in early childhood programming. Two potential roles have evolved over recent years for school psychologists: (a) evaluating the extent to which risk factors may be present in young children's lives, such as socioemotional, family, or biological factors, and (b) developing effective prevention and intervention programs to respond to the individual needs of preschoolers who may be at risk for later learning or behavior problems. Many of the same principles and concepts underlying the provision of services to school-age children are also important in providing early childhood services. Although the basic assessment, consultation, and intervention skills school psychologists already possess can be applied to their work with preschool-age children, the content of these practices may differ in several ways. First, early childhood services are likely to be delivered in nonschool contexts and typically involve parents and other significant influences in a child's environment. In that the major objective of early intervention is to promote optimal development and primary prevention within the natural learning and social environment, an emphasis on the contributions of parents is understandable. Another difference for many school psychologists in the provision of early childhood services is the need to work collaboratively with professionals from many different disciplines, each having specialized clinical skills and research perspectives on services to young children and families. To take advantage of current opportunities for extending their role and to meet the challenge of early childhood service delivery, school psychologists must expand their professional skills and broaden their knowledge base.

A need for school psychologists to examine and integrate current information related to early childhood issues from multiple perspectives—educational, sociological, as well as psychological—precipitated the development of this volume of *Advances in School Psychology*. Each chapter presents a comprehensive review of a special topic in the area of preschool and early childhood intervention. Six topics were identified that collectively represent important developments for school psychology. These include: (a) current early childhood education program models; (b) preschool handicapped children; (c) parental involvement; (d) peers and socialization; (e) stress and coping; and (f) computers and young children. Although measurement and assessment issues are addressed within each topic, the primary emphasis across all chapters is on *treatment directions* in preschool and early childhood. [See Paget & Bracken, 1983, for discussion of preschool assessment issues.]

OVERVIEW OF CHAPTERS

A number of different service delivery approaches and exemplary model programs in early childhood education exist today. Many model programs were developed initially in response to public policy and legislation concerning the nature and availability of early childhood services. Since the initiation of national efforts in the 1960s toward model program development, our knowledge concerning appropriate educational experiences and effective instructional strategies for preschool-age children has increased significantly. Early childhood education and intervention is a rapidly growing area of scientific inquiry. Increasingly, research and theoretical viewpoints concerning children's learning and development, more than just policy issues, guide program development. Although program evaluation research provides general empirical support for the efficacy of early childhood education, there remains some debate regarding which theoretical perspectives and which program features are most critical for long-term effectiveness. This volume begins with a comparative review and analysis of the various program models which have developed over the past 30 years. In Chapter 1, Ershler provides a brief historical overview and rationale for early childhood education. Next, major theoretical perspectives in program development are discussed in relationship to three common dimensions: (a) assumptions and goals underlying each perspective, (b) curriculum, teacher role, and instructional methods; and (c) exemplary model programs and evaluative research. Finally, Ershler discusses some implications and directions for school psychology in terms of consultation, assessment, intervention, research, and training in early childhood education.

The number of young children with special educational needs who are receiving psychoeducational services before age 5 has been steadily increasing, particularly since the passage of PL 99-457 in 1986. Service delivery for handicapped preschoolers poses a unique challenge to psychologists working in schools. Early childhood-special education is a field in which intervention priorities and assessment procedures often differ from those of either special education for school-age children or regular early childhood education for normally developing preschoolers. Chapter 2 by Telzrow addresses several issues surrounding intervention for preschool children with special needs. Included in this chapter is a discussion of relevant federal policy legislation and a review of classification systems for preschool handicapped children. Telzrow points out that many measurement problems complicate school psychologists' efforts to identify special needs among young children. Problems include inadequate measurement precision, marked developmental variability among children, and the interactive effects of multiple influences on children's development. As with early education programs, several service delivery alternatives for young children with special needs are being implemented today. Although consultation is a common service delivery approach among school psychologists, out-of-school, center-based, and home-based models are being used more frequently in conjunction with early childhood services. As Telzrow notes, school psychologists comprise one of many types of professionals who face challenges in the years ahead as early childhood-special education continues to grow as a field.

We know that children grow and develop in a social environment. Infant research, in fact, suggests that children are social beings at birth. Newborns, for example, are observed to behave in ways that promote social contact and interaction with others through discriminative crying or gazing (Ainsworth, 1979). Traditionally, considerable attention has often been given to external social factors that impinge on a young child's development in either positive or negative ways. More recent views of children's early socioemotional development, however, highlight the child's contributions to social relationships. Bell (1976) proposed an interactional model of early childhood development in which the child's characteristics and temperament interact with those of his or her social world, including parents, peers, and other social-emotional environmental conditions. All environments may present risks or opportunities for development in early childhood years. It is young children's interaction with their environments that underlies cognitive, social, and emotional growth.

Chapters 3, 4, and 5 authors collectively address young children's development within social environments. In these three chapters, theoretical and empirical perspectives are offered concerning the role of parental involvement, peer relations, and stress and coping in young children's development. In Chapter 3, Paget discusses parental involvement and early childhood issues. She describes the historical and current milieu of parental involvement in early childhood services. The passage of 99-457 reflects a growing emphasis on family- and parent-focused approaches to working with young children. Paget provides a discussion of ways in which parents can be involved in special areas of their children's education and development, and reviews research related to various types of effective parental involvement and training programs with young children. Paget encourages school psychologists to utilize the family system as a major source of support and resources for meeting young children's individual needs.

In Chapter 4, Howes, Droege, and Phillipsen address the contributions of peers to socialization in early childhood. The development of peer relationships and friendships in the preschool years has been the focus of considerable research in recent years. In their chapter, Howes and her colleagues delineate what is known about social development and the role peers play in the socialization of preschool-age children. They also review research regarding how to foster positive peer relations among young children and how school psychologists might involve themselves in that process. Peers, like parents, are viewed as a critical influential component of young children's personal social network.

In Chapter 5, Pianta and Nimetz examine the developmental aspects of stress, the effects of stressors on preschool children, and the ways in which school psychologists can facilitate coping and adaptation among young children. Pianta and Nimetz integrate findings from empirical studies concerning several diverse problem areas, including poverty, abuse and neglect, divorce, and academic stressors, that may affect young children and their families. If early intervention programs are to be optimally effective, they cannot operate in isolation of children's social environment. Currently, there is a movement in early childhood beyond viewing the child as the sole focus of intervention to a consideration of the role of multiple social influences. This new perspective recognizes the interrelationship among the child, family, and broader social community. As emphasized in Chapters 3, 4, and 5, being able to assess and respond to the influence of parents, peers, and related environmental conditions are critical skills for school psychologists.

Several early childhood programs, especially those for mildly handicapped youngsters, have exploited the inherent advantages and motivational appeal of microcomputer technology. There has been a great deal of practitioner-oriented literature concerning computers and young children. This volume concludes with a chapter by Clements and Nastasi on computers and early childhood education. In Chapter 6, Clements and Nastasi provide an integration of principles and theories of early childhood education with computer practices. They support and describe the utilization of computers to operationalize what we know about early childhood learning strategies and principles. The authors also describe the effects and applications of microcomputer experiences for young children, to enhance both socioemotional development as well as cognitive and academic achievement.

We are witnessing tremendous growth and interest in the provision of services to preschool-age children. To date, more efforts have been directed toward devising and validating instruments that predict failure or success among preschoolers than on designing and evaluating approaches for treating them (Peterson, 1987). Although assessment is critical for meeting individual needs, the primary focus of the chapters in this volume is on fostering cognitive, academic, social, and emotional growth of young children. With the current emphasis on development, implementation, and evaluation of instructional programs and intervention models, it is an opportune time for school psychology to consider its role in early childhood and preschool service delivery.

REFERENCES

Ainsworth, M. D. S. (1979). Infant crying and maternal responsiveness. *Child Development, 50,* 1171–1190.

Bell, R. Q. (1976). Toward more comparability and generalizability of developmental research. *Child Development, 47,* 6–13.

Castro, G., & Mastropieri, M. A. (1986). The efficacy of early intervention programs: A meta-analysis. *Exceptional Children, 52,* 417–424.

Guralnick, M. J., & Bennett, F. C. (Eds.). (1987). *The effectiveness of early intervention for at-risk and handicapped children.* New York: Academic.

Kirk, S. A. (1958). *Early education for the mentally retarded: An experimental study.* Urbana, IL: University of Illinois Press.

Ludlow, B. (1981). Parent-infant interaction research. The argument for earlier intervention programs. *Journal of the Division for Early Childhood, 3,* 34–41.

Paget, K. D., & Bracken, B.A. (Eds.). (1983). *The psychoeducational assessment of the preschool child.* New York: Grune & Stratton.

Peterson, N. L. (1987). *Early intervention for handicapped and at-risk children: An introduction to early childhood-special education.* Denver: Love.

Rutter, M. (1981). Stress, coping, and development: Some issues and some questions. *Journal of Child Psychology and Psychiatry, 22,* 323–356.

Skeels, H. M. (1966). Adult status of children with contrasting early life experiences. *Monographs of the Society for Research in Child Development, 31*(3).

1 Model Programs and Service Delivery Approaches in Early Childhood Education

Joan L. Ershler
University of Wisconsin–Madison

HISTORY AND RATIONALE
FOR EARLY CHILDHOOD EDUCATION

Discussions about the value of early education and how best to provide early education services have had a recurring presence in the literature. For over 2,000 years, issues related to the "why" and "how" of teaching preschool-aged children have engaged philosophers, psychologists, educators, and parents (Borstellman, 1983). Contemporary early educators attempt to grapple with issues similar to those that have occupied their predecessors. Because there are valuable insights to be gained by understanding "our professional ancestors," it is important to make note of some of the sources of the ideas and questions still being addressed in early childhood programs (Hooper, 1987).

One way to conceptualize the rationale for providing early education services is to contrast two historical schools of thought whose legacy is expressed in current service delivery approaches in early childhood education (Carter, 1987). Plato expressed the first of these perspectives, emphasizing the "equalizing" nature of public education (Plato, 1945). Advocating placing children early in life in state-run schools, he believed that educating children uniformly would promote the egalitarian growth of abilities and would diminish the influence of less than desirable home environments. In contrast, in the 17th century Comenius proposed that mothers were the best educators of their young children (Sadler, 1969). Comenius' belief in the educational benefits that mothers' emotional, energy, and time commitments provided to their children led him to formulate guidelines for educating young children in their homes.

Plato's and Comenius' views may be conceptualized as two poles on the continuum of school-based versus home-based approaches in early education. Current issues related to the school–home relationships in the education of young children reflect this continuum. Thus, some early educators express their concern with ways to involve parents in school programs to enhance their children's learning (e.g., Grotberg, 1972). Others are interested in developing programs that support or complement the training that families already provide (e.g., Shearer & Shearer, 1976). In either case, the nature of parental involvement in early education programs, an issue that is derived from varying perspectives along the Platonic–Comenian continuum, is still being discussed (see Meisels & Shonkoff, 1990, and Paget, chapter 3, this volume).

Historical discussions addressing the issue of "how" to educate young children may also be found. In the 1700s, Jean Jacques Rousseau's belief in the innate goodness of children led him to propose early schooling that enabled children to direct their own activities, free from the constraints imposed by "society" (Rousseau, 1961). Such child-centered education, emphasizing activity and the use of the senses, was thought to foster the development of each child's moral and intellectual potential.

Rousseau's idealism was embraced yet modified by Friedrich Froebel, who has been credited with establishing the kindergarten movement in early 19th-century Germany (Deasey, 1978). His advocacy of early education in the Rousseau tradition was carried to the United States by Elizabeth Peabody, who established the first Froebelian kindergarten in Boston in 1860. Many aspects of the Froebelian kindergartens are present today in preschool programs.

Following Rousseau's philosophy, Froebel advocated respect for young children's needs and the importance of sensory training. He specifically promoted the importance of play as the educational "medium" through which children could reach their intellectual and emotional potentials. Perhaps Froebel's major contribution to early education as a separate field of study and practice was his articulation of a theory of child development and a related theory of early childhood education. Suggesting that children progress through different age-related "phases," he proposed that certain materials, or "gifts," be incorporated into the kindergarten curriculum to correspond with these phases, hence enhancing development. This notion of appropriate "match" (Hunt, 1961) has been the cornerstone of many contemporary early education programs.

The final historical figure in this brief overview is Maria Montessori, who in the early part of this century continued the Froebelian tradition within a different context (Montessori, 1964). Concerned with the welfare of young, poor urban children in Italy, she established her "children's houses." Thus, reiteration of the Platonic notion of compensatory early education may be seen in Montessori's work. Like Froebel, Montessori implemented an early education curriculum that was founded on a developmental theory, employed play as the instructional method, and sequentially introduced developmentally appropriate materials designed to facilitate sensory and cognitive skills.

Although the historical overview presented is certainly not complete, it does represent much of the thinking that has shaped the field of early education. This thinking may be summarized as follows:

1. Early education at the very least may serve to complement what children learn in their homes. At the most, it may facilitate learning that has not yet occurred.
2. A useful approach for planning a curriculum for young children is to employ a theory of development or learning.
3. An important component of early education programs is active learning, or learning through play.

Each of the approaches described in this chapter has addressed these three points. In the first part of this chapter, the characteristics of these "models," or conceptual frameworks, are described, along with exemplary programs. As becomes evident, the application of these points differs among programs adhering to each conceptual model. Following a discussion of the model approach, issues related to the evaluation of model programs and representative research are presented. Finally, the third part of this chapter is devoted to issues related to the school psychologist's growing involvement in the field of early childhood education. This description is limited to service delivery for 3- to 5-year-old children who may be at risk because of economic hardship and/or family stress (see Telzrow, chapter 2, this volume, concerning children with special education needs for a description of special services).

THEORETICAL PERSPECTIVES IN PROGRAM DEVELOPMENT

Overview: The Model Approach

Although a steady stream of discussion about early education has been evident historically, there appears to have been a burst of energy in the area beginning in the 1960s that continues to this day (Johnson, 1988). This has been reflected in the number of publications devoted to various aspects of early childhood education. To a great extent, the onset of this period of growth was due to a societal commitment to improving the lives of economically disadvantaged children, articulated by President Johnson's War on Poverty. Concomitantly, the emergence of Piagetian theory in the fields of psychology and education fueled more discussions about the practical implications of various theoretical approaches. The increase in the demand for compensatory early education programs, as well as the re-introduction of cognitive-developmental theory as an alternative to psychodynamic and behavioral approaches, contributed to the increase in program research and development during the 1960s.

TABLE 1.1
An Overview of the Model Approach in Early Childhood Education

Theoretical Perspective	Curriculum Objectives	Curriculum Content	Instructional Techniques	Key Concepts
Maturationist	Qualitative skills	Determined by developmental level and individual interests	Teacher facilitates child initiated and directed play	Readiness
	Development of self-confidence and self-esteem	Spontaneous and planned experiences	Prepared environment	Experiential learning
	Social and cognitive development			
	Emphasis on current level of functioning			
Learning	Quantitative skills	Determined by teacher	Teacher directed instruction	Operant learning
	Behavior change	Varies; can include academic and social skills cultural information, and moral behavior	Strategies include task analysis, cuing and prompting, reinforcement procedures, and modeling	Reciprocal determinism
	Transmission of information			
	Emphasis on preparation for the future			
Interactionist	Qualitative skills	Determined by developmental level and interests	Child initiated and directed play	Sources of development
	Independent thinking and problem solving skills	Experiences that facilitate physical knowledge, logical thinking, and/or representational thinking skills	Teacher as coworker	Types of knowledge
	Moral autonomy		Prepared environment	Constructivism
	Emphasis on depth of understanding		Discovery learning (physical knowledge)	
			Construction of knowledge (logical and representational thinking)	
			Inquiry methods	

One outcome of the increase in activity in the 1960s was the articulation of the model approach in early education. Discussion centered in general around how best to translate psychological theory into educational practice, and specifically how best to derive early education principles from developmental and learning theories (e.g., Bloom, 1964; Day & Parker, 1977; Hunt, 1964; Kohlberg, 1968; Murray, 1979; Ripple & Rockcastle, 1964; Shapiro & Biber, 1972). Prescriptions for programs (i.e., how to teach and what to teach) were often defined by beliefs about the ways young children develop and learn. These beliefs were, in turn, derived from theory and supporting research.

An overarching assumption of the model approach is that a specific theory and the empirical work it generates may lend themselves to practical application. Obviously there is no single theory concerning how children develop and learn and, consequently, how they should best be taught. However, there are clusters of approaches that share assumptions about the nature of young children's development that have given rise to programs that are theoretically compatible. These clusters or theoretical frameworks may be categorized as *maturationist, learning,* and *interactionist* (Evans, 1975; Kohlberg, 1968). A summary of the characteristics of these models is presented in Table 1.1.

Maturationist View

Assumptions and Goals. The maturationist perspective is based on the belief that children's development is governed by a biologically based schedule. That is, children's abilities and the general timing of their appearance are essentially predetermined (cf. Nagel, 1957). Although maturational unfolding typically has been discussed in the context of gross and fine motor development (e.g., Shirley, 1931–1933), its principles may also be applied to understanding other developmental domains, such as social and emotional growth (e.g., Erikson, 1950, 1980; Isaacs, 1933) and cognition (Isaacs, 1930). Maturationists do not deny the importance of factors other than biological pre-programming in facilitating development, such as environmental stimulation or experience; they simply consider this pre-programming to be the most important factor in explaining development.

Programs derived from a maturationist perspective often place heavy emphasis on certain tenets of psychodynamic theories of development and progressive educational philosophy (Zimiles, 1987). The importance of early experience for subsequent emotional, social, and cognitive development is a core belief, reflecting the writing, for example, of Freud and Erikson. The influence of the psychodynamic tradition may also be seen in the frequently articulated relationship between emotional well-being and rationality, as if stable affect "fuels" intellectual thought (cf. Piaget, 1981). Finally, early education programs within this perspective advocate the pedagogically compatible notion of the importance of individual exploration as a means of tying direct experience with learning. These ideas are founded in the progressive educational philosophy exemplified by the writings of John Dewey (e.g., 1944).

The goal of the maturationist-inspired early education program, then, is to provide a nurturing and supportive environment, one in which the child's innate strengths (e.g., curiosity, desire for competency) will be allowed to blossom, while less desirable characteristics (e.g., lack of cooperation) will be brought under control (Kohlberg & Mayer, 1972). Thus, educational objectives are stated in global, qualitative terms, often related to the development of competency and self-esteem, which are considered necessary for cognitive and social development. The manner in which each child makes use of the available experiences to accomplish these objectives depends on his or her unique timetable of naturally unfolding developmental processes.

Curriculum, Teacher Role, and Instructional Methods.   The curriculum within the maturationist approach can best be described as child centered. That is, curriculum content is determined by both children's developmental levels and their interests. In terms of providing developmentally appropriate activities, this means that it is assumed that children cannot (indeed, should not) be "pushed" to learn or perform beyond their current abilities. There is an emphasis on "readiness," about which children are considered to be the best judges. Children are therefore expected to direct their own activities based on their interests. As much as possible, children's experiences are incorporated into the activities, which are supplemented with planned, shared experiences (e.g., field trips), providing a broader experiential base. In all, the curriculum is designed to facilitate each child's competency at his or her current level of functioning rather than offering specific skill training for the future, because a solid foundation is considered the best preparation.

Teachers working within the maturationist perspective are likely to possess a solid understanding of child development, enabling them to make appropriate choices when planning activities and providing materials. Although some of the experiences teachers present are those many preschool-aged children find interesting, others may be unique and reflect a particular child's interest or experience. Typically, activities are organized into interest centers, with related activities (e.g., animal care, large motor, art, small manipulative) located within these areas, and children are free to initiate and direct their own activities throughout the day.

Teaching techniques facilitate both individual expression and social development. Following the children's lead, teachers comment on their activities, similar to the behavioral strategy of attending (Forehand & McMahon, 1981). When new materials or activities are introduced, they are presented as options, ones in which the children have a choice to participate. Cooperation and getting along with others are facilitated through guided reasoning and modeling. Generally, teachers fulfill a supportive, nurturing role, providing an emotionally safe environment, one in which children feel secure and competent enough to explore and learn through playing (cf. Ainsworth, 1967).

Exemplary Programs.   Those familiar with early childhood classrooms are likely to see elements of the maturationist approach in many programs not explicitly driven by this perspective. The themes of supporting feelings of individual competence, social development, and tying experience to learning are familiar ones in early education. However, as "common sense" as these principles may seem, in programs explicitly derived from the maturation perspective, the rationale for these principles stems from a strongly articulated theory, and their expression is well-thought through and carefully implemented. Two such programs are The Children's Center, administered through Syracuse University, and the Bank Street Approach, administered through the Bank Street College of Education.

The Children's Center, originally established to help economically disadvantaged children in the 1960s (Caldwell et al., 1968), became the school-based arm of a larger intervention project, the Family Development Research Program (FDRP; Honig & Lally, 1982; Lally & Honig, 1977). The primary objectives of the FDRP were to: (a) provide parenting instruction and support to low-income parents with limited formal education, and (b) promote the development of emotionally healthy and competent young children. This was accomplished through both a home-based and a school-based approach.

The home-based component of the FDRP was implemented by trained paraprofessionals (Child Development Trainers) who fulfilled the roles of teacher, friend, and advocate for the participating families. Mothers, rather than their children, were the focus of this component, with the Child Development Trainers providing a myriad of support services, ranging from helping to gain access to community services to modeling appropriate interactions with children.

In contrast to the home-based program, The Children's Center was designed to facilitate children's development, adhering closely to an Eriksonian model. That is, objectives of the program emphasized age-appropriate psychosocial goals, such as developing trust and autonomy (Honig, 1987). These were considered crucial for the development of a positive self-concept and feeling of competence, personality characteristics that facilitate learning and cognitive growth.

The Children's Center employed a multi-aged, interest center approach for children from the time they were 6 months to 5 years old. While infants and toddlers were in age-segregated classes, preschool-aged children were grouped together in what was considered a "family" style. Preschoolers were free to select activities in any of the four interest areas available (large motor, small motor, sensory, and creative expression), where teachers were stationed. The daily schedule was thus organized spatially rather than temporally, as children directed their own play (Honig, 1987). Teachers facilitated this positive activity and social interaction by commenting about the activities, responding to children's needs, and following the children's lead in play. In addition, teachers incorporated language experiences and Piagetian-inspired concept activities in their interactions with the children. Although the FDRP is no longer operating in its entirety, many of its assumptions and procedures continue to be implemented in Syracuse University's early childhood education program.

A second program exemplifying the application of maturationist principles is the Bank Street Approach, which is currently in operation (Biber, 1984; Biber, Shapiro, & Wickens, 1977; Gilkeson & Bowman, 1976; Shapiro & Biber, 1972). Like The Children's Center, the Bank Street Approach's objectives include enhancing children's feelings of competence and self-esteem. Whereas The Children's Center drew its primary guidelines from Erikson's theories, the Bank Street Approach has emphasized the educational philosophy of John Dewey, which advocates (among other ideals) making learning meaningful to children by using their own experiences as curriculum content. Learning is conceived as the process of participating in multiple meaningful experiences, rather than achieving specific academic goals.

Activities in the Bank Street program are designed to help children understand first, the school environment, and subsequently their community. The classroom is organized into learning centers, which include reading, listening, writing, math, science, and art. Field trips help acquaint children with the world outside their classroom. Throughout these experiences, the necessity of active learning, the importance of concrete illustrations of concepts, and the functional utility of information are emphasized. For example, reading experiences may include making attendance charts, labeling materials on shelves, and dictating news articles about class activities. As in The Children's Center, teachers provide support and guidance, following the children's direction in play.

In summary, each of the programs described reflects the basic tenets of the maturationist model in early education, although each may stress different sources for their ideas and different practical applications. These basic tenets include a respect for each child's individuality, the notions of readiness and child-directed play, the importance of enhancing self-esteem and feelings of competency for cognitive, social, and emotional development, and the facilitation of development in a variety of domains rather than achievement of specific academic objectives. A useful way to conceptualize this approach is to remember that programs functioning within a maturationist perspective fit the program to the child, rather than teach a specific curriculum to all children (Zimiles, 1987).

Learning View

Assumptions and Goals. Within the learning perspective there are alternative ways of viewing behavior change in general (e.g., Sahakian, 1976) and those changes associated with age (e.g., Baer, 1970, 1973; Gagne, 1968; Spiker, 1966). One commonality among investigators of age-related change, however, is their reliance on antecedent–consequent relationships for explanation. That is, there is fundamental agreement that the essence of development is the sequence of environmentally produced changes in behavior. Thus, in contrast to the maturationist belief in an organismic regulatory process, the learning view is founded on the belief that children's development can best be understood through their experiential history.

White (1970) provided a simple "learning theory point of view" in an effort to describe the assumptions inherent in this position:

1. The environment may be described in terms of its stimuli.
2. Behavior may be described as responses.
3. When stimuli occur contingently and immediately following a response and there is a subsequent increase in that response, these stimuli may be considered reinforcers.
4. The various pairings of stimuli, responses, and reinforcers characterize learning.
5. If there is no evidence otherwise, it is safe to assume that behavior is learned and may be modified (e.g., trained, extinguished) by environmental events.

Despite this core belief in the power of the environment in influencing behavior, the theoretical subdivisions within the learning, or behaviorist, approach suggest different educational applications. Although not all (e.g., classical conditioning) may be equally useful (Nelson & Polsgrove, 1984), applications of operant conditioning and social learning theory are two approaches that have been widely used. In-depth description of the implications of these two learning theory variants is beyond the scope of this chapter. However, a brief description of their relevance is included as a backdrop against which to consider early education model programs.

Operant conditioning, with its emphasis on overt behavior and the functional relationship between antecedents and consequences, suggests that: (a) learning objectives should be stated in terms of observable behaviors, and (b) both aspects of the "equation" (i.e., antecedents and consequents) may be considered in an attempt to change behavior (see, e.g., Cooper, Heron, & Heward, 1987). Thus, the field of applied behavior analysis has investigated strategies for altering stimulus events. These strategies include breaking down learning objectives into smaller steps (in line with the notion of successive approximation), and providing cues and prompts. In addition, the arrangement of reinforcers has been varied, for example, through the use of token economies or group contingencies. These techniques have been used with preschoolers in an array of settings, with a wide assortment of problems, and by a variety of persons (parents, teachers, and peers) (Cooper et al., 1987).

Social learning theory differs from operant conditioning in an important way: Inferred cognitive activity is accorded an important role in behavior change. It is therefore assumed that learning occurs not only through trial and error and reinforcement contingencies, but through observation and imitation, as well. Thus, learning is accomplished through a more active and interactive exchange between the individual and the environment, in a process that has been termed *reciprocal determinism* (Bandura, 1978). Thoughts or ideas may function as stimuli, and efficient learning may be enhanced by the judicious use of modeling. Coupled with effective reinforcement strategies, providing appropriate models for imitative learning is considered a powerful method of instruction.

The goal of an early education program derived from any of the learning theories is to change behavior or transmit information in the most efficient and direct manner. Unlike the maturationist approach, no assumptions are made about the inherent nature of children's emotional, social, or cognitive development. Instead, there is the belief that children's learning in these areas may be most influenced by stimulus events. Although these stimulus events may include those that are internal (at least for the social learning theorists), they are still directly amenable to environmental influence (rather than, e.g., being under the control of a system of internal regulation).

Curriculum, Teacher Role, and Instructional Methods.   Because behavioral strategies comprise a technology that is considered unrelated to any particular theoretical context (Skinner, 1953), in principle, they can be applied to any instructional content. In other words, learning theories and the subsequent instructional theories they engender address the issue of "how" to facilitate learning and not the issue of "what" to teach. The content of a program driven by this perspective may typically include pre-academic and academic skills, moral behavior, and/or cultural information (Kohlberg & Mayer, 1972), but each program determines its own particular content (Spodek, 1973).

Teachers within the learning perspective possess a strong understanding of basic principles of behavioral analysis, enabling them to teach efficiently (facilitating learning as quickly as possible). Thus, they are likely to determine specific behavioral objectives for the classroom as a whole as well as for individual children. Teachers arrange these objectives in sequential steps, and they provide materials, activities, and appropriate reinforcers to enhance their acquisition. In general, the high degree of teacher direction characteristic of learning-oriented programs involves both consistency in interacting with children and sensitivity to the relationship between characteristics of the classroom and children's behavior (Spodek, 1973).

Teaching methods follow directly from empirically derived principles of learning (Bushell, 1973; Case & Bereiter, 1984) and include: (a) identifying desired behavioral outcomes, (b) identifying and utilizing effective and available reinforcers, (c) determining and hierarchically arranging learning goals that comprise the desired outcome, (d) identifying the skills in the sequence children already possess, and (e) determining mastery criteria and, through demonstration and verbal instruction, teaching each step that has not yet been acquired. In addition, programs that incorporate a social learning theory perspective use modeling as an instructional method.

Exemplary Programs.   Strategies for enhancing learning that are derived from behavioral research may be found in many early childhood programs. Breaking down larger tasks into their components, reinforcing appropriate behavior, and providing models of desired behavior are instructional techniques that have found their way into the programs of even decidedly nonbehavioral practitioners. Moreover, current computer-assisted learning programs in preschool are seen as an updated version of programmed instruction (Hutinger, 1987; Mounts & Roopnarine, 1987; see also Clements, chapter 6, this volume). Today, it is unlikely that programs employing behavioral principles do so to the exclusion of other theoretical approaches, instead incorporating these strategies into broader curricula. However, there have been model programs that have been solely derived from the learning perspective. Two such programs are the Bereiter–Engelmann Direct Instruction Program and the Demonstration and Research Center for Early Education program (DARCEE), administered through George Peabody College for Teachers.

The Bereiter–Engelmann Direct Instruction Program is probably the best known early education model based entirely on operant conditioning principles. Originally designed as a compensatory program for economically disadvantaged preschool-aged children (considered at the time to be "culturally deprived"), its objectives include specific language, mathematics, and reading skill acquisition (Bereiter & Engelmann, 1966). The language skills involve using "yes–no" statements and prepositions, identifying colors, and performing "if–then," "not," and "or" deductive reasoning. Mathematics objectives are primarily concerned with counting skills, and reading objectives involve recognizing letters, rhyming, and acquiring a minimal sight word vocabulary. The content of the Bereiter–Engelmann program is thus highly academic, and in keeping with the learning view, educational objectives are stated in clear, behavioral terms.

The objectives of the Bereiter–Engelmann program are met through a highly structured, teacher-directed program of instruction. It is believed that the unstructured, child-directed nature of traditional "enrichment" programs is inadequate for children who need to "make up" instruction they are lacking. Children are thus divided into "study groups" of not more than five children and participate in six activity periods. These include three, 20-minute periods, each devoted to the three academic areas, with "minor" activities, such as snack and music, scheduled as breaks in between academic periods. Instruction in the study groups involves rapid-fire drills in which the teacher presents a series of verbal statements and questions with a high degree of redundancy, and the children respond on cue. The verbal statements represent instructional objectives that are carefully arranged in hierarchical, small steps. The quick pace is intended to reduce distractions, and children's responses, performed in unison, are immediately reinforced with edibles or praise. The possibility of incorrect responding is greatly reduced by the repetitiveness of the material and the closed questioning techniques employed, so children are likely to experience a high degree of success and reward. The following excerpt concerning the concept of "part" illustrates this instructional technique (Bereiter & Engelmann, 1973, p. 180):

Teacher: (pointing) This is Tyrone. Now listen. (Holding up Tyrone's hand and speaking slowly and methodically in a way the children have learned to recognize as a signal that something new is being presented) This is a *part* of Tyrone. This part of Tyrone is a _____

Children: Hand.

Teacher: (pointing to Tyrone's nose) And this is a part of Tyrone. This part of Tyrone is a _____

Children: Nose.

Several other parts of Tyrone are introduced in this way and then the teacher alters the presentation to require the children to provide more of the statement.

Teacher: (pointing to Tyrone's ear) Is this a part of Tyrone?

Children: Yeah.

Teacher: Yes, this is a _____

Children: Part of Tyrone.

Progressively the children are led to the point where they are supplying the entire pair of statements. Negative instances are introduced.

Teacher: (pointing to Marie's nose) Is this a part of Tyrone?

Children: No, this is not a part of Tyrone.

Teachers in this program fulfill a role that is admittedly very different from that traditionally seen in early education. First, they are provided a script of lessons, and need to be well rehearsed. The spontaneous interaction with children that typically occurs in preschools is actively discouraged, because the program's focus on compensating for academic deficits precludes what is considered an inefficient use of time. Second, although not denying the importance of a good relationship between teacher and child, Bereiter and Engelmann considered the nurturing, affectionate role of the teacher irrelevant for direct instruction, suggesting instead that ". . . . . highly motivated long-term involvement in a common task tends to produce very strong bonds between the people involved— as witness combat teams in wartime compared to the more idle military groups in peacetime" (Bereiter & Engelmann, 1966, p. 59).

A second program that illustrates the learning view is the instructional program of DARCEE (Camp, 1973), which is in addition an example of the "learning to learn" programs developed in the 1960s and 1970s (e.g., Harter, 1968). Also designed as a compensatory early education program, DARCEE's goal was to teach preschoolers the skills and attitudes that had been shown to correlate with academic achievement. These information-processing skills included sensory skills (attention and discrimination through the use of the senses), abstracting and mediating skills (basic concepts, classification, sequencing, and critical thinking), and response skills (verbal and motor). Although specific content was selected to illustrate these processing skills, it was the processing skills themselves that were the focus of the curriculum.

Skills in each of the curriculum areas were arranged logically in order of increasing difficulty and then task analyzed to produce a hierarchical, sequential instructional program. Moreover, these skills were presented to the children in what was termed an interrelated unit approach, in which objectives were organized according to central themes. These themes also comprised learning experiences that progressed from simple to complex, building upon each other. For example, a beginning sensory unit was the child him or herself, which was followed by units on the family and home, the neighborhood, and the city. In this way, children were given the opportunity to transfer and generalize the component skills they were learning.

Children in the DARCEE program spent about two thirds of their time in small groups of five children and one teacher, where their lessons were presented. Although verbal expression was given a high priority, teacher-led small groups included activities and materials that would typically be found in a preschool classroom. In addition, a variety of reinforcers were used, including tangibles, physical gestures, and praise. As with the skill objectives, these reinforcers were also carefully programmed to facilitate performance that increasingly approximated desired outcome behaviors.

Despite some of their value-laden assumptions concerning cultural deprivation (discussed later), the Bereiter–Engelmann and DARCEE instructional programs exemplify well the use of operant techniques. The use of clear behavioral objectives, small instructional steps arranged sequentially, cuing and prompting, immediate and corrective feedback, and reinforcers all represent educational applications of this perspective. In addition, DARCEE's attempt to teach information-processing skills reflects the importance given to inferred, intervening factors in influencing behavioral outcomes, characteristic of the more cognitively oriented learning theories.

Interactionist View

Assumptions and Goals.   Also known as the cognitive-developmental view, the interactionist perspective in early childhood education has had a steadily increasing influence (Weber, 1984). The assumptions inherent in this position are rooted in the developmental theory of Jean Piaget. There have been and continue to be many discussions concerning the educational implications of Piagetian theory. This discussion is limited to three theoretical aspects that have particular relevance to early education programming. These are the sources of developmental change, types of knowledge, and constructivism. Each of these are discussed in turn.

Central to the Piagetian position is the belief that age-related changes may be attributed to five sources: biology (including maturation), experience, cultural and educational transmission, social factors, and equilibration (Piaget, 1964, 1971b). Maturation refers to abilities that have a strong biological basis, such as the growth of muscle strength during infancy, and as such involves internal processes. Experience refers to two types of opportunities: manipulating physical objects and observing their properties (which promotes physical knowledge), and thinking about and drawing conclusions from experiences with objects, events, and people (which promotes logico-mathematical knowledge). Cultural and educational transmission refers to instruction, both direct and indirect, whereas the notion of social factors implies the importance of social interchange. Thus, experiences with the physical, educational, and social worlds are acknowledged as necessary external processes for development. It is through the last, internal process of equilibration, or self-regulation, however, that cognitive development occurs. That is, given a child's maturational constraints or strengths and the general experiences or instruction he or she may have encountered, the equilibration process enables a child to make sense of those experiences. The meaningfulness of these experiences is influenced by the level of understanding or organization of knowledge (cognitive structure) that a child brings with him or her to each learning opportunity. When the "balance" of this internal organization is disrupted by the introduction of new information, the equilibration process allows a child to incorporate the new information in a way that makes sense, thereby creating a different, more mature level of knowledge.

Each of the five developmental components is thus necessary, but not alone sufficient, for cognitive growth. In this way, the cognitive-development perspective reflects a belief that the source for cognitive change is the interaction between internal processes and external experiences. Although this view acknowledges the roles of both maturational and environmental factors, it is their interaction that provides the essential ingredient for developmental change.

The second set of assumptions concerns the types of knowledge that children acquire: social, physical, and logicomathematical (Kamii, 1971; Kamii & Radin,

1970). Social knowledge refers to culturally based information, such as the names of objects, colors, and what is considered appropriate behavior. As such, it may differ across cultures, and is best acquired through direct instruction or feedback from people. Physical knowledge refers to information about the physical properties inherent in objects, and the effects of one's actions on those objects. Knowing that a golf ball is hard and will roll when pushed are examples of physical knowledge (but knowing it is called a golf ball is social knowledge). From a Piagetian perspective, this type of knowledge must be discovered through concrete manipulation and feedback from objects. The last category of knowledge, logicomathematical, refers to information comprised of systems of rules and relationships about objects, events, and people. Logicomathematical knowledge is exemplified by the now familiar notions of classification, relational thinking, number concepts, and conservation, among others. The relationships or rules with which it is concerned are not inherently part of the objects or events with which a child may interact. Rather, they must be constructed or invented by means of inferential reasoning. For example, although an impatient child may be told that being fourth in line means that there are only three people ahead (an example of relational thinking), a genuine understanding of that message can only be the result of prior experiences in which he or she has had the opportunity to "re-invent" the concept for him or herself. True acquisition of logicomathematical knowledge results in a qualitatively different form of knowing, referred to as a stage. Piaget was most interested in this last type of knowledge, but for pedagogical reasons it is important to note the existence of all three and the means by which each may be acquired.

Constructivism, the last theoretical assumption for purposes of this discussion, refers to a school of thought regarding the acquisition of logicomathematical knowledge. As previously described, from a Piagetian perspective this type of information must be re-invented by each child for him or herself, from information acquired from his or her experiences. Constructing information is often confused with discovering information, the means by which physical knowledge is believed to be obtained. However, Piaget provided a distinction, as Kamii (1970) reported: Piaget's ". . . . favorite example of 'discovery' is Columbus' discovery of America. Columbus did not invent America, he points out. America existed all along before Columbus discovered it. The airplane, on the other hand, was not discovered. It was invented because it did not exist before its invention" (p. 8). In like manner, for each child, logicomathematical knowledge constitutes a new invention; it simply does not exist in mature form before a child has made sense of his or her experiences, organizing the information acquired from these experiences through the equilibration process.

Several guiding principles have directed the ways that programs adhering to the interactionist view have "translated" the aforementioned theoretical assumptions into practice (Ginsburg & Opper, 1969). These include:

1. Young children think about the world differently than adults. Therefore, it is inappropriate to think that what is valid from an adult's perspective is valid from the child's. This means that *logical* organization of knowledge into instructional objectives (as in task analysis) does not necessarily correspond to a child's *psychological* organization of knowledge.

2. Young children learn best from active (physical and mental) involvement and experimentation with concrete materials. This means that for physical and logicomathematical knowledge development, verbal transmission of information is insufficient. It also means that information obtained from our senses is incomplete. Rather, information must be organized and structured, in other words, "thought about" (Forman, 1987).

3. Because true understanding evolves from the internal equilibration regulatory process, children should be allowed to progress at their own rates, ask their own questions, and direct their own activities.

4. Social interaction is important because it facilitates clarification of thoughts through defending one's own ideas and considering others'.

The overall goal of an early education program derived from the interactionist perspective is to facilitate the development of independent thinking and problem solving. As Piaget has stated:

> The principle goal of education is to create men who are capable of doing new things, not simply of repeating what other generations have done—men who are creative, inventive, and discoverers. The second goal of education is to form minds which can be critical, can verify, and not accept everything they are offered. . . So we need pupils who are active, who learn early to find out by themselves, partly by their own spontaneous activity and partly through material we set up for them; who learn early to tell what is verifiable and what is simply the first idea to come to them. (Duckworth, 1964, p. 5)

This objective is very different from that of traditional education, with its emphasis on transmitting cultural knowledge and values across generations (Kamii, 1984).

Although it appears that program objectives focus on cognitive abilities to the exclusion of other areas, such as social skills, language, and personality, this is not the case. Interactionist programs view these other areas through a cognitive "eye." That is, the same principles that explain cognitive development are applied to all areas of development without differentiating among the areas (Elkind, 1968). For example, cooperating with other children is viewed as involving the same ability as knowing that 10 pennies remains 10 pennies whether arranged in a pile or a line. (Both require thinking about more than one aspect of a problem and coordinating discrepancies.) In this way, program objectives are integrated, each with the others, just as children's abilities are integrated across different developmental domains.

Curriculum, Teacher Role, and Instructional Methods. Early educators functioning within the interactionist perspective have differed in their application of Piagetian theory to educational practice. One difference among programs has been in the theoretical constructs that have been selected as the primary focus, because Piaget's theory encompasses such a broad range of cognitive functioning. A second difference among programs has been the direction in which curriculum has been tied to theoretical constructs (Johnson, 1988). Some programs (e.g., Kamii & Radin, 1970; Sonquist, Kamii, & Derman, 1970; Weikart, Rogers, Adcock, & McClelland, 1971) have first looked at activities and materials that are being used and then have determined the ways in which they may be related to theoretical constructs (a "bottom-up" approach). Others (e.g., Forman & Kuschner, 1977; Furth & Wachs, 1974; Roeper & Sigel, 1970) have first derived objectives from theory and subsequently have planned activities and designed materials that meet those goals (a "top-down" approach). In between these two approaches lies a third, in which portions of a curriculum are derived from Piagetian theory. This last approach may involve including within a broader program nontraditional areas that reflect Piagetian-inspired content, such as physical knowledge (Kamii & DeVries, 1978). More commonly, it may involve traditional content that has been reinterpreted from a Piagetian perspective, such as mathematics (Copeland, 1974; Kamii & DeVries, 1976), large group experiences (Kamii & DeVries, 1980), or science (e.g., Karplus, 1970). Thus, there are numerous variations in curriculum practice that may be seen within the interactionist perspective.

Teachers working within this theoretical framework fulfill a supportive role, encouraging active involvement with the materials similar in manner to those working in the maturationist perspective. However, there are several important additions. First, in many cases activities and materials that are provided are designed to foster particular types of thinking skills. Although children are encouraged to direct their own play and teachers follow their lead, the availability of these activities and materials makes it likely that curriculum objectives will be met. Second, teachers are sensitive to the reasoning skills that children exhibit, planning activities that are optimally challenging, that is, neither too difficult to be beyond children's interests, nor too familiar to be considered boring. The intent is for "moderately novel" (Flavell, 1963) activities to provide just the right "match" (Hunt, 1961) to stimulate thinking. Third, teachers provide activities that will accommodate variability in the range of cognitive abilities within a classroom. Thus, materials are likely to be open-ended in nature, facilitating divergent thinking (i.e., multiple correct responses). Finally, although individual pacing of activity is encouraged, social interaction is encouraged as well. There is a strong belief in the importance of this interaction for facilitating cognitive growth, as Piaget stated:

> When I say "active," I mean it in two senses. One is acting on material things. But the other means doing things in social collaboration, in a group effort. This leads to a critical frame of mind, where children must communicate with each other. This is an essential factor in intellectual development. Cooperation is indeed co-operation. (Duckworth, 1964, p. 5)

The instructional method that is used can best be described as that of co-worker (Ginsburg & Opper, 1969; Hooper, 1968). Working alongside the children, teachers make every effort to understand their point of view, using that point of view as a starting point from which children are encouraged to "stretch" their thinking. Because teachers are aware of the types of knowledge that children acquire, their teaching techniques reflect this understanding. Although social knowledge lends itself to direct instruction, the source of physical and logicomathematical knowledge does not emanate from adults, but from the interactions that children have with the environment. Therefore, with physical and logicomathematical knowledge experiences, children are encouraged to reflect on their actions and relate them to past experiences. This is done through commenting about the children's activities and by asking open-ended, thought-provoking questions. In this way, teachers attempt to facilitate children's understanding and organization of information for themselves.

Exemplary Programs.   Programs derived from cognitive-developmental theory often appear to be like traditional, child-centered programs, with some similar materials available and children's play and self-direction as primary characteristics. However, the hallmarks of interactionist programs are the types of materials and experiences provided for the children and the substance of the teacher–child interactions. Both are designed to facilitate thinking and problem-solving skills in an effort to promote the discovery of physical knowledge and/or the construction of logicomathematical knowledge. Four representative approaches are the High/Scope Cognitively Oriented Curriculum, the Piaget-Derived Preschool Curriculum, the School for Constructive Play, and the Educating the Young Thinker Program.

The High/Scope Cognitively Oriented Curriculum was developed in 1962 by Weikart in response to the need to help young economically disadvantaged preschoolers (Weikart, Rogers, Adcock, & McClelland, 1971). It is currently used in many centers in the United States and throughout the world. Initially called the Perry Preschool Project (as part of the Perry Elementary School in Ypsilanti, Michigan), the High/Scope objectives include helping children learn from their experiences and engage in logical thinking. The program includes both a home-based component, in which teachers visit the children's homes weekly, as well as a center-based component. As one would expect, children are seen as active learners, and teachers are seen as facilitators, not directors, of their learning. Incorporating materials one would expect to typically find in a preschool classroom, the High/Scope program has evolved since the 1970s to employ a specific organizational framework for both the children and the teachers (Hohmann, Banet, & Weikart, 1979).

The children's day is organized according to a daily schedule that includes (a) a *planning* session, in which children decide which activities they will participate in for the day; (b) *worktime,* in which children carry out their plan in the available interest areas that teachers have established beforehand; (c) clean-up time; (d) *recall,* in which children report about their worktime activities; (e) small group; and (f) large group time. The emphasis on the *plan–do–review* routine is intended to give children the opportunity to practice representational skills as they reflect on their activities both before and after carrying them out. These representational skills may be further enhanced if, for example, they draw a picture for their plan or teachers record a dictated account during recall.

Curriculum content (i.e., activities and materials available during worktime, small group, and large group time) is determined by the teachers according to their knowledge of "key experiences." These are pedagogical principles derived from Piagetian theory that guide teachers' interactions with the children. The principles include active learning, using language, representing experiences and ideas, classification, seriation, time and number concepts, and spatial relations (Weikart & Schweinhart, 1987). Rather than representing behavioral objectives or target behaviors, these areas function as guideposts for teachers to use in planning and implementing curricular activities. For example, when discussing the introduction of a new type of blocks during a planning session, teachers make note of the ways in which these blocks may facilitate active learning, language development, and the other key experience objectives. Thus, teachers in the High/Scope program must be well aware of the theoretically derived principles, and be skilled in implementing them during their interactions with the children.

Similar to Weikart's High/Scope program, Kamii and DeVries' Piaget-Derived Curriculum evolved over a 20-year period. The overall objective of the Piaget-Derived Curriculum is the facilitation of independent, self-directed thinking, both intellectually and morally, in which children are able to take into consideration multiple viewpoints (Kamii, 1984). Piaget's theory was thus applied to facilitate the development of the "whole" child, including personality and cognitive aspects (Kamii & DeVries, 1977). Kamii and DeVries' early application of theory employed a "bottom-up" approach (e.g., Kamii, 1971; Kamii & DeVries, 1973; Kamii & Radin, 1970), but later work has included a "top-down" approach, as well, where specific aspects of Piagetian theory have functioned as sources for curriculum ideas (e.g., Kamii & DeVries, 1978).

One aspect of Piagetian theory that is highlighted in the Piaget-Derived Curriculum is its differentiation among the types of knowledge that children come to acquire. The construct of knowledge types has direct implications for educational programming. As discussed earlier, social, physical, and logicomathematical knowledge, because they are acquired through different mechanisms, are each addressed differently in the classroom (e.g., Kamii, 1970).

A second theoretical construct that is applied in the Piaget-Derived Curriculum is the integration of development across areas that are typically discussed separately, such as cognition, language, or memory. Hence, curriculum is integrated across instructional areas that in other approaches are considered separately, such as science, math, and language arts. In this way, it follows the example of the British Infant School curriculum (Silberman, 1973). Instead of planning activities with separate objectives for each of the possible subject areas, activities are considered in terms of their possibilities for facilitating thinking in a variety of ways. Multiple objectives are the norm, and the actual objectives that are met are determined by each child when he or she encounters the activity or the materials. Because of this view, teachers function as on-the-spot diagnosticians, determining how a child is thinking about an activity and adapting their interactions to make the activity meaningful (challenging, or moderately novel) from the child's perspective. Of course, this requires a great deal of foresight during planning and flexibility during teaching.

In addition to curriculum objectives in the physical and logicomathematical knowledge domains, the Piaget-Derived Curriculum includes objectives in the socioemotional and psychomotor domains, areas not directly addressed by Piagetian theory. It is in these areas that Kamii and DeVries have extended cognitive-developmental theory to provide a comprehensive curriculum framework. Although specific objectives in these areas have been drawn from other theories and educational practices (Roach & Kephart, 1966, for psychomotor objectives; Vinter, Sarri, Vorwaller, & Schafer, 1966, for socioemotional objectives), their inclusion is logically related to educational principles derived more directly from Piagetian theory (Kamii, 1971).

A classroom following the Piaget-Derived Curriculum is typically divided into interest areas, much as those in the maturationist tradition. Within the interest areas, however, materials that are typically present in preschool programs are considered in terms of their possibilities for enhancing thinking in the three knowledge areas. Others are deliberately selected that are especially likely to facilitate physical and logicomathematical knowledge development. Unlike Weikart's program, there is no suggested routine, although teachers working within Kamii and DeVries' framework may similarly organize the day. Teachers are available to help children reflect upon their actions and extend their thinking in line with the objectives activities appear to be serving for them. They are likely to encourage children to interact with each other, as well, to help meet these objectives. It should be remembered, however, that the objectives in the Piaget-Derived Curriculum are processes of thinking rather than behaviors to be achieved or facts to be remembered. Teachers have a strong understanding of ways to optimize children's interactions with the materials and with each other, remembering that it is this interaction that enhances development.

A third variant of the interactionist perspective in early education is the School for Constructive Play (Forman & Hill, 1984; Forman & Kuschner, 1977). Originating as a research-based application of Piagetian theory, this program is currently incorporated into the early education program at the University of Massachusetts. As its name implies, the theoretical principle it emphasizes is constructivism.

The curriculum in the School for Constructive Play is based on four thinking processes that comprise equilibration, or the means by which logicomathematical knowledge is constructed. These are as follows:

1. Correspondence: This involves understanding that an object remains the same object even if it changes location (qualitative or identity conservation). It also involves understanding that the quantity (e.g., number, volume, mass) of an object remains the same regardless of its physical configuration (the familiar notion of conservation).

2. Functions: This involves understanding direct functional relationships (as one factor increases, so does another), such as, "The harder I push, the farther it goes." It also involves understanding inverse relationships, such as "The harder I push, the less time I can maintain my effort."

3. Perspective: This involves acknowledging the existence of different viewpoints in what may be seen (visual perspective), as well as what may be felt (psychological perspective).

4. Transformation: This involves understanding the changes that an object may undergo, whether it is visually perceived or mentally inferred.

These four learning processes stem directly from Piagetian theory (Piaget, 1971a, 1977), and serve as the foundation for curriculum planning, a strong example of the top-down approach within the interactionist view.

The classroom in the School for Constructive Play consists of well-planned "learning encounters," in which unique activities are set out for the children (Forman & Kuschner, 1977). The activities are usually innovative combinations of materials to enable children to engage in the four learning processes. For example, an activity in which children reconstruct a model of their playground from miniature replicas of equipment is intended to facilitate correspondence of identity. A specially constructed chute with changing levels reduces the speed of a ball traveling down, so that children are better able to notice the ball's changing positions, facilitating their understanding of transformations. Activities such as these may be designed to address one or more of the learning processes, and, as in the Piaget-Derived Curriculum, the exact objective(s) is determined when each child encounters each activity.

Teachers in the School for Constructive Play may position themselves near the activities and begin using them in an effort to stimulate children's curiosity, or they may join children already engaged in play. In either case, their role is one of supporter or facilitator, helping children notice the results of their actions by verbal articulation or repetition of the children's actions. They may also suggest possible uses of the materials, keeping in mind the way each child appears to be using them and the learning processes that the activity may facilitate. Again, this requires that teachers understand the theoretical underpinnings of the curriculum and maintain a great deal of flexibility when working with the children.

The final example of a program within the interactionist view is Educating the Young Thinker, a research-based approach that evolved during the 1970s, first at the State University of New York at Buffalo and subsequently at the Educational Testing Service under the direction of Sigel (Copple, Sigel, & Saunders, 1984; Sigel, 1970; Sigel & Saunders, 1979). Like Forman's program, Educating the Young Thinker was founded on a firm belief in constructivism. However, it emphasized representational competence, the ability to think about and use symbols that stand for (represent) objects, events, and people not currently present. In addition to Piagetian notions of symbolic development (e.g., Furth, 1969), Sigel drew from the theories of Bruner (1973) and Kelly (1955).

There are two types of representational competence: *Internal* processes involve thinking, imagination, ideation, and the like. *External* processes involve conveying these internal representations to others or expressing them for one's own pleasure, through, for example, speaking, writing, drawing, music, or dance. Thus, there are different forms, or representational modes, through which the same event can be portrayed. The ability to understand that different modes can express the same event is one that children acquire through experience. For example, realizing that a silhouette of a child's face is a way of representing that person, as is a photograph or a painting, evolves as children resolve the apparent discrepancies that exist between what they already know (the actual person) and the new information (the representation). Generally, then, the Educating the Young Thinker program was founded on the theoretical constructs of representational competence (its objective), different representational modes, and discrepancy resolution (another way of describing the equilibration process).

In normative development, children acquire representational competence through experiences that require them to deal with objects, events, and people that are not immediately present. The first evidence of this emerging ability is, of course, the acquisition of object permanence. Sigel's research led him to conclude that some experiences are better than others for helping children acquire representational skills. These were circumstances that created the most demand to think about nonpresent events. Sigel and his co-workers applied these findings to the development of teaching strategies that required children to deal with objects or events removed (i.e., distant) in time or space (Sigel, 1970; Sigel & Cocking, 1977). This has been called the distancing model in early education (Sigel, 1987b).

The classroom in the Educating the Young Thinker program was organized both temporally and spatially. The daily routine included a series of periods alternating between group activities and free play. Activities in each of these time periods were designed to encourage children to practice representational skills. The materials that were available in the classroom were also meant to foster representational thinking and were arranged in eight interest areas: large wooden blocks, small blocks and manipulatives, water table, easel painting, art area, books, and clay.

The teaching technique that was used in this setting was the inquiry method. This method involved the skilled use of questioning to place a cognitive demand on children to think abstractly (Sigel & Saunders, 1979). Characteristics of this teaching strategy included using a judicious supply of open-ended questions that required children to think about past events, anticipate future ones, and create different modes for expressing current ones. Teachers were careful not to bombard children with questions, keeping their timing and number optimal so that the children's play was not interrupted. Teachers in this program were therefore viewed as thinkers themselves, making critical decisions as to how to implement distancing demands through inquiry.

Summarizing the interactionist view, it is apparent that, despite differences concerning which cognitive-developmental principles are applied, programs functioning within this perspective share a fundamental belief in the necessity of active, self-directed manipulation of materials for the construction of knowledge. Because children themselves ultimately re-invent knowledge, teachers are not seen as the source of information, but as the facilitators of intellectual development. They fulfill the role of co-workers, stimulating children's thinking by creating challenges to their organization of knowledge. In this way, their jobs are more indirect than teachers following the learning perspective, because they aspire to influence children through the experiences they provide for them rather than through direct instruction.

Summary of the Model Approach

Curriculum models have been called idealizations of the way programs may be structured (Evans, 1982). Their virtue is that they provide an organizational framework for making decisions about program objectives, content, instructional methods, and evaluation criteria and techniques. From the three curriculum models that have been presented, it is apparent that very different decisions may be made. Program goals or objectives may focus on facilitating general socialization to enhance current functioning, or on enhancing intellectual abilities as a means to prepare for the future. Program content may emphasize either affective/social development or intellectual development, and within the latter objective, the emphasis may be on either cognitive development or academic achievement. Finally, instructional methodology may be direct and didactic, or it may be indirect, using a prepared environment that children actively explore.

As useful as models may be for helping to organize a broad array of information, they bring with them several liabilities. First, models may take on a life of their own, narrowing the focus of program providers to remain within the domain of their respective frameworks. Several of the representative programs described exemplify this, emphasizing particular domains, such as certain academic skills or logicomathematical concepts, to the exclusion of others. Second, models may have distinct theoretical assumptions about children, yet in applying these assumptions to practice, a program representing one model may share many characteristics with a program representing another. Again, this may be seen in several of the programs derived from different models. In instances such as these, it is worth asking how useful the model is (cf. Reese & Overton, 1970). Third, because different models have different assumptions about children's development and behavior, the types of questions regarding program efficacy will differ, making comparability difficult. This point has often been overlooked or misunderstood. It is to these issues regarding the evaluation of model programs that the discussion now turns.

EFFECTIVENESS OF MODEL PROGRAMS

The question of program effectiveness may be conceptualized as comprised of four issues: (a) Are early childhood education programs effective? (b) Do children achieve the objectives of the individual model programs in which they participate? (c) Is one model more effective than another in the achievement of objectives? and (d) What aspects of early childhood model programs contribute to program effectiveness?

Information relating to the answers to these questions may be found in studies conducted during two "periods" of evaluative research. During the first period prior to the 1960s, research concerning the effectiveness of early childhood education was really concerned with documenting the lack of harmful effects of schooling for very young children (Condry, 1983). At that time, the objectives of early education were facilitating emotional well-being, decreasing separation anxiety, and broadening children's social worlds. Research addressing these issues was typically conducted in university- or church-based programs with middle-class children. During the second period beginning in the 1960s, research concerning early education effectiveness had as its focus the documentation of the ameliorative effects of early intervention and/or the explication of early cognitive development. These studies were usually conducted in community- or university-based programs with children (often minority) living in poverty. It is in the context of this second period of research that evaluation of program effectiveness typically (and in the present chapter) is discussed. In the following discussion, issues related to each of the above four questions are presented, as well as illustrative research. It should be emphasized that the research reviewed is not meant to be exhaustive, only representative.

Issue 1: The Effectiveness of Early Education

Although research related to the justification of compensatory early education has not had as its primary goal the evaluation of the effectiveness of specific model programs, it has nonetheless provided information regarding model evaluation. An example of this research is that conducted by the Consortium for Longitudinal Studies (Consortium for Longitudinal Studies, 1983; Lazar & Darlington, 1982). In 1975, 11 early education research groups decided to conduct a pooled, longitudinal posttest of the effects of their respective early education programs that had been implemented by the individual investigators from 1962 to 1972. Four outcome areas were selected and their measures were determined: school competence (measured by grade retention and special class placement); developed abilities (measured by standardized intelligence and achievement tests); children's attitudes (measured by child interviews regarding achievement motivation and self-esteem); and impact on the family (measured by parent interview regarding satisfaction with child school performance and vocational aspirations). To eliminate potential bias, the analysis of the pooled data was conducted by a 12th group of investigators who had been uninvolved in program implementation.

The Consortium found that, compared to children who had not participated in preschool programs (through randomly assigned control groups), children who had attended the research programs were less likely to be retained in a grade or to be in special education classes. In addition, the children expressed higher achievement motivation and school-related self-esteem, and their mothers had higher vocational aspirations for them. However, intelligence and achievement test scores did not differ significantly between participatory and control group children, despite initial gains (1 to 2 years following preschool) by the former.

The 11 research programs comprising the Consortium study represented different applications of the three model approaches. Although the outcome measures may not have been explicitly stated for each of the programs described, they were implicit goals, given the sociopolitical climate of the programs' inception. What is interesting from the model perspective is the uniformity of outcomes in each of the four areas measured across programs, regardless of their respective theoretical orientations. Thus, despite divergent rationale for program curricula and instructional methods, the goal of improving "social competence" (Zigler, 1970; Zigler & Trickett, 1978) was achieved, while insight was obtained regarding the inadequacy of global intellectual and academic measures for evaluating intervention effectiveness. As Lazar and Darlington (1982) concluded, any high quality early childhood education program could produce long-lasting, positive effects in the lives of young children.

These conclusions must be considered in light of the methodological flaws that are evident. These flaws include the fact that only 3 of the 11-member Consortium found significant effects, although the remaining programs showed the same general trends; there was a high attrition rate; and the number of children who were followed varied greatly in the length of time they were studied. Although the latter two problems are typical of longitudinal studies, these factors must be considered when evaluating the meaningfulness of the Consortium findings.

Issue 2: Effectiveness of Individual
Early Education Model Programs

One of the original intents of the model approach in early education was the articulation of theoretically derived curriculum content and instructional technique to enhance cognitive abilities. It was believed that the enhancement of cognitive abilities early in life would facilitate successful school performance. Standardized intelligence tests and achievement tests were selected as indices of program effectiveness, as were other measures of personality adjustment and achievement-oriented attitudes. The inclusion of these outcome measures reflects the historical period in which many of the model programs were planned and implemented, namely a time when government, university, and community efforts were engaged in a congruent and often collaborative effort to reduce the effects of poverty in the lives of young children (Condry, 1983). As discussed later, however, there was much disagreement concerning appropriate outcome variables, and, again, evidence of methodological problems.

The amount of research concerning individual program effectiveness is quite large. Research that is reviewed here is intended as a sample and as an illustration of methodological problems that have been associated with this area. For a more complete review of research since the 1980s, the reader is referred to Farran (1990).

In general, research findings have shown that over the long run scores on standardized tests do not differ significantly between children enrolled in early education programs and controls (e.g., see reports from individual programs in the Consortium for Longitudinal Studies, 1983). For those programs that show immediate gains (e.g., Lally, Mangione, & Honig, 1988), these effects were achieved by control group children after 2 or 3 years or were "washed out." On the other hand, indices of enhanced social productivity and adjustment were higher for children who participated in early education programs. For example, there were lower rates of special education placement, grade retention, juvenile delinquency, and school drop-out; as well as higher self, parent, and teacher ratings of positive academic attitude, and higher rates of returning to high school following pregnancy (e.g., Berrueta-Clement, Schweinhart, Barnett, Epstein, & Weikart, 1984; Gray, Ramsey, & Klaus, 1983; Lally et al., 1988; Palmer & Siegel, 1977). Thus, studies of individual program effectiveness show similar results regarding cognitive training (as measured by standardized measures) and later school and personality adjustment, regardless of theoretical orientation. However, there are several methodological points that bear addressing.

Summative evaluation (also called *outcome* or *impact* evaluation) includes several basic assumptions (Evans, 1982). First, the program should have goals or outcome objectives that can be attained by the program, and these goals should be linked to instruction. Second, there should be valid, reliable measures of program outcomes, and third, the program should be implemented as intended. These assumptions have not been equally met in evaluation studies.

Regarding the first assumption, hindsight has afforded analysts the luxury of realizing the naivete of an "inoculation" theory of early education, that is, that intervention during the preschool years in the form of schooling would in and of itself prevent academic failure during later years. Original early educators, however, conceived their programs with this goal in mind, assuming that this was a realistic objective. It is now realized that a sustained and broader ecological view of intervention is necessary, one that encompasses children's families, and the communities and sociopolitical climate in which they live (Zigler, 1990).

The second assumption is problematic, as well. As mentioned earlier, measures of cognitive objectives have typically been standardized intelligence and achievement tests. The validity of intelligence tests, especially, as appropriate outcome measures is questionable for several reasons. Although the correlation between intelligence test scores and indices of school performance may be as high as .70 (McClelland, 1973), this still means that intelligence (or what intelligence tests measure) accounts for only half of the variance in predicting school success. In addition, by their nature intelligence tests are insensitive to fine-grained gains in performance (e.g., Garwood, 1982), as well as less than desirable reflections of specific program content, compared to, for example, curriculum-based measures (Marston, 1989). Finally, noncognitive factors, such as motivation, may adversely influence intelligence test performance (Reynolds, Baker, & Levin, 1987; Zigler & Trickett, 1978), and may account for the typical immediate 10-point gain in IQ scores that disadvantaged preschoolers have shown following any length or kind of intervention (Zigler, 1990).

Measures of personality variables have also been questionable, with some programs employing psychometrically problematic projective techniques (e.g., Lally et al., 1988), or relying on self-report of delinquency and other antisocial behavior (e.g., Berrueta-Clement et al., 1984). In addition, programs whose goals are to improve process skills (e.g., Forman & Kuschner, 1977) require a different kind of evaluation procedure. A finer-grained observation of the *quality* of children's in-class behavior is considered to be more appropriate (Johnson, 1987), and this method differs from the psychometric tradition (Elkind, 1971).

Finally, there has been varying heeding of the third assumption regarding program fidelity. Some programs that have been quite detailed about their curriculum and instructional strategy have written little about ongoing checks concerning appropriate implementation (e.g., Bereiter & Engelmann, 1966). On the other hand, other projects have carefully described their monitoring procedures (e.g., Honig & Lally, 1982). In summary, although the findings from evaluations of individual programs are in general agreement, the quality of methodology employed by the programs has been quite variable and renders these findings less definitive.

Issue 3: Comparative Effectiveness of Model Programs

As it was originally conceived, the model approach did not involve a comparative analysis of programs that cut across theoretical boundaries. As noted before, researchers were interested in applying theory to instructional programs and measuring the various effects on children's cognitive development. However, during the 1970s, the sociopolitical climate of support changed, as Honig and Lally (1982) aptly described regarding their (FDRP): "As it started, the goals and values of the program were enthusiastically endorsed. When it ended, those same goals and values had to be defended to the same agencies that had previously endorsed them" (p. 43). It was within this context of diminishing funding and increasing demand for accountability that the goal of early educators was altered by government funding agencies to that of looking for "the one best way" (Cronbach, 1957), the traditional American educational research objective (House, Glass, McLean, & Walker, 1978; Weikart, 1981). This change in orientation was problematic in two ways.

First, the change to an evaluation perspective glossed over the differences between traditional empirical research and evaluation research (Burry, 1981). Traditional empirical research is conclusion-oriented, and it employs methodology that attempts to control for extraneous variables so that cause and effect relationships may be inferred. Evaluation research, on the other hand, is decision-oriented and as such examines phenomena as they exist at a certain point in time. The model approach in early education began with a traditional research orientation, with the expectation that findings would be used in a formative evaluation manner to improve program design (Bloom, Hastings, & Madaus, 1971). However, the change to (or imposition of) an evaluative orientation meant that decisions about the feasibility of programs could be made on the basis of premature research findings.

Second, the change to a comparative perspective ignored the lack of equivalence of model programs. By virtue of the theories from which they were derived, individual early education programs emphasized different goals, curriculum content, beliefs about how best to teach young children, and criteria for judging the effectiveness of intervention. Employing one evaluation research design and methodology to compare the effectiveness of programs based on disparate models would be inappropriate (Overton & Reese, 1973). On the other hand, it would be perfectly reasonable to evaluate the relative effectiveness of early education programs that were based on the same model. For the most part, however, comparative evaluation research has looked at programs across distinct theoretical models.

Given the methodological constraints of comparing models, researchers once again chose to evaluate general program influence on global measures of intelligence and academic achievement. Results from a variety of studies were remarkably similar: In the short- and long-run, children from each model program showed no significant differences in their test scores, although there was a tendency for children in Weikart's (1981) and Bereiter and Engelmann's (1966) programs to score higher (albeit nonsignificantly) than children from programs derived from the maturationist view (Karnes, Shwedel, & Williams, 1983; Miller & Dyer, 1975; Stebbins, St. Pierre, Proper, Anderson, & Cerva, 1977; Weikart, Epstein, Schweinhart, & Bond, 1978). Despite claims of serious methodological flaws (e.g., House et al., 1978), these findings are in agreement with results of individual investigations (Issue 2), as well as those evaluating general preschool effectiveness (Issue 1).

Issue 4: Aspects of Model Programs Contributing to Effectiveness

With consideration of this issue, the discussion of evaluating early education program effectiveness comes full circle, in that determining factors that contribute to program-specific outcomes was the original intent of investigators of model programs. From the perspective of process evaluation (Evans, 1982), change is assumed instead of derived (Reese & Overton, 1970), and the research question becomes, "How does this change come about?", rather than, "What is the one best way?"

There have been numerous attempts to study the myriad of variables comprising teacher behavior, curriculum content, and child behavior in the early education classroom, and to relate these variables to outcome measures in programs representing different model perspectives. For example, Soar and Soar (1972) conducted a fine-grained analysis of teacher-directed and supportive behavior, and children's directed learning, free choice, and cognitive behavior. Using detailed observation checklists, observers recorded frequencies of behavior categories in classrooms following different theoretical guidelines. Such use of low-inference, systematic observation revealed distinct differences in the relationship between teacher and child behaviors, and child cognition. Teacher behaviors that involved controlling and directing learning activities were related to children performing well in simple, concrete tasks, such as naming letters or matching shapes. On the other hand, supportive teacher behavior and child-direction of activity were related to children performing well in complex, abstract tasks, such as applying previous learning to new situations. However, this latter relationship was curvilinear in nature, indicating the importance of an optimal amount of child direction contributing to abstract learning. In addition, Soar and Soar found that programs following different theoretically derived guidelines promoted different types of cognitive activities. For example, as one would expect, children in the Bereiter–Engelmann classroom performed better on rote, concrete tasks, whereas those in the cognitively oriented classroom performed better on abstract tasks. Thus, theoretical models were reflected in teacher behavior, which was in turn related to specific outcomes in child behavior.

Findings similar to Soar and Soar's were reported by Stallings (1975). Using a different but similarly detailed systematic observation schedule of child and teacher behaviors in different model programs, she found that in classrooms where teachers exercised a high degree of control and used direct instruction and positive reinforcement, children had higher math and reading scores (rote skills measured on standardized instruments). In classrooms where teachers were flexible and provided more materials to explore and children had more choice in determining their activity, there were higher nonverbal reasoning skills, lower rates of absenteeism, and more students willing to work independently.

From Stallings' research and the work by Soar and Soar, it is evident that different theoretical approaches to working with children are reflected in classroom procedures and behavioral outcomes. However, discerning these program differences requires the use of careful observation of teacher and child behavior, not global measures of intelligence and achievement. More recent model programs have attempted to conduct systematic classroom observation to explicate the process of learning (e.g., Forman, 1987; Sigel, 1987b).

Conclusions About Model Program Effectiveness

Few would deny the justification of schooling for children above the ages of 6 or 7. Yet the contemporary history of schooling for children below this age has been marked by the nagging need to show first, that children are not harmed, and second, that school experiences can even be beneficial. Perhaps the necessity of showing that early school experiences may facilitate later personality and social adjustment is a reflection of the deeply ingrained cultural value that only families should care for and educate young children (Condry, 1983). Research since the 1970s has shown that early education experiences do promote social and emotional well-being. Research has also shown that the theoretical derivation of a curriculum matters less than the provision of high-quality educational experiences, that is, experiences that have well-articulated objectives, instructional techniques, and rationales for activities. However, strong conclusions about program effectiveness in general and model programs in particular must be tempered by the recognition of the conduct of often flawed research. Although some stress the unequivocal benefits of early education programs (e.g., Zigler, 1990), others are much more tentative in their conclusions (e.g., Farran, 1990).

In what ways related to cognitive skills, then, do model programs make a difference? What has been determined is that there is little long-lasting relationships between specific programs and standardized measures of intelligence and achievement. This is not to say, however, that there is no relationship between specific programs and intelligence and achievement. Research investigating the *process* of teaching and learning (i.e., teacher and child behaviors during program implementation) has revealed important differences among theoretically distinct models. Programs adhering to the belief that the source of knowledge is external have teachers who use direct instruction and reinforcement, and they have children who learn concrete skills efficiently. Programs based on the belief that knowledge is self-constructed have teachers who are less controlling and directing, and they have self-directing children who engage in more abstract reasoning.

Current Status of the Model Approach

From the 1960s to the early 1990s there was a "maturing" of thought concerning the model approach (Johnson, 1988). This change has been the result of a growing realization that several of the assumptions at the foundation of the model approach were limited in their usefulness or were prejudicial. First, the practical difficulty of determining optimally challenging activities (the "match") and knowing when an experience has been appropriate has revealed the vagueness of some theoretical beliefs as sources of curricula. Second, it has become evident that there are many interpretations and applications of theory to early education, and it is possible to find programs that are based on differing models that look alike in practice. Third, the belief that economically disadvantaged, minority children were culturally deprived with inferior language skills and cognitive abilities (e.g., Bernstein, 1968; Hess & Shipman, 1968) and therefore in need of special instructional techniques has given way to the belief that difference does not imply deficit (Cole & Bruner, 1972; Ervin-Tripp, 1972; Ginsburg, 1972). Therefore, programs designed to replace culturally different learning styles, language, and value systems with White middle class ones are now considered paternalistic, at best. Finally, the exclusively classroom-based nature of some model programs, separate from the rest of children's lives, has evolved into a realization that a contextual approach, one that includes families, is more effective (Honig & Lally, 1982; Lazar & Darlington, 1982; Weikart & Schweinhart, 1987).

The result of this change in thinking has been a movement toward "theoretical pluralism" (Johnson, 1988), as well as toward family and community involvement. This means first, that different theoretical approaches may be applied to different aspects of a program or to different child behaviors. Although early education programs may still emphasize one theoretical approach over others, it would be unusual today to see programs viewing children from a cognitive perspective alone (or any other single domain), or to be applying a single theory in their practice. Thus, determining the "best" model is no longer considered appropriate, because the selection of one is not founded in empiricism but in one's value system (Reese & Overton, 1970). The change in thinking about models also means that there have been increased efforts to not only include families in the education of their young children, but to change the nature of early intervention to that of family empowerment (Simeonsson & Bailey, 1990; Vincent, Salisbury, Strain, McCormick, & Tessier, 1990). In this way, many aspects of young children's lives—cognition, health, nutrition—may be improved.

Does this diminishing of the unitary model approach mean there is little need for deriving early education practice from theory? The answer to this question must be no. Developmental and learning theories provide the guiding frameworks for determining the "why" and "how" of early education. They enable teachers to plan thoughtfully, to provide clear objectives, and to determine criteria for meeting those objectives. Substituting a pluralistic model approach for a unitary one allows a much more useful application of theory to different behavioral domains, and is more likely to result in a comprehensive program of early education that addresses social, emotional, cognitive, and physical development. Moreover, it enables practitioners to provide more flexible programming to individual children who might learn more successfully with one approach than with another.

MODEL PROGRAMS IN EARLY EDUCATION
AND SCHOOL PSYCHOLOGY

In the past, preschool-aged children have not been included in the scope of service delivery by school psychologists. However, with the implementation of Public Law 99-457, children below the age of 6 who have disabilities are being provided services in public schools. Although this creates the need for the articulation of psychological services for young, developmentally disabled children, public school programs comprise only one arena in which these services can and should be provided. In the following discussion, two service delivery systems are described: the delivery system for providing early education programs to children who are developing normally but may be at risk because of economic hardship or family stress, and (b) the possibilities for psychological service delivery to these children. Throughout this discussion, implications from the model approach in early education are included.

Providing Early Education Programs
in the Community

Currently, the United States has no national policy for providing services to nondisabled children below school age that is comparable to the public school system. The closest approximation to a national policy may be Project Head Start, a federally funded program for economically disadvantaged children and their families that was initiated in 1965 (Zigler & Valentine, 1979). Currently,

Head Start serves 488,470 children (1990 projected figure), of whom 13.5% (1988–1989) have handicapping conditions (Project Head Start Statistical Fact Sheet, 1990). However, the number of children served represents less than 20% of the eligible children (Washington & Oyemade, 1987), with an estimated 2 million disadvantaged children without services (Day, 1988). The hallmarks of Head Start are its combination of center- and home-based approaches, as well as the active part that parents play in the planning and implementing of child and family support programs. In this way, Head Start exemplifies the contextual or ecological approach to serving children, in addition to helping families acquire more control over the nature of services that are financially provided (cf. Vincent et al., 1990).

With the exception of Head Start, a system of service delivery for early childhood education programs has evolved as a result of market need. This has been accomplished through a combination of federal, state, and local funding of programs serving families and/or children, and the provision of services through university laboratory programs, churches, private businesses, and private homes (Early Childhood Services, 1989). States especially have increased their funding of early education programs, with 28 states supplementing funds for Head Start programs or fully funding prekindergarten or parent education programs (see Day, 1988). This system has been considered less than ideal, however, because of its lack of policy coordination, lack of quality control, and shortfall of programs (e.g., Day, 1988; Vincent & Salisbury, 1988; Zigler, 1982).

Early education programs may be characterized by two service delivery dimensions: the *recipient* of service and the *location* of service delivery. A useful way to consider how young children are provided programming is to look at the intersection of different aspects of these service delivery dimensions (cf. Linder, 1983; see Fig. 1.1).

Early childhood education programs may serve children, their families, or both. Moreover, there is a gradation in the scope of services that may be provided to families, from teaching parents normative child development or strategies for coping with misbehavior, to helping parents become more powerful members of their community to effect social change (Simeonsson & Bailey, 1990). Programs that provide a combination of services to both children and their families may

	LOCATION OF SERVICE		
	Center-Based	Center & Home	Home-Based
Child			
Child & Family			
Family			

RECIPIENT OF SERVICE

FIG. 1.1.   A model of early childhood education service delivery.

also differ in their emphasis. At one end of the continuum, children may be the focus with their families drawn into their educational experiences. At the other end, families may be the primary focus and child care provided so that parents can participate.

The second dimension in early education services relates to the program site. Traditionally, educational programs have been conducted in schools or institutional settings. With the growth of compensatory early education and the realization of the necessity of ecologically valid programs, there has been a concomitant rise in home-based programs, as well as those that include a combination of a center-based and a home-based approach.

Programs may be found representing each of the cells in Fig. 1.1 (see Meisels & Shonkoff, 1990). The model programs discussed earlier may also be considered in this framework. It is not difficult to see that most of them are characterized by their focus on the child served in a school-based program, with the exception of Weikart's High/Scope curriculum and Honig and Lally's FDRP. This narrower focus may have been the result of programs being patterned after the academic orientation of the public school system, or the desire to empirically evaluate the effectiveness of intervention using a particular learning or child-development theory. Viewing the model approach in this way concretizes the shift in thinking that has occurred toward ecologically oriented programming. (However, several model programs not discussed in this chapter have incorporated a family component; see Consortium for Longitudinal Studies, 1983; Johnson, 1988; Pierson, 1988; Ramey, Bryant, Campbell, Sparling, & Wasik, 1988.)

Providing School Psychology Services to At-Risk Preschoolers in Early Education Programs

Although provisions for serving preschool-aged children considered at risk for later developmental and/or learning problems are included under Public Law 99-457, the decisions as to eligibility and institutional responsibility have been left to individual states. Therefore, service delivery to this population may be quite variable, and there may be many at-risk preschoolers without access to public school early childhood programs (Graham & Scott, 1988). Although at-risk preschoolers may also gain access to services through Head Start, as we have seen, the proportion of eligible children served is quite small. School psychologists can certainly provide services to at-risk children enrolled in both of these programs (Head Start requires that such services be available). However, there is the high probability that many young children who would benefit from services remain outside the reach of these two programs. For school psychologists, a prerequisite for providing early childhood services to this latter group of children is a commitment to extend their services to community-based programs. Assuming that this commitment exists for the moment, what lessons of the model approach are relevant for early childhood school psychologists and how may they influence the roles—assessment and intervention, consultation, inservice and preservice, and research (Morgan, 1979)—that school psychologists may perform in public school, Head Start, and community-based programs?

Lesson 1: The Preschool Classroom Cannot be Effective in Isolation. Services to young children, including school psychology services, must address family, community, and cultural issues, the "systems" within which children live. Although family involvement in the education of preschoolers with disabilities is legally mandated by Public Law 99-457, this same ecologically minded policy must be carried out with children at risk who do not fall within the public school service delivery system.

For school psychologists, an ecological perspective implies that the assessment process must entail obtaining information about children's functioning in the settings in which they typically occur (e.g., preschool classrooms, at home) and should incorporate information from a number of relevant sources (e.g., teachers, family members) (cf. Paget, 1990). In addition, family assessment techniques should be added to the school psychologist's repertoire for a variety of reasons (Simeonsson & Bailey, 1990). Related to screening, research suggests that for children age 3 and younger, parental factors are better predictors of later disability then child-centered skills (Kochanek, Kabacoff & Lipsitt, 1990). Other reasons for including family assessment include the importance of determining a family's strengths and needs, which are crucial to the planning and implementation of a child-oriented intervention program, as well as for determining family commitment to implementing treatment.

There is some evidence that suggests early education teachers view the assessment activities conducted by school psychologists as consisting primarily of norm-referenced testing, and that this function is not considered very useful (Widerstrom, Mowder, & Willis, 1989). Teachers' opinions may reflect the traditional classificatory function that school psychology assessment has played. Although this role continues to be important for determining elementary school program eligibility, school psychologists do have much to offer in the area of early childhood assessment as a continuous process related to intervention, and as it is currently being reconceptualized from a broader, contextual perspective. The importance of the school psychologist's assessment role is underscored by recent findings that teachers tend to rely on a narrow range of instruments, ones they have learned during preservice training or have relied on for a number of years (Johnson & Beauchamp, 1987). School psychologists may thus bring to teachers' attention a wider range of assessment techniques that may be more appropriate.

An ecological approach also implies that intervention techniques that are appropriate for one child or in one setting may not be effective for another child or in another setting (Reynolds, Gutkin, Elliott, & Witt, 1984). In addition, intervention programs should be carried out in multiple natural settings, and persons important in children's lives, such as family members, peers, and teachers, should participate in their implementation. This is especially important in families where culturally different philosophies exist regarding the role of the helping professions, and where there are differing views concerning which family members are responsible for the child (Vincent et al., 1990).

An ecological perspective also means that intervention programs must not be limited in their focus to changing child behavior, but should include family-focused intervention, as well, since the influence between child and family is reciprocal (Barnett & Paget, 1989; Mcloughlin, 1989). The range of family-focused intervention is broad. For example, intervention may include helping a family obtain services for their child, working in a partnership with a family to implement an intervention program, providing counseling to a family, or helping a family improve its advocacy skills for acquiring community services (Simeon-son & Bailey, 1990).

Providing indirect services through consultation, inservice, and preservice programs constitutes an especially important role for the practice of ecologically oriented early childhood school psychology. It is through the provision of indirect services that a wide range of people capable of influencing a wider range of children may be reached. Indirect services are particularly important in the area of prevention, which is, after all, one way of conceptualizing early education (Price, Cowen, Lorion, & Ramos-McKay, 1988). Thus, in addition to problem-oriented consultation with teachers and families, preventive consultation can help teachers in the processes of assessment and intervention through individual consultation about specific children, or through group consultation delivered through inservice programs for teachers.

Preventive consultative services are multifaceted. First, they may include discussion of procedures for child-focused as well as family-focused assessment and intervention (cf. Bailey, Palsha, & Huntington, 1990). A second function of consultation may be to help parents prepare their children for the transition from community-based preschool programs to public school-based kindergarten (e.g., Hamblin-Wilson, & Thurman, 1990). A third consultation role may involve working collaboratively with high school psychologists, offering adolescents the opportunity to discuss beliefs or "theories" about child development and parenting. Finally, school psychologists can provide workshops or community center-based courses for families. Of course, a community level of involvement by school psychologists requires a willingness to broaden one's consultative base. It may also require perseverence to convince community services personnel of the relevance of the school psychologist's skills as a proactive agent in the lives of young children. This broadening of consultative services from child-, to teacher-, to family-, and finally to community-focused delivery fits well within an ecological view of the school psychologist's roles.

Lesson 2: Theories of Development and Learning can Contribute to Formulating Effective Theories of Practice. An understanding of theory and how to apply it in practice facilitates the creation of effective intervention programs— ones that have objectives, activities related to these objectives, and methods for evaluating whether the objectives have been met. Although not all teachers in practice may articulate a particular theory and how it may be implemented, it is likely that they operate within an implicit guiding framework (Johnson, 1988). One's beliefs and values influence program objectives and the types of activities provided. As practitioners able to bridge the fields of psychology and education, school psychologists can work with early childhood education teachers, helping them make explicit their beliefs and assumptions about children to plan more effectively and evaluate children's progress. In addition, school psychologists can become involved in preservice programs in teacher training, fulfilling the same kind of function.

Lesson 3: Different Theoretical Frameworks may be Applied to Different Program Components.   The model approach has shown that theoretical perspectives influence program objectives, content, and outcomes. School psychologists (again in a consultative relationship) can help teachers incorporate different theoretical frameworks into different aspects of their program to serve the "whole child." Moreover, this multitheoretical perspective may be particularly useful for understanding individual differences among children and for developing individual programs. Related to this ideal of theoretical pluralism, school psychologists may also be helpful in bridging the differences that may exist between teachers trained in the child-centered approaches of early childhood education and teachers trained in the teacher-directed approaches of special education (Mowder & Widerstrom, 1986). Early education programs can certainly accommodate both approaches, and helping teachers from both traditions see the value of each perspective in relation to curriculum objectives for individual children is a role school psychologists could fulfill.

Lesson 4: The Processes of Intervention are Related to Behavior Outcomes.   The work of Soar and Soar (1972) and Stallings (1975) has shown that specific teaching behaviors can be related to specific outcomes in children's behavior. Because this research investigated group differences across programs, it represents only a beginning effort in understanding individual differences in learning. The task of researchers now is to determine, within the respective theoretical frameworks, the teaching practices that are related to learning outcomes for individual children in specific situations (cf. Paul, 1967). School psychologists, familiar with single subject designs in applied behavior analysis (see Cooper et al., 1987), can address this research need of determining effective instructional techniques for individual children. Moreover, as Paget (1985) has pointed out, in addition to behavioral technology, other intervention-linked assessment procedures such as curriculum-based assessment (Neisworth & Bagnato, 1986), dynamic assessment (Lidz, 1983), and test–teach–test approaches (Ysseldyke & Mirkin, 1982) may be studied in preschool intervention with individual children. In this way, school psychologists could contribute to both a methodology and a knowledge base concerning the conditions under which individual children successfully learn and develop.

New Directions in School Psychology Training. Because young children and their families are the focus of early childhood school psychology, professional practice does not merely involve a downward extension of services. Training programs must address the acquisition of different content necessary for working with this population.

A primary reason for the unique nature of early childhood school psychology is the importance of paying attention to children's development and learning (e.g., Barnett, 1986). Development in this instance refers to qualitative changes that can not be attributed to specific experiences, but result from the accumulation of experiences. Learning, on the other hand, refers to quantitative changes in behavior whose source can be traced to specific experiences (Wohlwill, 1970). Model programs in early education have typically placed themselves toward one end of the learning–development continuum, emphasizing one over the other. This has generated much discussion concerning the function of early education as a means to facilitate development via enrichment, or as a way to teach specific content through direct instruction (Elkind, 1973, 1987; Kohlberg & Mayer, 1972; Sigel, 1987a; Zigler, 1987). School psychologists working in the area of early education should have a clear understanding of the issues related to the development–learning controversy, for its resolution has implications for program objectives and content (see also Barnett, 1986). Thus, training programs should include coursework in both the developmental and learning traditions, as well as dialogue with students whose programs emphasize these separate areas, perhaps through interdisciplinary seminars. These training experiences will enable prospective school psychologists to develop and articulate their own organizational frameworks or "philosophies" of service, which should also enhance multidisciplinary teamwork in practice.

The ecological nature of school psychology practice in early education also has several implications for training. First is the importance of developing expertise in assessment methods more closely related to intervention and to the contexts in which children typically behave. This includes observation methods as well as family assessment methods. A second implication is the provision of increased opportunities for family-focused intervention through practicum experiences. Third, training should include coursework in consultation, including comparative consultative models, as well as experience in consultation. This is an especially important area, because so much of service delivery in early education is accomplished through collaboration with other professionals and with children's families (Barnett, 1986; Mcloughlin, 1989). A final area of training involves helping students acquire a broader vision of school psychology, one that involves an awareness of community services for young children and their families. Practicum experiences that are community based, that is, in community centers, on advisory boards, and the like, would familiarize students with many community programs for young children and their families. This community involvement would also provide students the training for influencing policy decisions when they are in practice.

In all, training programs for preparing school psychologists to work with early childhood programs should reflect the unique nature of young children. This includes the importance of addressing the issue of development as a curriculum goal, of considering the many contexts that influence young children's behavior, and of working collaboratively with families and within the community.

SUMMARY AND CONCLUDING REMARKS

The model approach in early education grew out of the desire to improve the academic performance of economically disadvantaged children during the 1960s. Three models (maturationist, learning, and interactionist) have generated a variety of programs, each with specific objectives, curriculum content, and teaching methods. These models represent differing views regarding the primacy of developmental versus learning processes for explaining children's behavior. Evaluation of early education model programs has shown that, despite theoretical differences in programs, children perform equivalently on broadly conceived measures of social competence. However, there has been little sustained influence on standardized intelligence and achievement test scores. Today, these measures are considered inadequate as means of evaluating cognitive outcomes. Research has turned instead to analyzing teacher and learner behaviors and individual differences in learning in relation to theoretical principles driving early education programs.

The model approach has changed since the 1970s. Currently, the notion of a single, best theoretical approach in early education has given way to the belief in theoretical plurality, where different theories may be applied to different aspects of a curriculum or to different behavioral domains. In addition, there has been a rediscovery of the influence of context on individual behavior and development. This has been translated in practice into an ecological perspective, the recognition of the mutually influential relationships among children, their families, and the communities in which they live.

For school psychologists the lesson to be learned from more than 20 years of studying model programs is the utility of a multitheoretical, ecological approach in providing services for young children (cf. Christenson, Abery, & Weinberg, 1986). School psychologists themselves have not typically worked within a theoretically pluralistic, context-oriented perspective. Traditionally, the school psychologist's focus has been child centered, although persons important in a child's life (teachers, parents) have been recipients of service. However, both theory and supporting research have moved early childhood education and school psychology toward incorporating a multitheoretical, ecological approach, which has important implications for training and practice for professionals in both fields.

REFERENCES

Ainsworth, M. D. (1967). Patterns of infantile attachment to mother. In Y. Brackbill & G. G. Thompson (Eds.), *Behavior in infancy and early childhood* (pp. 607–615). New York: The Free Press.

Baer, D. (1970). The control of developmental processes: Why wait? In J. R. Nesselroade & H. W. Reese (Eds.), *Life-span developmental psychology: Methodological issues* (pp. 185–193). New York: Academic Press.

Baer, D. (1973). An age-irrelevant concept of development. *Merrill–Palmer Quarterly of Behavior and Development, 16,* 238–246.

Bailey, D. B., Jr., Palsha, S.A., & Huntington, G. S. (1990). Preservice preparation of special educators to serve infants with handicaps and their families: Current status and training needs. *Journal of Early Intervention, 14,* 43–54.

Bandura, A. (1978). The self-system in reciprocal determinism. *American Psychologist, 33,* 344–358.

Barnett, D. W. (1986). School psychology in preschool settings: A review of training and practice issues. *Professional Psychology: Research and Practice, 17,* 58–64.

Barnett, D. W., & Paget, K. D. (1989). Alternative service delivery in preschool settings: Practical and conceptual foundations. In J. L. Graden, J. E. Zins, & M. J. Curtis (Eds.), *Alternative educational delivery systems: Enhancing instructional options for all students* (pp. 291–308). Washington, DC: National Association of School Psychologists.

Bereiter, C., & Engelmann, S. (1966). *Teaching the disadvantaged child in the preschool.* Englewood Cliffs, NJ: Prentice-Hall.

Bereiter, C., & Engelmann, S. (1973). Observation on the use of direct instruction with young disadvantaged children. In B. Spodek (Ed.), *Early childhood education* (pp. 176–186). Englewood Cliffs, NJ: Prentice-Hall.

Bernstein, B. (1968). A socio-linguistic approach to social learning. In J. L. Frost (Ed.), *Early childhood education rediscovered* (pp. 445–466). New York: Holt, Rinehart & Winston.

Berrueta-Clement, J. R., Schweinhart, L. J., Barnett, W. S., Epstein, A. S., & Weikart, D. P. (1984). *Changed lives: The effects of the Perry Preschool Program on youths through age 19* (Monographs of the High/Scope Educational Research Foundation No. 8, Ypsilanti, MI: High/Scope Press.

Biber, B. (1984). *Early education and psychological development.* New Haven, CT: Yale University Press.

Biber, B., Shapiro, E., & Wickens, D. (1977). *Promoting cognitive growth: A developmental interaction point of view* (2nd ed.). Washington, DC: National Association for the Education of Young Children.

Bloom, B. S. (1964). *Stability and change in human characteristics.* New York: John Wiley.

Bloom, B. S., Hastings, J. T., & Madaus, G. F. (Eds.). (1971). *Handbook on formative and summative evaluation of student learning.* New York: McGraw-Hill.

Borstellman, L. J. (1983). Children before psychology: Ideas about children from antiquity to the late 1800s. In P. H. Mussen & W. Kessen (Eds.), *Handbook of child psychology* (Vol. 1, 4th ed.) (pp. 1–40). New York: Wiley.

Bruner, J. S. (1973). *Beyond the information given: Studies in the psychology of knowing.* New York: W. W. Norton.

Burry, J. (1981). An introduction to assessment and design in bilingual program evaluation. *Bilingual Education Series, 5,* Los Angeles, CA: EDAC.

Bushell, D., Jr. (1973). The behavior analysis classroom. In B. Spodek (Ed.), *Early childhood education* (pp. 163–175). Englewood Cliffs, NJ: Prentice-Hall.

Caldwell, B. M., Richmond, J. B., Honig, A. S., Moldovan, S. E., Mozell, C., & Kawash, M. B. (1968). A day care program for disadvantaged infants and young children—Observations after one year. In G. A. Jervis (Ed.), *Expanding concepts in mental retardation* (pp. 103–115). Springfield, IL: Charles C. Thomas.

Camp, J. C. (1973). A skill development curriculum for 3-, 4-, and 5-year-old disadvantaged children. In B. Spodek (Ed.), *Early childhood education* (pp. 187–198). Englewood Cliffs, NJ: Prentice-Hall.

Carter, D. B. (1987). Early childhood education: A historical perspective. In J. L. Roopnarine & J. E. Johnson (Eds.), *Approaches to early childhood education* (pp. 1–14). Columbus, OH: Merrill.

Case, R., & Bereiter, C. (1984). From behaviourism to cognitive behaviorism to cognitive development: Steps in the evolution of instructional design. *Instructional Science, 13,* 141–158.

Christenson, S., Abery, B., & Weinberg, R. A. (1986). An alternative model for the delivery of psychological services in the school community. In S. N. Elliott & J. C. Witt (Eds.), *The delivery of psychological services in the schools* (pp. 349–391). Hillsdale, NJ: Lawrence Erlbaum Associates.

Cole, M., & Bruner, J. S. (1972). Preliminaries to a theory of cultural differences. In I. J. Gordon (Ed.), *Early childhood education: The seventy-first yearbook of the National Society for the Study of Education* (pp. 161–180). Chicago, IL: The National Society for the Study of Education.

Condry, S. (1983). History and background of preschool intervention programs and the Consortium for Longitudinal Studies. In Consortium for Longitudinal Studies, *As the twig is bent . . . Lasting effects of preschool programs* (pp. 1–32). Hillsdale, NJ: Lawrence Erlbaum Associates.

Consortium for Longitudinal Studies. (1983). *As the twig is bent . . . Lasting effects of preschool programs.* Hillsdale, NJ: Lawrence Erlbaum Associates.

Cooper, J. O., Heron, T. E., & Heward, W. L. (1987). *Applied behavior analysis.* Columbus, OH: Merrill.

Copeland, R. W. (1974). *How children learn mathematics—Teaching implications of Piaget's research* (2nd ed.). New York: MacMillan.

Copple, C., Sigel, I. E., & Saunders, R. (1984). *Educating the young thinker.* Hillsdale, NJ: Lawrence Erlbaum Associates.

Cronbach, L. (1957). The two disciplines of scientific psychology. *American Psychologist, 10,* 633–643.

Day, B. D. (1988). What's happening in early childhood programs across the United States. In C. Warger (Ed.), *A resource guide to public school early childhood programs* (pp. 3–31). Alexandria, VA: Association for Supervision and Curriculum Development.

Day, M. C., & Parker, R. K. (1977). *The preschool in action: Exploring early childhood programs* (2nd ed.). Boston, MA: Allyn & Bacon.

Deasey, D. (1978). *Education under six.* New York: St. Martin's Press.

Dewey, J. (1944). *Democracy and education.* New York: Macmillan Free Press.

Duckworth, E. (1964). Piaget rediscovered. In R. E. Ripple & V. N. Rockcastle (Eds.), *Piaget rediscovered* (pp. 1–5). Ithaca, NY: Cornell University Press.

Early childhood services: A national challenge. (1989). New York: Ford Foundation.

Elkind, D. (1968). Editor's introduction. In J. Piaget, *Six psychological studies* (pp. v–xviii). New York: Vintage Books.

Elkind, D. (1971). Two approaches to intelligence: Piagetian and psychometric. In D. R. Green, M. P. Ford, & G. B. Flander (Eds.), *Measurement and Piaget* (pp. 12–27). New York: McGraw-Hill.

Elkind, D. (1973). Preschool education: Enrichment or instruction? In B. Spodek (Ed.), *Early childhood education* (pp. 108–121). Englewood Cliffs, NJ: Prentice-Hall.

Elkind, D. (1987). Early childhood education on its own terms. In S. L. Kagan & E. F. Zigler (Eds.), *Early schooling: The national debate* (pp. 98–115). New Haven, CT: Yale University Press.

Erikson, E. H. (1950). *Childhood and society*. New York: W. W. Norton.

Erikson, E. H. (1980). *Identity and the life cycle*. New York: W. W. Norton.

Ervin-Tripp, S. M. (1972). Children's sociolinguistic competence and dialect diversity. In I. J. Gordon (Ed.), *Early childhood education: The seventy-first yearbook of the National Society for the Study of Education* (pp. 120–160). Chicago, IL: The National Society for the Study of Education.

Evans, E. D. (1975). *Contemporary influences in early childhood education*. New York: Holt, Rinehart, and Winston.

Evans, E. D. (1982). Curriculum models and early education. In B. Spodek (Ed.), *Handbook of research in early childhood education* (pp. 107–134). New York: The Free Press.

Farran, D. C. (1990). Effects of intervention with disadvantaged children: A decade review. In S. J. Meisels & J. P. Shonkoff (Eds.), *Handbook of early childhood intervention* (pp. 501–539). New York: Oxford University Press.

Flavell, J. H. (1963). *The developmental psychology of Jean Piaget*. Princeton, NJ: D. Von Nostrand.

Forehand, R. L., & McMahon, R. J. (1981). *Helping the noncompliant child*. New York: The Guilford Press.

Forman, G. (1987). The school for constructive play. In J. L. Roopnarine & J. E. Johnson (Eds.), *Approaches to early childhood education* (pp. 71–84). Columbus, OH: Merrill.

Forman, G., & Hill, F. (1984). *Constructive play: Applying Piaget in the preschool*. Menlo Park, CA: Addison Wesley.

Forman, G. E., & Kuschner, D. S. (1977). *The child's construction of knowledge: Piaget for teaching children*. Monterey, CA: Brooks/Cole.

Furth, H. G. (1969). *Piaget and knowledge*. Englewood Cliffs, NJ: Prentice-Hall.

Furth, H. G., & Wachs, H. (1974). *Thinking goes to school*. New York: Oxford University Press.

Gagne, R. (1968). Contributions of learning to human development. *Psychological Review, 75*, 177–191.

Garwood, S. G. (1982). (Mis)use of developmental scales in program evaluation. *Topics in early Childhood Special Education, 1*, 61–68.

Gilkeson, E. C., & Bowman, G. W. (1976). *The focus is on children*. New York: Bank Street Publications.

Ginsburg, H. (1972). *The myth of the deprived child*. Englewood Cliffs, NJ: Prentice-Hall.

Ginsburg, H., & Opper, S. (1969). *Piaget's theory of intellectual development*. Englewood Cliffs, NJ: Prentice-Hall.

Graham, M. A., & Scott, K. G. (1988). The impact of definitions of high risk on services to infants and toddlers. *Topics in Early Childhood Special Education, 8*, 23–38.

Gray, S. W., Ramsey, B. K., & Klaus, R. A. (1983). The Early Training Project. In Consortium for Longitudinal Studies, *As the twig is bent . . . Lasting effects of preschool programs* (pp. 33–70). Hillsdale, NJ: Lawrence Erlbaum Associates.

Grotberg, E. H. (1972). Institutional responsibilities for early childhood education. In I. J. Gordon (Ed.), *Early childhood education: The seventy-first yearbook of the National Society for the Study of Education* (pp. 317–338). Chicago, IL: The National Society for the Study of Education.

Hamblin-Wilson, C., & Thurmon, S. K. (1990). The transition from early intervention to kindergarten: Parental satisfaction and involvement. *Journal of Early Intervention, 14*, 55–61.

Harter, S. (1968). Learning to learn. In J. L. Frost (Ed.), *Early childhood education rediscovered* (pp. 322–326). New York: Holt, Rinehart & Winston.

Hess, R. D., & Shipman, V. C. (1968). Maternal influences upon early learning: The cognitive environments of urban pre-school children. In R. D. Hess & R. M. Baer (Eds.), *Early childhood education* (pp. 91–103). Chicago, IL: Aldine.

Hohmann, M., Banet, B., & Weikart, D. P. (1979). *Young children in action: A manual for preschool educators*. Ypsilanti, MI: High/Scope Press.

Honig, A. S. (1987). The Eriksonian approach: Infant–toddler education. In J. L. Roopnarine & J. E. Johnson (Eds.), *Approaches to early childhood education* (pp. 49–69). Columbus, OH: Merrill.

Honig, A. S., & Lally, J. R. (1982). The family development research program: Retrospective review. *Early Child Care and Development, 10,* 41–62.

Hooper, F. H. (1968). Piagetian research and education. In I. E. Sigel & F. H. Hooper (Eds.), *Logical thinking in children* (pp. 423–434). New York: Holt, Rinehart & Winston.

Hooper, F. H. (1987). Epilogue: Déja vu in approaches in early childhood education. In J. L. Roopnarine & J. E. Johnson (Eds.), *Approaches to early childhood education* (pp. 301–314). Columbus, OH: Merrill.

House, E. R., Glass, G. V., McLean, L. D., & Walker, D. F. (1978). No simple answer: Critique of the Follow Through evaluation. *Harvard Educational Review, 48,* 128–160.

Hunt, J. McV. (1961). *Intelligence and experience.* New York: The Ronald Press.

Hunt, J. McV. (1964). The psychological basis for using pre-school enrichment as antidote for cultural deprivation. *Merrill-Palmer Quarterly, 10,* 209–248.

Hutinger, P. L. (1987). Computer-based learning for young children with special needs. In J. L. Roopnarine & J. E. Johnson (Eds.), *Approaches to early childhood education* (pp. 213–236). Columbus, OH: Merrill Publishing.

Isaacs, S. (1930). *Intellectual growth in young children.* London: Routledge.

Isaacs, S. (1933). *Social development in young children.* London: Routledge.

Johnson, D. L. (1988). Primary prevention of behavior problems in young children. In R. H. Price, E. L. Cowen, R. P. Lorion, & J. Ramos-McKay (Eds.), *14 ounces of prevention* (pp. 44–52). Washington, DC: American Psychological Association.

Johnson, J. E. (1987). Evaluation in early childhood education. In J. L. Roopnarine & J. E. Johnson (Eds.), *Approaches to early childhood education* (pp. 15–34). Columbus, OH: Merrill Publishing.

Johnson, J. E. (1988). Psychological theory and early education. In A. D. Pelligrini (Ed.), *Psychological bases for early education* (pp. 1–21). New York: Wiley.

Johnson, J. L., & Beauchamp, K. D. F. (1987). Preschool assessment measures: What are teachers using? *Journal of the Division for Early Childhood, 12,* 70–76.

Kamii, C. K. (1970). Piaget's theory and specific instruction: A response to Bereiter and Kohlberg. *Interchange, 1,* 33–39.

Kamii, C. K. (1971). Evaluation of learning in preschool education: Socio-emotional, perceptual-motor, and cognitive development. In B. S. Bloom, J. T. Hastings, & G. F. Madaus (Eds.), *Handbook on formative and summative evaluation of student learning* (pp. 281–344). New York: McGraw-Hill.

Kamii, C. K. (1984). Autonomy: The aim of education envisioned by Piaget. *Phi Delta Kappan, 15,* 410–415.

Kamii, C., & DeVries, R. (1973). An application of Piaget's theory to the conceptualization of a preschool curriculum. In M. C. Day & R. K. Parker (Eds.), *The preschool in action* (pp. 91–131). New York: McGraw-Hill.

Kamii, C., & DeVries, R. (1976). *Piaget, children, and number.* Washington, DC: National Association for the Education of Young Children.

Kamii, C., & DeVries, R. (1977). Piaget for early education. In M. C. Day & R. K. Parker (Eds.), *The preschool in action* (2nd ed., pp. 365–420). New York: McGraw-Hill.

Kamii, C., & DeVries, R. (1978). *Physical knowledge in preschool education.* Englewood Cliffs, NJ: Prentice-Hall.

Kamii, C., & DeVries, R. (1980). *Group games in early education.* Washington, DC: National Association for the Education of Young Children.

Kamii, C. K., & Radin, N. L. (1970). A framework for a preschool curriculum based on some Piagetian concepts. In I. J. Athey & D. O. Rubideau (Eds.), *Educational implications of Piaget's theory* (pp. 89–100). Waltham, MA: Xerox College Publishing.

Karnes, M. B., Shwedel, A. M., & Williams, M. B. (1983). A comparison of five approaches for educating young children from low-income homes. In Consortium for Longitudinal Studies, *As the twig is bent . . . Lasting effects of preschool programs* (pp. 133–169). Hillsdale, NJ: Lawrence Erlbaum Associates.

Karplus, R. (1970). The science curriculum improvement study—Report to the Piaget Conference. In I. J. Athey & D. O. Rubideau (Eds.), *Educational implications of Piaget's theory* (pp. 241–246). Waltham, MA: Xerox College Publishing.

Kelly, G. A. (1955). *The psychology of personal constructs.* New York: W. W. Norton.

Kochanek, T. T., Kabacoff, R. I., & Lipsitt, L. P. (1990). Early identification of developmentally disabled and at-risk preschool children. *Exceptional Children, 56,* 528–538.

Kohlberg, L. (1968). Early education: A cognitive-developmental view. *Child Development, 39,* 1013–1062.

Kohlberg, L., & Mayer, R. (1972). Development as the aim of education. *Harvard Educational Review, 42,* 449–496.

Lally, J. R., & Honig, A. S. (1977). The family development research program: A program for prenatal, infant, and early childhood enrichment. In M. C. Day & R. D. Parker (Eds.), *The preschool in action* (2nd ed., pp. 149–194). Boston, MA: Allyn & Bacon.

Lally, J. R., Mangione, P., & Honig, A. S. (1988). The Syracuse University Family Development Research Program: Long-range impact of an early intervention with low income children and their families. In D. Powell (Ed.), *Parent education as early childhood intervention: Emerging directions in theory, research, and practice* (pp. 79–104). Norwood, NJ: Ablex.

Lazar, I., & Darlington, R. B. (1982). Lasting effects of early education. *Monographs of the Society for Research in Child Development, 47*(2–3, Serial No. 195).

Lidz, C. S. (1983). Dynamic assessment and the preschool child. *Journal of Psychoeducational Assessment, 1,* 59–72.

Linder, T. (1983). *Early childhood special education: Program development and administration.* Baltimore: University Park Press.

Marston, D. (1989). A curriculum-based measurement approach to assessing academic performance: What is it and why do it? In M. Shinn (Ed.), *Curriculum-based measurement: Assessing special children* (pp. 18–78). New York: The Guilford Press.

McClelland, D. (1973). Testing for competence rather than for "intelligence." *American Psychologist, 28,* 1–14.

Mcloughlin, C. S. (1989). Provision of psychological services to very young children and their families. In J. L. Graden, J. E. Zins, & M. J. Curtis (Eds.), *Alternative educational delivery systems: Enhancing instructional options for all students* (pp. 269–290). Washington, DC: National Association of School Psychologists.

Meisels, S. J., & Shonkoff, J. P. (Eds.). (1990). *Handbook of early childhood intervention.* New York: Cambridge University Press.

Miller, L. B., & Dyer, J. L. (1975). Four preschool programs: Their dimensions and effects. *Monographs of the Society for Research in Child Development, 40*(5–6, Serial No. 162).

Montessori, M. (1964). *The Montessori method.* New York: Schocken Books.

Morgan, V. (1979). Roles and status of school psychology. In G. D. Phye & D. J. Reschly (Eds.), *School psychology: Perspectives and issues* (pp. 25–47). New York: Academic Press.

Mounts, N. S., & Roopnarine, J. L. (1987). Application of behavioristic principles to early childhood education. In J. L. Roopnarine & J. E. Johnson (Eds.), *Approaches to early childhood education* (pp. 127–142). Columbus, OH: Merrill Publishing.

Mowder, B. A., & Widerstrom, A. H. (1986). Philosophical differences between early childhood education and special education: Issues for school psychologists. *Psychology in the Schools, 23,* 171–174.

Murray, F. B. (1979). Educational implications of developmental theory. In H. J. Klausmeier & Associates (Eds.), *Cognitive learning and development: Piagetian and information processing perspectives* (pp. 247–268). Cambridge, MA: Ballinger Publishing.

Nagel, E. (1957). Determinism and development. In D. B. Harris (Ed.), *The concept of development* (pp. 15–24). Minneapolis, MN: The Jones Press.

Neisworth, J. T., & Bagnato, S. J. (1986). Curriculum-based developmental assessment: Congruence of testing and teaching. *School Psychology Review, 15,* 180–199.

Nelson, C. M., & Polsgrove, L. (1984). Behavior analysis in special education: White rabbit or white elephant? *Remedial and Special Education, 5,* 6–17.

Overton, W. F., & Reese, H. W. (1973). Models of development: Methodological implications. In J. R. Nesselroade & H. W. Reese (Eds.), *Life-span developmental psychology: Methodological issues* (pp. 65–86). New York: Academic Press.

Paget, K. D. (1985). Preschool services in the schools: Issues and implications. *Special Services in the Schools, 2,* 3–25.

Paget, K. D. (1990). Best practices in the assessment of competence in preschool-age children. In A. Thomas & J. Grimes (Eds.), *Best practices in school psychology - II* (pp. 107–119). Washington, DC: The National Association of School Psychologists.

Palmer, F. H., & Siegel, R. (1977). Minimal intervention at ages two to three and subsequent intellective changes. In M. C. Day & R. K. Parker (Eds.), *The preschool in action* (2nd ed., pp. 3–26). Boston, MA: Allyn & Bacon.

Paul, G. P. (1967). Outcome research in psychotherapy. *Journal of Consulting Psychology, 31,* 109–118.

Piaget, J. (1964). Development and learning. In R. E. Ripple & V. N. Rockcastle (Eds.), *Piaget rediscovered* (pp. 7–20). Ithaca, NY: Cornell University Press.

Piaget, J. (1971a). *Biology and knowledge: An essay on the relations between organic regulations and cognitive processes.* Chicago, IL: University of Chicago Press.

Piaget, J. (1971b). *Psychology and epistemology.* New York: Viking Press.

Piaget, J. (1977). *The development of thought: Equilibration of cognitive structures.* New York: Viking Press.

Piaget, J. (1981). *Intelligence and affectivity.* Palo Alto, CA: Annual Reviews.

Pierson, D. E. (1988). The Brookline Early Education Project. In R. H. Price, E. L. Cowen, R. P. Lorion, & J. Ramos-McKay (Eds.), *14 ounces of prevention* (pp. 24–31). Washington, DC: American Psychological Association.

Plato. (1945). *The republic of Plato* (F. M. Cornford, Trans.). New York: Oxford University Press.

Price, R. H., Cowen, E. L., Lorion, R. P., & Ramos-McKay, J. (Eds.). (1988). *14 ounces of prevention.* Washington, DC: American Psychological Association.

Project Head Start Statistical Fact Sheet. (1990). Washington, DC: Department of Health and Human Services.

Ramey, C. T., Bryant, D. M., Campbell, F. A., Sparling, J. J., & Wasik, B. H. (1988). Early intervention for high-risk children: The Carolina Early Intervention Program. In R. H. Price, E. L. Cowen, R. P. Lorion, & J. Ramos-McKay (Eds.), *14 ounces of prevention* (pp. 32–43). Washington, DC: American Psychological Association.

Reese, H. W., & Overton, W. F. (1970). Models of development and theories of development. In L. R. Goulet & P. B. Baltes (Eds.), *Life-span developmental psychology: Research and theory* (pp. 116–149). New York: Academic Press.

Reynolds, C. R., Gutkin, T. B., Elliott, S. N., & Witt, J. C. (1984). *School psychology: Essentials of theory and practice.* New York: Wiley.

Reynolds, W. R., Baker, J. A., & Levin, D. C. (1987). Assessment of intellectual abilities of mentally retarded individuals. In R. S. Dean (Ed.), *Introduction to assessing human intelligence* (pp. 137–176). Springfield, IL: Charles C. Thomas.

Ripple, R. E., & Rockcastle, V. N. (Eds.). (1964). *Piaget rediscovered.* Ithaca, NY: Cornell University Press.

Roach, E. G., & Kephart, N. C. (1966). *The Purdue Perceptual-Motor Survey.* Columbus, OH: Merrill Publishing.

Roeper, A., & Sigel, I. (1970). Finding the clue to children's thought processes. In I. J. Athey & D. O. Rubideau (Eds.), *Educational implications of Piaget's theory* (pp. 75–88). Waltham, MA: Xerox College Press.

Rousseau, J. J. (1961). *Emile* (B. Foxley, Trans.). New York: E. P. Dutton.

Sadler, J. E. (Ed.). (1969). *Comenius*. London: Collier-MacMillan.

Sahakian, W. S. (1976). *Learning: Systems, models and theories* (2nd ed.). Chicago, IL: Rand McNally.

Shapiro, E., & Biber, B. (1972). The education of young children: A developmental-interaction approach. *Teachers College Record, 74*, 55–79.

Shearer, D., & Shearer, M. (1976). The Portage Project: A model for early childhood intervention. In T. Tjossem (Ed.), *Intervention strategies for high risk infants and young children* (pp. 335–350). Baltimore, MD: University Park Press.

Shirley, M. M. (1931–1933). *The first two years: A study of twenty-five babies* (Vols. 1 & 2). Minneapolis, MN: University of Minnesota Press.

Sigel, I. E. (1970). The distancing hypothesis: A causal hypothesis for the acquisition of representational thought. In M. R. Jones (Ed.), *The effects of early experience* (pp. 99–118). Miami, FL: University of Miami Press.

Sigel, I. E. (1987a). Early childhood education: Developmental enhancement or developmental acceleration? In S. L. Kagan & E. F. Zigler (Eds.), *Early schooling: The national debate* (pp. 129–150). New Haven, CT: Yale University Press.

Sigel, I. E. (1987b). Educating the young thinker: A distancing model of preschool education. In J. L. Roopnarine & J. E. Johnson (Eds.), *Approaches to early childhood education* (pp. 237–252). Columbus, OH: Merrill Publishing.

Sigel, I. E., & Cocking, R. R. (1977). *Cognitive development from childhood to adolescence: A constructionist perspective*. New York: Holt, Rinehart & Winston.

Sigel, I. E., & Saunders, R. (1979). An inquiry into inquiry: Question asking as an instructional model. In L. G. Katz (Ed.), *Current topics in early childhood education* (Vol. 2, pp. 169–193). Norwood, NJ: Ablex.

Silberman, C. E. (1973). *The open classroom reader*. New York: Vintage Books.

Simeonsson, R. J., & Bailey, D. B., Jr. (1990). Family dimensions in early intervention. In S. J. Meisels & J. P. Shonkoff (Eds.), *Handbook of early childhood intervention* (pp. 428–444). New York: Cambridge University Press.

Skinner, B. F. (1953). *Science and human behavior*. New York: MacMillan Publishing.

Soar, R. S., & Soar, R. M. (1972). An empirical analysis of selected Follow Through programs: An example of a process approach to evaluation. In I. J. Gordon (Ed.), *Early childhood education: The seventy-first yearbook of the National Society for the Study of Education* (pp. 229–259). Chicago, IL: The National Society for the Study of Education.

Sonquist, H., Kamii, C., & Derman, L. (1970). Piaget-derived preschool. In I. J. Athey & D. O. Rubideau (Eds.), *Educational implications of Piaget's theory* (pp. 101–113). Waltham, MA: Xerox College Publishing.

Spiker, C. (1966). The concept of development: Relevant and irrelevant issues. *Monographs of the Society for Research in Child Development, 31*(5, Serial No. 107).

Spodek, B. (Ed.). (1973). *Early childhood education*. Englewood Cliffs, NJ: Prentice-Hall.

Stallings, J. (1975). Implementation and child effects of teaching practices in Follow Through classrooms. *Monographs of the Society for Research in Child Development, 40*(7–8, Serial No. 163).

Stebbins, L. B., St. Pierre, R. G., Proper, E. C., Anderson, R. B., & Cerva, T. R. (1977). *Education as experimentation: A planned variation model. Vol. IV-A. An evaluation of Follow Through*. Cambridge, MA: ABT Associates.

Vincent, L. J., & Salisbury, C. L. (1988). Changing economic and social influences on family involvement. *Topics in Early Childhood Special Education, 8*, 48–59.

Vincent, L. J., Salisbury, C. L., Strain, P., McCormick, C., & Tessier, A. (1990). A behavioral-ecological approach to early intervention: Focus on cultural diversity. In S. J. Meisels & J. P. Shonkoff (Eds.), *Handbook of early childhood intervention* (pp. 173–195). New York: Oxford University Press.

Vinter, R. D., Sarri, R. C., Vorwaller, D. J., & Schafer, W. E. (1966). *Pupil Behavior Inventory*. Ann Arbor, MI: Campus.

Washington, V., & Oyemade, U. J. (1987). *Project Head Start: Past, present, and future trends in the context of family needs.* New York: Garland Publishing.

Weber, E. (1984). *Ideas influencing early childhood education: A theoretical analysis.* New York: Teachers College Press.

Weikart, D. P. (1981). Effects of different curricula in early childhood intervention. *Educational Evaluation and Policy Analysis, 3,* 25–35.

Weikart, D. P., Epstein, A. S., Schweinhart, L., & Bond, J. T. (1978). The Ypsilanti Preschool Curriculum Demonstration Project. *Monographs of the High/Scope Educational Research Foundation, 4,* Ypsilanti, MI: High/Scope Press.

Weikart, D. P., Rogers, L., Adcock, L., & McClelland, D. (1971). *The cognitively-oriented curriculum: A framework for preschool teachers.* Urbana, IL: University of Illinois.

Weikart, D. P., & Schweinhart, L. J. (1987). The High/Scope Cognitively-Oriented Curriculum in early education. In J. L. Roopnarine & J. E. Johnson (Eds.), *Approaches to early childhood education* (pp. 253–268). Columbus, OH: Merrill Publishing.

White, S. (1970). The learning theory tradition and child psychology. In P. Mussen (Ed.), *Carmichael's manual of child psychology* (Vol. 1, pp. 657–690). New York: Wiley.

Widerstrom, A. H., Mowder, B. A., & Willis, W. G. (1989). The school psychologist's role in the early childhood special education program. *Journal of Early Intervention, 13,* 239–248.

Wohlwill, J. F. (1970). The place of structured experience in early cognitive development. *Interchange, 1,* 13–27.

Ysseldyke, J. E., & Mirkin, P. K. (1982). The use of assessment information to plan instructional interventions: A review of the research. In C. R. Reynolds & T. B. Gutkin (Eds.), *The handbook of school psychology* (pp. 395–409). New York: Wiley.

Zigler, E. (1970). The environmental mystique. *Childhood Education, 46,* 402–412.

Zigler, E. (1982). Preventive intervention in the schools. In C. R. Reynolds & T. B. Gutkin (Eds.), *The handbook of school psychology* (pp. 774–795). New York: Wiley.

Zigler, E. F. (1987). Formal schooling for four-year-olds? No. In S. L. Kagan & E. F. Zigler (Eds.), *Early schooling: The national debate* (pp. 27–44). New Haven, CT: Yale University Press.

Zigler, E. F. (1990). Forward. In S. J. Meisels & J. P. Shonkoff (Eds.), *Handbook of early childhood intervention* (pp. ix–xiv). New York: Oxford University Press.

Zigler, E. F., & Trickett, P. K. (1978). IQ, social competence, and evaluation of early childhood intervention programs. *American Psychologist, 33,* 789–797.

Zigler, E. F., & Valentine, J. (Eds.). (1979). *Project Head Start: A legacy of the War on Poverty.* New York: The Free Press.

Zimiles, H. (1987). The Bank Street approach. In J. L. Roopnarine & J. E. Johnson (Eds.), *Approaches to early childhood education* (pp. 163–178). Columbus, OH: Merrill Publishing.

2 Young Children with Special Educational Needs

Cathy F. Telzrow
Cuyahoga Special Education Service Center, Cleveland, Ohio

Educational services to young children with special needs increased dramatically during the latter part of the 1980s, largely as a result of the impetus provided by the addition of the 1986 amendments to the Education of the Handicapped Act (EHA). Commonly referred to as Public Law 99-457, these amendments offered financial incentives to states for the provision of educational services to infants and preschool children with special needs (Garwood, Fewell, & Neisworth, 1988). This chapter describes the population of young children for whom such services are relevant and summarizes the research data supporting early intervention for these groups of youngsters. Special issues involved in providing services to young children with special needs are discussed, and implications for practice are outlined.

To begin this discussion, clarification of the concepts *prevention* and *intervention* may be helpful. The literature regarding prevention generally describes the triune model of primary, secondary, and tertiary prevention (Zins, Conyne, & Ponti, 1988). Within the present context of educational services to infants and preschool children with special needs, primary prevention is illustrated by medical and social programs that are designed to ameliorate the causes of those special needs. Examples might include carrier detection programs, rubella immunization, and parent education efforts (Guralnick & Bennett, 1987; Morrow & Morrow, 1987). Secondary prevention programs target identified subgroups of children considered to be at risk for some condition (e.g., school difficulty), and provide specific intervention strategies to ward off this condition. Screening newborns for phenylketonuria (PKU) and intervening with specialized diet therapy to prevent mental retardation is an example of a secondary prevention program (Guralnick & Bennett, 1987). Tertiary prevention programs focus on identified disorders and are designed to maintain or rehabilitate individuals. Infant stimulation programs for children with Down Syndrome are examples of tertiary prevention programs.

The distinction between prevention and intervention becomes increasingly difficult to make as one progresses from the primary to the tertiary level of prevention. Certainly some form of treatment or intervention occurs at all levels, particularly the secondary and tertiary stages of prevention. Indeed, many experts describe the treatments provided as preventive interventions (Knoff, 1987; Zins et al., 1988).

This chapter reviews educational programs for infants and preschool children with special needs. Some of these programs, particularly compensatory education programs targeted toward children who are at environmental risk, can be viewed as secondary prevention programs. Others (e.g., special education programs for preschoolers with biologically based handicaps) may be considered examples of tertiary prevention programs. Because both types of programs incorporate treatment or intervention, the generic term *early intervention* is employed in this chapter.

DEFINING THE POPULATION

Federal Guidelines Defining At Risk and Handicapped

Public Law 99-457, the EHA amendments of 1986, is the major source for federal guidelines regarding the identification and service delivery for young children with special needs. The scope of the amendments, as well as the speed with which they completed the legislative cycle and were enacted into law, was nothing short of extraordinary, and demonstrated a significant federal commitment to the provision of services to young handicapped children (Garwood et al., 1988). The amendments consist of four sections, two of which are relevant to this chapter: Title I. Handicapped Infants and Toddlers, and Title II. Handicapped Children ages 3 to 5.

The policy statement contained in Title I of Public Law 99-457 is remarkably broad, and reads, in part, "It is therefore the policy of the United States to provide financial assistance to States . . . (1) to develop and implement a statewide, comprehensive, coordinated, multidisciplinary, interagency program of early intervention services for handicapped infants and toddlers and their families" (Council for Exceptional Children, 1986, p. 1145). A broad definition of the population of handicapped infants/toddlers is contained in the legislation, and reads as follows:

> The term "handicapped infants and toddlers" means individuals from birth to age 2, inclusive, who need early intervention because they (A) are experiencing devel-

opmental delays, as measured by appropriate diagnostic instruments and procedures in one or more of the following areas: Cognitive development, physical development, language and speech development, psychosocial development, or self-help skills, or (B) have a diagnosed physical or mental condition which has a high probability of resulting in developmental delay. Such term may also include, at a State's discretion, individuals from birth to age 2, inclusive, who are at risk of having substantial developmental delays if early intervention services are not provided. (p. 1146)

Although this definition offers some direction for describing the infant and toddler population the legislation is intended to serve, operationalizing the definition is a task left to the states (Sheehan & Sites, 1989; Smith & Strain, 1988).

Title II of Public Law 99-457 is concerned with handicapped children ages 3 to 5. The major focus of this section of the legislation is on financial incentives to states for the development of services rather than on definition of the population to be served. Title II extends all "rights and protections" of Public Law 94-142 (EHA, Part B) to handicapped children ages 3 to 5 by 1990–1991 (or by 1991–1992 if federal financial allocations are not provided). This "extending downward" of elements of EHA, together with the absence of definitions in Title II, implies that "special education and related services" are as defined in EHA, Part B; in other words, definitions generally conceptualized for and considered more applicable for school-aged children. Although states are not required to report served children, ages 3–5, by disability category, some process for determining eligibility for special education must be employed.

Review of Classification Systems for Preschool Handicapped Children in Various States

Given the absence of precise definitions of the identified service populations in Titles I and II of Public Law 99-457, states were required to develop more specific definitions. According to Danaher's (1989) review of the approaches to defining handicapped preschool children used by the 50 states, two general types of responses are evident. Fewer than half the states employ categorical definitions as contained in EHA, Part B (i.e., mentally retarded, hard of hearing, deaf, speech impaired, visually handicapped, seriously emotionally disturbed, orthopedically handicapped, other health impaired, deaf–blind, multihandicapped, specific learning disabilities). A different type of approach is utilized by the remaining states, which employ definitions considered more suitable for very young children. Danaher's (1989) analysis of the eligibility criteria employed by these 29 states revealed approximately six different strategies, ranging from the use of categorical criteria with special preschool-specific options to a totally noncategorical approach to identification. Comparison of Danaher's 1989 survey results with data collected several months earlier (Danaher, 1988) suggests that increasing numbers of states are making efforts to accommodate the unique issues involved in the identification of special needs among young children in their definitional systems. This trend is gratifying, because, as Sheehan and Sites (1989) noted, "preschool measures simply do not provide a defensible basis for most of the diagnostic classification systems used with school-aged populations" (p. 106).

Measurement Issues in Identifying Special Needs in Young Children

As noted previously, states have responded to the challenge of defining special needs in young children in widely varying ways. The diversity of responses is one index of the complexity of the tasks involved in describing what constitutes a handicap in children of very young ages. Other issues, particularly those associated with the science and practice of measurement, further complicate the mission of defining special needs in young children. These difficulties are discussed in greater detail in the following sections.

Questionable Constructs: The Problem of the Mildly Handicapped.   In establishing whether or not a handicap exists in very young children, greatest concern is associated with those areas traditionally considered to be mild handicaps, such as mild mental retardation and specific learning disabilities. Categories associated with low incidence handicaps (e.g., visually handicapped, hearing handicapped, orthopedically handicapped), where physical evidence of the disability is identifiable, typically generate little disagreement about the presence of the handicap (although disagreement about appropriate interventions may occur). With regard to mild handicaps, however, where physical evidence associated with the condition may be absent or at best equivocal (e.g., soft neurologic signs), there is much more room for clinical judgment and accompanying difference of opinion. Most mild handicaps are defined contextually via sociopolitical influences such as governmental directives and pressures brought to bear by special interest groups (Keogh, 1988; Swanson, 1988). Consequently, the validity of the construct of mild handicaps has been called into question, and many would contend that these "politically manufactured" groups do not represent handicapping conditions at all.

Although the problems associated with the identification of mild handicaps are not observed exclusively in the early childhood population (e.g., Telzrow, 1990), they are of greater significance in this age group than others for several reasons. First, many of the signs of mild handicaps that may be useful in the identification of such conditions in older children have a high base-rate representation in young children. Letter reversals, for example, would be unusual among fourth graders, but occur in the majority of kindergartners (Chance, 1985). A second concern is that the behavioral repertoire of most preschool-aged children does not include many skills that are significant for identifying mild handicaps. For example, because absence of reading is the norm rather than the exception for preschool children, it is not possible to use reading performance as a means of differentiating between youngsters who have mild difficulties such as specific learning disabilities and those who do not. A third reason the identification of mild handicaps presents special problems for early childhood assessment relates to the high probability of children's experiences confounding the measurement of critical performance variables. Although this may occur among school-aged children as well, the influence of experience, including exposure to structured group activities and even test taking, on the performance of very young children can be profound.

Two contradictory viewpoints are relevant to the identification of mild handicaps concerning young children's access to special education services. On the one hand, as just noted, the validity of our identification systems is questionable due to the absence of objective validating criteria. Hence precision in locating and identifying very young children with mild handicaps is not an easy matter (Keogh & Becker, 1973). Furthermore, there is strong opinion in some quarters that the process of "handicapping" youngsters who exhibit mild disorders, even with the stated intention of providing intervention, in fact serves to limit opportunities and establish negative outcomes (Mercer, 1973; Smith & Schakel, 1987). Nonetheless, a label traditionally has been viewed as a prerequisite to receiving special services (Smith & Schakel, 1987). Young children in our largely politically defined mildly handicapped areas (mild mental retardation, specific learning disabilities), who are perhaps most vulnerable to misidentification, in fact may benefit the most from specific interventions such as can be offered through special education services (Barnett, 1988). Smith and Strain (1988), for example, advocate the extension of special education to all at-risk children from birth to age 5.

Inadequate Measurement Precision.   School psychologists, perhaps more than other specialists in the behavioral sciences, tend to be both enamored of and enslaved by test scores. It is remarkable that critical decisions about children's education and, consequently, their lives, often may rest on apparently insignificant variability in test scores. In Ohio, for example, an intelligence test score of 80, when co-occurring with deficits in adaptive behavior and academic achievement, makes a child eligible for a special education program for the developmentally handicapped; an IQ score of 81 excludes this youngster. There is no consideration given to the influence of different measures with different variances, publication dates, or standard errors of measurement. Instead, an almost mythical truth is ascribed to the derived test scores.

Other examples of this tendency to assume unerring precision of test data exist. Recently, a school psychologist whose job it was to establish the intelligence test score criterion for admission to her school district's preschool gifted program questioned the relative merits of employing age-based standard scores as opposed to normalized standard scores and age-based standard errors of measurement. The differences obtained from the application of these two methods were miniscule—in most cases well within the standard error of measurement. Yet the gravity of the decision within her setting demonstrated the extreme importance that had been attributed to such scores.

The myth of precise measurement of young children's abilities, as well as the fallibility of the instruments school psychologists commonly employ, was illustrated in a comparison of tests of early reading. Schultz (1988) demonstrated that essentially the same level of reading behavior (such as letter but no word recognition) may translate into standard scores on different reading tests that vary by more than 30 standard score points. Clearly our "truth" is a direct result of the yardstick we use to measure it.

Inadequate measurement precision is an important issue, particularly in the case of young children. The use of a discrepancy index (e.g., percent deviation of developmental age from chronological age or standard deviation units from the mean) is reported to be the procedure favored by states in identifying developmentally delayed infants and toddlers (Sheehan & Sites, 1989). When such objective, operational definitions of handicap or risk are employed (e.g., 1.5 standard deviations below the mean), there is a tacit assumption that measurement precision exists to implement such identification procedures. In practice, however, commonly employed preschool measures have been criticized rather severely because of poor technical adequacy and absence of convergent validity of like-named scales (Bracken, 1987; Poth & Barnett, 1988; Sommers, 1989). Although concerns about measurement have been raised with respect to children of all ages, these take on a special significance for the early childhood population because of concerns about the technical adequacy of the measures in common use, and the inexperience of many examiners in evaluating very young children (Sheehan & Sites, 1989).

Developmental Variability. Experts in early childhood assessment must have a good foundation in child development. Familiarity with the normal variability observed in the acquisition of major developmental milestones in infants and preschoolers provides a critical reminder that the distinction between normal and abnormal development is often imprecise. This may be particularly true in young children who have been hospitalized or have had ongoing medical or therapeutic interventions, because these experiences have been reported to constitute major stressors affecting children's behavior (Copeland & Kimmel, 1989).

Determining when a delay becomes a deficit, and when either a delay or a deficit warrants intervention, is an extremely delicate matter (Boehm & Sandberg, 1982). Such decisions are profoundly important, and the quicksands of error are present on both sides of the path. If we identify, label, or intervene, the possibility of family stress, secondary deviance, and narrowing of options may exist. In contrast, the failure to intervene for children who may benefit from special services is a potentially serious omission and may constitute a restriction of opportunity for the child and his or her family (Barnett, 1988).

Transition Issues in Definition

In identifying young children who should receive special education interventions, transition periods present some especially difficult problems (Wolery, 1989). During the period between infancy/toddler and preschool, and again from preschool to the early school years, both legal and philosophical influences are operative. Transition is complicated by issues such as the possibility of different lead agency responsibilities during the infant/toddler and preschool periods (Meisels, Harbin, Modigliani, & Olson, 1988), and by the hazy distinctions among medical, social, and educational services for many young children with special needs.

Federal law (Public Law 99-457) and most states' rules reflect a cascade model of service delivery, which results in the broadest range of special education services being afforded to infants and a subsequent gradual restriction of services to a smaller population of children through preschool to school-age years. Hence children with some presenting problems during infancy (e.g., at-risk conditions) may be excluded from special education services as preschoolers (Smith & Strain, 1988). A further reduction in the numbers of children with special needs served might be expected by school age.

This cascade model has both advantages and disadvantages. Presumably the rationale for such an approach is that intervention very early in life might serve to ameliorate identified problems, hence eliminating the need for subsequent special education. In addition, preschool and school-aged years are more closely linked to educational as opposed to medical and social services, which might be more paramount during infancy (e.g., Sheehan & Sites, 1989). Therefore, it might be argued that moving to a progressively more restrictive definitional model during this period, where educational needs are the primary focus, is legitimate.

Narrowing definitions that restrict services as children progress from the infancy/toddler to the preschool period and again from preschool to school-aged years, however, are not without problems (Barnett, 1988; Smith & Strain, 1988). Although it is optimistic to hope that intervention for children who may be at risk during infancy will eliminate subsequent educationally relevant needs, this is not always the case for individual children. In addition, maintaining efficient, cost-effective involvement of multiple service systems during the preschool and school-aged years is often problematic.

Defining the Population: Summary and Recommendations

In this section, it has been illustrated that federal guidelines concerning which young children are in need of special education services generally are vague and nonspecific. Consequently, definitions of preschool handicapped children must be operationalized by the states. As Danaher's (1989) report of states' eligibility determinations illustrates, a broad range of strategies have been employed. Although more than half the states have implemented procedures that appear to take into account the unique issues associated with identifying special needs in young children, others have simply adopted the EHA definitions, which generally were designed with school-aged populations in mind.

Regardless of the method used to determine special education eligibility for young children, the process requires sorting children into two groups: those who need special education and those who do not. Furthermore, nearly all definitions currently employed by states incorporate some normative index of performance, which means that the identification of special needs in young children introduces numerous measurement issues. The previous discussion describes several problems associated with identifying special needs in young children, including the double-edged sword of "mild handicaps," the lack of measurement precision for very young children, the perplexing judgment calls resulting from normal variability among preschoolers, and practical and public relations dilemmas arising from a cascade model that narrows the service populations from infancy/toddler years through the preschool to school-aged periods.

Although these problems do not have ready solutions, there may be some practical suggestions for minimizing difficulties that arise from definitional, measurement, developmental, and transitions issues. The following recommendations are offered to school psychologists and other professionals who are responsible for the design and implementation of early intervention programs for young children with special needs.

Advocate for Definitional Systems Appropriate for Young Children. In a thoughtful and practical article, Smith and Schakel (1987) offered a rationale for adopting noncategorical identification policies in the provision of services to young children with special needs. They offer four specific approaches to noncategorical identification that appear to be better suited to young children than the wholesale adoption of what appears in EHA. Increasing numbers of states are moving in this direction (Danaher, 1988, 1989), and policymakers are urged to consider definitional systems that are appropriate for early childhood populations. Alternatives such as those offered by Smith and Schakel (1987), for example, can obviate concerns associated with the identification of mild handicaps.

Incorporate Both Actuarial and Clinical Judgment Eligibility Approaches. Although measurement in the behavioral sciences is not without problems, investigators have demonstrated repeatedly the superiority of actuarial over clinical judgment criteria (Faust, 1986; Meehl, 1954; Sawyer, 1966). Weaknesses in available preschool measures make rejection of their use an appealing option. However, eliminating test-based measurement, albeit imperfect, does not do away with error, in that nonactuarial approaches to decision making have other weaknesses (Fagley, 1988; Faust, 1986). In general, decisions derived from both actuarial and clinical methods are most defensible (Willis, 1986).

Develop and Maintain Interagency Liaisons. Many young children could benefit from interventions that are more properly identified as medical or social rather than educational (Sheehan & Sites, 1989). When educational agencies have established means for linking such children and their families with these alternative systems, both children and families benefit (Meisels et al., 1988; Nordyke, 1982; Wolery, 1989).

EFFICACY OF EARLY INTERVENTION
FOR YOUNG CHILDREN WITH SPECIAL NEEDS

Implicit in the increasing momentum with which programs for young children with special needs are being expanded is the tacit assumption that such services are of benefit to children and systems. However, school psychologists and others should be aware that this viewpoint is not unanimous (White, 1985–1986; Woodhead, 1988). The following discussion summarizes the literature on the efficacy of early intervention for young children with special needs.

Efficacy of Early Intervention for Environmentally At-Risk Populations

Environmental risk is defined by several factors, including poverty and minority status. Minority group youngsters, especially Black and Hispanic, are disproportionately represented among poverty families; statistics dating from the mid-1980s indicate that one out of every two Black children and two of every five Hispanic children live in poverty ("Who's dependent," 1986). Educational risk is demonstrated by data indicating more than one fourth of Black children and one third of Hispanic youngsters fail to complete high school ("At risk," 1986). Schweinhart, Berrueta-Clement, Barnett, Epstein, and Weikart (1985) noted that one in five children in the United States lives in poverty, yet only a minority of preschoolers from poverty families attend preschool programs. Indeed, data have shown a positive correlation between family income and attendance in early childhood programs. This statistic harbors the suggestion of even greater disparity between the school performance of low and middle income children in the future, in that children most in need of a head start may be least likely to get it.

The effects of early intervention efforts (including educationally based programs) on altering outcomes for minority, low socioeconomic status (SES), and other high-risk populations have been studied for nearly 30 years—since Lyndon

Johnson's implementation of the Head Start program. Summarizing this massive literature in a cogent manner is not an easy matter; however, a brief historical review, with an emphasis on the most recent data, follows.

Compensatory education had its roots in the civil rights movement of the early 1960s, and such programs were offered as tonics to cure the ills associated with poverty and minority status (Jensen, 1985). In addition, there was considerable emphasis on conceptualizing the educational difficulties of this population as a failure in society (Bereiter, 1985), and thus intervention programs that could reverse these circumstances were heralded as a means of increasing IQ (Jensen, 1985; Zigler & Berman, 1983). As Zigler and Berman (1983) described the naive optimism of this era, "many expected that the brief preschool experience would be so potent a counteraction to the deficits in poor children's lives that it could prevent further attenuation in age-appropriate performance and a recurrence of the gap between the social classes" (p. 895).

Table 2.1 provides a brief summary of some key studies, including many literature reviews, which have examined the efficacy of early intervention efforts for young children who are at environmental risk. These investigations, which generally employed secondary prevention interventions, targeted infants, pre-schoolers, and young school-aged children who were at risk of developing learn-ing and behavior problems. Risk status was defined by such characteristics as family poverty, minority status (primarily Black), below average parental educa-tion level, and below average IQ scores for either children or parents.

The preventive intervention strategies employed in these investigations were diverse. Some provided parent-centered interventions during the infancy period. Others (e.g., Carter, 1984) consisted of pull-out compensatory education pro-grams that commenced during the early school years. The criterion measures used to judge effectiveness varied as well. Several of the studies (e.g., Bryant & Ramey, 1987; Schweinhart & Weikart, 1985; White, 1985–1986) utilized changes in IQ as at least one index of effectiveness. This criterion has been criticized because of its arguable insensitivity to the effects of early intervention for young children at environmental risk. Jensen (1985), for example, suggests that various aspects of information processing, especially meta-processes such as executive functions, are more appropriate targets for intervention and indices of change in compensatory education programs. Zigler (Zigler & Berman, 1983; Zigler & Trickett, 1978) favors social competence as an outcome measure for evaluating the effectiveness of compensatory education.

Several of the studies described in Table 2.1 incorporate a broader range of criterion measures than IQ alone. Indices of immediate effects such as changes in language, academic skills, and motor skills were employed by several investiga-tors (e.g., Carter, 1984; White, 1985–1986). Long-term academic and social outcomes, such as grade retentions, special education placements, school drop-out rates, and arrest incidents, were utilized as indicators of program effective-ness by others (e.g., Schweinhart et al., 1985; Schweinhart & Weikart, 1985).

Author	Sample Characteristics	Preventive Intervention Strategies	Results	Comments/Limitations
Bryant and Ramey (1987)	Socially, economically, and educationally disadvantaged infants and toddlers in 17 true experimental studies. Samples were characterized by low SES, mostly Black families.	Intervention approaches of variable models, intensity and duration. Both home-and center-based programs and both parent-and child-centered interventions were included.	Among infant programs, five of nine programs using Bayley showed significantly higher scores for experimental than control groups. An intensity hypothesis, suggesting home visits alone were not sufficient to produce change, was demonstrated. Programs that began during infancy and continued through the preschool years demonstrated positive effects on IQ at ages 3, 4, and 5. Gains in IQ also were demonstrated for children who entered programs at ages 3 or 4.	This analysis examined a wide variety of preventative intervention strategies. Delineation of the specific treatment effect associated with specific interventions is not possible. The index of efficacy used was increases in IQ scores, which may not be sensitive to the effects and potential benefits of preventive intervention programs.
Carter (1984)	120,000 students from a representative sample of over 300 elementary schools participating in the Sustaining Effects Study mandated by congress and funded by the U.S. Department of Education. The study included in-depth or ethnographic material from 55 high-poverty schools.	Compensatory education programs (Title I) delivered via diverse program models and employing variable interventions. The typical model employed a pullout setting with small instructional groups.	Students with mild to moderate achievement deficits showed improvement in reading and math. Students with the most severe deficits did not show improvement in relative achievement. There was no relationship between the cost of intervention and achievement.	The wide diversity in intervention programs complicated the interpretation of results from this analysis.

continued

TABLE 2.1 Continued

Author	Sample Characteristics	Preventive Intervention Strategies	Results	Comments/Limitations
Schweinhart, Berrueta-Clement, Barnett, Epstein, and Weikart (1985)	Graduates (N = 123) of Perry Preschool Project in Ypsilanti, Michiagn, who were 19 years old at follow-up. As preschoolers, these youngsters had numerous at-risk characteristics, including minority status (Black), below average parental education level, high incidence of single parent household, and below average IQ scores.	The Perry project employs a cognitively based organized educational model. Children attended school in half-day sessions 5 days per week, for 7 1/2 months each year. A teacher-child ratio of 1:5 or 6 was maintained. Weekly home visits were incorporated.	Relative to a comparison group, significantly more Perry Preschool graduates had completed high school, were enrolled in post secondary programs, and were employed. Significantly fewer had ever been detained by the police, been arrested, or were receiving public assistance. Cost effectiveness of the program was demonstrated by reduced costs for additional years of schooling (i.e., due to retention) as well as increased earnings.	This analysis and others reported by Schweinhart, Weikart, and their colleagues, employs a wide variety of outcome measures which may be particularly sensitive to change in environmentally at-risk populations.
Schweinhart and Weikart (1985)	Over 3,000 environmentally at-risk children. Samples were largely Black (at least 90%), characterized by family poverty, and were reported to have below average IQ scores for either mother or children.	Subjects were graduates of well-known early childhood programs initiated between 1962 and 1975 to ameliorate the negative educational, vocational, and social outcomes associated with poverty and minority status. Examples include the Perry Preschool Project (aforementioned), the Early Training Project, and the Milwaukee study. Diverse intervention models (e.g., child vs. parent centered, home vs. center-based) were employed.	Subject populations were followed to at least age 9, and in some cases to late teens or early 20's. Target populations were reported to show increases in IQ scores during early childhood, fewer grade retentions and special education placements, and lower incidences of school dropout during elementary and high school years.	Although there was wide variability among the program models analyzed, favorable outcomes were reported for target children across models.

| White (1985-1986) | Samples from 326 studies of at-risk, handicapped, or disadvantaged children who had been involved in early intervention programs. Nearly half the effect sizes involved disadvantaged populations; "disadvantaged children" were defined by low socioeconomic status. | All educational, psychological, or therapeutic interventions were included which were designed to prevent the onset or progression of a disability or improve functional ability. | mmediate effect sizes of half a standard deviation were demonstrated on most criterion measures, including intelligence, language, academic functioning, and motor functioning. Over time these effect sizes were substantially reduced. | The author cautions that this analysis did not include more recent, well-designed investigations. Most long-term data consisted of IQ and achievement measures, which may not be the most sensitive measures of change for children at environmental risk. |

The data reviewed suggest that early intervention programs for socially, economically, and educationally disadvantaged children have the potential to produce some significant main effects both on a short- and long-term basis. The immediate benefits reported in the literature include significant gains in IQ and academic achievement. Although these effects have been reported to be slight and to decline over time (White, 1985–1986), other indices of change have attributed lasting benefits to early intervention. These longitudinal effects include fewer retentions and special education placements, and long-term social benefits such as higher employment rates, higher postsecondary education levels, fewer arrest incidents, and fewer requirements for public assistance. A limited number of investigations have considered the cost–benefit ratio for early intervention programs, a necessary consideration for policymakers (Zigler & Berman, 1983). Schweinhart et al. (1985) reported optimistic cost benefits, as reflected in fewer years of additional schooling for children who had not been retained and increased earnings on the part of these individuals. In his analysis of compensatory education programs that did not commence until the early school years, Carter (1984) found no relationship between the cost of intervention and achievement.

Although these reviews provide generally positive support for the efficacy of early intervention programs for children at environmental risk, it is important to emphasize the specificity of the effect, because not all approaches were equally effective (e.g., Carter, 1984). Woodhead (1988) reported that although a variety of intervention techniques and approaches may be viable, not all can receive equal endorsement. Common features of successful programming include careful planning and implementation, well-supported educational staffs, low child to adult ratios, and careful program design within a clear philosophical framework. Schweinhart et al. (1985) hypothesized that two primary lessons are learned by disadvantaged children from well designed and implemented early childhood programs. The first is how to be a good learner, and might include such skills as persistence and attention, which have consistently been identified as predictors of school success (Bender, 1987; Horn & Packard, 1985; Martin, Drew, Gaddis, & Moseley, 1988). The second skill that Schweinhart et al. (1985) hypothesized is acquired by disadvantaged children who have been enrolled in quality early childhood programs is how to work with adults outside of the family. Such behaviors may be reflected in the approach dimension of temperament found to be significantly correlated with school achievement (Martin & Holbrook, 1985).

In conclusion, although the research data concerning early intervention programs for children at environmental risk are generally optimistic, we must be alert to a tendency to overgeneralize these data in an inappropriate manner (e.g., Woodhead, 1988). As Schweinhart et al. (1985) stated, "There is no intrinsic value in a young child's leaving home for a few hours a day to join another adult and a group of children. Unless the content of a program is carefully defined, a preschool is just another place for a child to be" (p. 553).

Efficacy of Early Intervention for Children with Biologically Based Handicaps

In reviewing efficacy studies of early intervention for children with biologically based handicaps, attention must be addressed to methodological and measurement issues associated with these investigations (Bailey & Bricker, 1984). One such issue concerns the indicators of change that have been employed in analyses of program effectiveness. Much of the research has incorporated specific, norm-referenced measures of individual mental ability such as IQ tests (Casto & Mastropieri, 1986; Zigler & Berman, 1983). The limitations of such measures in reflecting individual child growth have been described (Jensen, 1985; Zigler & Berman, 1983), and more appropriate alternatives have been suggested (Bagnato, 1981; Bricker & Gumerlock, 1988). A second limitation to studies of the efficacy of early intervention for handicapped children concerns the difficulties in obtaining comparable control groups. A number of well-regarded authorities in the field of early intervention with handicapped children (e.g., Bricker & Gumerlock, 1988; Guralnick & Bennett, 1987; Guralnick & Bricker, 1987) have argued that the realities involved in the delivery of intervention programs generally preclude the implementation of experimental research designs.

Although these methodological limitations impact the quality of the research, such that most investigations of early interventions with handicapped children are not experimentally elegant, it is often possible to make generalizations about program characteristics from available studies (Guralnick & Bennett, 1987). In particular, evaluation plans that employ a systematic interaction among child assessment, intervention delivery systems, and evaluation procedures can enhance our ability to test hypotheses about program efficacy (Bricker & Gumerlock, 1988).

Table 2.2 summarizes the results of 11 selected studies of the efficacy of early intervention for identified handicapped children. These studies, most of which are comprehensive literature reviews, were published between 1983 and 1987. Both mildly and severely handicapped subject populations were represented among these investigations, and children's presenting problems ranged from "at-risk status" to severe disorders such as autism and blindness. Wide variability in the age of program initiation (from infancy to as late as age 4), duration, and intensity of the interventions was evident across the studies. Similarly, curricular emphases and service delivery models were diverse. Outcome measures included indices of child progress (e.g., IQ), curriculum-referenced skills, achievement, need for special education services, and parent change variables.

Virtually all of the 11 studies reported at least some positive benefit that could be attributed to the intervention provided. One example of such benefit was evident in individual child progress, as reflected in both growth from baseline (Casto & Mastropieri, 1986; Guralnick & Bricker, 1987; Harris, 1987; Meadow-

TABLE 2.2
Summary of Selected Studies of the Efficacy of Early Intervention for Children with Biologically Based Handicaps

Author	Sample Characteristics	Intervention Strategies	Results	Comments/Limitations
Bailey and Bricker (1984)	Severely handicapped infants and preschool children in 13 programs which reported objective outcome data for child progress and published findings in professional literature between 1974 and 1983. Child characteristics were quite diverse.	Diverse treatment approaches were employed, including home-based, center-based, and combination models; wide variations in treatment intensity, and in curricular emphases.	A sizable majority of the programs (10 out of 13) reported child progress regardless of the length or intensity of intervention. Three of the programs reported significant benefits relative to controls.	The authors note two limitations: variability in program characteristics and methodological flaws such as absence of controls for some studies.
Castro and Mastropieri (1986)	Young handicapped children, ages birth through 5 years, including 44% with mental retardation, 29% with multiple handicaps, and 8% with speech/language handicaps.	Subjects participated in early intervention programs described in 74 studies conducted between 1937 and 1984 (majority occurring after 1970). Programs varied widely on such dimensions as degree of structure and degree of parental involvement. Review of data employed meta-analysis techniques.	Outcome measures included IQ (the modal variable), other child performance measures, and indices of parental change and parent-child interaction. Mean effect size of .68 was reported for all studies. This was reduced to .40 when only "good quality studies" (i.e., those with good internal validity indices) were included in the analyses.	The use of meta-analytic techniques and the interpretation of Castro and Mastropieri's results have been criticized (Strain & Smith, 1986).
Colorado Department of Education (1983)	Children who received preschool special education in four school districts in Colorado between 1974 and 1977, and controls who did not have such intervention (Total N = 518).	Program objectives included improving language, thinking, and social skills, and preventing handicaps in "at-risk" children. The IN class REactive Language program, which emphasized language development within the classroom was employed.	Target population demonstrated higher test scores (measures not specified), and fewer years of special education. A savings of over $1,5000 per handicapped pupil was attributed to the early intervention program.	The population characteristics were not thoroughly described.

Edgar, McNulty, Gaetz, and Maddox (1984)	2,752 graduates of early childhood special education programs in 22 school districts in Colorado and Washington in the early 1980s. Children met state special education eligibility criteria.	Variable treatment approaches provided in early childhood special education programs operated by public school districts in Colorado and Washington were employed.	15 to 20% of severely handicapped students received instruction in regular classrooms following graduation from early childhood special education programs, with greater proportions of mildly handicapped children being educated in these environments.	The authors caution that the absence of a control group limits the generalizability of the findings.
Guralnick and Bricker (1987)	Preschool children with Down syndrome and other biologically based developmental delays.	Treatment approaches incorporated widely diverse models with variability in the intensity and duration of intervention.	Decline in cognitive functioning which is frequently reported for Down syndrome population was ameliorated or prevented by early intervention during the period these services were provided. Long-term effects after intervention is discontinued are unknown. In children with other biologically based handicaps, specific curriculum-referenced skills attributable to the intervention occurred, although generalization to other measures was rarely demonstrated.	The authors note the following limitations: methodological weaknesses (e.g., absence of controls) and heterogeneity in subject population.
Harris (1987)	Young children with motor handicaps, including cerebral palsy, myelomeningocele, and Down syndrome	Therapy-based approaches to early intervention, such as neurodevelopmental treatment, sensorimotor therapy, and vestibular stimulation.	Review of 13 studies published between 1973 and 1986 suggested positive gains in individual motor, and visual perceptual performance, as well as parental caregiving variables, are associated with early intervention.	Limitations noted include inadequacy of sensitive outcome measures and methodological weaknesses.

continued

71

TABLE 2.2 Continued

Author	Sample Characteristics	Intervention Strategies	Results	Comments/Limitations
Meadow-Orlans (1987)	Preschool children with hearing impairments enrolled in 13 early intervention programs. Child characteristics regarding age of intervention, hearing status of parents, and degree and onset of hearing impairment were variable.	Intervention programs were variable, and included traditional oral-only preschools and home interventions of varying intensity and duration.	Very early intervention (i.e., before age 2) appears to be an important factor in subsequent achievement of children with hearing impairments. Studies comparing treatment methods demonstrated enhanced achievement for children exposed to oral-plus-visual as opposed to oral-only approaches.	The interaction of child variables (e.g., degree of hearing impairment) may interact with treatment variables, thus complicating interpretation.
Olson (1987)	Infants and preschool children with varying degrees of visual impairment who participated in seven early intervention programs.	Intervention programs were of varying intensity and duration, and included center-based programs and home visits.	A trend supporting the effectiveness of early intervention in helping children with visual impairments to achieve developmental expectations of sighted children was demonstrated. Intervention setting was unrelated to outcome.	Methodologically sound, large group investigations are not viable for this population because of the small number of affected children. Single-subject, longitudinal studies are recommended.
Simeonsson, Olley, and Rosenthal (1987)	Autistic children, ages 5 years or younger, who participated in 10 early intervention programs.	Diverse treatment approaches, which shared these features: identified goal of promoting children's development, analyzing change, employed experimental treatments, and objective outcome measures.	10 studies met selection criteria, but several were not included in analysis because of narrow or brief interventions. Review of three comprehensive studies found most positive outcomes were associated with such program features as structured, behavioral strategies, inclusion of a parental education component, highly intensive treatment, and the incorporation of generalization training.	The authors note that early identification of autism is difficult, and in fact this may interact with outcome (e.g., are children with the severest degrees of autism identified earliest?).

Snyder-McLean and McLean (1987)	Young children with language and communication disorders who participated in 30 early intervention programs.	Diverse treatment approaches that varied in focus, intensity, duration, and method of delivery were analyzed.	Review of 30 studies published since 1970 provided support for early intervention in ameliorating young children's communication disorders. Direct therapeutic interventions which targeted specific communication skills were especially effective.	The authors note that data regarding the maintenance or generalization of specific skills were not included.
White (1985-1986)	Samples from 326 studies of at-risk, handicapped, or disadvantaged children who had been involved in early intervention programs. "At-risk children" were those who suffered birth trauma. "Handicapped children" were defined by criteria outlined in EHA.	All educational, psychological, or therapeutic interventions were included which were designed to prevent the onset or progression of a disability or improve functional ability.	An immediate effect size of approximately .4 of a standard deviation was reported from an analysis of 20 effect sizes from 11 different studies.	The author reported that only 16% of the data for handicapped children in this analysis came from high quality studies. Virtually no methodologically sound followup data beyond 12 months following intervention were available.

Orlans, 1987; Olson, 1987; Simeonsson, Olley, & Rosenthal, 1987; Snyder-McLean & McLean, 1987; White, 1985–1986) and relativeness to controls (Bailey & Bricker, 1984; Colorado Department of Education, 1983). Another example of the efficacy of these interventions was reflected in evidence that fewer years of special education were required when such interventions were provided (Colorado Department of Education, 1983; Edgar, McNulty, Gaetz, & Maddox, 1984), which in turn resulted in a sizable cost benefit (Colorado Department of Education, 1983).

The interaction between specific intervention characteristics and outcome was complex, and was often highly specific to the population studied. Intervention setting was unrelated to outcome for children with visual handicaps, for example (Olson, 1987), but was found to be an important factor in progress for children with communication disorders (Snyder-McLean & McLean, 1987). Specific curricular emphases were often highly specific to the sample characteristics as well. Structured, behavioral approaches were demonstrated to be critical for young autistic children, for example (Simeonsson et al., 1987), and oral-plus-visual methods were superior to oral-only methods for preschoolers with hearing impairments (Meadow-Orlans, 1987).

In summary, the studies revealed are generally optimistic about the efficacy of early intervention for young children with biologically based handicaps. Although many of the studies lack elegant research designs, these analyses reported positive gains on child progress measures such as IQ, academic achievement, and specific developmental skills. Evidence of lasting benefits of early intervention was reflected in an amelioration of cognitive decline over time (Guralnick & Bricker, 1987) and fewer years of required special education (Colorado Department of Education, 1983; Edgar et al., 1984). Programmatic features that were most effective in producing child progress were often highly specific to the nature and severity of the handicapping condition.

Efficacy of Early Intervention: Summary

Research regarding the effectiveness of early childhood education is plagued by numerous methodological and measurement limitations, including difficulties in obtaining equivalent comparison groups and in selecting indices that are sensitive to treatment effects. Although the available literature might be considered flawed because few studies meet the necessary criteria for true experimental research, some interpretation of the reported data is possible. This brief review of research regarding the efficacy of early intervention for young children who have special needs as a result of environmental risks or biologically based handicaps has provided evidence that such services have the potential to enhance outcomes for children. All approaches to intervention, however, do not produce identical benefits. Data suggest that early intervention programs for handicapped and at-risk children that are planned and implemented carefully and link assessment directly to intervention and outcome data result in the most substantial benefits for children. The following section explores in greater detail some specific programmatic features associated with child progress.

ISSUES IN SERVICE DELIVERY
FOR PRESCHOOL CHILDREN WITH SPECIAL
EDUCATIONAL NEEDS

In this section, four major issues relative to the design and implementation of early intervention programs are discussed. The topics addressed, age at intervention, treatment intensity, parental/family involvement, and least restrictive environment, were chosen on the basis of their salience for school psychologists and others involved in developing and providing services to young children with special needs.

Age at Intervention

The popular trend among many experts in early childhood special education is that earlier is better. There is an intuitive sense that if interventions can be initiated during infancy, or at least when children are still quite young, demonstrably greater benefits can be achieved. However, as Galloway and Chandler (1978) noted, trends in service delivery, as well as public policies that often drive these systems, generally derive not from scientific evidence but from other nondata-based belief systems. The following data suggest that the commonly held premise that the earliest interventions produce the greatest benefits for children may not have empirical support.

In their longitudinal investigation of 118 children with severe and profound hearing losses, Musselman, Wilson, and Lindsay (1988) reported that age of intervention was significantly related only to a measure of receptive language during the first year of intervention. The authors concluded that early intervention with young hearing-impaired children is associated with short-term gains, and that by the school-aged years the benefits of earlier intervention are not distinguishable. Casto and Mastropieri's (1986) review of the literature resulted in similar conclusions, and in fact suggested that later intervention may produce more benefits. In his meta-analysis of the effects of early intervention, White (1985–1986) reported that although few data were available, those he analyzed did not support the premise that earlier intervention is superior to programs that are initiated later. White reported results from five studies (17 effect sizes) that manipulated starting age while holding constant all other possible intervening variables. His findings suggest a slight advantage for children who commenced their education programs later. Bryant and Ramey (1987) reviewed 17 experimental studies of the effects of early intervention for environmentally at-risk children. Their analysis suggests that benefits are evident whether intervention commences during the infancy or preschool periods. Furthermore, these authors concluded that there are no data to support very early (i.e., at birth or shortly after) intensive intervention with this population.

Although results such as those just cited have been challenged and interpreted as a negative blow to the early intervention movement by some (Strain & Smith, 1986), an alternative view is that such findings offer new optimism about maximizing the potential of young children who are handicapped or at risk, in that intervention that commences at any time during the early preschool period appears to offer positive benefit. Furthermore, for policymakers and school personnel who inevitably must make decisions based on cost–benefit ratios, evidence that even later intervention can be beneficial is good news indeed.

The practice implication that can be derived from this literature is that intervention initiated during the preschool years can be associated with positive benefits for children who are at environmental or biological risk. Although some exceptions are noteworthy (e.g., Meadow-Orlans, 1987), in general infant intervention has not been shown to be preferable to programs that are initiated somewhat later in achieving more substantial outcomes for children.

Treatment Intensity

In addition to determining when to initiate intervention, program planners must consider the issue of how much intervention to provide. Although this decision is often financially driven, it is helpful to consider data regarding what level of program intensity is associated with maximum benefit when establishing intervention models.

Musselman et al. (1988) found that program intensity, as reflected in the cumulative number of hours of specialized training, was related only to increased mother–child communication. However, other data contradict these conclusions suggesting program intensity results in only minimal effects. Fredericks, Moore, and Baldwin (1982) used ex post facto data to evaluate the long-term effects of early childhood education for a group of children diagnosed as trainable mentally retarded. Among the program features most predictive of success (as reflected by performance on a criterion-referenced developmental inventory) were the amount of time spent in individual instruction and ingroup instruction planned specifically to address individually identified needs.

Similar findings were reported by Bryant and Ramey (1987) in their review of 17 compensatory education programs for children at environmental risk. They noted that the intensity of the program (as defined by amount and breadth of contact) was an important factor in children's progress. Bryant and Ramey (1987) concluded that educationally oriented home visits as a sole intervention are probably not sufficient to produce significant effects.

The general trend in the data concerning program intensity is that greater benefits result from more intensive interventions. These findings are consistent with the literature on engaged learning time for school-aged children (Gettinger, 1984; Kavale & Forness, 1986), and suggest that programs that offer pre-schoolers more time in well-planned and executed interventions are more likely to demonstrate greater benefits.

The implication of these findings for practice is that, in general, more inten-sive treatments are associated with more positive benefits. The available data do not permit the development of specific guidelines regarding treatment intensity; however, the studies examined suggest it is generally true that more cumulative hours of intervention produce more substantial gains for target children. Al-though it is not possible to determine from the data reviewed, program intensity may reach an asymptote, such that benefits correlate with program intensity to an optimal level. In this case, programs of greater intensity would not produce additional gains, and may possibly reduce them. When considered in conjunction with data reviewed in the previous section, these results suggest that programs that delay intervention until the preschool period, and provide a more intensive intervention, will produce greater gains than programs that commence during infancy but offer less intensive interventions.

Parental/Family Involvement

Numerous models of early childhood intervention exist, and the degree of paren-tal/family involvement among these alternatives varies widely. The following section summarizes data regarding the effects of parental/family involvement in early childhood intervention programs, both on the target child and on the family.

Studies examining the effect of parent involvement on children's outcomes have not found involving parent(s) to be a significant treatment variable. In his meta-analysis of early intervention programs for disadvantaged children, White (1985–1986) concluded that there were no differences in children's performance between graduates of these programs where parents were intensively involved and those where they were not. Similar conclusions were reached by Casto and Mastropieri (1986) in their review of early intervention research for handicapped children. In their investigation of program characteristics associated with en-hanced benefits for a group of preschoolers with hearing impairments, Mus-selman et al. (1988) found no support for the value of direct parent instruction.

Such results suggest that, although there is intuitive appeal in emphasizing parental involvement/education in intervention programs for young handicapped and disadvantaged children (Hatch, 1984), data supporting the benefits of such involvement for enhancing outcomes for the target child are not automatically apparent. Furthermore, as Bryant and Ramey (1987) point out, programs for disadvantaged children that require intensive parental involvement traditionally have a high attrition rate. This finding suggests that requirements for extensive participation by parents may result in such programs becoming inaccessible to children who might otherwise benefit from them.

Although the data suggest that parental involvement is generally not an essential ingredient in achieving positive benefits for disadvantaged or handicapped children, parent participation in early childhood intervention may be associated with broader benefits to the parent(s) or the family unit (Kaiser & Hemmeter, 1989). Certainly the trend of the 1980s favored increased attention to parent/family needs. For example, in a review of characteristics of the Handicapped Children's Early Education Projects (HCEEP) funded between 1982 and 1986, Suarez, Hurth, and Prestridge (1988) reported that nearly half of those projects whose objectives included curriculum development targeted parents or families as the major recipients of services. Furthermore, only 20% of those projects identified handicapped children as the sole receiver of intervention services, with either the family or the child and his or her parents more commonly defined as the target of intervention. The strong focus on family services in Public Law 99-457 provides further evidence of increased attention to parent/family needs (Kaiser & Hemmeter, 1989; Vincent & Salisbury, 1988), and experts expect this emphasis to continue (Odom & Warren, 1988).

Fredericks et al. (1982) surveyed parents whose children had been enrolled in early childhood special education and compared the results with parents whose children had not received such services. The authors found that parents whose children had been involved reported that their handicapped children were less draining on their physical energies than 3 years previously, and that they felt no more anger toward their handicapped child than other children in the family. Such data suggest that one potential benefit to parents of handicapped children resulting from their involvement is increased understanding and satisfaction with their children.

Turnbull and Winton (1984) asserted that there is a contradiction between policy in early childhood intervention, which advocates active parental involvement, and actual implementation, where parental/family involvement is typically passive. They provide two reasons for this discrepancy between policy and implementation. First is the premise that all parents of handicapped children possess a strong desire for intense involvement with their children's intervention program. As Turnbull and Winton (1984) stated, "Because there is a group of parents who strongly desire to be actively involved in parent activities and in educational decision making, and these parents have been successful in making their needs known . . . , it has been assumed that all parents share this perspective" (p. 388). The second reason for the discrepancy between public policy and implementation with regard to parental/family involvement offered by Turnbull and Winton (1984) is that programs tend to emphasize parents' participating in highly involved roles, such as teacher and decision maker, for which some parents may not be suited.

As Turnbull and Winton's work suggests, much of the current literature regarding parent/family involvement favors a highly individualized approach, with the type and degree of participation suited to the particular parent(s) (Sheehan, 1988; Turnbull & Winton, 1984; Turnbull, Winton, Blacher, & Salkind, 1982).

Many experts recommend a continuum of involvement, such that participation varies from family to family, and even for the same family across time (Bristol & Gallagher, 1982; Kaiser & Hemmeter, 1989). The changing configuration of families (e.g., single-parent families, working mothers) must be considered, and care should be taken that requirements for parental participation are not so intensive or inflexible that program access is denied to families that may benefit most (Bristol & Gallagher, 1982; Mlinarcik, 1987; Vincent & Salisbury, 1988). The statistic indicating that "traditional" families (i.e., working father, mother at home with children) comprise only 4% of the U.S. culture today ("Traditional families," 1986) underscores the need for innovative patterns of service delivery to families.

Some evidence suggests that parents of young handicapped children favor involvement in a manner that affords less formal, more frequent contacts with the educational staff, such as might occur during drop-off and pick-up times (Winton & Turnbull, 1981). Although teachers also have reported favoring these types of contacts over more formal parent–teacher conferences, there is evidence that more time is spent in the latter, less desirable modes of communication (Fuqua, Hegland, & Karas, 1985). Factors associated with increased parent/family involvement have been investigated. Bristol and Gallagher (1982) reported that smaller, behaviorally oriented programs tended to have more parental involvement than school-based settings, perhaps as a result of the perceived bureaucratic, hierarchical structures of these latter programs. Incorporating features such as incentives, child care (Baker, 1984), or transportation (Bristol & Gallagher, 1982) also might enhance parental participation.

The implications of these findings are complex for school psychological practice. The data reviewed suggest parent participation in early intervention programs is unrelated to child outcome. However, it is possible that measures sensitive to these effects were not employed in the investigations cited. Furthermore, parent/family participation in early childhood intervention programs may be associated with enhanced benefits to the parent(s) or family unit. Most experts favor an individualized approach that can match the type and degree of involvement to parents' wishes. There is evidence that certain factors (e.g., child care, transportation, small program size, informal communication strategies) can enhance parent participation in early childhood education programs.

Least Restrictive Environment

One of the fundamental provisions in EHA is the least restrictive environment (LRE) provision. This assurance maintains that handicapped children will be educated with nonhandicapped children to the maximum extent appropriate, and presumes that handicapped children will be segregated from their nonhandicapped peers only when the severity of the handicap is such that education cannot be accomplished in a regular education setting.

Implementing the LRE provision of EHA for preschool children is complicated by the fact that few public schools serve populations of nonhandicapped
preschool children (Odom & Warren, 1988; Smith & Strain, 1988). This reality
often results in segregated programs for handicapped children, and for several
years this "screen and segregate" approach was the norm (Safford, 1989). More
recently, increased attention has been given to the effects of integrated programs
on the performance of handicapped children. In addition, evidence indicating
that benefits can result from integration has provided impetus for the design of
programs that can allow handicapped children access to their nonhandicapped
peers.

Using a multi-element baseline design, Esposito and Koorland (1989) analyzed the free-play behavior of two preschool children with severe to profound
hearing losses in both integrated and nonintegrated settings. The authors concluded that nonsocial, parallel play was evidenced to a greater degree in the
segregated setting. In contrast, more socially advanced, associative play occurred in the integrated setting.

Guralnick (1978) reported that integration of handicapped children with nonhandicapped children may produce positive effects on the former group. He
suggested that nonhandicapped children appear to act as models, instructors, and
providers of consequences. This results in such effects as fewer inappropriate
behaviors, and richer social, play, and linguistic environments. Guralnick and
Groom (1988) compared peer interactions and cognitive levels of play of mildly
developmentally delayed preschoolers in mainstreamed and specialized settings.
They reported that handicapped children demonstrated a substantially higher rate
of peer-related social behaviors and played more constructively in mainstreamed
settings. The rate of social interaction in the mainstreamed classroom was more
than twice that in the specialized setting, and there were higher rates of behaviors
associated with peer-to-peer social competence.

Although these results suggest that positive benefits can occur when handicapped children are educated with their nonhandicapped peers, there is considerable evidence to suggest that access alone is not sufficient to produce such
effects. Peterson (1982) noted that preschoolers' social groups are often child
directed, and there are considerable data to indicate that handicapped children are
less likely to be chosen as playmates in comparison to their nonhandicapped
peers. Such findings suggest that, unless children's social groups are subjected to
appropriate teacher manipulation, the major intent of mainstreaming will not be
achieved by merely placing handicapped youngsters in regular educational environments. That proximity alone is not sufficient to insure interaction between
handicapped and nonhandicapped children was demonstrated by Kugelmass
(1989) in her analysis of the behavior of six handicapped and six nonhandicapped
children during free play over a 9-month period. According to Kugelmass
(1989): "planned and systematic structure and curriculum were necessary ingre-
dients of the success of the program" (p. 42).

Similarly, Guralnick (1978) indicated that a setting that simply provides handicapped children access to their nonhandicapped peers is not sufficient to produce desirable gains. Systematic attention to structural, organizational, and programmatic features of the environment is essential. Examples include: (a) appropriate selection of toys, social activities, and games such that interaction is facilitated; (b) teacher-initiated modeling and prompting to encourage interaction; (c) well-structured but flexible curriculum that permits varying emphases according to children's needs; and (d) classroom organization to facilitate alternative social activities and groupings. The value of providing handicapped children access to nonhandicapped peer models in a carefully implemented manner was illustrated by the work of Schoen, Lentz, and Suppa (1988), who demonstrated that opportunities to observe nonhandicapped children, when accompanied by cuing and reinforcement of student attention, can produce significant gains in self-care skills for handicapped preschoolers.

Jenkins, Speltz, and Odom (1985) investigated the effects of mainstreaming on child development and social interactions. The authors reported that children in both integrated and segregated settings made gains on various indices of development (e.g., cognitive, language, motor, social behavior). The only significant main effect occurred on a measure of social play that was conducted in a discrete, specific "peer entry" situation. Jenkins et al. concluded: "a preschool following the proximity model of integration, in which handicapped and non nonhandicapped children are simply placed together without a systematic plan or curriculum for integration, produces developmental changes that are no different from those resulting from a preschool in which only handicapped children are enrolled" (p. 15).

Subsequent work by these investigators demonstrated the positive effects of carefully structured social interactions for preschool handicapped children. In this study (Jenkins, Odom, & Speltz, 1989), the behavior of 73 preschool children, including 56 with mild or moderate handicaps, was compared across settings (integrated vs. segregated) and play conditions (social interaction and child-directed play). The authors reported that the social interaction treatment (consisting of small-group, structured play situations that incorporated modeling and prompts as needed) resulted in more interactive play across settings, as well as more social interaction between handicapped and nonhandicapped children in integrated classrooms.

The successful use of nonhandicapped peers as models for handicapped children through a process of peer imitation training (PIT) was described by Apolloni and Cooke (1978). Through the use of verbal and physical prompts, which were subsequently faded, the authors reported that delayed toddlers and preschool children learned to imitate the motor, material use, and communication behaviors of nonhandicapped peers. Furthermore, generalization of imitative behaviors to nontraining settings and nontargeted responses was reported. The authors offered advice to educators regarding the integration of handicapped and nonhandicapped children. Their recommendations included the judicious use of teacher reinforcement to enhance and not interfere with social interactions, thoughtful selection of instructional and play materials and equipment, and the systematic organization of small social groupings to provide an optimal social climate.

In summary, integrated settings have been associated with enhanced outcomes for handicapped children. However, such settings might be described as necessary but not sufficient for achieving such benefits. Merely integrating handicapped and nonhandicapped children in the same space does not insure social interaction. Special attention to this objective in the instructional curriculum is necessary (Odom & Strain, 1984). Curricular strategies that have been shown to be effective include the use of appropriate toys and activities (Beckman & Kohl, 1984; Guralnick, 1978; Odom & Strain, 1984), the use of small, teacher-directed social groupings (Guralnick, 1978; Jenkins, Odom, & Speltz, 1989), and peer modeling with teacher-directed cues and reinforcement (Apolloni & Cooke, 1978; Schoen et al., 1988).

One practice implication that can be derived from this literature is that developers of early childhood special education programs should structure environments so that handicapped children can be integrated with their nonhandicapped peers. A practical issue in providing integrated educational programs for young handicapped children concerns how administrators can achieve integrated programs when the incentives for early childhood education apply only to handicapped children. Smith and Strain (1988) list several methods that can be utilized to provide handicapped preschoolers access to their nonhandicapped peers. These include developing liaisons with community day care or preschool programs (Odom & Warren, 1988) and "reverse mainstreaming" arrangements that enroll nonhandicapped children in specialized settings.

A second practice implication is that successful outcomes in the LRE require carefully planned and executed programs that include such features as effective teacher cuing and reinforcement, the selection of activities and toys to facilitate interaction, and flexible social groupings. Achieving successfully integrated education programs for young handicapped children requires the satisfactory resolution of philosophical differences between early childhood educators and special educators (Kugelmass, 1989). Safford (1989) conceptualized these differences as the contrast between a "developmentally appropriate practices" orientation and a "special education methods and procedures" or individual child study orientation. Such differences can result in conflict when one orientation masks or overshadows the other. However, Safford (1989) suggested that although differences between these two orientations exist, there are many areas of common agreement, and optimal benefits occur when both direct instruction and developmentally appropriate practices are considered.

Issues in Service Delivery: Summary

Four specific issues relating to the design and implementation of early childhood education (age at intervention, treatment intensity, parental/family involvement, and least restrictive environment) were explored. The literature reviewed is helpful in suggesting some guidelines for school psychologists and others who are developing and implementing early childhood programs for children who are handicapped or at-risk. Interventions that were initiated during the preschool period were associated with positive outcomes for target children, and in a few instances infant intervention was found to be superior. In general, programs characterized by more intensity produced more significant changes, although there may be an optimal level of intensity not yet defined. Parental/family involvement has not been associated with increases in child progress, although some enhancement of parent or family systems has been described. The type of parent/family involvement (i.e., less formal, more frequent contacts) may be of more relevance than the amount of involvement. Finally, early childhood environments that can provide handicapped children access to their nonhandicapped peers in a structured, teacher-directed manner appear to enhance outcomes for target children.

SUMMARY

Young children with special education needs include two major groups: those who are at risk because of specific environmental factors such as poverty or minority status and those who have biologically based handicaps. Identification of children who are handicapped or at risk is a complex matter because of the questionable validity of mild handicaps, the lack of measurement precision for very young children, and variability in definitions across ages and agencies. Problems in identifying special needs in young children may be minimized by employing definitional systems appropriate for the early childhood years, incorporating both actuarial and clinical judgment criteria, and developing and maintaining linkages among diverse service agencies.

Early interventions for young children with special needs have been associated with generally positive outcomes. Both short-term effects, such as gains in IQ and academic achievement, and long-term benefits, including fewer retentions and fewer years in special education, have been demonstrated. Not all programs are equally effective, however, and there is general agreement that a poorly conceived and implemented early childhood program is little better than none at all.

Several characteristics of effective early childhood programs for children with special needs have been identified. Evidence suggests, for example, that interventions should be of optimal intensity, such that there is maximum engaged time for learning. Involving parents and families in the interventions, particularly to a degree and in a manner that is determined to be appropriate for the individuals in question, may produce favorable changes for the parent or family. Programs that integrate handicapped and nonhandicapped children and incorporate systematic curricular goals to foster their interaction, are associated with enhanced social competence and play behavior on the part of target children.

REFERENCES

Apolloni, T., & Cooke, R. P. (1978). Integrated programming at the infant, toddler, and preschool levels. In M. J. Guralnick (Ed.), *Early intervention and the integration of handicapped and nonhandicapped children* (pp. 147–165). Baltimore: University Park Press.

At risk: Pupils and their teachers. (1986, May 14). *Education Week*, pp. 28–29.

Bagnato, S. J. (1981). Developmental scales and developmental curricula: Forging a linkage for early intervention. *Topics in Early Childhood Special Education, 1*, 1–8.

Bailey, E. J., & Bricker, D. (1984). The efficacy of early intervention for severely handicapped infants and young children. *Topics in Early Childhood Special Education, 4*(3), 30–51.

Baker, B. L. (1984). Intervention with families with young, severely handicapped children. In J. Blacher (Ed.), *Severely handicapped young children and their families: Research in review* (pp. 319–375). Orlando: Academic Press.

Barnett, W. S. (1988). The economics of preschool special education under Public Law 99-457. *Topics in Early Childhood Special Education, 8*(1), 12–23.

Beckman, P. J., & Kohl, F. L. (1984). The effects of social and isolate toys on the interactions and play of integrated and non-integrated groups of preschoolers. *Education and Training of the Mentally Retarded, 19*, 169–174.

Bender, W. N. (1987). Behavioral indicators of temperament and personality in the inactive learner. *Journal of Learning Disabilities, 20*, 301–305.

Bereiter, C. (1985). The changing face of educational disadvantagement. *Phi Delta Kappan, 66*, 538–541.

Boehm, A. E., & Sandberg, B. R. (1982). Assessment of the preschool child. In C. R. Reynolds & T. B. Gutkin (Eds.), *The handbook of school psychology* (pp. 82–120). New York: Wiley.

Bracken, B. A. (1987). Limitations of preschool instruments and standards for minimal levels of technical adequacy. *Journal of Psychoeducational Assessment, 4*, 313–326.

Bricker, D., & Gumerlock, S. (1988). Application of a three-level evaluation plan for monitoring child progress and program effects. *The Journal of Special Education, 22*, 66–81.

Bristol, M. M., & Gallagher, J. J. (1982). A family focus for intervention. In C. Ramey & P. Trohanis (Eds.), *Finding and educating the high risk and handicapped infant* (pp. 137–161). Baltimore: University Park Press.

Bryant, D. M., & Ramey, C. T. (1987). An analysis of the effectiveness of early intervention programs for environmentally at-risk children. In M. J. Guralnick & F. C. Bennett (Eds.), *The effectiveness of early intervention for at-risk and handicapped children* (pp. 33–78). Orlando: Academic Press.

Carter, L. F. (1984). The sustaining effects study of compensatory and elementary education. *Educational Researcher, 13*(7), 4–13.

Casto, G., & Mastropieri, M. A. (1986). The efficacy of early intervention programs: A meta-analysis. *Exceptional Children, 52*, 417–424.

Chance, P. (1985). Perception: Mirror mystery. *Psychology Today*, August, p. 16.

Colorado Department of Education (1983). *Effectiveness of early special education for handicapped children*. Denver: Author.

Copeland, M. E., & Kimmel, J. R. (1989). *Evaluation and management of infants and young children with developmental disabilities*. Baltimore: Paul H. Brooks.

Council for Exceptional Children (1986, October 8). *Public Law 99-457: The Education of the Handicapped Act Amendments of 1986*. Reston, VA: Author.

Danaher, J. (1988, June 10). *Six types of noncategorical and modified categorical eligibility requirements for preschool special education and related services*. Chapel Hill, NC: National Early Childhood Technical Assistance System.

Danaher, J. (1989, March 29). *Six types of noncategorical and modified categorical eligibility requirements for preschool special education and related services*. Chapel Hill, NC: National Early Childhood Technical Assistance System.

Edgar, E., McNulty, B., Gaetz, J., & Maddox, M. (1984). Educational placement of graduates of preschool programs for handicapped children. *Topics in Early Childhood Special Education, 4*(3), 19–29.

Esposito, B. G., & Koorland, M. A. (1989). Play behavior of hearing impaired children: Integrated and segregated settings. *Exceptional Children, 55,* 412–419.

Fagley, N. S. (1988). Judgmental heuristics: Implications for the decision-making of school psychologists. *School Psychology Review, 17,* 311–321.

Faust, D. (1986). Research on human judgment and its application to clinical practice. *Professional Psychology: Research and Practice, 17,* 420–430.

Fredericks, H. D., Moore, M. G., & Baldwin, V. L. (1982). The long-range effects of early childhood education on a trainable mentally retarded population. In E. B. Edgar, N. G. Haring, J. R. Jenkins, & C. G. Pious (Eds.), *Mentally handicapped children: Education and training* (pp. 173–199). Baltimore: University Park Press.

Fuqua, R. W., Hegland, S. M., & Karas, S. C. (1985). Processes influencing linkages between preschool handicap classrooms and home. *Exceptional Children, 51,* 307–314.

Galloway, C., & Chandler, P. (1978). The marriage of special and generic early education services. In M. J. Guralnick (Ed.), *Early intervention and the integration of handicapped and nonhandicapped children* (pp. 261–287). Baltimore: University Park Press.

Garwood, S. G., Fewell, R. R., & Neisworth, J. T. (1988). Public Law 94-142: You can get there from here! *Topics in Early Childhood Special Education, 8*(1), 1–11.

Gettinger, M. (1984). Measuring time needed for learning to predict learning outcomes. *Exceptional Children, 51,* 244–248.

Guralnick, M. J. (1978). Integrated preschools as educational and therapeutic environments: Concepts, design, and analysis. In M. J. Guralnick (Ed.), *Early intervention and the integration of handicapped and nonhandicapped children* (pp. 115–145). Baltimore: University Park Press.

Guralnick, M. J., & Bennett, F. C. (1987). A framework for early intervention. In M. J. Guralnick & F. C. Bennett (Eds.), *The effectiveness of early intervention for at-risk and handicapped children* (pp. 3–29). Orlando: Academic Press.

Guralnick, M. J., & Bricker, D. (1987). The effectiveness of early intervention for children with cognitive and general developmental delays. In M. J. Guralnick & F. C. Bennett (Eds.), *The effectiveness of early intervention for at-risk and handicapped children* (pp. 115–173). Orlando: Academic Press.

Guralnick, M. J., & Groom, J. M. (1988). Peer interactions in mainstreamed and specialized classrooms. A comparative analysis. *Exceptional Children, 54,* 415–425.

Harris, S. R. (1987). Early intervention for children with motor handicaps. In M. J. Guralnick & F. C. Bennett (Eds.), *The effectiveness of early intervention for at-risk and handicapped children* (pp. 175–212). Orlando: Academic Press.

Hatch, O. G. (1984). Environmental constraints affecting services for the handicapped. *Topics in Early Childhood Special Education, 4*(1), 83–90.

Horn, W. F., & Packard, T. (1985). Early identification of learning problems: A meta-analysis. *Journal of Educational Psychology, 77,* 597–607.

Jenkins, J. R., Odom, S. L., & Speltz, M. L. (1989). Effects of social integration on preschool children with handicaps. *Exceptional Children, 55,* 420–428.

Jenkins, J. R., Speltz, M. L., & Odom, S. L. (1985). Integrating normal and handicapped preschoolers: Effects on child development and social interaction. *Exceptional Children, 52,* 7–17.

Jensen, A. R. (1985). Compensatory education and the theory of intelligence. *Phi Delta Kappan, 66,* 554–558.

Kaiser, A. P., & Hemmeter, M. L. (1989). Value-based approaches to family intervention. *Topics in Early Childhood Special Education, 8*(4), 72–86.

Kavale, K. A., & Forness, S. R. (1986). School learning, time and learning disabilities: The dissociated learner. *Journal of Learning Disabilities, 19,* 130–138.

Keogh, B. K. (1988). Learning disability: Diversity in search of order. In M. C. Wang, M. C.

Reynolds, & H. J. Walberg (Eds.), *Handbook of special education: Research and practice* (Vol. 2, pp. 225–251). Oxford, England: Pergamon Press.

Keogh, B., & Becker, L. (1973). Early detection of learning problems: Questions, cautions, and guidelines. *Exceptional Children, 40,* 5–11.

Knoff, H. M. (1987). School-based interventions for discipline problems. In C. A. Maher & J. E. Zins (Eds.), *Psychoeducational interventions in the schools* (pp. 118–140). New York: Pergamon Press.

Kugelmass, J. W. (1989). The "shared classroom": A case study of interactions between early childhood and special education staff and children. *Journal of Early Intervention, 13,* 36–44.

Martin, R. P., Drew, K. P., Gaddis, L. R., & Moseley, M. (1988). Prediction of elementary school achievement from preschool temperament: Three studies. *School Psychology Review, 17,* 125–137.

Martin, R. P., & Holbrook, J. (1985). Relationship of temperament characteristics to the achievement of first-grade children. *Journal of Psychoeducational Assessment, 3,* 131–140.

Meadow-Orlans, K. P. (1987). An analysis of the effectiveness of early intervention programs for hearing-impaired children. In M. J. Guralnick & F. C. Bennett (Eds.), *The effectiveness of early intervention for at-risk and handicapped children* (pp. 325–362). Orlando: Academic Press.

Meehl, P. E. (1954). *Clinical versus statistical prediction: A theoretical analysis and a review of the evidence.* Minneapolis: University of Minnesota Press.

Meisels, S. J., Harbin, G., Modigliani, K., & Olson, K. (1988). Formulating optimal state early childhood intervention policies. *Exceptional Children, 55,* 159–165.

Mercer, J. R. (1973). *Labeling the mentally retarded.* Berkeley, CA: University of California Press.

Mlinarcik, S. (1987). Community partnerships: A collaborative approach for developing integrated preschool programs. In M. S. Berres & P. Knoblock (Eds.), *Program models for mainstreaming* (pp. 239–260). Rockville, MD: Aspen.

Morrow, L. W., & Morrow, S. A. (1987). Prevention, primary. In C. R. Reynolds & L. M. Mann (Eds.), *Encyclopedia of special education* (Vol. 3, pp. 1245–1246). New York: Wiley.

Musselman, C. R., Wilson, A. K., & Lindsay, P. H. (1988). Effects of early intervention on hearing impaired children. *Exceptional Children, 55,* 222–228.

Nordyke, N. S. (1982). Improving services for young, handicapped children through local, interagency collaboration. *Topics in Early Childhood Special Education, 2*(1), 63–72.

Odom, S. L., & Strain, P. S. (1984). Classroom-based social skills instruction for severely handicapped preschool children. *Topics in Early Childhood Special Education, 4*(3), 97–116.

Odom, S. L., & Warren, S. F. (1988). Early childhood education in the year 2000. *Journal of the Division for Early Childhood, 12,* 263–273.

Olson, M. (1987). Early intervention for children with visual impairments. In M. J. Guralnick & F. C. Bennett (Eds.), *The effectiveness of early intervention for at-risk and handicapped children* (pp. 297–324). Orlando: Academic Press.

Peterson, N. L. (1982). Social integration of handicapped and nonhandicapped preschoolers: A study of playmate preferences. *Topics in Early Childhood Special Education, 2*(2), 56–69.

Poth, R. L., & Barnett, D. W. (1988). Establishing the limits of interpretive confidence: A validity study of two preschool developmental scales. *School Psychology Review, 17,* 322–330.

Safford, P. L. (1989). *Integrated teaching in early childhood: Starting in the mainstream.* White Plains, NY: Longman.

Sawyer, J. (1966). Measurement *and* prediction, clinical *and* statistical. *Psychological Bulletin, 66,* 178–200.

Schoen, S. F., Lentz, F. E., & Suppa, R. J. (1988). An examination of two prompt fading procedures and opportunities to observe in teaching handicapped preschoolers self-help skills. *Journal of the Division for Early Childhood, 12,* 349–358.

Schultz, M. K. (1988, December). A comparison of standard scores for commonly used tests of early reading. *Communique,* p. 13.

Schweinhart, L. J., Berrueta-Clement, J. R., Barnett, W. S., Epstein, A. S., & Weikart, D. P. (1985). The promise of early childhood education. *Phi Delta Kappan, 66,* 548–553.

Schweinhart, L. J., & Weikart, D. P. (1985). Evidence that good early childhood programs work. *Phi Delta Kappan, 66,* 545–551.

Sheehan, R. (1988). Involvement of parents in early childhood assessment. In T. D. Wachs & R. Sheehan (Eds.), *Assessment of young developmentally disabled children* (pp. 75–90). New York: Plenum.

Sheehan, R., & Sites, J. (1989). Implications of P.L. 99-457 for assessment. *Topics in Early Childhood Special Education, 8*(4), 103–115.

Simeonsson, R. J., Olley, J. G., & Rosenthal, S. L. (1987). Early intervention for children with autism. In M. J. Guralnick & F. C. Bennett (Eds.), *The effectiveness of early intervention for at-risk and handicapped children* (pp. 275–296). Orlando: Academic Press.

Smith, B. J., & Schakel, J. A. (1987). Noncategorical identification of preschool handicapped children: Policy issues and options. *Journal of the Division for Early Childhood, 11,* 78–86.

Smith, B. J., & Strain, P. S. (1988). Early childhood special education in the next decade: Implementing and expanding P.L. 99-457. *Topics in Early Childhood Special Education, 8*(1), 37–47.

Snyder-McLean, L., & McLean, J. E. (1987). Effectiveness of early intervention for children with language and communication disorders. In M. J. Guralnick & F. C. Bennett (Eds.), *The effectiveness of early intervention for at-risk and handicapped children* (pp. 213–274). Orlando: Academic Press.

Sommers, R. K. (1989). Language assessment: Issues in the use and interpretation of tests and measures. *School Psychology Review, 18,* 452–462.

Strain, P. S., & Smith, B. J. (1986). A counter-interpretation of early intervention effects: A response to Casto and Mastropieri. *Exceptional Children, 53,* 260–265.

Suarez, T. M., Hurth, J. L., & Prestridge, S. (1988). Innovation in services for young children with handicaps and their families: An analysis of the handicapped children's early education program projects funded from 1982 to 1986. *Journal of the Division for Early Childhood, 12,* 224–237.

Swanson, H. L. (1988). Toward a metatheory of learning disabilities. *Journal of Learning Disabilities, 21,* 196–209.

Telzrow, C. F. (1990). Reducing error in identifying specific learning disabilities. In A. Thomas & J. Grimes (Eds.), *Best practices in school psychology* (Vol. 2, pp. 607–620). Washington, DC: National Association of School Psychologists.

Traditional families—A dying breed? (1986, May 14). *Education Week,* pp. 22–23.

Turnbull, A. P., & Winton, P. J. (1984). Parent involvement policy and practice: Current research and implications for families of young, severely handicapped children. In J. Blacher (Ed.), *Severely handicapped young children and their families* (pp. 377–397). Orlando: Academic Press.

Turnbull, A. P., Winton, P. J., Blacher, J., & Salkind, N. (1982). Mainstreaming in the kindergarten classroom: Perspective of parents of handicapped and nonhandicapped children. *Journal of the Division for Early Childhood, 6,* 14–20.

Vincent, L. J., & Salisbury, C. L. 1988). Changing economic and social influences of family involvement. *Topics in Early Childhood Special Education, 8*(1), 48–59.

White, K. R. (1985–1986). Efficacy of early intervention. *The Journal of Special Education, 19,* 401–416.

Who's dependent upon whom? (1986, May 14). *Education Week,* pp. 25–27.

Willis, W. G. (1986). Actuarial and clinical approaches to neuropsychological diagnosis: Applied considerations. In J. E. Obrzut & G. W. Hynd (Eds.), *Child neuropsychology: Vol. 2. Clinical practice* (pp. 245–262). Orlando: Academic Press.

Winton, P., & Turnbull, A. (1981). Parent involvement as viewed by parents of preschool handicapped children. *Topics in Early Childhood Special Education, 1*(3), 11–19.

Wolery, M. (1989). Transitions in early childhood special education: Issues and procedures. *Focus on Exceptional Children, 22*(2), 1–14, 16.

Woodhead, M. (1988). When psychology informs public policy: The case of early childhood intervention. *American Psychologist, 43*, 443–454.

Zigler, E., & Berman, W. (1983). Discerning the future of early childhood intervention. *American Psychologist, 38*, 894–906.

Zigler, E., & Trickett, P. (1978). IQ, social competence, and evaluation of early childhood intervention programs. *American Psychologist, 33*, 789–798.

Zins, J. E., Conyne, R. K., & Ponti, C. R. (1988). Primary prevention: Expanding the impact of psychological services in schools. *School Psychology Review, 17*, 542–549.

3 Parent Involvement in Early Childhood Services

Kathleen D. Paget
University of South Carolina

Recent years have witnessed increased interest and advancement in the intensity and quality of parent involvement in early childhood services. Expanded beyond a focus on parent education to enhance young children's cognitive development (Bronfenbrenner, 1975), the trend now reflects increased understanding of family influences during early childhood and the importance, not only of parent training and education, but also of support for the entire family during a young child's preschool years. Indeed, one cannot peruse recently published articles, book chapters, journals, and books on early childhood services without recognizing the intense emphasis on the role of families in these services and the challenge to develop professional–family partnerships (Jennings, 1990; Kagan, Powell, Weissbourd, & Zigler, 1987; Powell, 1989).

A multifold rationale exists to explain these advances from economic, legal, humanistic, empirical, theoretical, and common sense standpoints. Components of the rationale include the parent involvement mandates of Public Law 94-142, changing economic and social influences on contemporary family life, increasing support for the potent effects of family life on young children's development, and the recent passage of Public Law 99-457 (The Education of the Handicapped Amendments of 1986) targeting services to infants, toddlers, preschool children, and their families.

The purpose of this chapter is to discuss parent involvement in early childhood services from historical and contemporary vantage points. The chapter begins with an elaboration of the rationale for the involvement of parents in services for young children, followed by a discussion of the scope of parent involvement and the various roles played by parents. The next section critiques parent involvement and presents an overview of research into the effectiveness of various forms of involvement. Following these discussions is an analysis of the contemporary movement away from parent involvement per se to family support and family-focused intervention services. The scope of family-focused intervention is discussed, followed by a presentation of exemplary models. The chapter ends with a discussion of implications for school psychologists in the areas of service delivery, training, and research.

RATIONALE FOR PARENT INVOLVEMENT

Developmental theories have long suggested that the family is a primary context in which children's competencies develop, especially during the early years from birth through 5 years of age. Bronfenbrenner (1986) conceptualized the family as a system embedded in other systems, both formal (e.g., educational and medical services) and informal (e.g., a family's network of relatives, neighbors, and friends). He emphasized the indisputable influence these systems have on family life and asserts that children must be viewed as family members and that families must be viewed within a context of larger influences.

In a comprehensive review of current theory and research, Silber (1989) provided further analysis of multiple family dimensions affecting young children's development and emphasized that the precise manner in which these dimensions manifest themselves differs from one family to the next. The relevant dimensions illustrate the complexity of family life and include the presence of a responsive, warm, and attentive attachment figure, parental use of consistent disciplinary standards that involve explanation and the appropriate expression of affect, a well-organized and stimulating (but not overstimulating) environment, parental encouragement of learning through responsive feedback, parental expectations for child competence, harmonious relations among family members, and a positive relationship with the environment outside the family, including contact with extended family members and access to community services.

In addition to such influences from families on young children's development, children themselves exert a reciprocal influence on family life. Whenever a new birth occurs in a family, for example, anticipated and unanticipated effects occur, including additional demands on parents' time and energy, disruptions in schedules and routines, increased reason to interact with extended family members, and sibling rivalry when there is another child in the family. Thus, it is clear that unique conditions exist for any family after the birth of a young child.

Difficulties surrounding the birth and development of a young child create additional complications and challenges for a family. Peterson (1987) created a conceptual context for understanding these challenges and difficulties by synthesizing developmental theory and research. Unique conditions are created by reactions parents have to the unexpected difficulties of the birth process and the reality of having a child with a disability. These include:

1. Parental attempts to explore reasons for the disability, including blaming themselves.
2. Parental attempts to find a diagnosis and appropriate services.
3. Their need to learn special methods of caring for an infant with serious medical difficulties.
4. Being in the initial, vulnerable, stages of developing a bond and personal relationship with their child.
5. Their frustration if answers are not readily available, if the answers obtained conflict with one another, and/or if accessing services becomes a complicated, exhausting process.

These conditions contribute to a conceptual rationale for parent–professional communication in early childhood services and underscore the operative issue that the helpgiving/helpseeking context into which professionals and parents enter is an intensely emotional one requiring special understanding and skills.

In developing a rationale for parent involvement and education in early intervention services, Peterson and Cooper (1989) offer several premises upon which such involvement is based. These premises are summarized in Table 3.1.

The previous discussion establishes a sound rationale for parent involvement in early childhood services. In fact, the concept of parent involvement is so strongly supported by theory and logic that one may question the need to discuss it further. Paradoxically, however, the concept continues to generate much discussion and controversy in early intervention and related disciplines.

Changes in the composition of families contribute to the controversy by creating challenges to the notion that one frame of reference should be held by professionals toward families. Such changes are characterized by increases in the proportion of ethnic and racial minority families in the United States, increases in the incidence of single parenthood, the economic realities of single parenthood and the concomitant rise in the number of children being raised in poverty, and the increased need for childcare and scheduling demands experienced by families in which both parents work outside the home (Vincent & Salisbury, 1988). These societal influences contribute to the context in which early childhood services exist and assist in the creation of a relevant framework for understanding the complexities of parent involvement.

SCOPE OF PARENT INVOLVEMENT

An expansion in the number and type of roles played by parents in early childhood services have been associated with societal and demographic changes. Various roles have been created by parents and for parents since the time of the eugenics movement when, because of the belief in hereditary influences, parents

TABLE 3.1
Premises Related to Parent Involvement in Early Childhood Services

1. Parents (or their substitute caregivers) are the most significant teachers, socializing agents, and caregivers for children during their years from birth to age 5.

2. Parents are in a unique, strategic position to enhance or negate the potential benefits or an early intervention program.

3. Parents can act as key intervention agents in their child's life and can be primary teachers of the special skills their child needs to acquire.

4. Parent involvement and education offer a means for parents to build a positive perspective about their child and their position as parents.

5. Parents of young children with handicapping or at-risk conditions often face additional caregiving demands and stresses that demand new coping skills and parenting skills and may tax their emotional and coping systems.

6. The success of early intervention services and the duration of those benefits are directly related to the degree to which parents are part of the intervention process.

7. Intervention works best when parents and professionals are collaborating and working together toward common goals for a child.

8. Involving parents by educating them and helping them build new skills for dealing with their child's special needs from the onset has obvious economic benefits.

9. Involvement brings parents into contact with a variety of resources (caring people, agencies, materials, information, professionals) that they can draw upon to aid them in their parenting roles.

10. Parent education and involvement are advantageous simply because a great many parents are eager during their child's early life to be good parents, to nurture their child, and they are often not willing to relinquish control over a child so young to others.

11. Parent education and involvement foster parent and community support for early referral to early intervention programs.

Note. Adapted with permission from Peterson and Cooper (1989).

were viewed as the source of their children's problems, as victims, and as patients in need of treatment (Turnbull & Turnbull, 1986). The diversified roles and expansion in scope underscore the need to conceptualize parent involvement as a multidimensional construct.

Simeonsson and Bailey (1988) captured the multiple facets of parent involvement within the broad groupings of parents as participants in or recipients of professional services, whereas Peterson and Cooper (1989) enumerated various processes that take place between professionals and parents:

1. Processes involving what professionals do for parents or give to them (e.g., information, services, advice, consultation, training, or emotional support.

2. Activities that parents do for the intervention program, its staff, or the agency providing the services (e.g., fund raising, dissemination of information, advocacy, assistance to staff on various chores, financial contributions to the agency, or donated services to the center.

3. Activities parents do with or for their own child as an extension of the

intervention program carried out by professional staff members (e.g., teaching and tutoring the child on specific tasks at home or at the early childhood service center.

4. Activities that parents and staff do together, where both work on a common activity or task relating to the child, the program, or the center (e.g., planning, evaluating the child or program, participating in social activities, making joint presentations on the program, working on a project together to make something for the classroom or a child, or determining policy for a program or center).

Regardless of the precise manner in which the parameters of parent involvement are defined, the roles discussed range from passive to active involvement and underscore the importance of reciprocal interaction between parents and professionals. It is important to understand on both descriptive and interpretive levels the nature of the various roles played by parents and to guide a discussion of roles with information related to best practice. Because family circumstances and other variables affect how practical and desireable each role is for a given parent at any given time, best practice indicates that it is presumptuous for professionals to assume at the outset of our interactions with parents that one role is more desireable than another (Bailey & Simeonsson, 1988; Ehly, Conoley, & Rosenthal, 1985; Vincent & Salisbury, 1988).

Educational Decision Maker

A major role conferred upon parents by Public Law 94-142 has pertained to their participation in the development and implementation of their child's individualized educational plan (IEP). Associated with this role are due process procedures for protecting the rights of children and their parents and invoking accountability into special education procedures and practices (Turnbull & Turnbull, 1986). Although controversy exists regarding the benefits of this role and its impact on the relationship between schools and parents (Budoff & Orenstein, 1982; Strickland, 1983), implementation of this role has been important in giving parents a voice in decision making.

Advocate

Another role conferred upon parents of children with disabilities is that of advocate for their children's rights, as well as for their own. Advocacy activities have ranged from contesting decisions made by early childhood programs to attempting to influence legislation. As with educational decision making, the desire of parents to assume this type of role varies from parent to parent (Turnbull & Turnbull, 1986). Some parents have been very successful advocates for their children, whereas others have chosen not to engage in advocacy activities. As suggested by Turnbull and Turnbull (1986), this role requires considerable technical knowledge of available services, familiarity with statutes and laws, the ability to exercise sophisticated strategies of influence, and sometimes an assertive confrontational style. Parents with limited education and limited English proficiency, in particular, have voiced difficulty with such skills (Allen & Hudd, 1987).

Numerous perspectives exist on the appropriateness of parental advocacy activities. On the one hand, as articulated by Allen and Hudd (1987):

> to a legislator, a moving personal testimony from a parent is far more powerful than mountains of statistics. Administrators of many programs for children with handicaps, concerned about funding curtailment, are finding that parents can be the best advocates for program continuation. (p. 135)

On the other hand, professionals contend that because parents' own interests cannot be separated from those of their child, parents are not the most qualified to represent their child's needs. Thus, individual preferences are influenced by the purpose of the advocacy role and the conditions under which it exists for a particular parent.

Intervenor

The rationale for involving parents as teachers of their children is compelling, and the benefits of involving parents in such a way in early intervention programs have long been recognized (Bronfenbrenner, 1975). In a classic article by Johnson and Katz (1973), the rationale for involving parents as teachers or intervenors was clear: "The advantage of parents as change agents is that they constitute a cheap, continuous treatment resource which is able to augment existing therapeutic manpower capabilities and work conveniently within the home" (p. 181). Although the cost-effectiveness of parent training as a primary goal has been criticized (Wiegerink & Comfort, 1987), such training has provided a link between home and programs, thus creating the opportunity for reinforcement and generalization of skills across settings (Karnes & Teska, 1980; Shearer & Shearer, 1977).

Essentially, there have been two broad goals of parent training in early childhood programs. The first goal has been to ensure continuity between what occurs in the intervention program and the child's experiences at home. Exemplified by programs such as Head Start, such goals have been applied to populations of low socioeconomic status as well as those who are handicapped or biologically at risk. A second goal of parent training has been to place the parent in the role of direct teacher, where the parent is expected to carry out a prescribed curriculum, set aside specific times for teaching, keep records, and so forth. As suggested by Allen, Afflect, McGrade, and McQueeney (1984), such a role is based on several premises, including a relatively high level of parental verbal skill, confidence in the ability to function as a teacher, belief in the value of the intervention activities, a parent–child interactional style compatible with professional intervention methods, and living circumstances that afford the time and energy to follow through consistently on the child's teaching program.

Case Manager

Case management activities for parents involved in early intervention have arisen from problems in coordinating services among programs and agencies serving developmentally disabled children (Brewer & Kakalik, 1979; Dunst & Trivette, 1989). As with other roles, arguments and counterarguments exist about the appropriateness of this role for parents (Allen & Hudd, 1987). In support of such a role are contentions that because all services must be approved by parents and parents are closer to the situation than anyone else, they are most likely to be aware of the services their children are or are not receiving. Opposing contentions pertain to the time burden on parents, their lack of easy entry to service systems, and their lesser knowledge of both the resources available and the procedure for securing services (Allen & Hudd, 1987).

Program Evaluator

Based on the premise that sound program evaluation includes assessment of views from consumers of services (Wolf, 1978), parents have become increasingly involved in monitoring and evaluating programs, not only for their own individual children, but for groups of children as well. In this role, parents are asked to evaluate the quality of services offered to them on both formative and summative levels. This role affords parents an opportunity to contribute to program development via continual verbal feedback to staff members and completion of surveys assessing services on dimensions such as child progress, teaching methods, staff attitudes, parent involvement activities, and appropriateness and acceptability of recommendations. Also, when implemented on a summative basis, data collected from parents may be instrumental in determining the ultimate viability of a program. Thus, this form of communication holds potential for enhancing parents' sense of control and may be related to parental advocacy activities.

Team Member

Membership of parents on multidisciplinary teams is a recent role created to encourage full participation of parents in the assessment and intervention process for their children. Feedback from parents regarding delays in the receipt of information between diagnosis and treatment and inconsistencies in information received from multiple professionals (Anderson & Garner, 1973) have been instrumental in the creation of this role. Controversy surrounding this role results from the preference of some professionals to have a forum for the discussion of issues without parents present; the difficulties incorporating parental input into a team's structure, process, and language system; and ongoing developmental changes, within a team and a family, that influence ease of and desire for involvement (Nash, 1990). Consequently, considerable variation exists across programs regarding the manner in which this role is implemented, with some programs including parents in every team discussion (e.g., Dunst, Trivette, & Deal, 1988) and others determining more specific situations for the inclusion of parents as team members (Turnbull & Turnbull, 1986).

CRITIQUE OF PARENT INVOLVEMENT

Over the years, parents and professionals have voiced criticism of the parent involvement concept from conceptual, anecdotal, and empirical vantage points. Given the diversity of roles possible for parents, it is easy to understand the assertion, voiced years ago by Rutherford and Edgar (1979), that parent involvement may actually create stress for parents and thus interfere with the well-being of the child targeted for intervention. Other professionals have echoed this notion, suggesting that an inappropriate outcome of the parent involvement process may be to "professionalize parents" (Allen & Hudd, 1987) if parents are not explicitly offered the option not to become involved in early intervention services. Another inappropriate outcome of parent involvement, according to Winton and Turnbull (1981) results if parents are "locked" into one role with little opportunity to change from one role to another. Recent research into parents' needs for temporary respite (Salisbury & Itagliata, 1988) and opportunities to engage in recreational and leisure-time activities has served to increase professional awareness of these important issues.

Particular criticism has targeted the use of a "deficit model" for guiding the involvement of parents. This model is considered inappropriate because it establishes a hierarchy between professional and parent roles, with professionals holding a superior position to parents from the outset of the communication process (Dunst et al., 1988; Wiegerink & Comfort, 1987). Mahoney, O'Sullivan, and Dennebaum (1990) suggest that the use of such a model in early intervention evolved from medical science and learning theory models that conceptualized children's handicapping conditions in terms of their medical and physical complications. In view of the expanding scope of parent and family services, such a conceptualization is now considered to exclude important issues related to the realities of family life.

Empirical investigations into the effectiveness of parent involvement have examined the roles of parents as educational decision makers and intervenors, the satisfaction of parents with these roles, and the involvement of other family members in intervention. An overview of these current lines of research is provided below, with an understanding that more research is needed regarding the effectiveness of parents as advocates, program evaluators, case managers, and team members.

Participation in Educational Decision Making

Descriptive evidence regarding the participation of parents in educational decision making suggests their role is actually more passive than active. In an observational study of IEP conferences, Goldstein, Strickland, Turnbull, and Curry (1980) used a 2-minute coding system to record speaker contributions and topics discussed during such conferences. Results indicated virtually no contributions from parents regarding what, when, or how their child would be taught, with most of the topics being initiated by professionals at the conference. These topics included placement, related services, legal rights and responsibilities, the name of the individual responsible for implementing attaining goals and objectives, the child's health, future contacts, and future planning for the child. A primary message from this investigation was that the time spent in IEP conferences tends to be spent by parents listening to professionals. Employing an interview methodology, McKinney and Hocutt (1982) found that descriptive information reported by parents corroborated these observational data.

When investigators have moved beyond descriptive analyses to examine parental satisfaction, the results offer provocative explanations. Goldstein et al. (1980) gathered overwhelmingly positive data from parents who were asked eight satisfaction questions regarding their participation in educational decision making. Similarly, Lynch and Stein (1982) found that nearly three fourths of a sample of 400 parents perceived they were "actively" involved in their child's IEP—active involvement defined by them as expressing opinions and suggestions, working with and trusting the professionals, listening to and agreeing with the teacher's recommendations, and understanding what was going on. In studies conducted from 1977 to 1982, Hocutt and Wiegerink (1983) found similarly high levels of satisfaction among parents. In addition, Lusthaus, Lusthaus, and Gibbs (1981) found that many parents in their sample were not eager to assume an active role in educational decision making.

Collectively, these investigations into parent participation in decision making suggest that, although parents are observed to be relatively passive during conferences, they report satisfaction with this type of role. Such results underscore the importance of respecting the need of some parents for relief from educational responsibility for their children (Turnbull, Winton, Blacher, & Salkind, 1983; Winton & Turnbull, 1981) and encouraging informal interactions between professionals and parents.

Participation in Intervention

Although the rationale for involving parents as intervenors with their children appears to be sound, researchers have discovered a complex array of variables that mediate the overall effectiveness of this role. Considerable evidence suggests that parents can be effective intervenors with respect to teaching skills to and managing the behavior of their children. The literature is replete with studies indicating parental effectiveness as teachers of communication (Casey, 1978), self-help skills (Adubato, Adams, & Budd, 1981), academic skills (Wedel & Fowler, 1984), and compliant behavior (Breiner & Beck, 1984; Forehand & McMahon, 1981). Moreover, evidence suggests reasonable success from parents in following up with teaching sessions or behavior management programs after the completion of formal training (Baker, Heifetz, & Murphy, 1980).

In the developmental disabilities literature, researchers have endeavored to move beyond general questions, such as "Is parent training effective?" to ask specific questions regarding the frequency of home visits (Sandow & Clarke, 1978) and the effectiveness of home training with families of children with varying degrees and types of disabilities (Revill & Blunden, 1979). These investigations used single factor designs, measuring effectiveness in terms of child progress, operationalized by gains in IQ scores. Results indicated that outcomes were mediated by specific parental and family variables, such as attitudes toward professional services and support from informal networks of relatives and friends (Dunst & Rheingrover, 1981). A series of meta-analyses further suggested the need to expand the focus from IQ gains to include multiple outcomes, such as parent and family variables; to attend to internal validity issues such as maturation and attrition; and to conceptualize more broadly the complexities of parent involvement (Casto & Mastropieri, 1986; Dunst & Snyder, 1986; Shonkoff & Hauser-Cramm, 1988).

Research designed to measure parental satisfaction with an intervention role has caused professionals to question the assumptions that parents should assume the intervenor role and that "good" parents not only intervene, but do so frequently and with enthusiasm (Turnbull & Summers, 1987). Concerns expressed by parents pertain to their fear that acting as a teacher might interfere with some other behaviors as a parent and the family's quality of life. Studies of the unanticipated side effects of parental participation in behavioral training programs (e.g., Dubey & Kaufman, 1982; Griest & Forehand, 1982) have uncovered indirect effects on other relationships within families, such as disruption in the interactional patterns between parents and the amount of time spent with siblings.

Snell and Beckman-Brindley (1984) summarized limitations in parent training efficacy research by stating, in general, that:

1. The family's overall functioning has been tangential to the child's behavior change.

2. Intervention plans have not been assessed in the context of family priorities and routines.
3. Participants in the research have primarily been married, nonemployed mothers with ambulatory children having moderate deficiencies.
4. Little attention has been given to time and cost estimates.
5. The generalized effects of intervention on the child and family are unknown.

Expanding upon these conclusions, Paget (in press) presents a paradigm for the design and implementation of home-based intervention plans that are sensitive to family routines, values, beliefs, and life-cycle needs. Thus, it has become clear that, in contrast to the straightforward rationale stated earlier by Johnson and Katz (1973), parents do not always value a training role because teaching a child at home may contradict family belief systems and have indirect effects on the family as a whole. Collectively, research investigations into the effectiveness of parents as intervention agents with developmentally disabled young children strongly suggest that the long-term effectiveness of intervention plans depends on the extent to which the plans reflect family schedules and routines, family members' needs, and the satisfaction of parents with the role of intervenor.

Involvement of Other Family Members

Increased understanding of families as systems comprised of subsystems (Minuchin, 1985) and assertions that family functioning cannot be understood unless all interactions within and across subsystems are considered (Belsky, 1981) have led to conceptual and technical expansions in research with families. Bristol and Gallagher (1986) captured these advances by illustrating changes in research designs away from those where single deficits were isolated to those where multiple interactions were captured. Anchored at one end by relatively intrusive strategies in controlled analogue settings and at the other end by less intrusive strategies in naturalistic settings, Bristol and Gallagher (1986) presented a continuum of relational contexts in which research has been conducted. These are:

1. The unidirectional dyad, where the mother was thought to be responsible for a child's developmental problems.
2. The interactive dyad, where contributions of the child to mother–child interactions were recognized.
3. Multiple dyads, where interactions between father and child, mother and father, and mother and child were all considered.
4. The family system, where mediational influences of the parent's marital relationship and sibling relationships on a child's development were studied.
5. The family as an ecological system where the entire family is viewed as one of an interactive, interdependent set of systems nested within each other.

The continuum presented earlier formed the basis for a critical review of research by Paget (1988), who examined efficacy research in the context of the mother–child dyad, the father–child dyad, the father–mother–child triad, the sibling subsystem, and social support networks. Essential points raised in this review were:

1. All family members, including fathers, siblings, and grandparents can be effective trainers of developmentally disabled or at-risk children (Brody & Stoneman, 1986; Vadasy, Fewell, Greenberg, Dermond, & Meyer, 1986).

2. The quality of the marital relationship and the presence of a spouse during training sessions can influence the behavior of a parent during training sessions (Stoneman, Brody, & Abbott, 1983).

3. The success of intervention plans is influenced by the quality of informal support felt by family members from friends, neighbors, and relatives.

4. The motivation of parents to carry out an intervention plan is affected by informal and formal support from professionals regarding their own personal needs.

Although conceptual and methodological advances are evident in this literature, caveats are still necessary to guide proper interpretation. Most of the studies need to be replicated with similar samples, as well as across subjects, settings, and behaviors to strengthen confidence in the results. Also, much of the research suffers from classic problems with pre–post and retrospective research designs, inadequately matched control groups, and nonrandom assignment to treatment groups. Because an in-depth analysis of this literature is beyond the scope of the present chapter, the reader is referred to Paget (1988) for detailed information regarding specific studies.

FROM PARENT INVOLVEMENT TO FAMILY SUPPORT

Progress in the conceptualization and application of the parent involvement concept has led to the "family support" movement, derived essentially from the realization that parents and all significant others relating to children with developmental problems (e.g., siblings, grandparents) also possess special needs that require attention and support (Kagan et al., 1987). The movement from parent involvement to family support has been described by Turnbull and Summers (1987) as a "revolution," wherein the family is considered the center of the service delivery system, in contrast to the peripheral position heretofore held by parents. This change is also reflected in the provisions of Public Law 99-457, which advocate "the implementation of family-focused intervention services that address children's developmental needs by, in part, maximizing the effectiveness of their families" (Mahoney et al., 1990, p. 2). Provisions in the Preschool Program of the new law, which target children from 3 through 5 years of age, are a downward extension of those from Public Law 94-142, although financial costs incurred by parents for services to their child are covered more explicitly. The language of the Early Intervention Program, for handicapped and at-risk infants, toddlers, and their families, is a more dramatic departure from previous legislation, with emphasis on "families" in addition to "parents" and on concepts such as Individualized Family Service Plan (IFSP) and assessment of family strengths and needs (House of Representatives Report 99-860, 1986).

Although some political and social forces contributed to the family-focused agenda of the law, research relevant to families of children with disabilities was also an influencing factor. Mahoney et al. (1990) traced the evolution of this research and suggest that two sets of findings gave impetus to the family-focused agenda. First, they discussed the increasing awareness that children with disabilities often disrupt normal family functioning, and may even impede parental effectiveness, as indicated by studies of parental stress and coping (Beckman-Bell, 1981; Crnic, Friedrich, & Greenberg, 1983; Dyson & Fewell, 1986), family functioning and social support (Dunst, Trivette, & Cross, 1986), as well as parent–child interaction (Cunningham, Reuter, Blackwell, & Deck, 1981). Second, the authors described the increasing awareness of the impact that family factors have on the developmental functioning attained by children with handicaps, with emerging evidence that indices of family effectiveness (e.g., satisfaction with support and quality of parent-child interaction) may be causally linked to the developmental functioning of at-risk children or those with disabilities (Dunst et al., 1986; Mahoney, Finger, & Powell, 1985). Furthermore, a reconceptualization of early intervention by Dunst (1985) and data reported by Dunst et al. (1986) suggested rather provocatively that family factors may contribute even more to children's development than the involvement of parents in formal intervention activities. The definition of early intervention offered by Dunst (1985) captures the dramatic shift away from sole enrollment in a professional program to "the provision of support to families of infants young children from members of informal and formal social support networks that impact both directly and indirectly upon parental, family, and child functioning" (p. 179).

The legalized emphasis on family-focused intervention is posing numerous challenges to professionals to expand the parameters of their role and function. In response to these challenges, much energy is currently directed toward a reassessment of strategies for promoting family involvement, an examination of family assessment techniques, and extensive inquiry into the scope of family assessment. Feedback from parents of children with disabilities continues to be an important component of these investigations (Turnbull & Turnbull, 1986), and considerable progress is being made in the development of models for promoting family involvement.

Scope of Family-Focused Intervention

Emphasized throughout the early intervention literature is the fact that the new legislation does not require a broad-based family assessment; rather, the focus of assessment is on family strengths and needs (Whitehead, Deiner, & Toccafondi, 1990). This distinction is considered to be important to prevent the inappropriate application of mental health assessment techniques used with dysfunctional families to families with a young disabled child. Thus, although researchers recognize the probability of additional stress placed on family members and the need to adjust to unique demands on their time and energy (Frey, Fewell, & Vadasy, 1989), positive coping strategies and assumptions of competence form the parameters of family assessment procedures. A comprehensive model of adjustment proposed by Folkman, Schaefer, and Lazarus (1979), for example, is viewed as an appropriate framework within which to view families because of its emphasis on coping resources used to mediate stress (e.g., health/energy/morale, problem-solving skills, and social networks). Also important in understanding the scope of family assessment in early intervention is the increased awareness that individual family members may utilize different coping resources, thus leading to appraisals of resources used, not only by mothers, but also by fathers, siblings, and other significant family members (Bronfenbrenner, 1979; Frey et al., 1989). Researchers also emphasize the need to conduct such assessments over time, based on the assumption that family life is not static (Frey et al., 1989).

Empirical investigations are currently being conducted to examine professional and parental preferences regarding aspects of family life that are appropriate for intervention planning and characteristics of the communication process that are valued by parents. A recent study conducted by Able-Boone, Sandall, Loughry, and Frederick (1990) resulted in important findings related to families' views of essential aspects of family assessment and considerations for completing IFSPs. Families in the study revealed that financial resources, home environment, and getting to know the entire family were significant considerations. Regarding the IFSP, family members emphasized that the plan should be written with suggestions rather than definite goals, that it should be considered a working plan to be reviewed frequently, and that it should be designed to help families understand options for services leading to informed choices about services matched to their needs.

In a related study, Summers et al. (1990) used focus groups of professionals and parents to best identify areas to be addressed in family plans. The statements generated clustered into three major topic areas, including early intervention program principles, identification of family strengths and needs, and expected outcomes for families. With respect to program principles, the most frequently mentioned theme was sensitivity to families who are experiencing a wide range of emotions, reflected in an accepting and nonjudgmental approach and consideration of possible unintended consequences of casual comments or program expectations. Also emphasized was the importance of interacting with families in an unhurried atmosphere, providing emotional support that is responsive to rapid changes in families, and understanding "family readiness" to accept responsibility for decision making as a continuum along which families differ. With respect to identification of strengths and needs, Summers et al. (1990) report strong uniformity of opinion from families about the importance of informal methods of gathering information (e.g., open-ended conversations rather than structured interviews), with an additional emphasis on the development of friendships between professionals and family members. Regarding expected outcomes, families desired skills in negotiating and problem solving, information about services, increased self-confidence, and an enhanced sense of community through strengthening of social support networks.

Any consideration of the scope of family assessment must include differences in cultural and ethnic background between professionals and families. Hanson, Lynch, and Wayman (1990) emphasized that culture is an essential component of family assessment and suggest that cultural clashes in service delivery are likely unless differences in cultural and ethnic background are not only recognized, but also honored. Views of childrearing and children, disability and its causation, change and intervention, medicine and healing, family and family roles, and language and communication all become important when ethnic competence is valued by professionals. For example, a Native American family that views the cause of a disability as spiritual retribution for moral wrongdoing of a family member will likely hold special views regarding spiritual forms of intervention that are appropriate. This form of intervention may involve contact with a family or tribal member who is believed to possess special healing powers (Hanson et al., 1990). Also, a family of Asian American background may regard eye contact and question asking as threats to a person's authority and engage in these behaviors very infrequently during discussions with professionals. This communication style is easily misinterpreted as disinterest unless viewed within the context of the family's belief system. These examples underscore the importance of eliciting information from families regarding cultural beliefs and values to better understand a family's orientation to professional intervention.

Illustrative Models of Family-Focused Intervention

In the years succeeding the passage of Public Law 99-457, considerable energy has been directed toward the development of models or paradigms for guiding practice in family-focused early intervention. Because of variation in the interpretation of the law and philosophies about families, existing models reflect different approaches to the delivery of family-focused services. The models can be conceptualized broadly into three categories: (a) those that are strengths- and needs-based, (b) those that are values-based, and (c) those that are services-based. The following is a discussion of models representing each of these categories.

Strengths- and Needs-Based Models. Basing their principles about families on family systems theory (Bronfenbrenner, 1979), Dunst et al. (1988) propose that early intervention should focus on enabling parents to acquire for themselves the services and skills needed to facilitate adaptation and development of the family with a developmentally disabled child. At the heart of the model are the concepts of enablement and empowerment, which imply that assistance is provided by professionals in the identification and alignment of social support, with emphasis on family members feeling able to mobilize resources to strengthen the family unit. Also central to implementation of this model is the concept of functional plans for families; that is, those that are well-matched to family values, beliefs about intervention, schedules, and routines (Deal, Dunst, & Trivette, 1989). Implementation of this model has been associated with developmental gains in disabled children and an increase in the effective use of resources and supports by families (Dunst, Trivette, & Cornwell, 1989; Wilson, 1988; see Dunst et al., 1988 for a review of evaluation studies).

A second example of a needs-based model is the Family Focused Intervention Model of Bailey et al. (1986). Also functional in nature, this model consists of six steps:

1. comprehensive child and family assessment,
2. generation of initial hypotheses regarding intervention goals,
3. focused interview to discuss family needs and negotiate intervention goals,
4. operationalizing and scaling of goals,
5. implementation of intervention services, and
6. evaluation of goal attainment and documentation of child and family outcomes.

The model builds on the goodness-of-fit concept (Thomas & Chess, 1977), in which intervention is seen as a means for optimizing the fit between the capabilities of family members and the demands they face. Findings supportive of family involvement have emerged from implementation of the model in a state-wide network of home-based early intervention programs (Simeonsson, Bailey, Huntington, Isbell, & Brandon, 1988). The importance of involving the family in the negotiation of intervention goals was evident in the fact that the focused interview resulted in the deletion or modification of 20% of the original goals and the addition of 10% of the new goals (Simeonsson et al., 1988).

Values-Based Models. To provide guidance in designing methods for meeting family needs, Kaiser and Hemmeter (1989) offer a framework for analysing values related to family-focused interventions. The structure is derived from the work of Hobbs et al. (1984) and provides a mechanism for evaluating interventions according to level (e.g., does the family prefer a narrow, intense intervention targeting a specific need or a broad-based, less intense intervention targeting a range of needs?), scope (e.g., does the intervention include a balance of remedial and preventative strategies?), costs and efficiency (e.g., do the benefits derived outweigh the costs to the family in terms of time, money, intrusiveness, and disruption of normal family functions?), and acceptability (e.g., is the intervention matched to the family's values, social norms, and readiness for change?). The effectiveness of a values-based approach to family assessment awaits investigation and is a promising avenue for future research.

Services-Based Models.   A model proposed by Mahoney et al. (1990) is based on the premise that children's functioning is strengthened by providing services designed to enhance family effectiveness. Six categories of family-focused intervention services offered by early intervention and early childhood programs are described. First, programs provide assistance and information that help engage parents in the early intervention system. Systems engagement activities include information about laws, parental rights, and community systems, as well as case management services that help parents coordinate and implement their child's early intervention services (Landerholm, Karr, & Abrams, 1988). Second, programs provide families with information about the child's handicapping condition, health, current and expected developmental status, and the philosophy concerning their intervention services (Turnbull & Turnbull, 1986). Third, programs provide information and assistance to families for implementing instructional activities for the child at home. Fourth, programs provide personal and family assistance, including counseling and various types of social activities to help family members cope more effectively with the psychological and social stresses associated with caring for their children (Dunst, 1985). Fifth, programs provide resource assistance to help families obtain financial, medical, respite, and other community resources that might be needed for the daily care of children with disabilities (Bailey & Simeonsson, 1988).

Mahoney et al. (1990) developed and validated the Family-Focused Intervention Scale (FFIS), which examines maternal responses to family services. During the development of this scale, a national sample of 503 mothers of children with handicaps in early intervention programs completed a questionnaire assessing the number of family intervention services they had received. A factor analysis revealed that the items assessed five independent components of family-focused intervention, including the efforts of intervention programs to engage parents in the early intervention system, provide parents with information about their children, help parents implement instructional activities at home, attend to the well-being of parents and families, and assist parents to obtain community resources needed for their children. These results were used to construct the FFIS, which consists of 40 items and five subscales. Psychometric data generated by the authors suggest that each of the subscales is internally consistent (Chronbach's alpha values ranging from .78 to .89), and that the scale is sensitive to variations in the intensity of family-focused intervention services resulting from differences in the age of children being served (i.e., services were reported to be most intense at the birth-to-3-year level). Although currently limited to maternal perceptions, the FFIS is a promising format for conducting program evaluations at state and regional levels and for conducting research into the effectiveness of family-focused intervention services.

IMPLICATIONS FOR SCHOOL PSYCHOLOGISTS

The theoretical principles, paradigms, and empirical research discussed in this chapter hold numerous implications for school psychologists with respect to service delivery, training, and research. A major overriding implication results from the fact that services to families cross disciplinary boundaries and should be delivered in a context of shared expertise among social workers, special educators, psychologists, and medical personnel (Bagnato, Neisworth, Paget, & Kovaleski, 1988). Thus, activities in the areas of service delivery, training, and research should be carried out with an attitude of "de-disciplining" (Caldwell, 1978) wherein the pooling of knowledge and expertise about parents and families from multiple disciplines is considered a requisite to full understanding.

School psychologists involved in service delivery to very young children need to be aware of the expansion of family-based services which has occurred since the enactment of Public Law 94-142 and its parent involvement mandates. Because this expansion is represented legislatively in the provisions of Public Law 99-457 targeting infants and toddlers, we need to be knowledgeable about the law and its influence on service delivery. In addition, we need to be aware of certain distinctions between the Preschool Program (Part B) and the Early Intervention Program (Part H) of the law regarding the scope of services to families. Although such knowledge of the law is essential, we also need to complement our understanding of legislative realities with recognition of relevant theoretical principles and empirical findings that support the letter as well as the spirit of the new law.

To assist in the development of appropriate knowledge and skills, school psychologists who are already employed need to pursue continued professional development training through inservice offerings sponsored by universities, professional organizations, state-level agencies, and local staff development programs. Individuals interested in graduate study in this area need to choose programs that offer specialty training in family-based service delivery to very young children (Bagnato et al., 1988). Such training needs to be done in an interdisciplinary context to encompass such topics as the risk factors associated with families in poverty, the impact of an at-risk or developmentally disabled child on family life, parental and professional preferences regarding parent and family-based services, and the theoretical and empirical underpinnings of high quality family-focused assessment and intervention strategies.

Finally, researchers in school psychology need to develop expertise in quantitative and qualitative research designs that capture the systems-level intricacies of parenting and family life over time. Methodological improvements need to be made through the use of prospective, longitudinal, multivariate research designs with adequate comparison groups and attention to the replication of results. Promising avenues of research include:

1. continuities and discontinuities that occur within families who have a very young child with special needs;
2. differences among families with respect to values and beliefs, coping strategies, and preferences regarding forms of involvement and case management practices;
3. differences in needs among family members, including mothers, fathers, siblings, and relatives;
4. multiple impacts of the birth of an at-risk or developmentally disabled child on specific dimensions of family life, such as finances and socialization (Summers, 1987);
5. determinants of parental effectiveness as advocates, program evaluators, case managers, and team members; and
6. the comparative effectiveness of various models of family-focused intervention.

In addition to a focus on the effectiveness of various forms of involvement and intervention, we need to continue gathering data regarding the reactions of family members to professional services. Research designs attempting to answer any of these questions need to capture socioeconomic and ethnic differences among families. With a multifold emphasis in research, we should attempt to capture the conditions under which an optimal amount of reciprocal communication exists among professionals, parents, and other family members. Concomitant with advances made through research activities is the challenge to integrate empirical findings with training, service delivery, and future policy decisions. Accompanying the advances in the arenas of research, training, service delivery, and policy should be the development of models to facilitate coherent integration of information across these separate arenas.

REFERENCES

Able-Boone, H., Sandall, S. R., Loughry, A., & Frederick, L. L. (1990). An informed, family-centered approach to Public Law 99-457: Parental views. *Topics in Early Childhood Special Education, 10,* 100–111.

Adubato, S. A., Adams, M. K., & Budd, K. S. (1981). Teaching a parent to train a spouse in child management techniques. *Journal of Applied Behavior Analysis, 14,* 193–205.

Allen, D. A., Afflect, G., McGrade, B. J., & McQueeney, M. (1984). Factors in the effectiveness of early childhood intervention for low socioeconomic status families. *Education and Training of the Mentally Retarded, 19,* 254–260.

Allen, D. A., & Hudd, S. S. (1987). Are we professionalizing parents: Weighing the benefits and pitfalls. *Mental Retardation, 25,* 133–139.

Anderson, K., & Garner, A. (1973). Mothers of retarded children: Satisfaction with visits to professional people. *Mental Retardation, 22,* 36–39.

Bagnato, S. J., Neisworth, J. T., Paget, K. D., & Kovaleski, J. (1988). The developmental school psychologist: Professional profile of an emerging early childhood specialist. *Topics in Early Childhood Special Education, 7,* 75–89.

Bailey, D. B., Simeonsson, R. J., Winton, P. J., Huntington, G. S., Comfort, M., Isbell, P., O'Donnell, K. J., & Helm, J. M. (1986). Family-focused intervention: A functional model for planning, implementing, and evaluating individualized family services in early intervention. *Journal of the Division for Early Childhood, 10,* 156–171.

Bailey, D. J., & Simeonsson, R. J. (1988). *Family assessment in early intervention.* Columbus, OH: Merrill.

Baker, B. L., Heifetz, L. J., & Murphy, D. (1980). Behavioral training for parents of retarded children: One year follow-up. *American Journal of Mental Deficiency, 85,* 31–38.

Beckman-Bell, P. (1981). Child-related stress in families with handicapped children. *Topics in Early Childhood Special Education, 1,* 45–54.

Belsky, J. (1981). Early human experience: A family perspective. *Developmental Psychology, 17,* 3–23.

Breiner, J., & Beck, S. (1984). Parents as change agents in the management of their developmentally delayed children's noncompliant behaviors: A critical review. *Applied Research in Mental Retardation, 5,* 259–278.

Brewer, G., & Kakalik, J. (1979). *Handicapped children: Strategies for improving services.* New York: McGraw-Hill.

Bristol, M. M., & Gallagher, J. J. (1986). Research on fathers of young handicapped children: Evolution, review, and some future directions. In J. J. Gallagher & P. M. Vietze (Eds.), *Families of handicapped persons: Research, programs, and policy issues* (pp. 81–100). Baltimore: Paul H. Brooks.

Brody, G. H., & Stoneman, Z. (1986). Contextual issues in the study of sibling socialization. In J. J. Gallagher & P. M. Vietze (Eds.), *Families of handicapped persons: Research, programs, and policy issues* (pp. 197–218). Baltimore: Paul H. Brooks.

Bronfenbrenner, U. (1975). Is early intervention effective? In B. Z. Friedlander, G. M. Sterritt, & G. E. Kirk (Eds.), *Exceptional infant: Assessment and intervention* (Vol. 3; pp. 449–475). New York: Brunner/Mazel.

Bronfenbrenner, U. (1979). *The ecology of human development: Experiments by nature and design.* Cambridge: Harvard University Press.

Bronfenbrenner, U. (1986). Ecology of the family as a context for human development: Research perspectives. *Developmental Psychology, 22,* 723–742.

Budoff, M., & Orenstein, A. (1982). *Due process in special education: On going to a hearing.* Cambridge, MA: The Ware Press.

Caldwell, B. M. (1978). Foreword. K. E. Allen, V. A. Holm, & R. L. Schiefelbusch (Eds.), *Early intervention: A team approach* (pp. i–vi). Baltimore: University Park Press.

Casey, L. (1978). Development of communicative behavior in autistic children: A parent program using signed speech. *Devereux Forum, 12,* 1–15.

Casto, G., & Mastropieri, M. A. (1986). The efficacy of early intervention programs for handicapped children: A meta-analysis. *Exceptional Children, 52,* 417–424.

Crnic, K., Friedrich, W. N., & Greenberg, M. T. (1983). Adaptation of families with mentally retarded children: A model of stress, coping, and family ecology. *American Journal of Mental Deficiency, 88,* 125–138.

Cunningham, C. E., Reuter, E., Blackwell, J., & Deck, J. (1981). Behavioral and linguistic developments in the interactions of normal and handicapped children with their mothers. *Child Development, 52,* 62–70.

Deal, A. G., Dunst, C. J., & Trivette, C. M. (1989). A flexible and functional approach to developing Individualized Family Support Plans. *Infants and Young Children, 3,* 32–43.

Dubey, D. R., & Kaufman, K. F. (1982). The "side effects" of parent implemented behavior modification. *Child and Family Behavior Therapy, 4,* 65–71.

Dunst, C. J. (1985). Rethinking early intervention. *Analysis and Intervention in Developmental Disabilities, 5,* 165–201.

Dunst, C. J., & Rheingrover, R. M. (1981). Analysis of the efficacy of infant intervention programs for handicapped children. *Evaluation and Program Planning, 4,* 287–323.

Dunst, C. J., & Snyder, S. W. (1986). A critique of the Utah State University early intervention meta-analysis research. *Exceptional Children, 53,* 269–276.

Dunst, C. J., & Trivette, C. M. (1989). An enablement and empowerment perspective of case management. *Topics in Early Childhood Special Education, 8,* 87–102.

Dunst, C. J., Trivette, C. M., & Cornwell, J. (1989). Family needs, social support, and self-efficacy during a child's transition to school. *Early Education and Development, 1,* 7–18.

Dunst, C. J., Trivette, C. M., & Cross, A. (1986). Mediating influences of social support: Personal, family and child outcomes. *American Journal of Mental Deficiency, 91,* 403–417.

Dunst, C. J., Trivette, C. M., & Deal, A. G. (1988). *Enabling and empowering families.* Cambridge, MA: Brookline Books.

Dyson, L., & Fewell, R. R. (1986). Stress and adaptation in parents of handicapped and non-handicapped children: A comparative study. *Journal of the Division for Early Childhood, 10,* 25–35.

Ehly, S. W., Conoley, J. C., & Rosenthal, D. (1985). *Working with parents of exceptional children.* St. Louis, MO: Times Mirror/Mosby College Publishing.

Folkman, S., Schaefer, C., & Lazarus, R. C. (1979). Cognitive processes as mediators of stress and coping. In V. Hamilton & D. W. Warburton (Eds.), *Human stress and cognition* (pp. 50–79). New York: Wiley.

Forehand, R. L., & McMahon, R. J. (1981). *Helping the noncompliant child: A clinician's guide to parent training.* New York: Guilford Press.

Frey, K., Fewell, R. R., & Vadasy, P. (1989). Parental adjustment and changes in child outcome among families of young handicapped children. *Topics in Early Childhood Special Education, 8,* 38–57.

Goldstein, S., Strickland, B., Turnbull, A. P., & Curry, L. (1980). An observational analysis of the IEP conference. *Exceptional Children, 46,* 278–286.

Griest, D., & Forehand, R. (1982). How can I get any parent training done with all these other problems going on? The role of family variables in child behavior therapy. *Child and Family Behavior Therapy, 4,* 73–80.

Hanson, M. J., Lynch, E. W., & Wayman, K. I. (1990). Honoring the cultural diversity of families when gathering data. *Topics in Early Childhood Special Education, 10,* 112–131.

Hobbs, N., Dokecki, P. R., Hoover-Dempsey, K. V., Moroney, R. M., Shayne, M. W., & Weeks, K. H. (1984). *Strengthening families.* San Francisco: Jossey-Bass.

Hocutt, A., & Wiegerink, R. (1983). Perspectives on parent involvement in preschool programs for handicapped children. In R. Haskins & D. Adams (Eds.), *Parent education and public policy* (pp. 211–229). Norwood, NJ: Ablex.

House of Representatives Report 99-860. (September, 1986). Education of the Handicapped Act Amendments of 1986. Washington, DC: 99th Congress.

Jennings, L. (1990, August). Parents as partners: Reaching out to families to help students learn. *Education Week,* pp. 23–32.

Johnson, C. A., & Katz, R. C. (1973). Using parents as change agents for their children: A review. *Journal of Clinical Psychology and Psychiatry, 4,* 181–200.

Kagan, S. L., Powell, D. R., Weissbourd, B., & Zigler, E. F. (1987). *America's family support programs: Perspectives and prospects.* New Haven, CT: Yale University Press.

Kaiser, A. P., & Hemmeter, M. L. (1989). Value-based approaches to family intervention. *Topics in Early Childhood Special Education, 8,* 72–86.

Karnes, M. B., & Teska, J. A. (1980). Toward successful parent involvement in programs for handicapped children. In J. J. Gallagher (Ed.), *New directions for exceptional children: Parents and families of handicapped children* (pp. 85–109). San Francisco: Jossey-Bass.

Landerholm, E., Karr, A., & Abrams, P. (1988). Survey of parent involvement program activities offered at early intervention centers in a seven state area. *ICC Quarterly, 37,* 24–29.

Lusthaus, C. S., Lusthaus, E. W., & Gibbs, H. (1981). Parents' role in the decision process. *Exceptional Children, 48,* 256–257.

Lynch, E. W., & Stein, R. (1982). Perspectives on parent participation in special education. *Exceptional Education Quarterly, 3,* 56–63.

Mahoney, G., Finger, I., & Powell, A. (1985). The relationship of maternal behavioral style to the developmental status of mentally retarded infants. *American Journal of Mental Deficiency, 90,* 296–302.

Mahoney, G., O'Sullivan, P., & Dennebaum, J. (1990). Maternal perceptions of early intervention services: A scale for assessing family-focused intervention. *Topics in Early Childhood Special Education, 10,* 1–15.

McKinney, J. D., & Hocutt, A. M. (1982). Public school involvement of parents of learning-disabled children and average achievers. *Exceptional Education Quarterly, 3,* 64–73.

Minuchin, P. (1985). Families and individual development: Provocations from the field of family therapy. *Child Development, 56,* 289–302.

Nash, J. K. (1990). Public Law 99-457: Facilitating family participation on the multidisciplinary team. *Journal of Early Intervention, 14,* 318–326.

Paget, K. D. (1988). Early intervention: Infants, preschool children, and families. In J. C. Witt, S. N. Elliott, & F. M. Gresham (Eds.), *Handbook of behavior therapy in education* (pp. 569–600). New York: Plenum.

Paget, K. D. (1991). Treatment acceptability and early intervention: Multiple perspectives for improving service delivery in home settings. *Topics in Early Childhood Special Education, 11,* 3–17.

Peterson, N. L. (1987). *Early intervention for handicapped and at-risk children: An introduction to early childhood-special education.* Denver: Love.

Peterson, N. L., & Cooper, C. S. (1989). Parent education and involvement in early intervention. In M. J. Fine (Ed.), *The second handbook on parent education: Contemporary perspectives* (pp. 197–236). San Diego: Academic Press.

Powell, D. R. (1989). *Families and early childhood services.* Washington, DC: National Association for the Education of Young Children.

Revill, S., & Blunden, R. (1979). A home training service for preschool developmentally handicapped children. *Behavior Research and Therapy, 17,* 207–214.

Rutherford, R. B., Jr., and Edgar, E. (1979). *Teachers and parents: A guide to interaction and cooperation.* Boston: Allyn & Bacon.

Salisbury, C., & Itagliata, J. (1988). *Respite care: Support for persons with developmental disabilities and their families.* Baltimore: Paul H. Brookes.

Sandow, S., & Clarke, A. D. (1978). Home intervention with parents of severely sub-normal preschool children: An interim report. *Child: Care, Health and Development, 4,* 29–39.

Shearer, M. S., & Shearer, D. E. (1977). Parent involvement. In J. B. Jordan, A. H. Hayden, M. B. Karnes, & M. M. Woods (Eds.), *Early childhood education for exceptional children* (pp. 208–235). Reston, VA: Council for Exceptional Children.

Shonkoff, J., & Hauser-Cramm, P. (1988). Early intervention for disabled infants and their families—A quantitative analysis. *Pediatrics, 80,* 650–658.

Silber, S. (1989). Family influences on early development. *Topics in Early Childhood Special Education, 8,* 1–23.

Simeonsson, R. J., & Bailey, D. J. (1988). Family dimensions in early intervention. In S. J. Meisels & J. P. Shonkoff (Eds.), *Handbook of early childhood intervention* (pp. 100–125). Cambridge, MA: Cambridge University Press.

Simeonsson, R. J., Bailey, D. B., Huntington, G. S., Isbell, P., & Brandon, L. (1988). *Scaling and attainment of goals in family-focused intervention.* Unpublished manuscript. Frank Porter Graham Child Development Center. Chapel Hill, NC: University of North Carolina.

Snell, M. E., & Beckman-Brindley, S. (1984). Family involvement in intervention with children having severe handicaps. *Journal of Speech and Hearing, 3,* 213–230.

Stoneman, Z., Brody, G. H., & Abbott, D. (1983). In-home observations of young Down Syndrome children with their mothers and fathers. *American Journal of Mental Deficiency, 87,* 591–600.

Strickland, B. (1983). Legal issues that affect parents. In M. Seligman (Ed.), *The family with a handicapped child: Understanding and treatment* (pp. 27–39). New York: Grune & Stratton.

Summers, J. A. (1988). Family adjustment: Issues in research on families with developmentally disabled children. In V. B. Van Hasselt, P. S. Strain, & M. Hersen (Eds.), *Handbook of developmental and physical disabilities* (pp. 79–90). New York: Pergamon.

Summers, J. A., Dell'Oliver, C., Turnbull, A. P., Benson, H. A., Santelli, E., Campbell, M., & Siegel-Causey, E. (1990). Examining the Individualized Family Service Plan Process: What are Family and Practitioner Preferences? *Topics in Early Childhood Special Education, 10,* 78–99.

Thomas, A., & Chess, S. (1977). *Temperament and development.* New York: Bruner/Mazel.

Turnbull, A. P., & Summers, J. A. (1987). From parent involvement to family support: Evolution to revolution. In S. P. Pueschel, C. Tingey, J. E. Rynders, A. C. Crocker, & D. M. Crutcher (Eds.), *New perspectives on Down Syndrome* (pp. 289–306). Baltimore: Paul H. Brookes.

Turnbull, A. P., & Turnbull, H. R. (1986). *Families, professionals, and exceptionality: A special partnership.* Columbus, OH: Merrill.

Turnbull, A. P., Winton, P. J., Blacher, J. B., & Salkind, N. (1983). Mainstreaming in the kindergarten classroom: Perspectives of parents of handicapped and nonhandicapped children. *Journal of the Division for Early Childhood, 6,* 14–20.

Vadasy, P. F., Fewell, R. R., Greenberg, M. T., Dermond, N. L., & Meyer, D. J. (1986). Follow-up evaluation of the effects of involvement in the fathers program. *Topics in Early Childhood Special Education, 6,* 16–31.

Vincent, L. J., & Salisbury, C. L. (1988). Changing economic and social influences on family involvement. *Topics in Early Childhood Special Education, 8,* 48–59.

Wedel, J. W., & Fowler, S. A. (1984). "Read me a story, mom" A home-tutoring program to teach prereading skills to language delayed children. *Behavior Modification, 8,* 245–266.

Whitehead, L. C., Deiner, P. L., & Toccafondi, S. (1990). Family assessment: Parent and professional evaluation. *Topics in Early Childhood Special Education, 10,* 63–77.

Wiegerink, R., & Comfort, M. (1987). Parent involvement: Support for families of children with special needs. In S. L. Kagan, D. R. Powell, B. Weissbourd, & E. F. Zigler (Eds.), *America's family support programs: Perspectives and prospects* (pp. 182–206). New Haven, CT: Yale University Press.

Wilson, L. L. (1988, April). Promoting and strengthening family functioning and maternal competencies: A case study. *Zero to Three,* pp. 19–21.

Winton, P., & Turnbull, A. P. (1981). Parent involvement as viewed by parents of preschool handicapped children. *Topics in Early Childhood Special Education: Families of Handicapped Children, 1,* 11–19.

Wolf, M. M. (1978). Social validity: The case for subjective measurement or how applied behavior analysis is finding its heart. *Journal of Applied Behavioral Analysis, 11,* 203–214.

4

Contribution of Peers to Socialization in Early Childhood

Carollee Howes
Kristin Droege
Leslie Phillipsen
University of California

Preschool and younger children often spend 8 or more hours a day in the company of unrelated peers. These children are in full-time child care—in child-care centers or in family day-care homes. Virtually all other preschool and toddler-age children in the Western developed countries spend from 5 to 10 hours a week in part-day child care—nursery schools, preschools, and formal or informal playgroups. This increase in peer contacts has occurred because mothers are returning to work in ever larger numbers when their children are very young. One of the fastest growing sectors of the labor pool in the United States is mothers of children under 12 months of age. Children are also enrolled in child care or playgroups because of a maternal belief system that emphasizes the importance of early peer relations. In a recent study, mothers of 4-year-olds told interviewers that children should be able to make friends before their second birthdays, share by the time they are 2½, and successfully lead or influence others before their third birthday (Rubin, Mills, & Rose-Krasnor, 1989).

A growing body of literature on children's peer social skills and relationships parallels societal changes in the peer contacts of young children. This literature was fueled by reports in the 1970s of linkages between social relations with peers in middle childhood and adult social adjustment (e.g., Roff, Sells, & Golden, 1972). Most of this research has focused on school-age children (cf. Berndt & Ladd, 1989), particularly school-age children rejected by their peer group (cf. Asher & Coie, 1990).

Fortunately, for the purposes of this chapter, other, more recent literature has focused on the social experiences with peers of younger children. The increase in peer contacts of younger than school-age children permits observational studies in children's natural environments. In addition, modifications of standard sociometric methodology (Asher, Singleton, Tinsley, & Hymel, 1979; Howes, 1988a) extend social status research into the preschool. Careful behavioral definitions of friendship (Hinde, Titmus, Easton, & Tamplin, 1985; Howes, 1983) provide researchers access to early affective relationships between peers.

The purpose of this chapter is to review research on the development of social competence with peers in early childhood. Social competence has been defined in many different ways, ranging from what a given society or researcher considers socially desirable to a more inclusive notion of the child's social functioning including children's structuring and understanding their social contexts, the ways in which they perceive and understand themselves and their roles within contexts, and their ability to interact with others (Oppenheim, 1989). In this chapter we define social competence in a somewhat more narrow fashion. That is, social competence with peers represents successful social functioning with peers. We consider peer interactions and relationships to be dyadic rather than individual. Each partner contributes to the interaction and relationship. We also consider peer interactions and relationships to be reciprocal. That is, to understand the actions of one partner one must consider the preceding and subsequent actions of the other. Therefore, success in social functioning with peers implies that the child is accepted by peers, that the child is able to meet social goals within a peer's context, and that the child accommodates his or her goals and behaviors to the goals and behaviors of the partner. Other definitions of social competence emphasize cognitive skills such as information processing (Dodge, 1985; Gottman, Gonso, & Rasmusen, 1975) and sociocognitive skills (Rubin & Daniels-Beirness, 1983). However, this chapter is limited to two aspects of social competence with peers: social interaction and friendship formation.

We consider social interaction and friendship formation as independent and interacting aspects of social competence with peers. Competent social interaction is defined as social behaviors used to engage a peer and maintain a mutually satisfying encounter. Five domains of social interaction have received the most research attention: gaining entry to peer groups, social play, social pretend play, social problem solving, and conflict.

Friendships between children are defined as stable and affective dyadic relationships. Friendships are mutual preferences. Each child in a friendship prefers the other as a partner over other children in the group at least at some time during the contact and/or for some activities. Friendships are characterized by reciprocity. The children select each other as partners rather than just one child selecting the other as a friend. Finally, friendships are marked by positive affect—the children enjoy each other's company.

We begin the discussion of social competence with peers in early childhood by focusing on sequences for the development of social interaction and the development of friendships. We then turn to individual differences in young children's peer relations. These sections provide descriptions of the kind of peer interactions and friendships that are normative for young children, the range of individual differences, and indicators of what types of behaviors with peers may indicate that intervention is advisable. The final two sections of the chapter are concerned with antecedents and intervention. In the antecedents section, we examine theoretical and empirical perspectives that help explain social competence and social maladjustment in young children's peer engagement. Finally, we review strategies for enhancing and intervening in peer relations.

THEORETICAL AND EMPIRICAL PERSPECTIVES ON DEVELOPMENTAL SEQUENCES IN THE DEVELOPMENT OF PEER INTERACTION SKILLS

The development of peer behaviors has been a topic of concern of several developmental theorists. The central argument has rested on the independence of the peer system from the mother or adult child system. Lamb and Nash (1989) identify four alternative hypotheses: sociability or relationships with mother serve as precursors to sociability with peers (cf. Sroufe, 1983); characteristics of peer relationships affect infant–mother relationships and vice versa (cf. Rubenstein & Howes, 1976; Vandell, 1979); capacities for relationships with peers and mothers develop concurrently from the beginning of life within the context of generalized developing sociability (cf. Hay, 1985); and the skills that are needed to interact with peers are distinct in ontogeny and function from the skills needed to interact with mothers (cf. Mueller, 1979). The first three of these hypotheses are discussed in a later section of this chapter when we discuss antecedents of individual differences. In this section we discuss the development of social interaction with peers as if it developed completely within the peer system.

Developmental Models

Howes (1987) proposed a model for socially competent behaviors in preschool and younger children. Marker behaviors are used to define the central social task of four developmental periods. Social competence in interaction with peers at 12 months is defined by interest in potential play partners (Howes, 1987).

Social competence in interaction with peers in the early toddler period (13–24 months) is defined by complementary and reciprocal play. Complementary and reciprocal play occurs when children exchange roles and turns in action. Children engage in different but complementary activities, such as run and chase, hide and seek, or offer and receive. These activities represent the capacity to assume the role of the other in action.

Social competence in interaction with peers is defined in the late toddler period (25–36 months) by the communication of meaning. The communication of meaning is defined as the joint understanding of the theme of interaction. It has been operationalized as engaging in cooperative social pretend play (Howes, 1985, 1987; Howes, Unger, & Seidner, 1989). In cooperative social pretend play children must sustain complementary and reciprocal interaction while sharing the nonliteral themes of the play. When children are engaged in cooperative social pretend play they are communicating the nonliteral meaning of their actions. These communications do not necessarily have to be verbal or signed, but the children must indicate from their actions that they understand that the partner is acting out a role. For example, one child may "pour the tea" while the other holds out her cup and then "sips the tea."

In the Howes' (1987) model, social competence with peers in preschoolers (3- to 5-year-olds) is defined as social knowledge of and acceptance by the peer group. Social knowledge is the ability to define the group, differentiate between the various play styles and characteristic behaviors of children in the group, and make stable evaluative judgements about the members of the group. Social acceptance is operationalized by sociometric ratings and social status. Empirical support for the model is provided in at least one longitudinal study (Howes, 1988a). Children observed to be more competent in the play behaviors of one period were observed to be more competent in the play behaviors of the next period. At least one other research project has found support for the continuity of observed social competence with peers over the toddler to preschool periods (Cummings, Iannotti, & Zahn-Waxler, 1989; Denham & Zahn-Waxler, 1989).

Howes is neither the first nor the only researcher to focus on children's play as an important task of early childhood peer interactions. In 1932, Partens identified a developmental progression in children's play. In the Partens (1932) scheme, children move from unoccupied to solitary play, from parallel play to associative, and finally to cooperative play. Unfortunately, Partens' developmental progression has not been replicated by subsequent researchers (Bakeman & Brownlee, 1980; Goldman, 1981; Rubin & Krasnor, 1980; Rubin, Watson, & Jambor, 1978; Smith, 1978). The main reason for the failures to replicate the Partens scheme appears to be that the play forms represent play states or strategies rather than different levels of complexity (Bakeman & Brownlee, 1980; Fein, Moorin, & Enslein, 1982; Goncu, 1989).

The Howes (1987, 1988a) model for sequences in socially competent interaction with peers represents an attempt to define markers of the most competent behaviors possible in a period. Eckerman in the United States and Nadel and Baudonniere in France have addressed the problem of developmental progressions in social interaction with peers in an alternative yet complementary manner. Their focus has been to identify modal patterns of interaction rather than most competent interactions. This is analogous to the performance versus competence distinctions made in language assessment. Eckerman's work (Eckerman, Davis, & Didow, 1989; Eckerman & Didow, 1988; Eckerman & Stein, 1982; Eckerman, Whatley, & McGhee, 1979) also begins with the earliest encounters between toddler peers. She reported an increase between 16 and 32 months in acts coordinated with unfamiliar peers. In Eckerman's work as well as the work of French theorists Nadel (Nadel & Fontaine, 1989; Nadel-Brulfert & Baudonniere, 1982) and Baudonniere (Baudonniere, Garcia-Werebe, Michel, & Liegeois, 1989), imitation of the peer's nonverbal actions is central to achieving coordination with a peer. Nadel and Baudonniere extended their model of the development of social competence to preschoolers arguing that children make a transition from imitation to role identification, role differentiation, and complementarity.

Social pretend play might be considered the modal play form of preschoolers. Certainly, social pretend play becomes a nearly universal activity whenever preschoolers are in the company of other children. Children "become" mothers and fathers, doctors and fire fighters, monsters or wonder women. Social pretend play in preschoolers has been extensively studied and several researchers have suggested developmental progressions within the preschool period. Connolly, Doyle, and Ceschin (1983) noted that older preschoolers engage in more social pretend play than younger children. Older preschoolers (more often than younger) used functional (nonspecific) rather than familial identities. They more often used object replicas and their play was more complex and involved multiple elements. Thus, the older preschoolers' social pretend play was less structured and stereotypical than that of the younger children.

Goncu (1989) suggested that children's social pretend play becomes increasingly intersubjective with age. Intersubjectivity is defined as children establishing common features of their individual experiences. For example, when two children negotiate how to pretend to be mothers or doctors, they attempt to reach consensus on what is a mother or a doctor (Goncu, 1987). After about age 2, children use an effective and explicit play language. Between the ages of 3 and 5 children become increasingly able to communicate and interpret their play intentions. They extend the play ideas of their partners and increasingly establish connection and relevance in their play turn taking.

Connolly and Doyle (1984) suggested that social pretend play mediates between peer experience and more general social competence. They argued that it may not be sufficient to merely make sure that a child has peer contact, but that it may be important to ensure that fantasy play occurs. As we discuss later, adults can enhance social pretend play by manipulating the environment.

In summary, there are several models explaining developmental changes in children's social interactions with peers from the infant through the toddler and preschool periods. These models have in common a focus on the complexity of play and assume a general progression from increasingly complex forms of social play to increasingly complex forms of social pretend play.

Playgroup Entry

Children's strategies for entering ongoing peer groups have been considered markers of competent social interaction with peers. Corsaro (1981) and earlier observers (e.g., McGrew, 1972; Washburn, 1932) identified group entry as one of the more difficult tasks facing preschool children. Developmental trends in entry behavior have been noted for elementary children (Putallaz & Wasserman, 1989) but have not been studied in younger children (Howes, 1988a).

Social Problem Solving

Many theorists and researchers identify social problem solving as an important aspect of social competence. A child who is effective in social problem solving is more frequently able to meet social goals. Early research on social problem solving focused on its cognitive aspects (e.g., Spivack & Shure, 1974). A review of this literature is beyond the scope of the current chapter. However, one drawback to the cognitive approach is that children who can produce socially competent responses in hypothetical situations have not always been observed to do so in natural settings (Rubin & Krasnor, 1986). More recent work in the area of social problem solving has shifted to include direct observation of children's social problem solving. Krasnor and Rubin (1983) have presented a framework for such investigations. Within this framework, children's social goals, social strategies, and outcomes are assessed. This approach is effective in studying the social problem solving of preschool-age children. Preschool children are observed to modify their social goals and strategies according to the age and sex of their partners (Krasnor & Rubin, 1983). With age, young children become more adept in producing alternative strategies when the initial strategy does not work (Rubin & Krasnor, 1986).

Conflict

Conflict among peers is frequent. Conflicts are defined, not as aggressive encounters, but episodes in which children disagree. Thus, two children who are willing to play pretend together but are in disagreement about role assignment, script, or enactment are considered to be in conflict. Children quarrel and disagree about how to play, "who owns" what, who broke what rule, and who is a member of the group and who is not. As uncomfortable as these conflicts are for the participants and for the adults who supervise children, they appear to be important arenas for the development of negotiation and problem-solving skills, and ultimately for the development of relationships.

There are clear developmental trends in conflict topics and strategies. Toddler and young preschool children's conflicts are predominantly object control and secondarily social control (Shantz, 1987). Object control conflicts are usually struggles over toys or other possessions. Social control conflicts are most often over a child refusing to play a particular role in social pretend play, failing to enact the role as the other child would like, or refusing to play with another child. By late preschool children shift to approximately equal proportions of object and social control conflicts (Shantz, 1987). Children tend not to use aggressive strategies in conflicts, and the use of aggression decreases with time from close to 25% of toddlers' conflicts to only 5% of 6-year-olds' conflicts (Shantz, 1987). Large individual differences exist in children's conflict resolution strategies. Children who become friends (Gottman, 1983) are more articulate about their disagreements and are more likely to compromise. It is important to note that it is the manner of negotiating conflict rather than the presence or absence of disagreement that distinguishes successful relationships (friendships) from less successful ones (acquaintances) (Hartup, 1989; Hartup, Laursen, Stewart, & Eastenson, 1988). Furthermore, children able to sustain social interaction prior to a conflict are more likely to resolve the conflict and continue playing together than children who begin their engagement with a conflict (Laursen & Hartup, 1989).

THEORETICAL AND EMPIRICAL PERSPECTIVES ON THE DEVELOPMENT OF FRIENDSHIP RELATIONS

Theoretical writings by Sullivan (1953) and more recently by Buhrmester (Buhrmester & Furman, 1987) and by Parker and Gottman (1989) have suggested that friendship quality is an important aspect of children's social competence with peers. Friendships are opportunities for children to participate in collaborative, intimate personal relationships. Asher and Parker (1989) have identified seven functions of children's friendships: fostering the development of social skills, serving as sources of ego support and self-validation, providing emotional security, serving as sources of intimacy and affection, providing guidance and assistance, providing a sense of reliable alliance, and providing companionships and stimulation. Two separate literatures trace developmental shifts in children's friendships. One body of literature consists of examining developmental changes in children's conceptions of their friendships. This literature (e.g., Furman & Bierman, 1984) has usually been conducted with older children, as preschool and younger children lack the language and cognitive skills to talk about relationships. The other set of literature examines changes in friendships based on observations.

Howes (1983) investigated developmental patterns of friendship by observing behavior in groups of very young children, 5 to 49 months of age. Friendships were defined as interactions in which there was a mutual preference for interaction, skill at complementary and reciprocal peer play, and positive affect. Infants, toddlers, and preschoolers all engaged in friendships. Infants had a few stable partners with whom they primarily engaged in object exchanges, toddlers formed more than one friendship in which the interactions were neither completely object-oriented nor verbal, and preschoolers were involved in short-term and stable friendships based on verbal exchanges. In all three groups of children, the greatest increases in complexity of interaction occurred within maintained friendship dyads.

Gottman and Parkhurst (1980, cited in Roopnarine & Field, 1984) coded the home verbal interactions of friendships in children from 2 to 6 years of age and found younger children to have friendships that were marked by less conflict, more compliance, and more fantasy than those of older children. When interactions with friends were compared to interactions with a stranger, younger children engaged in more fantasy play, were more respondent and compliant, and were more willing to resolve disagreements with friends than with strangers, whereas older children were more willing to resolve disagreements with strangers than with friends.

Identification of Friendships

Friendship pairs have been identified in three different ways: adult informants, behavioral observation, and sociometric techniques. There is relatively high agreement among these three methods (Howes, 1988a). If the adult informant method is used, a teacher or a parent is asked to identify the target child's friend.

Behavioral observations to identify friendships assume that friends will behave differently than other pairs of children. There is support for this assumption especially in toddler and young preschool-age children. Friends, as compared to playmates, exchange more positive and less negative behaviors (Masters & Furman, 1981), show more reciprocity (Foot, Chapman, & Smith, 1980; Lederberg, Rosenblatt, Vandell, & Chapin, 1987), and are more responsive (Howes, 1983). Furthermore, the behavior within dyads of even toddler-age children differs from the behaviors that both partners give and receive in other social contexts (Ross & Lollis, 1989). This last finding validates the use of observational methods to identify friendships as particular relationships rather than two sociable and friendly children who happen to play together.

To identify friendships with behavioral observations the researcher must determine behavioral criteria for friendships. Several researchers have been successful in using mutual preference and shared positive affect as criteria for identifying friendships (Hinde et al., 1985; Howes, 1983; 1988a; Vandell & Mueller, 1980). The criterion of shared positive affect appears to best distinguish friendships (Howes, 1983).

Identifying friendships by behavioral observation is most effective in younger children. As children reach the end of their preschool years they are more likely to play with nonfriend playmates as well as with friends (Howes, 1983; Tessier & Bovin, 1985). Fortunately, as children get older they become more reliable informants in sociometric interviews (Hymel, 1983). Sociometric interviews with school children ask the children to nominate peers who are friends or who have particular behavioral attributes (Coie & Dodge, 1983; Newcomb & Bukowski, 1983; Perry, 1979). Sociometric nominations are most frequently used to obtain social status classifications (e.g., Coie & Dodge, 1983) but mutual nominations may also be used to identify friendships (Berndt, Hawkins, & Hoyle, 1986; Howes, 1988a).

An alternative sociometric assessment specifically designed for preschool children is a picture-rating sociometric (Asher et al., 1979). This procedure has acceptable test–retest reliability in preschool samples (Hymel, 1983). Friendships have been successfully identified using a combination of the nomination and rating procedures (Berndt, 1981; Howes & Wu, in press). Children are considered friends if they nominate each other or if one child nominates the other and the partner gives the nominating child the highest rating.

Predictive Validity of Friendships

Researchers have asked if having friends really does make a difference for young children. Their results suggest that friends among preschool children and toddlers do fill important functions. Howes (1988a), observing children aged 1 to 6 years, found some young friendships to be maintained over a 2- or 3-year period. Children who maintained a larger proportion of reciprocal friends over several years were more socially competent than children who lost reciprocal friends. Mutual friends were also found to facilitate the acquisition of developmentally appropriate social skills. Moreover, children who moved between classrooms or child-care centers with friends were more socially competent than children who moved alone.

Roopnarine and Field (1984) observed toddlers and preschoolers in free play. Dyads were considered friends if they interacted more than 66% of the 108 observation hours over a period of 4 months, and nonfriends if they interacted less than 25% of the time. Children who had close friends (57% of the sample) were more verbal and extraverted than those who did not have close friends. They also took more turns directing and submitting during interactions, engaged in more fantasy play, and did less passive watching of other children playing than did children who lacked close friends. This investigation looked at interactions with close friends, acquaintances, and nonfriends as well, finding that children engaged in fantasy play a greater proportion of the time when playing with friends than with acquaintances or nonfriends.

Preschool friends appear to use social pretend play to initiate and maintain their friendships (Howes, Unger, & Matheson, in press; Parker & Gottman, 1989). One of the functions of social pretend play in preschoolers may be to provide an avenue for exploring self disclosure and intimacy with friends. Preschool children in friendship dyads who had been friends for several years were observed to engage in more cohesive social pretend play and to more often self-disclose during pretend play than either children who were in more short-term friendships or who were not friends (Howes, Matheson, & Wu, in press).

Friendships also appear to aid in children's school transitions. Ladd and Price (1987) found that children who began kindergarten with familiar classmates were more accepted by their classmates and were more positive toward school. These familiar classmates were children from preschool and were not necessarily friends. In a second study of the transition between preschool and kindergarten,

Ladd (in press) found that children who either maintained the friendships with whom they entered school or who formed friendships within the first 2 months of school had the easiest adjustment to school.

INDIVIDUAL DIFFERENCES IN YOUNG CHILDREN'S PEER RELATIONS

Research into individual differences in early social competence with peers has focused on differences in children's acceptance by peers or their status in the peer group, differences in children's social activity with peers, and the interaction between social status and friendships.

Peer Acceptance and Social Status

Children's acceptance or social status within their peer group is an indication of how well they are liked or disliked by their peers. The study of social status or popularity has a long history as a predictor of social adjustment (see Parker & Asher, 1987, for a review). Social status in preschool children has been less well-studied because of concerns over measurement reliability and concurrent and predictive validity. Recent methodological changes in the assessment of social status and a series of studies suggesting that preschool status may be a valid measure have renewed interest in the social status of preschoolers.

Measurement of Social Status.   Most studies of preschool sociometric status use the picture nomination and rating methods described earlier. In an early review of studies using these measures, Hymel (1983) suggested that the picture-rating method was reliable for preschoolers, but that the picture nomination method fell below acceptable standards for reliability. Recent work with children in child-care centers suggests that acceptable reliability on sociometric nominations may be obtained when children are cared for in well-established groups (Howes, 1988a; Olson & Lifgren, 1988; Poteat, Ironsmith, & Bullock, 1986).
    Sociometric nominations may be used in a standardized way to form social status groups—popular, rejected, neglected, controversial, and average children (e.g., Coie & Dodge, 1983). Because preschool sociometric nominations even within well-established groups seem less reliable than sociometric ratings, alternative classification systems have been proposed. Howes (1988a; Howes & Wu, in press) used such a classification system based on ratings rather than nominations and found similar differences between social status groups as classifications based on nominations.

Concurrent Validity: Play and Entry Behaviors of Children with Differing Social Status.   Several investigators have examined the play patterns and entry strategies of children with differing social status. In general, popular children are most competent. First graders report that popular children participate in play, accept others' play invitations, engage in altruistic and entertaining behaviors, choose topics and language viewed as positive by peers, and have good conversation skills (Dygdon, Conger, & Keane, 1987). According to the child informants, rejected children behave aggressively, refuse to play, choose topics and language not liked by peers, and speak in a displeasing manner. Children classified as neglected were believed to break school rules, perform inefficiently in academic tasks, and lack attention to peers and the teacher when those persons were speaking.

Popular, rejected, and neglected children differ in their peer group entry strategies. Popular children are the most effective at gaining entry into groups, often using statements about the group activity or the peer hosts, whereas children classified as rejected are more likely to use statements that bring attention to themselves and disruptions of the group's activity (Dodge, Schlundt, Schocken, & Delugach, 1983; Howes, 1988a; Putallaz & Wasserman, 1989). Rejected children are more likely to respond negatively to peer hosts' statements. Other children are more likely to behave negatively toward rejected children's entry behaviors. Neglected children tend to wait or hover around groups. Peers are likely to ignore this behavior. Once high-status children enter peer groups they are more likely to engage in sustained group interaction than are children of low status (Putallaz & Wasserman, 1989). Over time, rejected children become less successful in their entries into play groups and less positive in their affect when engaged with peers (Howes, 1988a).

Preschoolers were identified as either popular or unpopular by sociometric nominations, and then observed during free play over a 4-month period in a study by Masters and Furman (1981). Their overall rates of receiving and dispensing reinforcing and neutral acts were associated with peer popularity. Interestingly, however, the selection of specific liked peers was not related to overall social behavior, but rather to specific interactions between children. Children's interactions with disliked peers were not different than those with peers who were neither liked nor disliked.

Head Start classrooms were used by Gottman (1977) in another study of sociometric status in which the construct of social isolation was specifically investigated. The relative frequency of peer interaction was not related to children's acceptance by peers. Socially isolated children seemed to be those with low peer acceptance and high rates of exhibiting shyness, anxiety, and fearfulness and were frequently "tuned out" or off task when alone.

Predictive Validity.   Sociometric ratings and social status classifications remain modestly stable within the preschool period (Howes, 1988a; Kempe, Speranza, Matula, & Hazen, 1989; Ladd, Price, & Hart; 1988), between kindergarten and first grade (Ladd & Price, 1987; Rubin & Daniels-Beirness, 1983; Vitaro,

Gagnon, & Boivin, 1989), and between kindergarten and third grade (Howes, in press). Approximately one third to one half of popular, rejected, and average children maintain their social status. Children classified as neglected or controversial are less likely to maintain a stable social status. Although social status in these younger children is less stable than in older elementary children, it is sufficiently stable to justify early intervention (Vitaro et al., 1989).

Preschool sociometric ratings and social status classifications have also been used to predict an array of social adjustment measures in subsequent years. Olson and Lifgren (1988) reported that preschoolers who received high levels of negative nominations from their peers were judged to have poor impulse control and gave forceful aggressive solutions to social problems in a subsequent year. Ironsmith and Poteat (in press) found that preschool sociometric ratings and social status predicted kindergarten teachers' ratings of social adjustment. Similarly, Rubin and Daniels-Bierness (1983) reported that in first grade, children who were popular kindergartners engaged in more mature cooperative activities, whereas children who were rejected as kindergartners were aggressive, hyperactive, and distractible in the first grade.

Interaction Between Social Status and Friendships

Some recent work by Parker and Asher (1989) and Bukowski and Hoza (1989) suggests that close friendships may buffer even negative social status. In their review of literature related to popularity and friendship, Bukowski and Hoza pointed out that there is a crucial distinction between the two constructs. Popularity refers to a group aspect of children's social experience (i.e., children's acceptance by the peer group), whereas friendship is an intense, mutual peer relation that develops between two individuals. Sociometric status measures may confound the distinction between the two constructs by using methodology in which friends are named rather than using general liking as a criterion; however, both friendship and social status need to be separately assessed to understand the full spectrum of children's peer relationships.

Preschoolers were identified by Masters and Furman (1981) as popular or unpopular, and their friendship selections and peer interactions were examined. Children's selections of liked peers were based on specific interactions between children, rather than on overall social behavior. Howes' (1988a) longitudinal study also examined the relation between friendship and social status classification in children aged 1 to 6 years. Of popular, average, rejected, neglected, and controversial children, those classified as rejected were observed during free play to have a more difficult time entering groups than popular and neglected children. Generally, children had a tendency to enter into play with acquaintances rather than friends. Children classified as rejected who had reciprocated friendships entered into play groups more easily than rejected children without reciprocated friendships. Rejected children were more likely to have ease in entering into play with friends than with acquaintances, whereas popular and average children had proportionally more ease of entry with acquaintances than with friends.

More recently reported longitudinal research from Howes (in press) of the link between social status and friendship in children from kindergarten through third grade discovered that children classified as popular in the third grade were more likely to maintain stable friendships from kindergarten to third grade than rejected children. Popular kindergartners were more likely to form friendships with rejected children than were popular third-grade children. Popular–popular dyads were more likely to remain stable friends from kindergarten to the third grade than popular–other dyads.

Isolation from Peers: Social Withdrawal

Teachers and parents often notice vast individual differences in young children's sociability. Some children spend virtually all of their time engaged with peers whereas other children rarely initiate peer contact and tend to withdraw from it if at all possible. The identification of social withdrawal has been a pervasive problem in the research literature (Rubin & Lollis, 1988; Rubin & Mills, in press). Only recently has it become clear that social withdrawal is a multidimensional construct and may change form with development (Rubin & Mills, in press). This understanding helps explain why several studies have reported that social withdrawal is unstable during preschool (Howes, 1988a) and between preschool and kindergarten (Rubin & Krasnor, 1986).

Rubin and Mills (in press) identified two subtypes of socially withdrawn children. Passive-isolated children usually engage in quiet, constructive, or exploratory play, and are usually sedentary. In early childhood these behaviors may be appropriate as children master impersonal tasks (Rubin, 1982). However, in elementary school passive-isolation may reflect social anxiety and negative self-perceptions of competence (Rubin, 1985).

A second subtype of social isolation is labeled active isolation. This form is characterized by cognitively immature and rambunctious behavior. In preschool, children who are classified as actively isolated produce high frequencies of solitary-sensorimotor play and solitary-dramatic play (Rubin, 1982). They are viewed by teachers as aggressive and impulsive (Rubin & Clark, 1983) and are disliked by their peers (Rubin & Daniels-Beirness, 1983). This form of social isolation, given the predictive validity of preschool sociometric ratings, is more problematic.

Sex and Ethnic Differences

Numerous studies suggest that preschool children prefer to play with same-sex peers (Hartup, 1983). As increasing numbers of younger children are enrolled in peer groups, several studies have examined preferences for same-sex playmates in toddler play groups. Toddler-age children also are observed to prefer same-sex play partners, with girls differentiating by sex before boys (Howes, 1988b; La Freniere, Strayer, & Gauthier, 1984). In at least one study, toddler-age boys tended to ignore or refuse girls' invitations to play. Simultaneously girls exhibited same-sex play partner preferences (Howes, 1988b). This suggests that play styles as well as differential maturation rates may underlie explanations for the girls' earlier same-sex preferences.

When friends are behaviorally identified, toddler and preschool-age children have both same and cross-sex friends (Howes, 1988b). When preschoolers select friends in sociometric nominations, they are more likely to select same-sex friends (Gottman, 1986). Although the predominant pattern is same-sex friendships, cross-sex friendships do exist in preschool peer groups (Gottman, 1986; Howes, 1988b). Children who have cross-sex friendships appear to be more socially skilled than those with only same-sex friendships (Gottman, 1986; Howes, 1988b). We suspect that they appear more socially skilled because of the greater flexibility in play style needed for having both same- and cross-sex friends.

Young children are more likely to have same-sex playmates and friends than they are to have same-ethnic playmates and friends (Hartup, 1983). Most studies of same and ethnically different playmates and friendships have examined elementary school children. Within these older children, same-ethnicity preferences increase with age (Asher, Singleton, & Taylor, 1983, Howes & Wu, in press).

Research on ethnic differences in the interactive play of preschool children suggests that Afro-American, Mexican-American, and Euro-American children may engaged in different styles of interactive play (Finkelstein & Haskins, 1983; Zimmerman & Brody, 1975). Perhaps because of these differences in play style Lederberg and colleagues (Lederberg, Chapin, Rosenblatt, & Vandell, 1986) reported that same-ethnic peers engaged in more interactive play than cross-ethnic peers. The Lederberg et al. study is particularly important because it included Mexican-American as well as Afro-American and Euro-American children. In most urban centers, children's peer groups are increasingly diverse. In some of our Los Angeles child care centers children collectively speak as many as 20 different home languages. We know relatively little about patterns of peer interaction and friendship among these ethnically diverse peer groups.

THEORETICAL AND EMPIRICAL PERSPECTIVES ON ANTECEDENTS OF INDIVIDUAL DIFFERENCES IN YOUNG CHILDREN'S RELATIONS WITH PEERS

Current developmental theories suggest that children develop competence with peers through experiences with adults and with peers mediated by dispositional characteristics. According to a framework suggested by Parke (Parke, Mac-

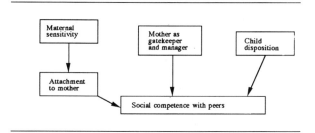

FIG. 4.1.   Model for the development of social competence with peers.

Donald, Beitel, & Bhavangari, 1986) and attachment theorists (La Freniere & Sroufe, 1985; Sroufe, 1983), adults shape peer relationships by socialization, and through the security of the child's attachment to the caregiver. According to a framework suggested by Howes (1987, 1988a) and work on children's social status within peer groups (Asher & Dodge, 1986; Coie & Dodge, 1983; Rubin & Lollis, 1988), children's social competence with peers is also enhanced or inhibited by experiences within the peer group. Characteristics of the child may also contribute to social competence with peers. Figures 4.1 and 4.2 represent schematically hypothesized major contributions to social competence with peers.

The models are different for children who enroll in child care at different ages. Figure 4.1 represents the model most characteristic of children who enroll in child care and thus begin regular experiences with a stable group of peers as preschoolers. In this model the mother is the most important adult socializer of peer relations. Also, the mother's sensitivity predicts the child's attachment security to the mother that in turn predicts social competence with peers. The mother's skill as gatekeeper and manager of peer contacts also predicts the child's social competence with peers. Finally the nature of the child, particularly

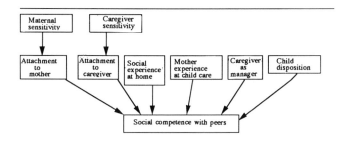

FIG. 4.2.   Model for the development of social competence with peers for children enrolled in child care as infants.

his or her temperament and communicative competence, will predict social competence with peers.

Figure 4.2 represents the model most characteristic of children enrolled in child care as infants. These children have at least two important adult socializers of peer relations, the mother and the child-care caregiver. Children who enroll in child care early in life also have social experiences with peers in child care that predict social competence with peers. In Fig. 4.2 the child has two sets of attachment relationships assumed to be relatively independent of each other. For each relationship the sensitivity of the adult predicts the quality of the child's attachment relationship that in turn predicts the child's social competence with peers. The mother within this model still serves as gatekeeper, providing experiences with peers at home and (as manager of peer contacts) when she is the adult present with peers. The child-care provider serves as a manager of peer contacts in the child-care setting. Individual differences in both the mother's and the child-care provider's skills in managing peer contacts predict social competence with peers. The child-care arrangement itself provides a variety of experiences with peers. The size and age mix of the peer group, as well as the structure of play materials, may all contribute to social competence with peers.

Adults as Socializers of Peer Contacts

Early peer relations are embedded within the process of parental and teacher socialization patterns that are in turn embedded within a cultural milieu (Maccoby & Martin, 1983). Within this cultural milieu, physical, social, and economic factors are recognized as having a considerable impact on the parent–child and presumably the teacher–child relationship (Maccoby & Martin, 1983) and on the developmental process itself (Mussatti, 1986). In this context two theoretical perspectives, ecocultural theory (Weisner, 1984; Whiting & Whiting, 1975) and social network theory (Cochran & Brassard, 1979), provide explanations for the process of adult socialization of peer relations.[1]

Ecocultural Theory.   Ecocultural theory is derived from the psychocultural model of the Whitings and their colleagues (LeVine, 1977; Super & Harkness, 1980; Weisner, 1984; B. Whiting, 1980; B. Whiting & Edwards, 1988; J. Whiting & B. Whiting, 1975). The strength of ecocultural theory for the understanding of the development of children's peer relations comes from the identification of ecocultural or environmental variables. Ecocultural variables are features of the environment that affect children directly or indirectly through children's participation in the family or community (Weisner, 1984). Ecocultural niche variables include income, public health conditions, housing, transportation, domestic work load, and household and family composition. Variations in these

---

[1]We are indebted to Olivia Unger for suggesting this perspective.

variables and combination of variables provide different contexts for the development of peer relations. For example two families with 4-year-old children might have similar incomes and domestic work loads, but if one family lived within an extended family so that the child had daily contact with same-age cousins and the other family was isolated from extended family so that the child was alone each day with a housekeeper, the children's experiences with peers would be very different.

Ecocultural theory proposes that social-ecological influences on the family are influenced through activity settings (Weisner & Gallimore, 1985). Activity settings provide a context for social interaction. In other words, ecocultural theory argues that social interaction is embedded within such everyday activities as eating dinner. Activity settings may be defined by (a) who is present, (b) their values and goals, (c) what tasks are performed, (d) why they are performed—the motives and feelings surrounding the action, and (e) what scripts govern interactions including those that shape and constrain the child's participation. Activity settings are useful in explaining socialization of the child's peer relations by adults, particularly parents and teachers. The activity setting of parental socialization of peer relations differs on several dimensions from the activity setting of teacher socialization of peer relations (see Fig. 4.2). The parental activity setting usually contains only a few children invited by the parent to play with their child. Therefore, the parent's values and goals are more salient in the selection of the peer group. The school activity setting probably contains more children and usually a peer group that is not selected according to the values and goals of the teacher. The parent may have invited children to play so that he or she could be uninvolved with the children and "get some work done," whereas a teacher may see his or her role as moderating peer interactions. The scripts of the participants at home when the toys belong to one child and must be shared are different than in school when the toys belong to the school and must be shared. Ecocultural theory and the construct of activity settings can be a useful framework for exploring socialization practices and differences in socialization practices.

Social Network Theory. Social network theory, a conceptual framework developed by sociologists and social psychologists, has been adapted by developmental psychologists to study the social ecology of socialization (Cochran & Brassard, 1979). Social network theory assumes that repeated contacts between individuals establish links. A social network consists of the way in which these links are distributed around an individual or within a population (Salzinger, Hammer, & Antrobus, 1988). The social network of a child includes everyone the child knows, the relationships among these persons, and the child. Thus, peers and the adults who arrange and supervise peer play are part of the social networks of young children. According to Cochran and Brassard (1979), the extent of influence by a network member is determined by what the network members do together (the activity setting), reciprocity (how members engage in exchanges of goods, services, information, and emotional support), and the intensity of their commitment. Mapping or describing a social network provides information on activity settings, reciprocity, and intensity and thus the influences of members.

There have been relatively few attempts to map or describe the social networks of children. Ellis, Rogoff, and Cromer (1981) described play groups of 1- to 12-year-old children. The youngest children in the study, ages 1 to 2, were most frequently in the presence of adults, but after infancy the presence of peers in the network increased dramatically. Increasing age networks contained more same-age and same-sex unrelated peers. Across all age groups, children were most likely to be in groups that contained at least one relative. Lewis et al. (Feiring & Lewis, 1988; Lewis & Feiring, 1979; Lewis, Feiring, & Kotsonis, 1984) followed a sample of families from infancy through the children's ninth year. Initially, children had more frequent contacts with adults than with peers and peer contacts were always mediated by adults. By age 6 children were spending more time with peers than with family members. By age 9 children's friendship patterns were particularly influential parts of their social networks; functions once filled by adults such as protection were filled by friends.

Using the frameworks of ecocultural and social network theory it is possible to conceptualize parents, teachers, and other adult socialization of peer relations through three functions: beliefs, gatekeepers, and managers.

Parental Beliefs and Values.   A number of authors have suggested that one of the determinants of parental behavior is parents' beliefs and values about how children become socially competent. Recent attention to parental beliefs has focused on children's cognitive development (e.g., Miller, 1988). In these new studies parents are asked directly about their beliefs. There are few comparable studies for peer socialization. Rose-Krasnor and Rubin (Rose-Krasnor, 1988; Rubin et al., 1989) asked mothers about the development of social skills with peers and how they would react if their child engaged in maladaptive peer behavior, and then observed their children in preschool. Mothers' beliefs were linked to their children's social competence.

In examining links between parental beliefs and social competence with peers we can draw on older literature in which parental beliefs and values were inferred by the researchers to examine relations between parental value systems and children's behavior with peers. In this literature, children who were rated as highly socially competent had parents who were rated as high in both warmth and control. The classic study in this area was completed by Baumrind (1967, 1971, 1973). She identified and studied longitudinally three groups of families: authoritarian (high control and low warmth), authoritative (high control and high warmth), and permissive (low control and low warmth). The authoritative parents were most likely to have socially successful children. Similarly, Hinde and

Tamplin (1983) found that authoritarian mothers were associated with hostile children who were unfriendly to peers, whereas authoritative mothers were associated with children high in friendliness to peers. Roopnarine (1987) reported that mothers who were highly involved with their children and who used reasoning as a disciplinary technique were associated with children who were positive toward peers.

Parent beliefs and values are most often associated with parental discipline style as in the Baumrind authoritative, authoriarian, and permissive styles. An alternative approach to inferring parental beliefs and values has been to examine relations between parent–child interaction and children's behavior with peers. This literature supports the premise that more socially competent parents are associated with children higher in social competence with peers. For example, Putallaz (1987; Putallaz & Heflin, in press) reported that parents of first graders with higher sociometric status were more competent in their interaction with adult peers, more positive and focused on feelings, and less disagreeable and demanding when interacting with their own children than parents of lower status children. Work by MacDonald (MacDonald, 1987; MacDonald & Parke, 1984) suggests that fathers' play with the child may be particularly important for the peer interaction skills of preschool-age children. His work suggests that fathers of neglected boys engage in less affectively arousing, physical play than do fathers of popular and rejected boys, but that fathers of rejected boys are more likely to either overstimulate or avoid stimulating their sons during play than fathers of popular boys. This work has particular implications for the growing number of children who are raised in households with single mothers and attend child care centers with a predominantly female teaching staff.

Adults as Gatekeepers. Adults function as gatekeepers when they arrange peer contacts (see Figs. 4.1 and 4.2). Parents vary greatly in their role as gatekeepers. Although many infants are enrolled in family day care homes or child care centers and thus spend their days in close contact with peers, others have child care arrangements that exclude peers such as a grandmother or a sitter coming to the child's home. Some families are integrated into social networks based on family or friends that include peer contacts, whereas other families are more isolated. Some working parents arrange playdates for their children and others do not.

Few studies have directly explored the role of social networks in children's development of social competence with peers. Ladd, Hart, Wadworth, and Golter (1988) explored relations between characteristics of preschool children's peer networks in nonschool settings and their social functioning in school. Younger preschool children (23–40 months) who played with older peers outside of school were more socially competent in school. For older preschool children (41–55 months) experiences with same-age peers outside of school were positively related to social competence. Older preschoolers who had spent more time in social network members' homes had higher sociometric ratings. These findings suggest that broadening children's social exposure is related to their social competence.

A second study by Ladd and Golter (1988) found that preschool children (49–68 months) whose parents provided more out-of-school peer contacts had a larger range of playmates and more consistent play companions. Boys with parents who initiated peer contact were found to be better liked and less rejected by classmates than boys with parents who did not initiate peer contact.

The personal networks of parents may also influence their role as gatekeepers. Parental network members indirectly influence the child by affecting the opportunities parents make available to their children for peer interaction. For example, children may be regular playmates because the parents are friends. Parental network members may also directly influence the child by serving as sources for cognitive and social stimulation, serving as role models for the child and parent, and directly engaging with the child and his or her peers. Cochran and Brassard (1979) suggested that through participation in parental social networks, the children observe reciprocal relationships.

Parents serve as gatekeepers not only for their child's peer contacts but for context of these experiences. Parents select the child-care arrangement. Thus Ladd, Hart, Wadworth, and Golter (1988) found that children from families with two working parents tended to have a larger peer network. An extensive body of literature links family characteristics and child care quality. More stressed families tend to place their children in lower quality child care (Goelman & Pence, 1987; Howes & Stewart, 1987; Phillips, McCartney, & Scarr, 1987). The literature linking child care quality and children's competence in peer relations is mixed. Howes and Stewart (1987) and Lamb et al. (1988) found no relationship between child care quality and children's play with peers. However, Vandell, Henderson, and Wilson (1988) found that children who had been in low quality child care as preschoolers had difficulty with peers as third graders.

Adults as Managers.   Parents and other adults become managers of children's peer contacts when they intervene and attempt to influence the direction and nature of peer contacts. Parents and child-care providers do directly influence their children's peer relations by mediating the child's activities with peers (Finnie & Russell, 1988; Ladd & Golter, 1988; Parke & Bhavanagri, 1988; Rubenstein & Howes, 1979). (See Figs. 4.1 and 4.2.) Although the idea of adults mediating children's peer contacts is gaining acceptance, relatively little is known about what adults actually do and how such behaviors relate to the child's competence. Extant studies have relied on parent reports (Ladd & Golter, 1988) or watched mothers in laboratory settings (Finnie & Russell, 1988; Parke & Bhavanagri, 1988). Even less is known about differences between the social mediation behaviors of parents and child care providers or these individuals' relative influence on the child. Casual observation suggests that the two groups may have very different socializing techniques. For example, parents may ignore or encourage hitting back whereas child-care providers may forbid it.

Parents and other socializing adults may modify their manager behaviors depending on the age of the child. Lollis and Ross (1987) and Halverson and Waldrop (1970) have observed that when toddler-age children are playing, mothers intervene fairly often, but only in conflict situations and most often when their own child is the aggressor. Ladd and Golter (1988) in studying preschool children found that mothers often used indirect supervision of peer contacts; that is, they were aware of the children's activity but were not consistently present or involved. School-age children receive even less direct supervision (Bryant, 1985).

Several studies have linked parental management techniques to children's social skills. Parke and Bhavanagri (1988) in a laboratory study of maternal management of toddler-age children found that children were more socially competent in peer play when mothers were supervising their play. Bhavanagri (1987) extended this research to preschool- as well as toddler-age children. She found that although the younger children (2 to $3\frac{1}{2}$ years of age) played more competently in mothers' presence, older children ($3\frac{1}{2}$ to 6) were able to maintain their levels of interaction when maternal intervention was removed. Similarly, Ladd and Golter (1988) reported that those preschool children whose parents directly supervised (maintained a presence or participated in the children's activities) versus indirectly supervised their play at home were more frequently rejected by their classmates in school and rated as more hostile toward peers by their teachers. Finally, Finnie and Russell (1988) compared maternal management style in two groups of preschool children: high and low social status. Mothers were asked to help their child enter a playgroup. Mothers of high-status children used behaviors such as assessing the group's frame of reference and encouraged the child to integrate into the play without changing the nature of the play. In contrast, mothers of low-status children avoided the task, were hostile and intrusive, or asked questions that disrupted the ongoing play. Thus, mothers of high-status children tended to coach their children in successful techniques, whereas mothers of low-status children suggested techniques known to be unsuccessful in the peer culture.

Adults as Attachment Figures

Attachment theory is derived from the work of Bowlby (1982). Central to the theory is the idea that through experiences with caregiving adults the child derives an internal working model of the self and others (Bretherton, 1985). This internal working model of self and other is theoretically responsible for the child's orientation to peers (see Figs. 4.1 and 4.2). If a child's internal working model incorporates security, then the child is likely to approach peer relationships with a positive orientation. In contrast, if a child is insecure with the caregiver he or she may avoid or resist peer contact (Cohn, 1990). There are several studies that suggest that in general, the nature of the child's attachment relationship with the mother predicts the child's relationship with peers. Children rated as secure with their mothers are observed or rated to be more competent with peers (Easterbrook & Lamb, 1979; La Freniere & Sroufe, 1985; Lieberman, 1977; Pastor, 1981; Sroufe, 1983; Waters, Wippman, & Sroufe, 1979). The precise nature of the linkage between the security of maternal attachment and children's behaviors and relationships with peers is less clear. As Lamb and Nash (1989) pointed out, most of the studies linking maternal attachment and later peer skills have not separated early maternal influences from concurrent ones, have not examined bi-directional effects, and do not consider growth of skills within the peer system independent of the mother–child system.

Considering adults as attachment figures become more complicated in light of the large number of infants, toddlers, and preschoolers who are cared for by other than parents for a large part of their days. Relatively little is known about the child who forms a nonparental attachment. According to attachment theory, children will form attachment relationships with all adults who are caregivers (Bretherton, 1985). These concurrently formed attachments are not necessarily concordant or similar in quality (Colin, 1986; Howes, Rodning, Galluzzo, & Myers, 1988; Lamb, 1977; Main & Weston, 1981). Attachment theory is less than clear about the consequences of multiple and nonconcordant attachments for the construction of the child's internal working model of self and other (Bretherton, 1985).

At least three logical alternatives exist for the internal working model for social relationships with others in a child with multiple attachments: hierarchically organized, integrated, and internal working models specific to activity settings. In a hierarchically organized model, the attachment figure who is the most emotionally salient or who was temporally first becomes the dominant representation in the model. This hierarchical model is best represented by Fig. 4.1. Bowlby (1982) assumed that maternal attachments would precede alternative attachments. The maternal attachment may also be the most important because of its emotional salience. Using the hierarchical model we would expect children's orientation to peers to be best predicted by their attachments to their mothers regardless of the quality of their attachment to others. There is a body of empirical literature from samples of children who had mothers as their primary caregivers and who did not enter peer groups until well after maternal attachments were established that supports this hypothesis (Easterbrook & Lamb, 1979; La Freniere & Sroufe, 1985; Lieberman, 1977; Pastor, 1981; Sroufe, 1983; Waters et al., 1979).

In an integrative model the child would combine his or her internal representations of attachment figures to form one integrated internal working model. The integrative model is represented in Fig. 4.2. Therefore, children with concordant secure attachments would have a different internal working model than children who had nonconcordant attachments (secure and insecure). Within this framework we would expect children who had secure attachments to both their mothers and their caregivers to be more positively oriented to peers than children who had one secure and one insecure attachment relationship. Support for the integrative model comes from one study of infants in child care. The child's involvement with adults and peers in child care was a function of both attachment security with mother and with caregiver (Howes, et al., 1988).

A third possibility for children with multiple and nonconcordant attachments is that the internal working model may be specific to particular activity settings. This model was stimulated by ecocultural theory. Because the child usually constructs internal representations of the mother and of the caregiver within distinct activity settings (e.g., child care center vs. home), the child's internal model of self and others might also be nested within these settings. Within this framework we would expect children whose main social contacts with peers were within child care to have peer relations that were more dependent on their relationship with the child-care provider than with the mother. If the child constructed peer relationships within the context of the caregiver attachment relationship, the child-care provider is the most salient attachment figure. Support for this framework comes from two studies. Oppenheim, Sagi, and Lamb (1988) in a study of Israel infants found that 4-year-olds' behaviors with peers were better predicted by the child's infant attachment to the metapelet (alternative caregiver) than the child's infant attachment to the mother or the father. Howes, Galluzzo, Hamilton, Matheson, and Rodning (1989) assessed security of attachment to mother and to a child care caregiver in infancy and again at age 4. Children's sociometric ratings and play with peers were best predicted by the child's relationship with the infant's child-care caregiver.

Experience in the Peer Group

Early and intimate experiences with peers are not well understood. Kibbutz studies in Israel suggest that when the peer group is stable and the contact is extensive, peers are important in the emotional lives of children (Oppenheim et al., 1988). Ecologically based studies of children's peer contact suggest that children form peer relationships in both schools and neighborhoods and their behavior may differ across contexts (Gump, Schoggen, & Refl, 1963). Three types of experiences within peer groups are expected to influence competence with peers: the age of entry, peer group stability, and friendships (see Figs. 4.1 and 4.2). The literature on age of entry is mixed. Several studies of competence with peers in younger children suggest that complexity of play with peers is dependent on experience within peer groups rather than on age, with more experienced children engaging in more complex play (Howes, 1988a; Mueller & Brenner, 1977). In contrast, some studies of early child-care report that children who enter center care (and thus peer groups) as infants are more aggressive with peers (Haskins, 1985), whereas others suggest that only children who enter low-quality child care as infants have more problematic relationships with peers (Howes, 1990).

The literature on the stability of the peer group and the stability of the child is more consistent. Increased stability is associated with increased competence with peers (Howes, 1988a; Howes & Stewart, 1987). This may not be as true for older children. Children neglected in one peer group may be accepted in another (Coie & Kupersmidt, 1983).

We know from studies of newcomers to peer groups that peer groups of young children are sufficiently coherent that access is not always easy. Feldbaum, Christenson, and O'Neal (1980) observed preschool children over their first four weeks of enrollment in established preschool classrooms. Initially, the newcomers were isolated, hesitant, and nonassertive with classmates and in attempts to join playgroups. Host children appeared disinterested in playing with them. After 4 weeks, the male newcomers were similar in their peer interactions to the host children. After 6 to 8 weeks, the female newcomers were assimilated.

Young children do form stable friendships (Hartup, 1989; Howes, 1988a). The literature is not clear about whether children form friendships because they are socially competent or become competent because they have friends (Howes, 1988a, in press; Parker & Asher, 1989). If children's child-care experience is characterized by stable groups of children sharing the experience of separation from parents, and if early friendships represent a form of emotional security, we might expect children who have had positive child-care experiences to especially value the social support provided by close friends.

Contribution of the Child

Children's temperament may mediate the child's development of social competence with peers by influencing the child's approach or withdrawal from peers (Parker-Cohen & Bell, 1988) (see Figs. 4.1 and 4.2). Rubin and Lollis (1988) suggest that peer rejection may be linked to withdrawal from social contact with peers and behavioral isolation. Work by Kagan, Reznick, Clarke, Snidman, & Garcia-Coll (1980) suggests that behavioral inhibition or shyness does indeed affect 4-year-olds' initial sociability with unfamiliar peers.

Children may also have difficulty with peers because their own social communication or their interpretation of the social communication of others lacks clarity (Dodge, 1985). A child who miscommunicates or misinterprets may be more likely to attribute hostile instead of positive intent to peers. Hazen and Black (1989) have pursued these hypotheses by examining discourse processes in free-play interaction of preschool children. Children who were liked by their peers were more likely than those who were disliked to direct communication to others clearly, to attend to all others involved in the interaction, to respond contingently to the initiations of others, to acknowledge the initiations of others, and to provide turnabout rather than minimal rejections. In a follow-up study the children who became more disliked also became less likely to direct their initiations to a specific listener or listeners and to respond contingently to the initiations of others. Children who became more liked by peers became more likely to accept rather than reject peers' initiations (Kempe et al., 1989).

ENHANCING AND INTERVENING IN PEER RELATIONS

Despite growing research literature on young children's peer relations, there is scant literature on programs to enhance or intervene in early peer relations. This is in contrast to the vast literature on intervention and prevention at the elementary school level (e.g., Schneider, Rubin, & Ledingham, 1985). We suspect that a long history of ignoring peer relations in children under 3 years old, combined with a societal notion that play is the natural activity of the preschool child have limited the development of programs of assessment and intervention in early peer relations. In the concluding section of this chapter, we survey the available literature on intervention.

Manipulating the Physical Setting

One of the easiest interventions that can be accomplished in a school setting may be manipulation of the physical setting. Unfortunately, literature is limited pertaining to environmental influences on children's interactions with peers. However, studies have shown that toys and materials available to children in child care settings influence the play and social interactions that occur (Quilitch & Risley, 1973; Scholtz & Ellis, 1975). Additionally, toy structure as an influential factor in pretend play has been examined by several investigators (Elder & Pederson, 1978; McGhee, Etheridge, & Benz, 1984; McLoyd, 1983; Pulaski, 1970).

In their investigation, Quilitch and Risley (1973) found extreme differences in social play dependent only on the toys that were provided for play. The investigators provided the children with toys that either encouraged social play (games whose directions called for two or more participants) or encouraged isolate play (books, puzzles, building, and art supplies). Substitution of one group of toys for the other had an immediate and dramatic effect on the level of social play of the children. This study contributes to the argument that the materials made available to children can influence their sociability.

Scholtz and Ellis (1975) concluded that children's overt preferences for toys decreased with exposure. The decrease, however, was inversely proportional to the level of complexity of the toys. In other words, children take longer to satisfy their curiosity with high complexity toys than with low complexity toys, and take longer to begin to involve the high complexity toys in social play. The study showed that high complexity settings fostered greater interaction with materials, and less interaction with peers than did the low complexity settings.

The two studies discussed earlier differ largely in their choice of materials. Quilitch and Risley (1973) provided predominantly fine motor materials, whereas Scholtz and Ellis (1975) provided gross motor apparatus. Vandenberg (1981) concluded that fine motor materials fostered more solitary and parallel play whereas gross motor materials fostered more associative play. With this in mind, it is possible that Quilitch and Risley's (1973) toys that encouraged solitary play had a strengthened effect due to their fine motor orientation. Similarly, it is possible that Scholtz and Ellis' (1975) findings would not generalize to fine motor materials.

There are several studies that attempt to examine toy structure's effects on play. Pulaski (1970), using 5- to 7-year-olds, found that minimally structured toys elicited a greater variety of themes in fantasy play than did highly structured toys. However, structure did not affect the "richness" of themes, which Pulaski scored by determining the distance of the fantasy from the reality of the child's life. There was some concern expressed that the minimal and high structure toys, despite differences in detail, were too closely matched. More extreme differences in the materials presented could result in a broader range of play behaviors, and perhaps increase both the variety and the richness of theme.

Beyond Pulaski's study, most of the work covering preschoolers focuses on the quantity of pretend play rather than the quality. Elder and Pederson (1978) concluded that children under 3 years of age were dependent on toys that resembled their referents to elicit pretend play. Children $3\frac{1}{2}$ years and older, however, were able to pretend equally well in situations with toys of progressively less structure, and even in situations with no toys at all. Although this is an interesting experimental result, it may not accurately portray what occurs during children's play. McGhee et al. (1984) discovered that 4-year-olds showed more frequent pretend behavior with unstructured toys but chose to play much longer with high structured toys. Unstructured toys were associated with a greater amount of playing time only when they were presented to the child before moderate or high structure toys. Despite the children's fantasy abilities, unstructured toys held less appeal. It is suggested by McGhee et al. (1984) that regardless of the fact that children spend more time with toys that look like what they represent, when preschoolers want to pretend they prefer the toy that matches their highest level of pretend capabilities, or the toy with less resemblance to its real-life counterpart.

In contrast to some of these findings, McLoyd (1983) found that high structure toys, as opposed to low structure toys, increased the noninteractive pretend play of $3\frac{1}{2}$-year-olds. High structure toys also elicited more associative pretend play among both $3\frac{1}{2}$-year-olds and 5-year-olds. Obviously, with this wide range of results across the various studies, the effect of toy structure on pretend play in preschools is still unclear.

Another area of research examines children's use of activity centers within their classrooms (Brenner & Omark, 1979; Innocenti et al., 1986; Pellegrini & Perlmutter, 1989; Shapiro, 1975). These studies are particularly relevant because observations were made in naturalistic settings.

Pellegrini and Perlmutter (1989) looked at the effects of age, gender, and play area on preschoolers' social play. They concluded that in 3- to 5-year-olds, block and art areas produce more constructive and solitary play, whereas replica areas (equivalent to this study's indoor/high structure area) produce more dramatic and interactive play. However, they discovered that, with age, children tend to use low structure toys more frequently to engage in pretend play. Using a slightly different approach, Shapiro (1975) looked at children's behavior in four play areas and found that social interaction was higher in the block and doll areas than in the art and table game areas. However, block and doll areas were also higher in social deviancy or aggression. Surprisingly, Shapiro (1975) noted that although children showed a clear preference for these two areas, amounting to 35% of their free-play time, teacher interactions with children were lower in these areas than in the remaining play areas. These two findings, the high peer interactions and low teacher interactions, are more easily understood in view of the finding that teacher interactions with a child in any activity area significantly decreased that child's peer interactions (Innocenti et al., 1986).

Brenner and Omark (1979), although they supported the notion that house areas produce more interactive and dramatic play, focused their study on the gender differences within play areas. Examining the house, block, and truck areas, the investigators found that boys and girls appeared with equal frequency, and that both sexes apportioned their time equally between make-believe and exploratory play in all the areas. Other results clearly differentiate the play of boys and girls. Boys engage in more active fantasy play, more fantasy play outdoors, and in more interactive fantasy play than girls (Sanders & Harper, 1976). Girls, however, displayed more role-taking pretend play, which the investigators attributed to greater time spent in the house area.

A large percentage of the literature discussing environment deals with issues of physical space (Field, 1980; Phyfe-Perkins, 1980). These studies present issues of concern including crowding, class size, student/teacher ratio, and arrangement of equipment. Although results have been mixed, reviews of the literature have been able to draw some broad summarizations. Phyfe-Perkins (1980) concluded that physically bounded spaces may increase work-related behavior by decreasing distractions. Small, enclosed areas encourage quiet activity and small group interaction. Variations in seating arrangements can either encourage or discourage conversation. Provisions for privacy, softness, and low noise level tend to encourage desired behaviors. Additionally, Field (1980) noted that the optimal classroom for encouraging peer interactions and fantasy play among middle-class, preschool children is a room featuring a low teacher–child ratio and partitioned special play areas.

Manipulating the Curriculum

Play has also been linked to curriculum or school programs in child-care settings. Johnson and Ershler (1981) examined the effect of classroom program, or curriculum, on the social play of preschoolers. They compared a formal education classroom (with small-group instruction and one free-play period) to a discovery classroom (with twice as much free-play time) in terms of Smilansky's (1968) cognitive play categories of functional, constructive, and dramatic play. Over time the formal education classroom shifted from predominantly constructive play to increased dramatic play. In contrast, the discovery classroom shifted from functional to constructive play. Although one study cannot be conclusive, it does appear that play development can be influenced by the educational program.

More research has been conducted on elementary school programs that encourage or discourage peer interaction than on preschool programs. Three basic approaches have been used. One common method is peer tutoring. In peer tutoring one child instructs and drills another child in material on which the first child is an expert and the second is a novice. In cooperative learning, children in a classroom are divided into teams of four to five children. Each team is given a project to complete. Usually the components of the project are divided among team members so that each team member becomes an expert in one piece of the whole. In peer collaboration children work in pairs to solve tasks that neither could do previously. In all programs the children appear to benefit both socially and cognitively from the discussions necessary to solve the problem (Dammon & Phelps, 1989).

In recent years the curriculum of early childhood has been the subject of great debate (cf. Bredekamp, 1988). Many preschool programs are now teaching formal academics in a drill and practice manner. This teaching method requires children to work individually, usually at desks, and dramatically decreases the amount of interactions with peers. Many educational experts have become alarmed over what they consider miseducation (e.g., Katz, 1985). The National Association for the Education of Young Children, the National Association of School Boards, and many state departments of education and school boards have issued position papers on developmentally appropriate programs for young children. In developmentally appropriate programs children are encouraged to collaborate with their peers on age-appropriate projects that encourage experiential learning. Although developmentally appropriate programs do not use the terms *cooperative learning* or *peer collaboration*, the principles underlying the approach are similar. Unfortunately, there have been few research evaluations of the processes or outcomes of these educational approaches.

Social Skills Training

Throughout this section of the chapter we have discussed interventions in the classroom setting and climate that enhance the development of social competence with peers. Along with these more global interventions researchers have also studied the effects of more direct intervention in the form of social skills training. According to Ladd (1985) social skills training relies on three assumptions: (a) many children experience difficulties in peer relations because they lack basic interpersonal skills, (b) social skills can be learned, and (c) the social skills that children acquire in training programs generally will be used and will resolve their difficulties with peers.

Social skills training can take place at the classroom level and involve all children in the group or they can be targeted for particular children. The training programs teach children the concepts underlying the skills. Examples of skillful and unskillful behavior are provided, and children are asked to generate additional examples. The children practice the skills in actual peer interaction and are given feedback and reinforcement for their performance. In general, research on intervention programs supports Ladd's assumptions. Children who experience social skills training programs do acquire social skills and they become better accepted by their peers (Furman & Gavin, 1989; Ladd, 1985).

The social skills training model is not a developmental model. Although social skills training studies are done with preschoolers as well as older children, there is little attempt to adjust the content, teaching method, or reinforcement to the age of the child. The predictive validity of preschool sociometric status as discussed earlier suggests that early intervention is warranted. We need a series of studies that examine whether general classroom interventions are as effective as targeted interventions for preschool children. Studies are also needed that examine age-appropriate and age-inappropriate intervention programs for early childhood.

CONCLUSION

Peer relationships in toddler and preschool children are important for children's socialization. As we have argued within peer groups and friendship dyads, children acquire important social skills for achieving and maintaining intimacy, for getting along in social groups, and for resolution of conflicts.

There are predictable sequences in the development of social interaction and friendships with peers. When teachers and school psychologists are aware of the marker behaviors of these sequences, they are able to assess the maturity of the child and plan appropriate interventions. Without this knowledge, adults working with children tend to underestimate the abilities of infants and toddlers and thus are unaware of the potential for early enhancement and intervention with peer relations. Teachers and school psychologists who attempt to generalize knowledge of school-age children's interactions with peers may overestimate the capacities of preschool children. A common result of this error is to highly structure preschool children's peer contacts and fail to provide sufficient time for free play and the development of elaborated pretend sequences.

Individual differences in children's social competence with peers begin to emerge as early as the toddler period. These individual differences have reasonable predictability for later maladjusted peer relations. These research findings suggest that careful observation of young children's peer play, and early preventative work with children may be justified. Teachers and school psychologists may need to take the lead in designing classrooms that include an awareness of the importance of early peer relations. There is little evaluative research to guide these interventions. Such a research direction would be fruitful and important.

We have suggested a complex model that combines the influences of parents and child care to predict social competence with peers. More research is needed to elucidate the additive and interactive influences of families and child care assumed in this model. We suspect that sensitive teachers and high-quality child-care settings may be able to compensate for disadvantaged relationships in the home. As most peer contacts occur in the school and child-care environment, we are less optimistic about the ability of advantageous family life to offset the influences of poor quality child care on peer relations. Teachers and schools may play a critical role in enhancing peer contacts and relationships.

REFERENCES

Asher, S., & Coie, J. (1990). *Peer rejection in childhood.* New York: Cambridge University Press.

Asher, S., & Dodge, K. A. (1986). Identifying children who are rejected by their peers. *Developmental Psychology, 22,* 444–449.

Asher, S. R., & Parker, J. G. (1989). Significance of peer relationship problems in childhood. In B. H. Schneider, G. Attili, J. Nadel, & R. Weissberg (Eds.), *Social competence in developmental perspective* (pp. 5–27). Dordrecht: Kluwer.

Asher, S. R., Singleton, L. C., & Taylor, A. R. (1983, April). *Acceptance versus friendship: A longitudinal study of racial integration.* Paper presented at the annual meeting of the American Educational Research Association, New York.

Asher, S. R., Singleton, L. C., Tinsley, B. R., & Hymel, S. (1979). A reliable sociometric measure for preschool children. *Developmental Psychology, 15,* 443–444.

Bakeman, R., & Brownlee, J. R. (1980). The strategic use of parallel play: A sequential analysis. *Child Development, 51,* 873–878.

Baudonniere, P. M., Garcia-Werebe, M. J., Michel, J., & Liegeois, J. (1989). Development of communicative competencies in early childhood: A model and results. In B. H. Schneider, G. Attili, J. Nadel, & R. Weissberg (Eds.), *Social competence in developmental perspective* (pp. 175–195). Dordrecht: Kluwer.

Baumrind, D. (1967). Child care practices anteceding three patterns of preschool behavior. *Genetic Psychology Monographs, 75,* 43–88.

Baumrind, D. (1971). Current practices of parental authority. *Developmental Psychology Monograph, 4*(1, Pt. 2).

Baumrind, D. (1973). The development of instrumental competence through socialization. In A. D. Pick (Ed.), *Minnesota Symposium on Child Psychology*, (Vol. 7, pp. 3–46). Minneapolis: University of Minnesota Press.

Berndt, T. J. (1981). Age changes and changes over time in prosocial intentions and behavior between friends. *Developmental Psychology,* 408–416.

Berndt, T., Hawkins, J. A., & Hoyle, S. G. (1986). Changes in friendship during a school year: Effects on children's and adolescents' impressions of friendship and sharing with friends. *Child Development, 57,* 1284–1297.

Berndt, T., & Ladd, G. W. (1989). *Peer relationships in child development* (Vol. 17). New York: Wiley.

Bhavanagri, N. (1987). *Parents as facilitators of preschool children's peer relationships.* Unpublished doctoral dissertation, University of Illinois at Champaign-Urbana.

Bowlby, J. (1982). *Attachment and loss.* New York: Basic.

Bredekamp, S. (1988). *Developmentally appropriate practices in early childhood programs serving children from birth through age eight.* Washington, DC: National Association for the Education of Young Children.

Brenner, M., & Omark, D. R. (1979). The effects of sex, structure, and social interaction on preschoolers' play behaviors in a naturalistic setting. *Instructional Science, 8,* 91–105.

Bretherton, I. (1985). Attachment theory retrospect and prospect. *Monographs of the Society for Research in Child Development, 50*(1–2, Serial No. 209).

Bryant, B. K. (1985). The neighborhood walk: Sources of support in middle childhood. *Monograph of the Society for Research in Child Development, 50*(3, Serial No. 210).

Buhrmester, D., & Furman, W. (1987). The development of companionships and intimacy. *Child Development, 58,* 1101–1113.

Bukowski, W. M., & Hoza, B. (1989). Popularity and friendship: Issues in theory, measurement, and outcome. In T. J. Berndt & G. W. Ladd (Eds.), *Peer relationships in child development* (pp. 15–45). New York: Wiley.

Cochran, M. M., & Brassard, J. A. (1979). Child development and personal social networks. *Child Development, 50,* 601–616.

Cohn, D. A. (1990). Child–mother attachments in six-year-olds and social competence at school. *Child Development, 61,* 152–162.

Coie, J. D., & Dodge, K. A. (1983). Continuities and changes in children's social status: A five-year-longitudinal study. *Merrill Palmer Quarterly, 29,* 261–282.

Coie, J. D., & Kupersmidt, J. B. (1983). A behavioral analysis of emerging social status in boys' groups. *Child Development, 54,* 1400–1416.

Colin, V. L. (1986, April). *Hierarchies and patterns of infant's attachments to employed mothers and alternative caregivers.* Paper presented at the International Conference on Infant Studies, Los Angeles.

Connolly, J., & Doyle, A. B. (1984). Relations of social fantasy play to social competence in preschoolers. *Developmental Psychology, 20,* 797–806.

Connolly, J., Doyle, A. B., Ceschin, F. (1983). Forms and functions of social fantasy play in preschoolers. In M. Liss (Ed.), *Children's play: Sex differences and the acquisition of cognitive and social skills* (pp. 83–97). New York: Academic Press.

Corsaro, W. A. (1981). Friendship in the nursery school. Social organization in a peer environment. In S. R. Asher & J. M. Gottman (Eds.), *The development of children's friendships* (pp. 207–241). New York: Cambridge University Press.

Cummings, E. M., Iannotti, R. J., & Zahn-Waxler, C. (1989). Aggression between peers in early childhood: Individual continuity and development change. *Child Development, 60,* 887–895.

Dammon, W., & Phelps, E. (1989). Strategic uses of peer learning in children's education. In T. J.

Berndt & G. W. Ladd (Eds.), *Peer relationships in child development* (pp. 135–157). New York: Wiley.

Denham, S., & Zahn-Waxler, C. (1989, April). *Social competence in young preschoolers: Continuity and change from two to five years.* Paper presented at the biennial meeting of the Society for Research in Child Development, Kansas City, MO.

Dodge, K. (1985). Facets of social interaction and the assessment of social competence in children. In B. Schneider, K. Rubin, & J. Ledeingham (Eds.), *Children's peer relations: Issues in assessment and intervention* (pp. 3–22). New York: Springer-Verlag.

Dodge, K., Schlundt, D., Schocken, I., & Delugach, J. (1983). Social competence and children's sociometric status: The role of peer group entry. *Merrill Palmer Quarterly, 29,* 309–336.

Dygdon, J. A., Conger, A. J., & Keane, S. P. (1987). Children's perceptions of the behavioral correlates of social acceptance, rejection, and neglect in their peers. *Journal of Clinical Child Psychology, 16,* 2–8.

Easterbrook, A., & Lamb, M. (1979). The relationship between the quality of the infant–mother attachment and infant competence in initial encounters with peers. *Child Development, 50,* 380–387.

Eckerman, C. O., Davis, C. C., & Didow, S. M. (1989). Toddlers' emerging ways of achieving social coordinations with a peer. *Child Development, 60,* 440–453.

Eckerman, C. O., & Didow, S. M. (1988). Lessons drawn from observing young peers together. *Acta Paediatrica Scandinavica, 77* (Suppl. 344), 55–70.

Eckerman, C. O., & Stein, M. R. (1982). The toddler's emerging interactive skills. In K. H. Rubin & H. S. Ross (Eds.), *Peer relationships and social skills in childhood* (pp. 41–72). New York: Springer-Verlag.

Eckerman, C. O., Whatley, J. L., & McGhee, L. J. (1979). Approaching and contacting the object another manipulates: A social skill of the one-year-old. *Developmental Psychology, 15,* 585–593.

Elder, J., & Pederson, D. (1978). Preschool children's use of objects in symbolic play. *Child Development, 49,* 500–504.

Ellis, S., Rogoff, B., & Cromer, C. C. (1981). Age segregation in children's social interactions. *Development Psychology, 17,* 349–401.

Fein, G., Moorin, E. R., & Enslein, J. (1982). Pretense and peer behavior: An intersectoral analysis. *Human Development, 25,* 392–406.

Feiring, C., & Lewis, M. (1988). The child's social network from three to six years: The effects of age, sex, and socioeconomic status. In S. Salzinger, J. Antrobus, & M. Hammer (Eds.), *Social networks of children, adolescents, and college students* (pp. 97–110). Hillsdale, NJ: Lawrence Erlbaum Associates.

Feldbaum, S., Christenson, P., & O'Neal, K. (1980). An observational study of the assimilation of the newcomer to preschool. *Child Development, 51,* 497–507.

Field, T. (1980). Preschool play: Effects of teacher/child ratios and organization of classroom space. *Child Study Journal, 10,* 191–205.

Finkelstein, N. W., & Haskins, R. (1983). Kindergarten children prefer same-color peers. *Child Development, 54,* 502–508.

Finnie, V., & Russell, A. (1988). Preschool children's social status and their mothers' behavior and knowledge in the supervisory role. *Developmental Psychology, 24,* 789–801.

Foot, H. C., Chapman, A., & Smith, J. (1980). Patterns of interaction in children's friendships. In H. C. Foot, A. Chapman, & J. Smith (Eds.), *Friendship and social relations in young children* (pp. 267–293). New York: Wiley.

Furman, W., & Bierman, K. L. (1984). Children's conceptions of friendships: A multimethod study of developmental changes. *Developmental Psychology, 20,* 925–931.

Furman, W., & Gavin, L. A. (1989). Peers' influences on adjustment and development: A view from the intervention literature. In T. J. Berndt & G. W. Ladd (Eds.), *Peer relationships in child development* (pp. 319–340). New York: Wiley.

Goelman, H., & Pence, A. R. (1987). Some aspects of the relationships between family structure and child language development in three types of day care. In D. L. Peters & S. Kontos (Eds.), *Advances in applied developmental psychology: Continuity and discontinuity of experience in child care* (pp. 67–79). Norwood, NJ: Ablex.

Goldman, J. (1981). Social participation of preschool children in same- versus mixed-age groups. *Child Development, 52,* 644–650.

Goncu, A. (1987). Towards an interactive model of developmental change in social pretend play. In L. Katz (Ed.), *Current topics in early childhood education* (pp. 108–125). Norwood: Ablex.

Goncu, A. (1989, April). *Models of social play: Towards a dialogic analysis of constructing intersubjectivity.* Paper presented at the biennial meeting of the Society for Research in Child Development, Kansas City, MO.

Gottman, J. M. (1977). Towards a definition of social isolation in children. *Child Development, 48,* 513–517.

Gottman, J. M. (1983). How children become friends. *Monographs of the Society for Research in Child Development, 48*(3, Serial No. 201).

Gottman, J. M. (1986). The world of coordinated play: Same and cross-sex friendship in young children. In J. M. Gottman & J. G. Parker (Eds.), *Conversations of friends: Speculations on affective development* (pp. 139–191). Cambridge: Cambridge University Press.

Gottman, J. M., Gonso, J., & Rasmusen, B. (1975). Social interaction, social competence and friendships in young children. *Child Development, 46,* 709–718.

Gump, P., Schoggen, P. R., Redl, F. (1963). The behavior of the same child in different milieu. In I. R. Barker (Ed.), *Stream of behavior* (pp. 169–202). New York: Meredith Publications.

Halverson, C. F., & Waldrop, M. F. (1970). Maternal behavior towards own and other preschool children: The problem of "ownness." *Child Development, 41,* 839–845.

Hartup, W. W. (1983). Peer relations. In E. M. Hetherinton (Ed.), *Handbook of child psychology: Vol 4. Socialization, personality, and social development* (pp. 103–196). New York: Wiley.

Hartup, W. W. (1989). Behavioral manifestations of children's friendships. In T. Berndt & G. Ladd (Eds.), *Peer relationships in child development* (pp. 46–70). New York: Wiley.

Hartup, W. W., Laursen, B., Stewart, M. I., & Eastenson, A. (1988). Conflict and the friendship relations of young children. *Child Development, 59,* 1590–1600.

Haskins, R. (1985). Public school aggression among children with varying day care experience. *Child Development, 56,* 698–703.

Hay, D. F. (1985). Learning to form relationships in infancy: Parallel attainments with parents and peers. *Developmental Review, 5,* 122–161.

Hazen, N., & Black, B. (1989). Preschool peer communication skills: The role of social status and interaction context. *Child Development, 60,* 867–876.

Hinde, R., & Tamplin, A. (1983). Relations between mother–child interaction and behavior in preschool. *British Journal of Developmental Psychology, 1,* 231–257.

Hinde, R. A., Titmus, G., Easton, J., & Tamplin, A. (1985). Incidence of friendship and behavior towards strong associates vs. nonassociates in preschools. *Child Development, 55,* 234–245.

Howes, C. (1983). Patterns of friendship. *Child Development, 54,* 1041–1053.

Howes, C. (1985). Sharing fantasy: Social pretend play in toddlers. *Child Development, 56,* 1253–1258.

Howes, C. (1987). Social competence with peers in young children: Developmental sequences. *Developmental Review, 7,* 252–272.

Howes, C. (1988a). Peer interaction of young children. *Monographs of the Society for Research in Child Development, 53*(1, Serial No. 217).

Howes, C. (1988b). Same and cross-sex friend: Implications for interaction and social skills. *Early Childhood Research Quarterly, 3,* 21–37.

Howes, C. (1990). Can the age of entry and quality of child care predict behavior in kindergarten? *Developmental Psychology, 26,* 292–303.

Howes, C. (in press). Social status and friendship from kindergarten to third grade. *Journal of Applied Developmental Psychology.*

Howes, C., Galluzzo, D., Hamilton, C. E., Matheson, D., & Rodning, C. (1989, April). *Social relationships with adults and peers within child care and families.* Paper presented at Society for Research in Child Development, Kansas City, MO.

Howes, C., Matheson, C., & Wu, F. (in press). In C. Howes, O. A. Unger, & C. Matheson (Eds.), *The collaborative construction of social pretend: Social pretend play functions.* Albany, NY: SUNY Press.

Howes, C., Rodning, C., Galluzzo, D., & Myers, L. (1988). Attachment and child care relationships with mother and caregiver. *Early Childhood Research Quarterly, 3,* 403–416.

Howes, C., & Stewart, P. (1987). Child's play with adults, toys, and peers: An examination of family and child care influences. *Developmental Psychology, 23,* 423–430.

Howes, C., Unger, O., & Matheson, C. (in press). *The collaborative construction of social pretend: Social pretend play functions.* Albany, NY: SUNY Press.

Howes, C., Unger, O. A., & Seidner, L. B. (1989). Social pretend play in toddlers: Parallels with social play and with solitary pretend. *Child Development, 60,* 77–84.

Howes, C., & Wu, F. (in press). Peer interactions and friendship in an ethnically diverse school setting. *Child Development.*

Hymel, S. (1983). Preschool children's peer relations: Issues in sociometric assessment. *Merrill Palmer Quarterly, 29,* 237–260.

Innocenti, M., Stowitschek, J., Rule, S., Killoran, J., Striefel, S., & Boswell, C. (1986). A naturalistic study of the relation between preschool setting events and peer interaction in four activity contexts. *Early Childhood Research Quarterly, 1,* 141–153.

Ironsmith, M., & Poteat, G. M. (in press). Behavioral correlates of preschool sociometric status and the prediction of teacher ratings of behaviors in kindergarten. *The Journal of Clinical Child Psychology.*

Johnson, J., & Ershler, J. (1981). Developmental trends in preschool play as a function of classroom program and child gender. *Child Development, 52,* 995–1004.

Kagan, J., Reznick, J. S., Clarke, C., Snidman, B., & Garcia-Coll, C. (1980). Behavior inhibition to the unfamiliar. *Child Development, 55,* 2212–2225.

Katz, L. (1985). Dispositions in early childhood education. *ERIC/EECE Bulletin, 98,* 1–3.

Kempe, K., Speranza, H., Matula, K., & Hazen, N. (1989, April). *Peer social status and discourse skills: Stability and change in the preschool years.* Paper presented at the biennial meeting of the Society for Research in Child Development, Kansas City, MO.

Krasnor, L. R., & Rubin, K. H. (1983). Preschool children's problem solving: Attempts and outcomes in young children. *Child Development, 54,* 1545–1558.

Ladd, G. W. (1985). Documenting the effects of social skill training with children: Process and outcome assessment. In B. H. Schneider, K. H. Rubin, & J. E. Ledingham (Eds.), *Children's peer relations: Issues in assessment and intervention* (pp. 243–270). New York: Springer-Verlag.

Ladd, G. W. (in press). Having friends, making friends, and being liked by peers in the classroom: Predictors of children's early school adjustment? *Child Development.*

Ladd, G., & Golter, B. (1988). Parents' management of preschooler's peer relations: Is it related to children's social competence? *Developmental Psychology, 24,* 109–117.

Ladd, G. W., Hart, C. H., Wadworth, E. M., & Golter, B. (1988). Preschoolers' peer network in nonschool settings. Relations to family characteristics and social adjustment. In S. Salzinger, M. Antrobus, & J. Hammer (Eds.), *Social networks of children, adolescents, and college students* (pp. 23–54). Hillsdale, NJ: Lawrence Erlbaum Associates.

Ladd, G. W., & Price, J. M. (1987). Predicting children's social and school adjustment following the transition from preschool to kindergarten. *Child Development, 58,* 1168–1189.

Ladd, G. W., Price, J. M., & Hart, C. H. (1988). Predicting preschoolers' peer status from their playground behaviors. *Child Development, 58,* 986–992.

La Freniere, P. J., & Sroufe, L. A. (1985). Profiles of peer competence in the preschool: Interrelations between measures, influence of social-ecology, and relations to attachment. *Developmental Psychology, 21,* 56–69.

La Freniere, P. J., Strayer, F. F., & Gauthier, R. (1984). The emergence of same-sex affiliative preferences among preschool peers: A developmental/ethological perspective. *Child Development, 55,* 1958–1965.

Lamb, M. E. (1987). The development of mother–infant and father–infant attachments in the second year of life. *Developmental Psychology, 13,* 637–648.

Lamb, M. E., Hwang, C. P., Bookstein, F. L., Broberg, A., Hult, G., & Frodi, M. (1988). Determinants of social competence in Swedish preschoolers. *Developmental Psychology, 24,* 58–70.

Lamb, M., & Nash, A. (1989). Infant–mother attachment, sociability, and peer competence. In T. J. Berndt & G. W. Ladd (Eds.), *Peer relationships in child development* (pp. 219–245). New York: Wiley.

Laursen, B., & Hartup, W. W. (1989). The dynamics of preschool children's conflicts. *Merrill Palmer Quarterly, 35,* 281–297.

Lederberg, A. R., Chapin, S. L., Rosenblatt, S., & Vandell, D. (1986). Ethnic, gender, and age preferences among deaf and hearing preschool peers. *Child Development, 57,* 375–386.

Lederberg, A. R., Rosenblatt, S., Vandell, D. L., & Chapin, S. (1987). Temporary and long term friendships in hearing and deaf preschoolers. *Merrill Palmer Quarterly, 33,* 515–534.

LeVine, R. (1977). Child rearing as cultural adaptation. In P. Leiderman, S. Tulkin, & A. Rosenfield (Eds.), *Culture and infancy* (pp. 15–27). New York: Academic.

Lewis, M., & Feiring, C. (1979). The child's social network: Social object, social functions, and their relationship. In M. Lewis & L. Rosenblum (Eds.), *The child and its family* (pp. 9–27). New York: Plenum.

Lewis, M., Feiring, C., & Kotsonis, M. (1984). The social networks of the young child. In M. Lewis (Ed.), *Beyond the dyad* (pp. 129–160). New York: Plenum.

Lieberman, A. F. (1977). Preschoolers' competence with a peer: Relations with attachment and peer experience. *Child Development, 48,* 1277–1287.

Lollis, S., & Ross, H. S. (1987, April). *Mothers' interventions in toddler-peer conflicts.* Paper presented at the biennial meeting of the Society for Research in Child Development, Baltimore.

Maccoby, E., & Martin, J. A. (1983). Socialization in the context of the family: Parent–child interaction. In P. H. Mussen (Ed.), *Handbook of child psychology* (Vol. IV, pp. 1–102). New York: Wiley.

MacDonald, K. (1987). Parent–child physical play with rejected, neglected, and popular boys. *Developmental Psychology, 23,* 705–711.

MacDonald, K., & Parke, R. (1984). Bridging the gap: Parent–child play interaction and peer interactive competence. *Child Development, 55,* 1265–1277.

Masters, J. C., & Furman, W. (1981). Popularity, individual friendship selection, and specific peer interaction among children. *Developmental Psychology, 17,* 344–350.

McGhee, P., Etheridge, L., & Benz, N. (1984). Effect of level of toy structure on preschool children's pretend play. *Journal of Genetic Psychology, 144,* 209–217.

McGrew, W. C. (1972). *An ethological study of children's behavior.* New York: Academic Press.

McLoyd, V. (1983). The effects of the structure of play objects on the pretend play of low-income preschool children. *Child Development, 54,* 626–635.

Miller, S. A. (1988). Parents' beliefs about children's cognitive development. *Child Development, 59,* 259–286.

Mueller, E. (1979). (Toddler + toys) = (An autonomous social system). In M. Lewis & L. A. Rosenblum (Eds.), *The child and its family* (pp. 169–194). New York: Plenum.

Mueller, E., & Brenner, M. (1977). The origins of social skills and interaction among playgroup toddlers. *Child Development, 48,* 854–861.

Mussatti, T. (1986). Early peer relations: The perspectives of Piaget and Vygotsky. In E. Mueller & C. Cooper (Eds.), *Process and outcome in peer relations* (pp. 25–54). New York: Academic.

Nadel, J., & Fontaine, A. M. (1989). Communicating by imitation: A developmental and comparative approach to transitory social competence. In B. H. Schneider, G. Attili, J. Nadel, & R. Weissberg (Eds.), *Social competence in developmental perspective* (pp. 131–144). Dordrecht: Kluwer.

Nadel-Brulfert, J., & Baudonniere, P. M. (1982). The social function of reciprocal imitation in two-year-old peers. *International Journal of Behavioral Development, 5,* 95–109.

Newcomb, A. F., & Bukowski, W. M. (1983). Social impact and social preference as determinants of children's peer group status. *Developmental Psychology, 19,* 856–867.

Olson, S. L., & Lifgren, K. (1988). Concurrent and longitudinal correlates on preschool peer sociometrics: Comparing rating scale and nomination measures. *Journal of Applied Developmental Psychology, 9,* 409–420.

Oppenheim, L. (1989). The nature of social action: Social competence versus social conformism. In B. H. Schneider, G. Attili, J. Nadel, & R. P. Weissberg (Eds.), *Social competence in developmental perspective* (pp. 41–70). Dordrecht: Kluwer.

Oppenheim, D., Sagi, A., & Lamb, M. (1988). Infant–adult attachments on the kibbutz and their relation to socioemotional development four years later. *Developmental Psychology, 24,* 427–433.

Parke, R. D., & Bhavanagri, N. P. (1988). Parents as managers of children's peer relationships. In D. Belle (Ed.), *Children's social networks and social supports* (pp. 241–259). New York: Wiley.

Parke, R. D., MacDonald, K. B., Beitel, A., & Bhavanagri, N. (1986). The role of the family in the development of peer relationships. In: R. J. McMahan (Ed.), *Marriages and families* (pp. 102–137). New York: Brunner.

Parker, J. G., & Asher, S. R. (1987). Peer relations and later personal adjustment: Are low-accepted children at risk? *Psychological Bulletin, 102,* 357–389.

Parker, J., & Asher, S. R. (1989, April). *Peer relations and social adjustment: Are friendship and group acceptance distinct domains?* Paper presented at the biennial meeting of the Society for Research in Child Development, Kansas City, MO.

Parker, J., & Gottman, J. (1989). Social and emotional development in a relational context: Interactions from early childhood to adolescence. In T. J. Berndt & G. W. Ladd (Eds.), *Peer relationships in child development* (pp. 95–130). New York: Wiley.

Parker-Cohen, N. Y., & Bell, R. Q. (1988). The relationship between temperament and social adjustment to peers. *Early Childhood Research Quarterly, 3,* 179–192.

Partens, M. B. (1932). Social participation among preschool children. *Journal of Abnormal Psychology, 27,* 243–269.

Pastor, D. L. (1981). The quality of the mother–infant attachment and its relationship to toddler initial sociability with peers. *Developmental Psychology, 17,* 326–335.

Pellegrini, A. D., & Perlmutter, J. C. (1989). Classroom contextual effects on children's play. *Developmental Psychology, 25,* 289–296.

Perry, J. C. (1979). Popular, amiable, isolated, rejected: A reconceptualization of sociometric status in preschool children. *Child Development, 50,* 1231–1234.

Phillips, D. A., McCartney, K., & Scarr, S. (1987). Child care quality and children's social development. *Developmental Psychology, 23,* 537–543.

Phyfe-Perkins, E. (1980). Children's behavior in preschool settings—the influence of the physical environment. In L. G. Katz (Ed.), *Current topics in early childhood education* (Vol. 3, pp. 218–231). Norwood, NJ: Ablex.

Poteat, G. M., Ironsmith, M., & Bullock, M. (1986). The classification of preschool children's sociometric status. *Early Childhood Research Quarterly, 1,* 349–360.

Pulaski, M. A. S. (1970). Play as a function of toy structure and fantasy predisposition. *Child Development, 41,* 531–537.

Putallaz, M. (1987). Maternal behavior and children's sociometric status. *Child Development, 58,* 324–340.

Putallaz, M., & Heflin, A. H. (in press). Parent–child interaction. In S. R. Asher & J. D. Coie (Eds.), *Peer rejection in childhood.* New York: Cambridge University Press.

Putallaz, M., & Wasserman, A. (1989). Children's naturalistic entry behavior and sociometric status: A developmental perspective. *Developmental Psychology, 25,* 297–305.

Quilitch, H., & Risley, T. (1973). The effects of play materials on social play. *Journal of Applied Behavior Analysis, 6,* 573–578.

Roff, M., Sells, S., & Golden, M. (1972). *Social adjustment and personality development in children.* Minneapolis: University of Minnesota Press.

Roopnarine, J. L. (1987). Social interaction in the peer group: Relationship to perceptions of parenting and to children's interpersonal awareness and problem-solving ability. *Journal of Applied Developmental Psychology, 8,* 351–362.

Roopnarine, J. L., & Field, T. (1984). Play interactions of friends and acquaintances in nursery school. In J. L. Roopnarine and & M. Segal (Eds.), *Friendships in normal and handicapped children* (pp. 81–88). Norwood, NJ: Ablex.

Rose-Krasnor, L. (1988, May). *Maternal beliefs and preschool social skill.* Paper presented at the Fifth Biennial University of Waterloo Conference on Child Development, Waterloo, Ontario.

Ross, H., & Lollis, S. (1989). A social relations analysis of toddler peer relationships. *Child Development, 60,* 1082–1091.

Rubenstein, J., & Howes, C. (1979). Caregiving and infant behavior in daycare and homes. *Developmental Psychology, 15,* 1–24.

Rubin, K. H. (1982). Non-social play in preschoolers: Necessarily evil? *Child Development, 53,* 651–657.

Rubin, K. H. (1985). Socially withdrawn children: An "at risk" population? In B. H. Schneider, K. H. Rubin, & J. E. Ledingham (Eds.), *Peer relationships and social skills in childhood: Issues in assessment and training* (pp. 125–139). New York: Springer-Verlag.

Rubin, K. H., & Clark, M. L. (1983). Preschool teachers' ratings of behavioral problems: Observational, sociometric, and social-cognitive correlates. *Journal of Abnormal Child Psychology, 11,* 273–285.

Rubin, K. H., & Daniels-Beirness, T. (1983). Concurrent and predictive correlates of sociometric status in kindergarten and grade 1 children. *Merrill-Palmer Quarterly, 29,* 337–351.

Rubin, K. H., & Krasnor, L. (1980). Changes in the play behaviors of preschoolers: A short-term longitudinal investigation. *Canadian Journal of Behavioral Sciences, 12,* 278–282.

Rubin, K. H., & Krasnor, L. R. (1986). Social-cognitive and social behavioral perspectives on problem solving. In M. Perlmutter (Ed.), *Minnesota Symposium on Child Psychology* (pp. 1–68). Hillsdale, NJ: Lawrence Erlbaum Associates.

Rubin, K. H., & Lollis, S. (1988). Origins and consequences of social withdrawal. In J. Belsky & T. Nezworski (Eds.), *Clinical implications of attachment theory* (pp. 219–252). Hillsdale, NJ: Lawrence Erlbaum Associates.

Rubin, K. H., & Mills, R. S. L. (in press). The many faces of social isolation in childhood. *Journal of Consulting and Clinical Psychology.*

Rubin, K. H., Mills, R. S. L., & Rose-Krasnor, L. (1989). Maternal beliefs and children's competence. In B. H. Schneider, G. Attili, J. Nadel, & R. P. Weissberg (Eds.), *Social competence in developmental perspective* (pp. 313–331). Dordrecht: Kluwer.

Rubin, K., Watson, K., & Jambor, T. (1978). Free-play behaviors in preschool and kindergarten children. *Child Developmental Psychology, 21,* 233–240.

Salzinger, S., Hammer, M., & Antrobus, J. (1988). *Social networks of children, adolescents and college students.* Hillsdale, NJ: Lawrence Erlbaum Associates.

Sanders, K., & Harper, L. (1976). Free-play fantasy behavior in preschool children: Relations among gender, age, season, and location. *Child Development, 47,* 1182–1185.

Schneider, B. H., Rubin, K. H., & Ledingham, J. E. (1985). *Children's peer relations: Issues in assessment and intervention.* New York: Springer-Verlag.

Scholtz, G. J. L., & Ellis, M. J. (1975). Repeated exposure to objects and peers in a play setting. *Journal of Experimental Child Psychology, 19,* 448–455.

Shantz, C. (1987). Conflicts between children. *Child Development, 58,* 283–305.

Shapiro, S. (1975). Preschool ecology: A study of three environmental variables. *Reading Improvement, 12,* 236–241.

Smilansky, S. (1968). *The effect of socioeconomic play on disadvantaged preschool children.* New York: Wiley.

Smith, P. (1978). A longitudinal study of social participation in preschool children: Solitary and parallel play reexamined. *Developmental Psychology, 5,* 517–523.

Spivack, G., & Shure, M. B. (1974). *Social adjustment of young children.* San Francisco: Jossey Bass.

Sroufe, L. A. (1983). Infant caregiver attachment and patterns of adaptation in preschool. In M. Perlmutter (Ed.), *Minnesota symposium in child psychology* (Vol. 16, pp. 41–83). Hillsdale, NJ: Lawrence Erlbaum Associates.

Sullivan, H. S. (1953). *The interpersonal theory of psychiatry.* New York: Norton.

Super, C., & Harkness, S. (Eds.). (1980). *Anthropological perspectives on child development: New directions for child development.* San Francisco: Jossey Bass.

Tessier, O., & Bovin, M. (1985, April). *The coherence of sociometric nominations and the preschooler's understanding of friendship.* Paper presented at the biennial meeting of the Society for Research in Child Development, Toronto.

Vandell, D. (1979). Effects of play group experience on mother–son and father–son interaction. *Developmental Psychology, 15,* 379–385.

Vandell, D., Henderson, V. K., & Wilson, K. S. (1988). A longitudinal study of children with daycare experiences of varying quality. *Child Development, 59,* 1286–1292.

Vandell, D. L., & Mueller, E. (1980). Peer play and friendship during the first 2 years. In H. C. Foot, A. Chapman, & J. Smith (Eds.), *Friendship and social relations in young children* (pp. 267–293). New York: Wiley.

Vandenberg, B. (1981). Environmental and cognitive factors in social play. *Journal of Experimental Child Psychology, 31,* 169–175.

Vitaro, F., Gagnon, C., & Boivin, M. (1989, April). *Multiple sources behavior correlates of stable sociometric status from kindergarten to grade one.* Paper presented at the biennial meeting of the Society for Research in Child Development, Kansas City, MO.

Washburn, R. W. (1932). A scheme for grading the reactions of children in a new social situation. *Journal of Genetic Psychology, 40,* 84–99.

Waters, E., Wippman, J., & Sroufe, L. A. (1979). Attachment, positive affect and competence in the peer group: Two studies in construct validation. *Child Development, 50,* 829.

Weisner, T. (1984). Ecocultural niches of middle childhood: A cross cultural perspective. In W. A. Collins (Ed.), *Development during middle childhood: The years from 6 to 12* (pp. 335–369). Washington, DC: National Academy of Sciences Press.

Weisner, T., & Gallimore, R. (1985). *The convergence of ecocultural and activity theory.* Paper read at the annual meeting of the American Anthropological Association, Washington, DC.

Whiting, B. (1980). Culture and social behavior: A model for the development of social behavior. *Ethos, 8,* 95–116.

Whiting, B., & Edwards, C. (1988). *Children of different worlds: The formulation of social behavior.* Cambridge, MA: Harvard University Press.

Whiting, J., & Whiting, B. (1975). *Children of six cultures: A psychocultural analysis.* Cambridge, MA: Harvard University Press.

Zimmerman, B., & Brody, G. H. (1975). Race and modeling influences on interpersonal play patterns of boys. *Journal of Educational Psychology, 14,* 591–598.

5

Development of Young Children in Stressful Contexts: Theory, Assessment, and Prevention

Robert C. Pianta
Sheri L. Nimetz
University of Virginia

Since the 1980s a number of phenomena have set the stage for school psychologists to become involved in the assessment and prevention of stressors experienced by preschool children. For example, stressors on children such as divorce, child maltreatment, and poverty have been implicated as causes of school failure. Basic research on children's stress has identified the extent to which stressful experiences are related to school outcomes such as behavioral and emotional problems, and academic failure (e.g., Pianta, Egeland, & Sroufe, 1990). Moreover, the education of preschoolers has emerged as a means of preventing failure (e.g., Pianta, 1990).

Although many practitioners readily acknowledge the detrimental effects stressors have on young children, identification and intervention programs are not strongly supported by empirical evidence. We hope to bridge the gap between research on children's stress and the needs of practitioners to ameliorate the detrimental effects of stress in their work with young children. Toward this end, we address four major themes: conceptual issues underlying the relation between stress and children's competence, empirical findings relevant to this relation, assessment of stress in preschool children, and programs of prevention and intervention for children exposed to stress.

CONCEPTUAL ISSUES

Perspectives on Stress in Developmental Contexts

Intervening with young children is currently seen as a primary means of reducing failure in the schools (e.g., Ramey, Bryant, & Suarez, 1986). We believe that

TABLE 5.1
A Framework for Environmental Developmental Relations[a]

Age	Salient Issue/ Competent Outcome	Incompetent Outcome	Adaptive Context	Maladaptive Context
0 - 3 months	Homeostasis, physiological regulation	Arrythmic, unregulated, high irritability, withdrawn	Regular, predictable management of tension, established routines, sensitive, invested, warm caretaking	Hypo/hyper stimulating, irregular responsiveness, abusive, unavailable, cold
2 - 7 months	Attachment, formation of a deep, emotional relationship with animate world, sense of basic trust	Lack of, nonaffective, or shallow involvement, autistic patterns	In love with infant, pleasurable multimodal involvement which is regular and predictable	Emotionally distant, inconsistent, impersonal, ambivalent caretaking
3 - 10 months	Somatopsychological differentiation, development of contingent, reciprocal, multisystem exchange with caretakers	Behavior and affects unrelated to each other or input, or rigid and stereotyped	Reads and responds contingently to infant's multimodal cues	Ignores or misreads infant's behaviors
10-30 months	Autonomy and exploration, mastery of object world, initiative, maintaining behavioral organization apart from caregivers	Excessive dependency, disintegration under stress, polarized affect or behavior	Encourages exploration, firm support and limit setting, teaching impulse control, respect for autonomy, structured, tolerant environment	Intrusive, overprotective, shaming. Poor role models, punitive or chaotic environment
2 - 5 years	Emerging representational capacity, move toward impulse control, peer relations, self-concept, identification	Lack of symbolic use, impulse/mood instability fragmented, undifferentiated self	Fosters internalization, organization, and differentiation. Supportive to phase appropriate regressions. Encourage use of symbols and affective expression	Restrictive, fearful of regression, misreads behavior, or engages around one mode/system. Punitive, shaming, or poor models
6 - 12 years	Extended representational capacity, self-control industry/mastery, self-concept, gender identification, same-sex "chums"	Lack of peer relations, poor coping capacity, problems with impulses, learning/self-sex concept	Appropriate peer, intellectual, and motivational stimulation. Supportive education, tolerant of autonomy	Lack of, or inappropriate stimulation, withdrawn or conflicted about emerging capacities

[a]From Greenspan and Porges (1964); Sroufe and Rutter (1984).

developing and implementing valid and useful identification procedures and intervention programs for stressed youngsters requires an appreciation of the complexity of the problems these programs attempt to prevent. If new initiatives lack adequate grounding, or are misconceived, they may yield poor evaluations and thereby deter subsequent funding efforts. Research and theory on child development provide the backdrop necessary for program development.

Recent developmental perspectives have been extremely useful in understanding the linkage between child adjustment and environments that support or inhibit adjustment (Greenspan & Porges, 1984; Sroufe & Rutter, 1984). Most developmental theorists view child competence as a function of (a) the developmental task that is appropriate for that period, (b) the child's history of adaptation to previous developmental tasks, and (c) the support provided by the environment to master competently the current task. Table 5.1 is a synthesis of models proposed by Greenspan and Porges (1984) and Sroufe and Rutter (1984). In this representation, specific developmental tasks are described, along with characteristics of environments that contribute either to adaptive or maladaptive outcomes with respect to these tasks. At each point in time the child's behavior, affect, and cognition are organized around a particular task. For example, the competent 12-month-old's behavior is organized around the task of maintaining an effective attachment relationship while exploring the environment; for the 3-year-old, behavior is organized around self-control, development of representational capacities, and mastery of the object world. The nature of the child's affective experience in meeting these developmental challenges is central to the degree to which the child's development will proceed effectively (Greenspan & Porges, 1984). For children for whom interactions with their environments raise unpleasant affects, or where affective expression is blunted or distorted, problems in development are likely to emerge.

For example, in cases of child maltreatment, the attempts of the 12-month-old child to seek assistance are often met with unpredictable anger or violence (Egeland & Sroufe, 1981). Over time, children may learn a strategy of denying their emotional needs, or may become preoccupied with concerns about safety and stability, both of which will compromise the extent to which they learn to explore their world in a secure fashion. Similarly, infants of depressed mothers learn to regulate their affect in a very constricted manner, in a sense denying their own needs for communication and reciprocity (Field et al., 1988). For young infants and preschoolers, one cannot underestimate the extent to which relationships with people and environments support or inhibit development. In a larger sense, we view the child's competence as relationally bound—that is, for the most part, young children are only as competent as their context affords them the opportunity to be. In short, young children are contextually dependent. Because young children have not internalized the psychological structures necessary for functioning more autonomously from their context, they are more vulnerable to contextual stresses and strains. The contextual dependency of preschoolers leads logically to the study of children's stress and its effect on school adjustment.

A developmental perspective suggests that periods of heightened sensitivity to certain environmental stressors may occur. For example, the literature on divorce suggests that the preschool and adolescent years are periods during which the child is especially sensitive to martial discord and breakup (Emery, 1982; Hetherington, 1989). Certainly, the preschool period is one of increased sensitivity relative to other developmental phases. In the age range from 2 to 5, children's development and competence are closely tied to the extent to which their context provides them with support for the developmental tasks of attachment, autonomy, mastery, communication, and self-control (Greenspan & Porges, 1984; Sroufe & Rutter, 1984). Environments that are structured, reciprocal, sensitive to the child's cues, and provide affectively positive stimulation support positive adaptation in the preschool years. For the preschooler, stressors that are most likely to have a strong impact are those altering the quality of affective stimulation available, those inducing changes or inconsistencies in contextual structure (e.g., rules), and those impacting the organization and structure of cognitive stimulation. Despite the myriad of possible stressors that impact children at this age, it is the way in which these stressors are mediated by interpersonal and social relationships that primarily determines the salience of their impact.

The dependence of younger children on relationships with people and environments makes it likely that the stress they experience will be the product of stress experienced by persons on whom they are dependent. For example, the single event of divorce impacts adversely the life of a preschool child. However, more important for a child's adjustment is how his or her parents (especially the custodial parent) deal with the divorce and subsequent stressors of lower income and fewer resources (Hetherington, 1989). Thus, it is important for practitioners not only to look at the experiences of the child when assessing and intervening with children's stress, but to evaluate the stresses experienced within the broader context of the people on whom the child is dependent for nurturance, structure, and stimulation.

Another important issue for understanding the effects of stress on young children is an appreciation of the linkage or connection that exists among stressors. Sameroff and Siefer (1984), in their work on low socioeconomic status (SES) and other high-risk children, have advanced the notion that psychosocial stress exists with systemic properties. Numerous environmental conditions and events that stress children are so closely linked with one another that this linkage itself is an important cause of pathology. For example, poverty is often cited as a cause of school failure for many children (Birch & Gussow, 1970). However, closer examination of children living in poverty who actually fail in school indicates that many conditions associated with poverty (i.e., single teen-age parenting, maltreatment, marital or family violence, lack of stimulation) may account for failure. Simply looking at poverty (or family violence, divorce, or parental psychopathology) will produce only a simplistic idea of who is most at risk. Moreover, when considering interventions for individuals exposed to stress, interrupting the link between a stress experience (e.g., unemployment) and subsequent stressors (e.g., marital discord, substance abuse, poverty) is a primary goal. The concept of linkage among stressors is important. The idea of creating interventions that interrupt these links also deserves attention.

Key Concepts in the Study of Children and Stress

In addition to the importance of a developmental perspective, the contextual dependency of young children, and the idea of linkage among stressors, a number of other concepts are applicable to children's stress. Among the concepts referred to frequently in the study of children and stress are the ideas of risk, vulnerability, and protective factors, as well as the distinction between stress and stressors.

Risk and Risk Research.   Risk is an epidemiological construct referring to the increased likelihood that a person (or group) will show a particular outcome of interest (e.g., psychopathology, school failure). Risk factors are events, conditions, and characteristics that increase the likelihood of attaining a particular outcome. Most of what we consider to be the salient stressors of childhood (e.g., divorce, maltreatment, parental death) are linked empirically to problem outcomes and can be considered risk factors for these outcomes.

Risk research involves longitudinal study of a group of children exposed to risk factors. This involves assessment of subsequent exposure to additional risk, stress or protective factors, and the positive or negative outcome status attained by individuals in the group (Garmezy, 1977). Risk research holds considerable promise for developing prevention and early intervention strategies. Identifying children who do well despite their risk status, and the factors distinguishing them from their peers who do not do well, are components of prevention and early intervention strategies (Rutter, 1987).

What is interesting then, to both scientists and practitioners, are the variations in individuals' responses to exposure to risk (or stress). These variations suggest how the risk situation is modified to produce positive and negative outcomes— that is, why some people cope well with particular stressors whereas others do not. Rutter (1987) has termed these positive and negative responses to risk and stress as *protective* and *vulnerability mechanisms,* respectively. For Rutter, protective mechanisms operate to ameliorate or reduce the reaction to risk, which in ordinary circumstances leads to a negative outcome. In contrast, vulnerability mechanisms intensify the reaction to stress and risk and lead to poor outcomes. Vulnerability mechanisms are similar to the concept of linkages between stressors mentioned earlier (Sameroff & Siefer, 1984) because when stress exposure causes additional stress (such as divorce leading to loss of income), a vulnerability mechanism is present in the link between these stressors. For practitioners, Rutter has identified a window of opportunity into the risk-outcome relation that affords the possibility of altering that relation. In Rutter's view, interrupting vulnerability mechanisms involves assessing not only stress exposure, but the capacity of the individual and system to respond adaptively to the stressor. Intervention can be seen as interrupting vulnerability mechanisms by promoting positive coping responses (e.g., social skill groups for children of divorce), or providing resources to stress-exposed individuals (e.g., child care for single mothers who need to work).

Stress and Stressors.   A variety of definitions of stress have guided its assessment and the interpretation of its effects. Most recent definitions of stress emphasize the interaction among a person's physiological response, characteristics of the stressful stimulus, and psychological processing of the stimulus (Lazarus, 1970).

This interactional definition of stress, which we adopt in this chapter, is based on the fact that reactions to an environmental event vary with the individual's cognitive appraisal (Derogatis, 1982). However, processes other than cognitive appraisal also have a moderating influence on a person's response to an event. For example, Egeland, Breitenbucher, and Rosenberg (1980) demonstrated that when mothers scored high on measures of anxiety, aggression, and suspiciousness, the relation between their stressful life events scores and caretaking was much higher than for mothers with low scores on these personality traits. The literature on stressful life events suggests that a comprehensive list of factors affecting the processing of a stressful event would include personality, intelligence, cognitive style, attitudes, social skills, and developmental history (e.g., Derogatis, 1982).

The interactionist position is consistent with Rutter's emphasis on the person's modification of risk situations as a means of accounting for individual variability in outcomes. The processes identified as mediators of stress in the interactionist framework (e.g., cognitive appraisal, personality, mood, social skills, developmental history) might function as protection or vulnerability mechanisms to the extent that they affect the person's response to stress. Again, for the practitioner, this suggests a number of individual and contextual processes that may be altered so that the likelihood of a positive outcome might be increased.

Summary

In considering children's stress and its detrimental effects on school adjustment, we argued that a number of conceptual issues underlie any attempt to assess or intervene in this area. A developmental perspective is necessary in terms of identifying the developmental tasks affected by stress exposure, and for appreciating the contextual dependency of young children. Moreover, developmental theorists have provided a framework for describing the child and environmental factors affecting the extent to which children master particular developmental tasks in a competent manner. Finally, concepts such as linkage between stressors, risk factors, vulnerability mechanisms, and protective factors help close the gap between theory and practice. We now review empirical evidence for the relation between stress and child adjustment.

EMPIRICAL STUDIES OF STRESS AND COPING IN THE PRESCHOOL YEARS

In this section, our goal is to review the empirical evidence for the belief that stress has a detrimental impact on child adjustment. Using an ecological perspective to classify stressors, we organize this discussion around environmental or contextual stressors, relationship-based stressors, stressors that are due to characteristics of an individual, and stressors that are due to factors present in schooling. The studies reviewed are largely descriptive and vary widely in methodological sophistication.

Environmental or Contextual Stressors

Environmental or contextual stressors primarily are present as a property of the family system, or systems external to the family (e.g., workplace, etc.). In this discussion we concentrate on the consequences of stress exposure for children and families, and the factors that appear related to positive outcomes in stress-exposed persons (i.e., protective factors). Readers may then apply these results to their own work in assessment, intervention, and prevention. Our discussion is intended as illustrative and not exhaustive.

Poverty.   Parents living below the poverty line conceive, bear, and rear children under particularly stressful conditions (Birch & Gussow, 1970; Sameroff, Seifer, Barocas, Zax, & Greenspan, 1987). Many researchers agree that poverty represents the single most negative stressor to which children are exposed (e.g., Sameroff & Chandler, 1975). The 30% increase in childhood poverty between 1979 and 1983 has hit young children hardest. For example, more than one quarter of children below age 6 are poor, infant mortality reductions slowed dramatically in the 1980s with the United States ranked last among 19 developed countries, and the Center for Disease Control reports a 69% increase in preventable cases of measles among children aged 16 months to 4 years from 1980 to 1985 (Hughes, 1988).

Public health statistics on young children in poverty highlight their need. Children reared in poverty tend to have lower birth weights, have an increased probability of death due to disease, have increased susceptibility to disease agents, receive poor prenatal care, have decreased gestational spacing, and have younger mothers (Birch & Gussow, 1970; Sameroff & Chandler, 1975). In addition, these children are at greater risk for difficulties in neurological functioning, prematurity, and malnutrition than children born and raised in nonpoverty households (Birch & Gussow, 1970; Hughes, 1988).

Poverty also stresses caretakers and households in ways that impact children's development. Parents of low income and poverty families tend to exhibit a more restrictive, punitive caretaking style, and perceive the child as a stressful burden upon their already taxed capacities (Egeland & Sroufe, 1981). Low income is associated with child abuse and neglect; social deprivation and general environmental inadequacy; maternal unresponsivity and passivity; and the child characteristics of negative mood, greater intensity, clinginess, lower cognitive functioning, and higher scores on behavior problem scales (e.g., Egeland & Sroufe, 1981; Sameroff, Seifer, & Zax, 1982).

In a study of children reared in poverty, Tonge, James, and Hillam (1975) described a disorder of lifestyle characterized by insularity, economic hardship, low social organization, adults who are marginally depressed and maladjusted, and children who, at the least, suffer from material deprivation, neglect, and lack of supervision. Mothers in these families were depressed and fathers were seen as impulsive and prone to aggression. Children had a higher mortality rate than the general population, more discipline problems, and poor academic skills. Exceptions to these patterns of development appeared to be a function of the children having positive school experiences.

Many investigators have noted that the linkage between poverty and poor child outcomes is not universal in some countries. This is largely because the effects of poverty on children are mediated by the presence or absence of stressors associated with poverty. Consequently, unlinking low income from these associated stressors has been described as a major preventive influence (Garbarino, 1982).

Social Support Versus Insularity. Investigators have distinguished between two major types of social support, emotional and instrumental, which both play a role in the amelioration of stress (Belle, 1982). Both act on different forms of stress, yet contribute to the psychological resources available in the home. For example, Belle (1982) noted that when poverty mothers were provided with material goods (instrumental support), the quality of care they were able to provide their children increased.

Engaging in and maintaining nurturing and supportive social contacts have been linked to numerous positive outcomes for children and parents in high risk samples (Crnic, Greenberg, Ragozin, Robinson, & Basham 1983; Crockenberg, 1981). Garbarino (1982) described support as links that occur whenever individuals (e.g., parents, teachers) or systems (schools, churches, families) have ongoing contacts with each other that are organized around concern for the welfare of the child. The value of social support, for caregivers or individuals under stress, appears to be in its provision of psychological or emotional resources. Conversely, obtaining transportation, needed food, clothing, or child care, is of tremendous value in shielding many caregivers (and in turn their children) from the negative impact of stress.

Isolation of a caregiver from the support of family and friends is a major stressor for children, characterized by significantly lower social contacts per day, social contacts with nonfriends such as agency representatives, and negative contacts with extended family members (Wahler, 1980). Coercive parenting and child aggression appear related directly to mothers' insularity: Lack of social support has been associated with child abuse (Pianta, Egeland, & Erickson, 1989) and marital violence (Strauss, Gelles, & Steinmetz, 1980). Conversely, parent training techniques intended to reduce coercion and aggression are most effective on days of low insularity (Wahler, Leske, & Rogers, 1979).

Unemployment.   Parental, especially paternal, unemployment is a highly visible and potent stressor on families and children. With an annual incidence rate estimated at nearly 20% of the male work force, and with most of these being younger, less experienced workers who tend to have children, it has been estimated that nearly 10 million children annually experienced some form of paternal unemployment in the early–mid 1980s (Margolis, 1982). These children are now in elementary school. More recent estimates of parental unemployment and underemployment suggest an incidence rate of between 10% and 15% (Hughes, 1988). However, there is evidence that unemployment and underemployment rates are higher in many minority groups and are concentrated in certain areas of the country (Hughes, 1988). In many schools across the country, parental unemployment and underemployment are a fact of life for the students.

Elder's studies of the Great Depression (Elder, 1974) indicate a lack of marked negative outcomes due to paternal unemployment for boys in that era as they showed increased independence and earlier heterosexual experiences. For girls, paternal unemployment resulted in greater participation in domestic activities. This reflected a reorganized family system with mothers taking a central decision-making and breadwinner role with the remainder of the family concerned with homemaking. This is an example of child outcomes to stress exposure being mediated by the adults' response to the stressor—in this case unemployment. The general conclusion of Elder's research is that these children fared rather well as adults, despite family reorganization.

Whereas during the 1930s unemployment cut across all segments of the population, in recent years unemployment occurs with much greater frequency among younger, less-skilled, less-educated, Black workers (Dooley, Catalano, Jackson, & Brownell, 1981). This sociological fact translates into unemployment being a potentially more potent stressor for afflicted individuals now than in 1930. Dooley et al. (1981) noted that unemployed workers seemed to experience greater self-blame and were likely to experience several instances of unemployment over the years. In 1989 unemployment was strongly associated with lack of education (for children and parents), homelessness, and social isolation. The alienation and segmentation of American social structure along lines of employed and unemployed (or other income-based strata) is one explanation given by some for the flourishing of alternative economies (e.g., the drug trade; Hughes, 1988).

In terms of its more direct effects on children, paternal unemployment has been associated with material deprivation (Horowitz & Wolcock, 1981), child abuse (e.g., Belsky, 1980), increased rates of parental mental health admissions (Catalano & Dooley, 1977), family violence (Strauss et al., 1980), marital discord, and depressed mood in mothers and fathers (Dooley et al., 1981). Unemployed single mothers are at increased risk for depression (Brown & Harris, 1978) and child abuse (Horowitz & Wolcock, 1981), and are at risk for their inability to meet the nurturing needs of other family members (Belle, 1982). Unemployment has been implicated as a major risk event in intergenerational cycles of poverty, poor education, and poor work skills (Birch & Gossow, 1970). Interestingly, raising children is viewed as a major stressor by women who are themselves unemployed and wanting to work (Canam, 1986).

Household Organization and Stimulation.   One stressor often overlooked on most measures of children's stress, but nevertheless one that has a strong impact on child development, is the degree of organization and structure available in the household. The dimension of household organization is also related to the extent to which the child receives developmentally appropriate stimulation for learning and cognitive development. Bradley, Caldwell, and colleagues have researched this area for the past 15 years and identified characteristics of the home environment that both underlie cognitive development and predict a range of school outcomes (Bradley, Caldwell, & Rock, 1988). Using the Home Observation for the Measurement of the Environment (HOME; Caldwell & Bradley, 1984), scales such as maternal responsivity, household organization, and provision of appropriate play materials were found to be moderately predictive of cognitive development across the preschool years and well into the primary grades. More importantly, changes in ratings on these scales correlated with improvements and decrements in intellectual test scores across the same developmental period (e.g., Bradley & Caldwell, 1976).

In a recent study, Bradley et al. (1988) analyzed the longitudinal effects of the preschool home environment on academic and behavioral adjustment in school. Their findings indicated that parental responsivity measured as early as infancy predicted classroom behavior in elementary school. Other aspects such as parental involvement in school, provision of play materials, and support for learning acted to maintain cognitive growth. These analyses indicate an interaction among phases of development, aspects of the home environment, and outcomes in school.

Neighborhood Stressors.   Although professionals who work with children readily acknowledge that living in a particular neighborhood can affect a young child, there has been little empirical work on this important influence on children. Garbarino and Sherman (1980) were among the first to document the effects of a neighborhood as a unit of analysis. In this study, neighborhoods of equivalent SES were examined for rates of child maltreatment, and then interviews were conducted with residents to establish what factors were associated with differential rates of maltreatment. The comparisons revealed the importance of informal support networks within these neighborhoods. "Safe" and "dangerous" neighborhoods were readily identified by postal carriers, children, and adult residents. The "safe" neighborhoods had reduced rates of child maltreatment and were those in which more neighborhood services were available (e.g., a recreational center) and caregivers had regular contact with one another and could count on others providing them with help in the form of transportation or child care. Interestingly, these networks were apparent to visitors and residents despite the equivalent poverty of the neighborhoods.

Relationship Stressors

Death of a Parent.   Parental death produces an unalterable and dramatic shift in caretaking resources requiring extensive reorganization and adaptation. According to Bowlby (1980) the presence of a warm, nurturant caretaker is the central means by which the child develops a sense of self and competence in interpersonal relationships. Disruption to that relationship, and the experience of loss due to death, places the child in a state of vulnerability.

In his book entitled *Loss,* Bowlby (1980) recounted the effects on the attachment behavior system that occur when a child loses a parent to death. Bowlby described the short-term effect of loss as one of disorganization in which the child's attachment behaviors (proximity-seeking when distressed, exploration when secure) are not organized around interaction with a central attachment figure. The task for the child and remaining caregivers becomes one of affording the child the opportunity to organize these behaviors around a new attachment figure. Bowlby described a number of cases in which the child is able to reorganize attachment behaviors around a new figure and move on with subsequent developmental tasks. This occurs when the surviving caregiving environment is supportive, available, responsive, structured, and gives the child accurate information regarding the loss of the parent. In pathogenic surviving environments, the remaining caregiver may be unavailable or depressed, the child may believe he or she was the cause of the parent's death, or the child may be exposed to additional stressors. Main and Solomon (1986) have identified a specific attachment classification that corresponds to children experiencing some form of trauma in the attachment relationship. These children are described as having disorganized attachments in which multiple behavioral systems (e.g., approach and avoidance) are simultaneously activated in response to the caregiver. When separated from parents in the strange situation (a procedure for assessing child–parent attachment in which children are separated from their parents in the presence of a stranger), children with disorganized attachments often look depressed or confused as infants, and in later years adopt a controlling or passive stance.

Epidemiological research indicates that bereavement does not always have long-term negative consequences for children (Van Eedewegh, Bieri, Parilla, & Clayton, 1982). Bereaved children and matched controls selected randomly from an urban population were interviewed at 1 and 13 months postbereavement concerning their perceptions of death, school and home behavior, and psychiatric symptoms. The bereaved children showed marked signs of behavioral disturbance for both follow-up assessments including grief reactions, sadness, irritability, depressive symptoms, and school behavior problems. However, there was also a decrease in the overall frequency of negative signs over the time period reviewed. The children's reactions suggest a general trend of marked short-term behavioral deviance and diminishing overt reactions to parental death.

Parental loss may also have negative effects if it results in prolonged maternal depression. Depressed mothers have been described as inadequate in their caretaking skills and interactive behavior, promoting an environment characterized by hostility and rejection, or lack of regulation (Orvaschel, Weissman, & Kidd, 1980). Children exposed to this caretaking pattern in depressed mothers have themselves been described as having more depressive symptoms and behavior problems (Orvaschel et al., 1980).

Marital Relationships.   Belsky (1984) claimed that the marital relationship serves as the principal support system for parents in their development of caretaking skills. Overt discord, violence, or lack of support between spouses or partners can be major stressors for young children. Low support or emotional tension in the marital dyad is associated with less affectionate and sensitive, and more punitive and restrictive parenting styles (Crnic, Greenberg, Ragozin, Robinson, & Basham, 1983). Spousal violence is associated with authoritarian and restrictive parenting styles, and child abuse within the immediate family (Strauss et al., 1980). Moreover, boys who have witnessed spousal violence have elevated incidence of abusing their own spouses and children when they become husbands and fathers (Rosenbaum & O'Leary, 1981).

Discord.   Most authors (e.g., Block, Block, & Gjerde, 1986; Emery, 1982) concluded that discord, not divorce or separation, is the marital variable having the greatest effect on children's competence. Marital discord has been linked with aggression and acting out behavior in boys (Rutter et al., 1975) and difficulties with sexual and social development in girls (Hetherington, 1989). Rutter et al. (1975) noted that antisocial behavior in boys was linked to broken homes due to lack of appropriate role models and inadequate socialization processes.

In a unique, prospective study on the effects of parental divorce versus discord, Block, Block, and Gjerde (1986) examined the effects of predivorce family arrangements on socioemotional development. Their results showed that conditions prior to divorce accounted for differences between children of divorced and intact families. In particular, boys were more vulnerable to parental discord and unavailability. These results confirmed findings from a poverty sample reported by Pianta, Egeland, and Hyatt (1986). They found that children of mothers with a history of chronic relationship instability and discord were initially indistinguishable from a control group. However, they became progressively less and less competent, and at school age these children were clearly less well adjusted than control subjects.

Single-Parent Families. The conditions associated with raising a child alone, one product of separation or divorce, put significant strain on personal, financial, and emotional resources, especially when they occur during the years in which the child is most needful of caretaking (Belle, 1982). The stresses of single parenthood become even worse when combined with poverty or insularity.

Hetherington (1989) summarized literature on divorce noting that middle-lcass, single parents who were recently divorced found child care particularly taxing and stressful, especially with their sons, and tended to be more angry, restrictive, punitive, and less structured in household operations than control parents. In poverty samples, single parenting is associated with poor child outcomes, but this association disappears after controlling for income (Munroe, Boyle, & Offord, 1988). Weissman, Leaf, and Bruse (1987) noted that single and married mothers are very similar on many psychological and social functioning variables except when there are large financial differences between them.

Single parents tend to be more isolated from the benefits of social support (Belle, 1982; Tonge et al., 1975; Wahler, 1980), exacerbating the taxing effect of raising children alone. This isolation of single-parent families is associated with child abuse in some populations (Garbarino, 1982), and parental health risks such as heart disease (Belle, 1982).

Divorce. Almost all children experience divorce as painful and show some type of short-term effects. These effects include lowered self-esteem, anger toward the custodial and noncustodial parent, decreased school adjustment and achievement, self-deprecation and blame, increased dependency on teachers and custodial parents, and increased depressive mood and acting out behavior (e.g., Emery, 1982; Hetherington, 1989).

Whereas the short-term consequences of divorce are primarily the product of the marital separation, the long-term consequences are a function of the quality of postdivorce relations between the parents and with their children (Hetherington, 1989). In fact, for some families, divorce or separation is a positive action perceived with relief and hope for positive change. Divorce can precipitate the stress of raising a child in a single-parent family, downward drift in terms of occupational and social status, decreased social support and income, parenting a child dealing with parental loss, and battles over custody and visitation. Furthermore, these potential outcomes of divorce have been associated with greater home disorganization, diminished quality and quantity of adult attention and caretaking, lack of role models, and custodial parent experiences of anxiety, helplessness, depression, and family discord (e.g., Hetherington, 1989).

Child Maltreatment.   It is important to identify the different forms of child maltreatment. Although traditionally attention is focused on acts of physical or sexual abuse, for many children these are not the most detrimental experiences. Most researchers recognize at least four forms of maltreatment: physical abuse, sexual abuse, physical neglect, and emotional neglect. Common across each form of maltreatment is a negative psychological effect (Garbarino & Vondra, 1987). In fact, Garbarino and Vondra (1987) suggest the term *psychological maltreatment* as a construct describing the psychological effects of all forms of maltreatment. School psychologists should understand each type of maltreatment, because the consequences for children can be equally devastating for the more unseen forms (e.g., neglect).

Erickson, Egeland, and Pianta (1989) tracked the consequences of four different forms of maltreatment (physical abuse, neglect, psychological unavailability, and sexual abuse) from birth through the first grade in a poverty sample. Physically abused children, as opposed to those who were well cared for, functioned poorly on a variety of assessments. At 18 months they were overrepresented among anxiously attached children, and at 24 months they were angry and noncompliant when interacting with their mothers. By 42 months they showed low self-esteem, poor self-control, were less effective problem solvers, and did not use their mothers as an effective resource. In preschool these children remained negativistic, angry, noncompliant, and hostile toward peers. These children were more aggressive and noncompliant in the primary grades (compared to controls) and had poor peer relations and problems with attention and academic achievement in the classroom. Approximately 50% of the physically abused children were referred for special education by the end of first grade.

A mother's emotional and psychological availability and involvement with her child were also shown to have enormous consequences for the child's development. Erickson et al. (1989) documented the progressive decline in competence during the preschool years that is associated with psychologically unavailable caregiving. Unavailable mothers were unresponsive and passively rejecting toward their children. They did not appear to display pleasure when interacting with their child nor did they respond positively to the child's attempts to elicit nurturance. Although these mothers met the child's physical needs, they did not appear to desire emotional involvement with their children. They failed to comfort the child in times of emotional distress and appeared depressed.

All of the children of psychologically unavailable mothers were anxiously attached at 18 months (86% anxious avoidant). At 24 months, when compared to children receiving adequate care, these children were angry, noncompliant, frustrated, and showed a marked decline in intelligence test scores. By 42 months they were less persistent and enthusiastic than controls, noncompliant, negativistic, and avoidant of their mothers. In preschool they had problems relating to adults and peers and were poor problem solvers. Generally, these children showed declines in functioning through 42 months, which exceeded those of the physically abused group. Once they reached school, however, this relative decline slowed. In the first 2 years of school, children of psychologically unavailable mothers were very similar to children who were physically abused. They were unpopular, noncompliant, aggressive, and had difficulty attending to academic work. Nearly 50% of this group was referred for special education by the end of the first grade.

Interestingly, it was the children of neglectful mothers who were the least competent in school. These children were exposed to chronic lack of material resources for the preschool period. In addition, their mothers were less intelligent than the mothers in the other maltreatment groups and their caretaking environments were characterized as unhealthy, unsafe, and lacking in supervision or stimulation. As with the other maltreatment groups, relative to controls, these children were insecurely attached at 12 and 18 months, performed poorly in problem-solving tasks with their mothers at 24 and 42 months, and were characterized by a lack of persistence, motivation, positive affect, or enthusiasm. In kindergarten and first grade, they were profoundly maladjusted. Socially, these children were rejected and unpopular, they displayed a mixture of aggression and withdrawal, and lacked social skills necessary to engage peers competently. They responded to teachers with a similar lack of skill, displaying a marked maladaptation to academic and pre-academic tasks. The neglected children were observed to lack persistence, attentiveness, or motivation, often simply wandering around the room aimlessly. Of these children, 80% had been referred for special education by the end of the first grade.

Erickson et al. (1989) also studied the effects of sexual abuse on children. Eleven children (9 girls and 2 boys) were identified when they were 5 years old as having been sexually abused within the last year. The experiences of these children all involved coerced sexual contact with an older male. The sexually abused children tended to come from homes in which the mother was highly stressed, often by a violent male partner or her own psychopathology. Adult supervision was low, and the ability of the mothers of this group of children to protect their children was questionable. The sexually abused children showed marked extremes in behavior in school. Individually, they would fluctuate from extreme aggression to marked passivity and dependence. Nearly all were characterized by extreme anxiety and marked dependence on adults. They all performed poorly on academic tasks and half were referred for special education by the end of first grade.

A child's age is a major factor influencing the occurrence and effects of child maltreatment. Steele (1987) noted that the likelihood of maltreatment is considerably higher for preschool than school-age children and adolescents. Preschool children are also just beginning to form models of the self and world and remain dependent on the smaller social network of the family, especially parents. For preschool children, maltreatment within the family may have the doubly negative effect of producing psychological disturbance in the child, which in turn impedes the child's ability to form more positive relationships with adults or peers.

Parental Deviance.   Parental psychological disorder is a major stressor for children due to possible genetic transmission and effects on the psychosocial environment (e.g., Field et al., 1988; Orvashel et al., 1980). A variety of studies have focused on the quality of caretaking provided by a deviant parent. Depressed parents have been shown to create a more hostile and rejecting home environment for their children than controls (Orvaschel et al. 1980). Sameroff et al. (1982) suggested that children of neurotic, depressed parents are at greater risk for psychological and social problems than children of schizophrenic parents. Children of depressed parents in their study demonstrated more bizarre and depressed behavior and less cooperation in interaction with parents at 30 months than controls or children of schizophrenics. Sameroff et al. concluded that it was the affective nature of parental deviance that accounted for deviant child outcomes. These conclusions concerning clinically depressed parents are very similar to those of the psychologically unavailable parents discussed earlier, and emphasize the importance of emotionally involved caretaking. Data on the importance of emotionally involved caretaking suggest that contextual stressors such as unemployment or poverty, which affect a parent's level of emotional resources, may also have effects on child outcomes.

Peer Rejection.   Although many of the child stressors discussed previously can be mediated by the parent–child relationship, it is important also to recognize the role of peer relations as the child approaches school age. There is no question that peer-based stressors are often the product of the child's maladjustment due to previous exposure to stressors (e.g., child maltreatment), which are carried forward into new relationships (Sroufe, 1983). In turn, peer relations then take on meaning as additional stressors in these children's lives. This is a clear example of the kind of linking or chaining that occurs for most stressed children, in which previous exposure to stress leads to exposure to new stressors. For this reason, the transition to peer contexts may be a critical juncture for intervention aimed at unlinking this chain and establishing a new trajectory of development.

Without intervention, incompetence in peer relations is a highly stable factor in children's lives as early as the preschool years, and can predict many negative future outcomes (Ladd, Price, & Hart, 1988). Conversely, when adults intervene to guide, but not direct, young children's peer relations, chances are greater that these children will form better relations in the future. Sroufe's (1983) data on the preschool adjustment of maltreated children are strongly supportive of the fact that there will be continuity in the types of relations formed by stressed children between parents and peers. Sroufe's (1983) data also suggested that new relationships with teachers and well-adjusted peers can begin to counteract some of these earlier models of the self and the world, which may improve the child's adjustment.

Child and Adult Characteristics

Conditions in children such as illness and developmental problems are additional sources of childhood stress. Characteristics of adults, such as psychopathology, may also be stressors. Again, evidence is strong that individual child or adult characteristics are stressors on the child to the extent that they negatively impact caretaking.

Child Illness and Developmental Problems.   There are a large number of illnesses and developmentally related problems that impact children and families (Yogman & Brazelton, 1987). Our brief focus on this area of stress will highlight a limited sample of such problems.

The presence of a severe anomaly at birth is a particularly potent stressor for the infant and family. There is a clear indication that these factors, from a probabalistic point of view, are risk factors for a large number of negative outcomes. Infants and young children with cerebral palsy, myleomenigocele, and cystic fibrosis, for example, have been shown to have increased prevalence of insecure attachments, difficulty with interactional patterns with caregivers, problems in learning social cues and skills, and difficulty establishing a sense of autonomy and mastery (e.g., Blacher & Meyers, 1983; Marvin & Pianta, 1989). In addition children having physical and developmental impairments are more often socially isolated in school and reported by teachers as displaying poor work attitudes. These child outcomes are usually a function of how well the parent(s) copes with the child's handicap and the level of resources and assistance available to the family.

Data from studies of premature children and children with temperamental variation converge with the findings on physiological and developmental handicapping conditions, although risk in these latter populations is measurably smaller for some outcomes. Other conditions being equal, risk from prematurity or temperament is somewhat elevated for certain problems. For example, children with shy or irritable characteristics tend to have difficulty in social relations and premature children may show some developmental lags behind their chronological age peers. However, the majority of the variance in most outcomes appears largely due to SES (Ramey et al., 1986; Sameroff & Chandler, 1975), family stability, and parent–child interaction patterns (Feiring, Fox, Jaskir, & Lewis, 1987; Field et al., 1988).

Finally, children with other life-threatening or serious illnesses (i.e., cancer, epilepsy, and diabetes) show some elevated risk for problem outcomes, with the magnitude of individual risk being dependent on a number of mediating factors. For the vast majority of cases in which child illness, handicap, or physical deviance plays a role in development, there have been beneficial effects cited for the presence of social support networks (e.g., Feiring et al., 1987). The more risk, the more support is needed to achieve an equivalent outcome (Crockenburg, 1981).

School-Based Stressors for the Preschool Child

We believe that school professionals should take note of the extent to which educational factors play a role in increasing the vulnerability of stressed children. Many children in preschool programs are in school because of past stress exposure. Therefore these first educational experiences can introduce demands for which they may not have competencies.

We know that the transition to school can be a major stressor due to problems in separation (Erickson & Pianta, 1989). Moreover, for many stressed children the school context is dramatically different than the home context. Schedules, dealings with peers, task demands, and press for increased autonomy are just some of the contextual shifts that may occur and for which the stressed child will need support (Alexander & Entwistle, 1988; Katz, 1988). Data from the Beginning School Study strongly suggest that this initial transition to school is a critical factor in determining a developmental trajectory that will constrain or enhance academic progress (Alexander & Entwistle, 1988).

Other issues may increase risk among these children. The first issue focuses on the need for a well-trained cadre of personnel able to program and interact successfully with these children and families (Kontos & Dunn, 1989). Simply taking the fragmented and differentiated special services often present in most elementary schools and extending them downward to even younger, more needy children, is likely to replicate and intensify the problems already present in delivering these professional services (e.g., Gartner & Lipsky, 1987).

The focus on academic outcomes is also likely to increase failure unless attention is paid to the developmental processes from which academic attainment normally grows (Katz, 1988). For most children, motivation to academically achieve, the ability to sit and concentrate on a task, to solve problems, and to plan, are prerequisites for success on more purely academic tasks. These dispositions build naturally out of a matrix of social interactions with competent adults and peers in which the child experiences both a sense of personal worth and security and a challenge to his or her current level of competence. As we know from the review of child stressors, this social matrix is extremely fragile and often maladaptive.

The first goal of preschool education for stressed children must be to enrich and stabilize this matrix. Preschool practices and policies that emphasize academics, alienate parents, and neglect the need for stability and acceptance in social relationships are likely to increase risk. In contrast, those that reach out to parents, stabilize student–teacher relationships for longer than 1 year, and emphasize nonrejecting discipline practices are examples of policies and practices that may reduce risk (Erickson & Pianta, 1989).

Summary

There is considerable empirical evidence that stressful environmental conditions and events can have a negative impact on child development in the preschool years. Moreover, individual child characteristics as well as factors reflective of the school environment can also mitigate against school success. Because of the critical nature of the transition to school, especially for children from stressful environments (Alexander & Entwistle, 1988), it is important to examine the extent to which schools can play a role in reducing the cycle of stress and poor outcome (vulnerability mechanisms). In the next major section of this chapter we review literature on assessment and intervention practices that show promise for reversing the stress–poor school outcome cycle.

IDENTIFICATION AND INTERVENTION PRACTICES

As we have stated, stress for young children occurs in and around the family and its relationships. For identification and intervention actions to be effective, they must be delivered in a fashion that is accessible, available on need, and salient for the recipients; the agents of change also need to be viewed as part of the relational context (Erickson, 1989). Traditional assessment and intervention practices are limited in the extent to which they can deal with stressors in natural contexts because they require documentation of failure before delivery, are usually available only in the school itself, and are often concerned primarily with narrow scope academic goals.

We believe efforts that enhance child competence and prevent behavioral and emotional difficulties can save time and resources in the intervention process and encourage school professionals to redesign traditional intervention strategies (Roberts & Peterson, 1984). Cost–benefit analyses indicate that for every $1 invested in early intervention, there is a $3 reduction in long-term educational costs (Berreuter-Clement, 1984). The resolution for increasing preventive efforts in education adopted by the National Association of School Psychologists (Advocacy for Appropriate Educational Services, 1985) signals a shift from intervening to manage already existent and defined problems to providing more diffuse, indirect services (Graham, 1987). Unfortunately most school psychologists do not identify preventive activities as part of their role (Zins & Forman, 1988). In a stressed service delivery system, and in light of the growing dissatisfaction with special education service delivery, preventive services demand consideration as a viable alternative to prevailing models of intervention (Gartner & Lipsky, 1987; Pianta, in press).

Prevention Versus Remediation

Although services lie on a continuum from prevention to remediation (Keogh, Wilcoxen, & Bernheimer, 1986), it is still useful to distinguish between them. The literature on prevention describes three levels: primary, secondary, and tertiary.

Primary Prevention.   Primary prevention efforts aim at reducing the incidence of a particular problem in the population. Examples of primary prevention in the schools include curriculum in social-cognitive problem solving to enhance children's coping and social skills (Elias & Clabby, in press; Spivack & Shure, 1974; Weissberg, 1985), and educational programs designed for children to decrease the incidence of sexual abuse (Tharinger et al., 1988).

Primary prevention work involves the reconceptualization of school psychologists' roles (Zins, Conyne, & Ponti, 1988). A focus on providing services to specific groups and populations rather than only to individuals is characteristic of this work. Services are not offered on the basis of individualized eligibility formulas. Finally, Zins, Conyne, and Ponti (1988) pointed out that school psychologists function in both indirect (consultative) and direct capacities in primary prevention efforts, such as leading social skills training groups or running parent support groups, teaching developmental guidance curricula to teachers, or providing leadership in the design and administration of preventive actions. The strategies of primary prevention (education, community organization and systems interventions, competency promotion, natural caregiving, and consultation and collaboration) identified by Zins et al. (1988), provide a focus for specific action by school personnel.

Secondary Prevention.   Secondary prevention programs aim intervention at particular groups of a population who have the highest likelihood of experiencing a target outcome (a high-risk group). Secondary prevention involves early identification and treatment of problems before they develop into handicapping or debilitating conditions (Keogh et al., 1986). Individuals are identified for secondary prevention in two ways: by manifesting early signs of later dysfunction, or by being members of a high-risk group that has an elevated likelihood of developing the dysfunction but as yet shows no signs of problems (Pianta, 1990). Examples of secondary prevention in the schools include group counseling for children from recently divorced families to reduce potential behavioral problems (Pedro-Carroll & Cowen, 1985), academic tutorial programs for students who are beginning to fail (Shapiro, 1988), and prekindergarten programs for children from low income or culturally disadvantaged families who may be unprepared for entering school.

Most preschool education programs fit the description of secondary prevention as they work with groups of children most likely to experience problems in school. However, the academic focus of the programs often diverts attention from social and ecological factors affecting the child. Again, even in preschool programs where prevention is an emphasis, the ecological considerations identified in our discussion of stress on the young child suggest that for a preschool program to be truly comprehensive and maximize its preventive impact, addressing the stressors in the child's life needs to be a program component.

Tertiary Prevention. Tertiary prevention consists of remedial efforts designed to prevent further deterioration in individuals with a specified problem. Tertiary prevention is the most common form of formal intervention services delivered in the public schools. Special education as it now exists in the schools uses a tertiary prevention or remedial model for service delivery because the documentation of disability or failure is the mechanism by which individuals gain access to services (Pianta, 1990). As we know, many children identified for special education programs fail in school due in large part to exposure to the kinds of stresses already discussed. We believe the disability/failure focus of eligibility rules and intervention in these programs obscures the ecological and developmental dimensions that are necessary in understanding and helping these children.

Assessing the Preschool Child Vulnerable to Stress

There are a multitude of stressors to which preschool children are exposed. Whether exposure to a stressor results in pathology depends on mediating vulnerability and protective mechanisms that determine the response to stress. It is in this intermediate process, characterized by links to new and often more debilitating stressors or to supportive resources, that assessment and intervention or prevention activities of the school play a role.

What do these vulnerable children look like in school? These are children whose matrix of social experiences has not contributed to a sense of basic trust in a safe, nurturing, and regulated environment (Erickson & Pianta, 1989). Vulnerable children are not likely to have interacted on a frequent basis with structured learning materials. Consequently, they may appear to have motivational, attentional, social, or skill deficits, and appear to be rather unregulated behaviorally.

It is not useful to view these children as deficient, but rather to understand their behavior as the best available response by an organism under stress. For most vulnerable children, their behavior represents a good "fit" or adaptation to the context in which they spend the most time. They represent a challenge to schools simply because the school environment is different for them and places new and, in many cases, unreasonable demands upon them. Appropriate assessment must identify the environmental, child, and relational processes involved in the adaptation process and predict whether these will serve the child well in school.

Traditional assessment techniques do an excellent job of describing one aspect of the adaptational system: the child's intellectual and academic skills and abilities. Assessment and identification practices need to be expanded to assess characteristics of the environment and relationships as well. These might include measures of parent–child interaction, social support available for parents, family stress, and peer relations.

Environmental Measures. Strong support exists for the use of environmental or contextual measures in identification of at-risk individuals. For example, Sameroff et al. (1987) describe a 30-point IQ difference for high-risk and nonrisk children using strictly environmental variables (e.g., parental education, social support). Pianta and Ball (in press) used an interview to assess levels of parental support. Mothers (and fathers) were asked to identify the persons who they felt they could talk to and feel understood, or someone who offered help. The number of persons listed, and how frequently they were in contact with the parents (daily, weekly, monthly), was coded. The score reflecting the total number of persons listed as supportive, obtained at school entry, added significant incremental validity to the prediction of kindergarten teachers' ratings of behavioral and academic competence, especially for boys and low SES children.

Interview and questionnaire techniques can yield rich data concerning the environment. In most preschool screening procedures there are questions regarding family income, educational level, household size, and so on. These can form the basis of a family demographic measure for identification of risk families. In addition, it is also possible to include, usually in interview form, a measure of parental emotional and instrumental support (Pianta & Ball, in press), and a measure of recent stressful life events (e.g., Egeland et al., 1980).

A variety of social support measures developed recently have been used widely with families with a handicapped or chronically ill child (e.g., Kazak, Reber, & Carter, 1988). These measures can be either interview based or in questionnaire form and involve the parent identifying persons who provide them with emotional or instrumental support, and the frequency with which they see these persons. In evaluation of social support for the purpose of subsequent intervention or referral, some measure of the recipient's perceived satisfaction is important because many families with chronically ill or handicapped children report being stressed by the number of support personnel providing services to their child and family (Kazak & Marvin, 1984).

The Parenting Stress Index (PSI, Abidin, 1983) is one example of a questionnaire designed to capture these factors, as well as information about family relationships. As a predictive indicator of risk, the PSI has been validated in a number of studies of school outcomes, and its usefulness as a screening tool for risk has been supported (Abidin, 1983). A measure of family social and demographic variables should include basic demographic information, information on family social networks (number of support figures and frequency of contact with them), and stressful experiences that have occurred within the family in the past 12 months (Egeland et al., 1980). It is most useful for the school professional to spend time individually with each family and go over these areas with them, whether in a semistructured interview or in a follow-up discussion after a questionnaire has been completed. In our experience, the more individual time spent with a family, the more likely they are to confide and trust in the professional.

The HOME (Bradley et al., 1988) is another example of a measure of environmental characteristics. This instrument has versions for infancy, preschool, and elementary school students and requires the assessor to obtain data during a home visit. The scale itself is a series of yes/no items reflecting dimensions such as parental involvement, organization of the home, and quality of stimulation available for the child. The assessor asks several broad questions of the caregiver concerning the activities involved in a usual day and elicits information for relevant items using probe questions. The assessor also makes observations of the physical environment and any social interaction that occurs between the caregiver and child. This instrument has been widely used in research on cognitive development and school success and is well validated (e.g., Bradley et al., 1988).

Life event scales are the most popular tools used to assess adult and child stress. Life event researchers have defined stressful life events as any events requiring adaptation on the part of the person. Thus any event can be experienced as stressful. Most life event scales consist of a list of items varying in their degree of stressfulness. Respondents indicate whether they have experienced each item within the past 6 or 12 months. Usually these endorsements are summed or subjected to a weighting procedure to assign a total score to the individual. Research on these scales indicates that simply summing item endorsements is as useful as complex weighting schemes (Derogatis, 1982). Although these checklists are used frequently in research, they have been less useful in practice. Most researchers and clinicians agree that a semistructured interview is more useful, in which respondents are asked questions corresponding to the life event scale items and are probed regarding their subjective experience of the event (Egeland et al., 1980). Several of these checklists have been developed for children, although they are not usable with children younger than 8 or 9 (Coddington, 1972). With younger children, assessment of the parent's stressful experiences is recommended.

Relationship Measures. A major source of stress on children comes from family relationships, either between parents, or parent and child. The prevention-oriented school psychologist may view these as important components of assessment, and will feel comfortable in broaching these issues with families.

A growing body of literature suggests that observations of family interaction patterns may provide unique and useful data for the identification of high-risk children and families. Observations of parent–child interaction in problem-solving and attachment paradigms have been predictive of preschool and school competence (Pianta et al., 1990; Pianta, Smith, & Reeve, 1991; Stroufe, 1983). These assessment activities are designed to be appropriate for the child's developmental status. A standard laboratory paradigm is set up to observe interaction in these tasks, and the participants' behavior is rated on scales designed to capture dimensions of interest at that age. For example, Pianta et al. (1986) reported on a series of four problem-solving tasks, completing a block tower, a matrix sorting task, a word categorization task, and a fine motor task, in which the parent was instructed to help the child in whatever way she felt necessary. Observations of the child's compliance and positive affect and the mother's support and quality of instruction were predictive of teachers' ratings of the child's behavior in kindergarten. Similarly, Pianta et al. (1991) used a block tower and word categorization task to screen 360 parents and children at kindergarten entry and found significant relations between parent and child competence in interaction and teachers ratings of the children in the classroom. For young children, these parent–child interaction measures provided data on the child's functioning in an important developmental context, and informed the school professional regarding the expectancies, beliefs, feelings, and behaviors that the child may transfer to the classroom context.

Interview data can also be obtained from parents regarding their own relationships. However, success in obtaining interview data depends on the school psychologist being comfortable in the interviewer role, and viewing the information to be provided by the parent as important. Data regarding whether a spouse or partner is a source of support, or if conflicts are present that interfere with child rearing, can be obtained in a fashion that normalizes the response, yet elicits important information. Obtaining such information makes it possible for the school professional to refer the parent for appropriate services, thereby serving as a link to supportive resources. Most importantly, the process of obtaining this information requires building trust between the parent and school professional, and can serve as the beginning of a supportive relationship.

Summary

A number of assessment techniques exist that make it possible to obtain information regarding a child's experience of stress and the vulnerability or protective mechanisms operating in the child's life. For preschool children, these techniques most often involve collecting data from parents, or directly observing parent–child interaction. Using these data sources well requires the school psychologist to be comfortable in working with parents, and to enter the family ecosystem in a supportive manner. Finally, it is the overriding goal of these assessment techniques to create a picture of the relational context in which the child is developing.

Schools as Protective Mechanisms for Preschool Children: Strategies for Prevention and Intervention

There is a growing body of literature on children who have been exposed to stress but do not subsequently exhibit vulnerabilities. These studies are the result of the recent interest in stress-resistant and invulnerable children. Garmezy, (1984) in summarizing this literature, identified three factors that are repeatedly associated with positive outcomes in stress exposed children. These are: (a) positive personal characteristics of the child (sociability, even-tempered, intelligent), (b) a supportive relationship with an adult or older peer (e.g., teacher, parent, sibling), and (c) an extended social network that supports the child's efforts to cope with stress (e.g., involvement between school and home, community groups, church). These factors moderate the effects of stress exposure by interrupting the link between initial exposure to stress or risk conditions and subsequent exposures to additional stressors. By interrupting this link and introducing new links to supportive elements, these factors divert developmental trajectories that otherwise would be directed toward negative outcomes.

We view the preventive efforts of school professionals and educational policies as formal efforts toward building these types of protective mechanisms. In a review of 18 longitudinal experimental studies on preschool education programs for disadvantaged children, sustained child and family participation was found to enhance success in child-centered and family-focused programs (Ramey et al., 1986). Clearly, these programs can succeed, and much of their success represents intentional enhancement of positive child characteristics, building of supportive adult–child relationships, and creating supportive social networks. Through intentional enhancement of these three factors, schools can begin to operate as protective mechanisms. Several promising avenues for intervention are reviewed in the paragraphs that follow.

Advocacy and Attitude Change.   For school psychologists to function preventively, it is important that they see prevention within the nature and breadth of their professional role. The present service delivery system in schools is based primarily on a special education model, which is set in motion by failure and focuses on diagnosing, labeling, and providing remedial services to individual children (Gartner & Lipsky, 1987). Interventions to promote mental health and competence before failure are rarely provided, nor are services that involve and support the child's family (Cowen, 1980). With a growing number of preschool-age children exposed to increasingly debilitating stressors, prevention is a viable and productive alternative for school psychologists (Pianta, 1990). Having prevention as a goal, emphasis on assessment, diagnosis, and remediation of dysfunction is shifted to an emphasis on families, environments, and indirect services. The initial preventive activity for the psychologist becomes convincing other educators within the system to attenuate the special education mindset and consider alternative intervention and prevention strategies. Working toward this type of attitude change is an active preventive effort. Its goal is the organization of resources and system-level commitment to the task, without which the school psychologist's efforts at prevention will be less effective.

Within Garmezy's three protective mechanisms, attitude change on the part of psychologists in schools contributes to a system that supports children's coping efforts. The need for working to counter the special education mindset, especially in the preschool years, is supported by data indicating that educators can easily identify family and environmental stressors producing risk in children, yet do not view intervention or prevention actions addressing these stressors as part of their role or the school's role (Pianta & Nimetz, 1989).

Finally, children's efforts to cope with stress and adversity are reinforced by the broader social network (Garmezy, 1984), and community policies are important parts of these networks (Garbarino, 1982). School psychologists have a role in influencing community and national policies that support children and families, such as funding for quality and affordable day care. At the local level this may involve community organizing activities in which the psychologist assists in unifying professionals and community members to influence policy decisions. Legislative lobbyists at the state and national level can work to create policy initiatives that support preventive interventions. Recent efforts by school psychologists to abolish corporal punishment in the schools are an excellent example of the extent to which school psychologists, through influencing community policies, can work to increase the role of the school as a protective mechanism.

Educational Strategies.   Educational strategies are designed to transmit information to children, teachers, and/or parents, and influence subsequent attitudes or behaviors. School psychologists can be involved in educational strategies that prevent stress exposure in several ways: (a) they may help teachers or schools design and implement developmentally appropriate curricula to be used with children in the classroom, (b) they may provide instruction and training to teachers, parents, or administrators, and (c) they may themselves provide education or training directly to children. These various roles may be illustrated by school psychologists' involvement in programs to prevent child sexual abuse, a problem that is often dealt with using an educational approach.

Over the past 10 years, the number of school-based child abuse prevention education programs has increased substantially (Tharinger et al., 1988). School psychologists play an important role in this prevention effort. At the level of tertiary prevention, school psychologists educate school staff and parents about the emotional and behavioral effects of sexual abuse, such as guilt, depression, fear, sleep difficulties, inappropriate sexual acting out, school problems, and poor peer relations (Browne & Finkelhor, 1986). This enables school staff and parents to identify and intervene with possible cases of abuse after they have occurred. The intent of such intervention is to reduce the debilitating effects associated with abuse. School psychologists can also serve as a valuable resource for teachers and other school personnel on current child abuse reporting laws.

At the level of primary prevention, school psychologists provide education for parents and teachers on the etiology of sexual abuse as well as suggestions on how to decrease the chances of its occurrence. In this way, parents exposed to this information can better act to protect their child from the chances of abuse occurring. School psychologists are also able to develop, implement, and evaluate school-based sexual abuse prevention programs that educate children (Tharinger et al., 1988). A variety of prepackaged, commercially available programs exist for young children through adolescents. Tharinger et al. (1988) emphasized that a weakness of many of these programs is that information is often not presented in a manner that is understandable to children. For example, explanations of sexual abuse may not be tailored to the developmental level of the intended recipients of this information. In addition, child abuse prevention programs that seek to empower children by teaching them to be assertive, trust their feelings, and say "no" can be detrimental, because they may increase feelings of self-blame in children who are abused (Tharinger et al., 1988). It is more appropriate to teach children to seek help and disclose abuse than it is to increase their sense of responsibility. As experts in social, emotional, and cognitive development, school psychologists perform a valuable function in identifying problems with the developmental appropriateness of curricula and helping design, implement, and evaluate more appropriate curricula for the education of children.

Indirect Services and Consultation. By developing collaborative relationships with parents, teachers, and administrators, school psychologists can share their knowledge and skills with other professionals who work with children. As described previously, school psychologists can consult with school staff in curriculum and program development and evaluation. They can also provide support and assistance to teachers who may be working with children who are experiencing behavioral or emotional difficulties and thus help these front-line professionals work more effectively with children and their parents. In addition, school psychologists can work as a part of an interdisciplinary team that designs prevention or intervention programs. For example, school psychologists, along with teachers, administrators, school board members, counselors, health educators, school and public health nurses, social workers, and parents, could assemble a team for AIDS education, prevention strategies, and working with affected children and family members (Zins, Curtis, Graden, & Ponti, 1988).

Indirect services and consultation are essential parts of the role school psychologists may play in dealing with preschool children under stress. Unlike most consultation models, in which the school psychologist's work is limited to consultation with school professionals (mostly teachers), we view the scope of consultative services to preschool children as including services to parents and families. Again, this is because of the extent to which young children are context dependent. To deal with the stresses experienced by preschool children, the school psychologist must become active in the relational contexts involving the child.

As we have emphasized, support to the adults who deal with these children, either parents or teachers, serves an essential role in strengthening protective mechanisms. Included in this role are activities such as referral for marital or family therapy, referral to appropriate programs for family violence or substance abuse, work with parent groups on parenting skills and support, and providing links to other support services. We believe referral is often overlooked as an intervention for stressed families and is not seen as an intervention. Working to know the needs of a family, building trust so that a referral can be successful, and providing follow-up services are major components of the concept of linkage that has been emphasized. For many stressed families who receive referrals to numerous programs, failure to receive services is often a function of lacking organization or planning skills, or physical means (e.g., transportation) to take advantage of such services. We view the linkage provided by good, supportive referrals to be an intervention in itself, and one that is easily identifiable within the scope of services provided by school psychologists.

Competence-Enhancement Strategies.   Competence-enhancement strategies are designed to help children develop skills that will enable them to deal more effectively with the demands and stresses in their lives. The goal of these strategies is to protect children against future dysfunction by building positive personal characteristics (Garmezy, 1984). Broadly defined competencies, such as interpersonal communication and problem-solving skills, are often the focus of competence enhancement programs. An example of a competence enhancement strategy is Spivack and Shure's (1974, 1985) program in social-cognitive problem-solving and decision-making skills. Social skill programs generally focus on children's affective reactions to and appraisal of interpersonal situations as well as their ability to set goals and carry out a planful sequence of behaviors to reach those goals (Elias & Branden, 1988). Programs exist for children of different ages, and Spivack and Shure (1974) have developed curriculum materials for children as young as preschool and kindergarten. School psychologists can be involved in developing programs, reviewing and choosing appropriate programs to implement in schools, training teachers or other school personnel to implement these programs, or working directly with children in these programs.

In working with families, Dunst and Trivette (1987) described an intervention model for families based on the concepts of enabling and empowering. They described four principles of this type of intervention: (a) basing intervention on the family's identified needs, personal agendas, and priorities, (b) using existing family functioning style as a basis for mobilizing resources, (c) maximizing the family's personal social network as a source of support and resources, and (d) employing helping behaviors that promote the family's acquisition of competencies and skills. This intervention model focuses on the promotion of growth (competence enhancement) in individual and family functioning rather than on the remediation of problems. The ultimate goal is to help families mobilize their own resources and skills to be able to deal more effectively with future problems. From their research and clinical experience with families of preschool retarded, handicapped, and developmentally at-risk children, Dunst and Trivette have developed Project SHaRE (Sources of Help Received and Exchanged). The project consists of a network of individuals and families of varying ages, backgrounds, needs, and strengths who exchange goods and services to get needs met; for instance, exchanging babysitting services for food. This type of exchange network, consisting of parents, teachers, high school students, and other community members, could be coordinated throughout a school system to capitalize on existing skills and resources and would serve to strengthen community cohesion.

Relationship-Based Strategies.   Strategies involving relationship-based interventions have as their focus building social support systems and fostering nurturant relationships for children and parents (Zins, Curtis, Graden, & Ponti, 1988). These types of interventions often have several components and involve both individual children and their families. Numerous intervention and prevention methods can be a part of these strategies, and they often include both educational and skills-based training for children and parents as well as supportive services to caregivers. Frequently, these types of interventions are targeted for children and families who are at risk for dysfunction by virtue of demographic or family characteristics, such as low SES, teenage parents, or special needs children, and thus represent examples of secondary prevention. Although numerous prevention and intervention programs now exist for at-risk children and their families, a review of several programs geared toward a preschool population serves to highlight some of the goals and results of these types of programs.

The Preschool Mental Health Project (PreMHP), based on the Primary Mental Health Project (PMHP; Cowen, 1980), is a preventive mental health program for preschool children and their parents (Rickel, Dyhdalo, & Smith, 1984). This program provides early screening and intervention to high-risk children who are experiencing learning and/or behavioral problems. In addition to helping these children, the PreMHP also includes a primary prevention parent training program to enhance parent–child interaction skills. By providing these services before a child even enters school, the PreMHP attempts to prevent more serious difficulties from developing as the child enters school (Rickel et al., 1984). Outcome research on the program indicated both short-term and long-term advantages for program children over control children (Rickel, Smith, & Sharp, 1979). In addition, after the intervention, the performance of treated high-risk children was not significantly different from that of low-risk children, who did not experience learning or behavioral problems (Rickel et al., 1984).

The Parent–Child Development Centers (PCDC; Andrews et al., 1982) have also shown much promise as a prevention strategy. These programs tailor their services to low income families of particular ethnic groups and consist of three components: (a) improving mother–child interaction through in-home, curriculum-based sessions, (b) bringing mothers and children to the center, where the children participate in a school program and the mothers attend home management sessions, and (c) using the PCDC as a resource center and support to parents and families (Elias & Branden, 1988). In a follow-up study of children in the PCDC program, a significantly lower incidence of behavioral problems and higher academic test scores were found for the participant children (Johnson & Walker, 1987).

The Steps Toward Early, Effective Parenting (STEEP) program, based on findings from the University of Minnesota Mother–Child Interaction Project, is an infant intervention program designed to offer support and educational services to high-risk mothers (Erickson, 1989). Both home visits and group sessions are provided to mothers, beginning in the second trimester of pregnancy, before the participants can experience having "failed" as a mother. Home visits focus on the mother's feelings about the pregnancy and planning for being a parent. Building a warm and supportive relationship with the mother is emphasized. Group sessions focus on child-care skills, education on infant development, and learning to understand and respond appropriately to the infant's needs. There is also time for the mothers to interact and build support networks with each other. Erickson (1989) stressed the relationship component of this program as essential, as most of the mothers have themselves experienced a history of abuse or neglect and have no models for nurturant relationships. Through the mothers' experience with a stable, supportive, and nurturant facilitator in the program, they can begin to modify their models of relationships and be better able to parent their own children.

Establishing helping networks and relationship-based interventions are perhaps the most comprehensive of the intervention strategies with which school psychologists can become involved. The role of the school psychologist in these programs can vary from developer to consultant to educator to direct service provider. These types of interventions are also the most likely to take the school psychologist out of the school and into the community to work with families. Although it may be a new role for many to play, well-trained school psychologists with a strong background in developmental theory and interventions seem likely and qualified persons to fulfill these new roles.

What School Psychologists Can Do

Clearly, the demands of educating preschoolers require that school psychologists master a broad scope of knowledge and skills. The school psychologist working with young children must be a skilled professional with comfortable access to the important contexts in the child's life. This means many things in addition to administration of standardized tests: entering a home and putting a stressed caregiver at ease, identifying strategies of child–caregiver interaction that are contributing to problems, and then using that information to help the dyad. This work involves identifying and linking sources of emotional or instrumental support for families in need, being knowledgeable about pediatrics and medical conditions, and organizing groups of diverse professionals in a manner that supports a family in need (i.e., good case management). The most critical aspect of the school psychologists' role in assessment and prevention/intervention with young children is insuring that they, or some other school professional, have a means by which they get to know the high-risk families in their school.

It is important that school psychologists working in preschool settings identify themselves primarily as psychologists. Few, if any, other professionals have the educational background in child development or skill training in observation, assessment, and intervention. It is with reference to psychological processes that the impact of different environments on children can be understood and communicated. There needs to be a spokesperson within the school setting for the psychological impact of stress on young children. Otherwise it becomes very easy for other agendas to overcome our understanding of the child and the preschool environment. Rather than being a protective mechanism, the school environment can introduce new stresses on the child in the form of rejection-based behavior management techniques, or an inappropriate emphasis on academics. Clearly, the school psychologist has an essential role in building preschool environments that operate as protective mechanisms in the lives of stressed children.

ACKNOWLEDGMENTS

The authors wish to acknowledge the helpful comments of an anonymous reviewer. Production of this chapter was supported in part by the Commonwealth Center for Teacher Education, University of Virginia and James Madison University.

REFERENCES

Abidin, R. R. (1983). *The Parenting Stress Index*. Charlottesville, VA: Pediatric Psychology Press.
Advocacy for Appropriate Educational Services for all Children. (1985). *Communique, 13*, 9.

Alexander, K., & Entwistle, D. (1988). Achievement in the first two years of school. *Monographs of the Society for Research in Child Development. 53*(2, Serial No. 218).

Andrews, S., Blumenthal, J., Johnson, D., Kahn, A., Ferguson, C., Lasatee, T., Malone, P., & Wallace, D. (1982). The skills of mothering: A study of Parent–Child Development Centers. *Monographs of the Society for Research in Child Development, 47*(6, Serial No. 198).

Belle, D. (1982). The stress of caring: Women as providers of social support. In L. Goldberger & S. Breznitz (Eds.), *The handbook of stress* (pp. 496–505). New York: The Free Press.

Belsky, J. (1980). Child maltreatment. *American Psychologist, 35,* 320–335.

Belsky, J. (1984). The determinants of parenting: A process model. *Child Development, 55,* 83–96.

Berreuter-Clement, J. (1984). Changed lives. The effects of the Perry Preschool Program on youths through age 19. *Monographs of the High Scope Educational Research Foundation, 8*(whole issue).

Birch, H., & Gussow, J. (1970). *Disadvantaged children.* New York: Grune and Stratton.

Blacher, J., & Meyers, C. E. (1983). A review of attachment formation and disorder of handicapped children. *American Journal of Mental Deficiency, 87,* 359–371.

Block, J. H., Block, J., & Gjerde, P. (1986). The personality of children prior to divorce: A prospective study. *Child Development, 57,* 827–840.

Bowlby, J. (1980). *Loss.* New York: Basic Books.

Bradley, R. H., & Caldwell, B. M. (1976). Early home environment and changes in mental test performance from 6 to 36 months. *Developmental Psychology, 12,* 93–97.

Bradley, R. H., Caldwell, B. M., & Rock, S. L. (1988). Home environment and school performance: A ten year follow up and examination of three models of environmental action. *Child Development, 59,* 852–867.

Brown, G., & Harris, T. (1978). *The social origins of depression.* New York: The Free Press.

Browne, A. B., & Finkelhor, D. (1986). Impact of child sexual abuse: A review of the research. *Psychological Bulletin, 99,* 66–77.

Caldwell, B., & Bradley, R. H. (1984). *Home observation for measurement of the environment.* Little Rock: University of Arkansas.

Canam, C. (1986). Perceived stressors and coping responses of employed and non-employed career women with preschool children. *Canadian Journal of Community Health, 5,* 49–59.

Catalano, R., & Dooley, D. (1977). Economic predictors of depressed mood and stressful life events in a metropolitan community. *Journal of Health and Social Behavior, 18,* 292–307.

Coddington, R. (1972). The significance of life events as etiologic factors in the diseases of children. *Journal of Psychosomatic Research, 16,* 7–18.

Cowen, E. L. (1980). The Primary Mental Health Project: Yesterday, today, and tomorrow. *Journal of Special Education, 14,* 133–154.

Crnic, K., Greenberg, M., Ragozin, A., Robinson, N., & Basham, R. (1983). Effects of stress and social support on mothers and premature and full term infants. *Child Development, 54,* 209–217.

Crockenburg, S. (1981). Infant irritability, mother responsiveness, and social support influences on the security of infant–mother attachment. *Child Development, 52,* 857–865.

Derogatis, L. (1982). Self report measure of stress. In L. Goldberger & S. Breznitz (Eds.), *The handbook of stress* (pp. 270–294). New York: The Free Press.

Dooley, D., Catalano, R., Jackson, R., & Brownell, A. (1981). Economic, life and symptom changes in a nonmetropolitan community. *Journal of Health and Social Behavior, 22,* 144–154.

Dunst, C. J., & Trivette, C. M. (1987). Enabling and empowering families: Conceptual and intervention issues. *School Psychology Review, 4,* 443–456.

Egeland, B., Breitenbucher, M., & Rosenberg, D. (1980). Prospective study of the etiology of child abuse. *Journal of Consulting and Clinical Psychology, 48,* 195–205.

Egeland, B., & Sroufe, L. A. (1981). Developmental sequelae of maltreatment in infancy. In R. Rizley & D. Cicchetti (Eds.), *New directions in child development: Developmental perspectives on child maltreatment* (Vol. 11, pp. 77–92). San Francisco: Jossey-Bass.

Elder, G. (1974). *Children of the Great Depression*. Chicago: University of Chicago Press.

Elias, M. J., & Branden, L. R. (1988). Primary prevention of behavioral and emotional problems in school-aged populations. *School Psychology Review, 17*, 581–592.

Elias, M. J., & Clabby, J. F. (in press). *Social skills and social decision-making skills for the elementary grades: A curriculum guide for educators*. Rockville, MD: Aspen.

Emery, R. (1982). Interparental conflict and the children of divorce. *Psychological Bulletin, 92*, 310–330.

Erickson, M. F. (1989). Infant intervention: Role for a school psychologist. *Communique, 17*(6), 4.

Erickson, M. F., Egeland, B., & Pianta, R. (1989). The effects of maltreatment on the development of young children. In D. Cicchetti & V. Carlson (Eds.), *Child maltreatment: Research on consequences and theoretical perspectives* (pp. 647–684). New York: Cambridge University Press.

Erickson, M. F., & Pianta, R. (1989). New lunchbox, old feelings: What children bring to school. *Early Education and Development, 1*, 11–19.

Feiring, C., Fox, N. A., Jaskir, J., & Lewis, M. (1987). The relation between social support, infant risk status and mother–infant interaction. *Developmental Psychology, 23*, 400–405.

Field, T., Healy, B., Goldstein, S., Perry, S., Bendell, D., Schanberg, S., Zimmerman, E. A., & Kuhn, C. (1988). Infants of depressed mothers show "depressed" behavior even with non-depressed adults. *Child Development, 59*, 1569–1579.

Garbarino, J. (1982). *Child and families in the social environment*. New York: Aldine.

Garbarino, J., & Sherman, D. (1980). High-risk neighborhoods and high-risk families: The human ecology of child maltreatment. *Child Development, 51*, 188–198.

Garbarino, J., & Vondra, J. (1987). Psychological maltreatment: Issues and perspectives. In M. R. Brassard, R. Germain, & S. Hart (Eds.), *Psychological maltreatment of children and youth* (pp. 254–266). New York: Pergammon.

Garmezy, N. (1977). On some risks in risk research. *Psychological Medicine, 7*, 1–6.

Garmezy, N. (1984). Stress-resistant children: The search for protective factors. In J. E. Stevenson (Ed.), *Aspects of current child psychiatry research* (pp. 213–233). Oxford: Pergammon Press.

Gartner, A., & Lipsky, K. K. (1987). Beyond special education: Toward a quality system for all students. *Harvard Educational Review, 57*, 368–395.

Graham, M. A. (1987). *The social and fiscal implications of the definition of high-risk for pre-K handicapped education in Florida*. Unpublished doctoral dissertation, University of Miami, Miami, FL.

Greenspan, S. I., & Porges, S. W. (1984). Psychopathology in infancy and early childhood: Clinical perspectives on the organization of sensory and affective-thematic experience. *Child Development, 55*, 49–70.

Hetherington, E. M. (1989). Coping with family transitions: Winners, losers and survivors. *Child Development, 60*, 1–14.

Horowitz, B., & Wolcock, I. (1981). Material deprivation, child maltreatment, and agency interventions among poor families. In L. Pelton (Ed.), *The social context of child abuse and neglect* (pp. 137–184). New York: Human Sciences Press.

Hughes, D. (1988). What about American children? *Child World, 14*, 8.

Johnson, D., & Walker, T. (1987). Primary prevention of behavior problems in Mexican-American children. *American Journal of Community Psychology, 15*, 375–386.

Katz, L. G. (1988). Engaging children's minds: The implications of research for early childhood education. In S. L. Kagan & E. Zigler (Eds.), *Early schooling: The national debate* (pp. 151–167). New Haven: Yale University Press.

Kazak, A., & Marvin, R. S. (1984). Differences, difficulties and adaptation: Stress and social networks in families with a handicapped child. *Family Relations, 33*, 67–77.

Kazak, A., Reber, M., & Carter, A. (1988). Structural and qualitative aspects of social networks in families with young chronically ill children. *Journal of Pediatric Psychology, 13*, 171–182.

Keogh, B. K., Wilcoxen, A. G., & Bernheimer, L. (1986). Prevention services for risk children: Evidence for policy and practice. In D. Farran & J. McKinney (Eds.), *Risk in intellectual and psychosocial development* (pp. 287–315). New York: Academic Press.

Kontos, S., & Dunn, L. (1989). Characteristics of the early intervention workforce: An Indiana perspective. *Early Education and Development, 1,* 141–157.

Ladd, G. W., Price, J. M., & Hart, C. H. (1988). Predicting preschoolers' peer status from their playground behaviors. *Child Development, 59,* 986–992.

Lazarus, R. (1970). Cognitive and personality factors underlying threat and coping. In S. Levine & N. Scotch (Eds.), *Social stress.* New York: Aldine.

Main, M., & Solomon, J. (1986). Discovery of an insecure-disorganized/disoriented attachment pattern. In T. B. Brazelton & M. Yogman (Eds.), *Affective development in infancy* (pp. 95–124). Norwood, NJ: Ablex.

Margolis, L. (1982). Help wanted. *Pediatrics, 69,* 816–818.

Marvin, R. S., & Pianta, R. (1989). *Patterns of attachment in children with motor impairments.* Unpublished manuscript, University of Virginia, Charlottesville.

Munroe, B. M., Boyle, M. H., & Offord, D. R. (1988). Single parent families: Child psychiatric disorder and school performance. *Journal of the American Academy of Child and Adolescent Psychiatry, 27,* 214–219.

Orvaschel, H., Weissman, M., & Kidd, K. (1980). The children of depressed parents; the childhood of depressed parents; depression in children. *Journal of Affective Disorders, 2,* 1–16.

Pedro-Carroll, J. L., & Cowen, E. (1985). The Children of Divorce Intervention Program: An investigation of the efficacy of a school-based prevention program. *Journal of Consulting and Clinical Psychology, 53,* 603–611.

Pianta, R. (1990). Widening the debate on educational reform: Prevention as a viable alternative. *Exceptional Children, 56,* 306–313.

Pianta, R., & Ball, R. (in press). Maternal social support as a predictor of children's adjustment to kindergarten. *Journal of Applied Developmental Psychology.*

Pianta, R., Egeland, B., & Erickson, M. F. (1989). The antecedents of child maltreatment in high risk families: The results of the Mother–Child Interaction Research Project. In D. Cicchetti & V. Carlson (Eds.), *Child maltreatment: Research on consequences and theoretical perspectives* (pp. 203–253). New York: Cambridge University Press.

Pianta, R., Egeland, B., & Hyatt, A. (1986). Maternal relationship history as an indicator of development risk. *American Journal of Orthopsychiatry, 56,* 385–398.

Pianta, R., Egeland, B., & Sroufe, L. A. (1990). Maternal stress and children's development: Prediction of school outcomes and identification of protective factors. In J. Rolf, A. Masten, D. Cicchetti, K. Neuchterlein, & S. Wienraub (Eds.), *Risk and protective factors in the development of psychopathology* (pp. 215–235). New York: Cambridge University Press.

Pianta, R., & Nimetz, S. L. (1989). Educators' beliefs about risk and prevention: The context of reform. *Early Education and Development, 1,* 115–126.

Pianta, R., Smith, N., & Reeve, R. (1991). Using child–parent interaction data in kindergarten screening procedures. *School Psychology Quarterly, 6,* 1–15.

Ramey, C., Bryant, D. M., & Suarez, T. M. (1986). Preschool compensatory education and the modifiability of intelligence: A critical review. In D. Detterman (Ed.), *Current topics in human intelligence* (pp. 247–292). Hillsdale, NJ: Lawrence Erlbaum Associates.

Rickel, A. U., Dyhdalo, L. L., & Smith, R. L. (1984). Prevention with preschoolers. In M. C. Roberts & L. Peterson (Eds.), *Prevention of problems in childhood: Psychological research and applications* (pp. 74–102). New York: Wiley.

Rickel, A. U., Smith, R. L., & Sharp, K. C. (1979). Description and evaluation of a preventive mental health program for preschoolers. *Journal of Abnormal Child Psychology, 7,* 101–112.

Roberts, M. C., & Peterson, L. (1984). *Prevention of problems in childhood.* New York: Wiley.

Rosenbaum, A., & O'Leary, K. (1981). Children: The unintended victims of marital violence. *American Journal of Orthopsychiatry, 51,* 692–699.

Rutter, M. (1987). Psychosocial resilience and protective mechanisms. *American Journal of Ortho-psychiatry, 57*, 316–331.

Rutter, M., Yule, B., Quinton, D., Rowlands, O., Yule, W., & Berger, M. (1975). Attainment and adjustment in two geographical areas III: Some factors accounting for area differences. *British Journal of Psychiatry, 126*, 520–533.

Sameroff, A., & Chandler, M. (1975). Reproductive risk and the continuum of caretaking casualty. In F. Horowitz, E. M. Hetherington, S. Scarr-Salapatek, & G. Siegel (Eds.), *Review of child development research* (Vol. 4, pp. 187–244). Chicago: University of Chicago Press.

Sameroff, A., & Seifer, R. (1984). Familial risk and child competence. *Child Development, 54*, 1254–1268.

Sameroff, A., Seifer, R., Barocas, R., Zax, M., & Greenspan, S. (1987). Intelligence quotient scores of 4-year-old children: Social-environmental risk factors. *Pediatrics, 79*, 343–350.

Sameroff, A., Seifer, R., & Zax, M. (1982). Early development of children at risk for emotional disorder. *Monographs of the Society for Research in Child Development, 47*(Serial No. 199).

Shapiro, E. S. (1988). Preventing academic failure. *School Psychology Review, 17*, 601–613.

Spivack, G., & Shure, M. (1974). *Social adjustment of young children: A cognitive approach to solving real-life problems.* San Francisco: Jossey-Bass.

Spivack, G., & Shure, M. (1985). ICPS and beyond: Centripetal and centrifugal forces. *American Journal of Community Psychology, 13*, 226–243.

Sroufe, L. A. (1983). Infant–caregiver attachment and patterns of adaptation in preschool: The roots of maladaptation and competence. In M. Perlmutter (Ed.), *The Minnesota Symposium on Child Psychology* (Vol. 16, pp. 41–83). Hillsdale, NJ: Lawrence Erlbaum Associates.

Sroufe, L. A., & Rutter, M. (1984). The domain of developmental psychopathology. *Child Development, 55*, 17–29.

Steele, B. F. (1987). Abuse and neglect in the earliest years: The groundwork for vulnerability. *Zero to Three, 7*, 14–15.

Strauss, M., Gelles, R., & Steinmetz, S. (1980). *Behind closed doors.* New York: Doubleday.

Tharinger, D. J., Krivacska, J. J., Laye McDonough, M., Jamison, L., Vincent, G. G., & Hedlund, A. D. (1988). Prevention of child sexual abuse: An analysis of issues, educational programs, and research findings. *School Psychology Review, 17*, 614–634.

Tonge, W., James, D., & Hillam, S. (1975). Families without hope. *British Journal of Psychiatry Special Publication #11.* Ashford, England: The Royal College of Psychiatry.

Van Eedewegh, M., Bieri, M., Parilla, R., & Clayton, P. (1982). The bereaved child. *British Journal of Psychiatry, 140*, 23–29.

Wahler, R. (1980). The insular mother: Her problems in parent–child treatment. *Journal of Applied Behavioral Analysis, 13*, 207–219.

Wahler, R., Leske, G., & Rogers, E. (1979). The insular family: A deviance support system for oppositional children. In L. Hamerdynck (Ed.), *Behavioral systems for the developmentally disabled I: School and family environments* (pp. 102–127). New York: Brunner-Mazel.

Weissberg, R. P. (1985). Designing effective social problem solving programs for the classroom. In B. Schneider, K. Rubin, & J. Ledingham (Eds.), *Children's peer relations: Issues in assessment intervention* (pp. 225–242). New York: Springer-Verlag.

Weissman, M. M., Leaf, P. J., & Bruse, M. L. (1987). Single parent women: A community study. *Social Psychiatry, 22*, 29–36.

Yogman, M., & Brazelton, T. B. (1987). *In support of families.* Cambridge, MA: Harvard University Press.

Zins, J. E., Conyne, R. K., & Ponti, C. R. (1988). Primary prevention: Expanding the impact of psychological services in schools. *School Psychology Review, 17*, 542–549.

Zins, J. E., Curtis, J. J., Graden, J. L., & Ponti, C. R. (1988). *Helping students succeed in the regular classroom: A guide for developing intervention assistance programs.* San Francisco: Jossey-Bass.

Zins, J. E., & Forman, S. G. (1988). Primary prevention in the schools: What are we waiting for? *School Psychology Review, 17*, 539–541.

6 Computers and Early Childhood Education

Douglas H. Clements
State University of New York at Buffalo

Bonnie K. Nastasi
Illinois State University*

YOUNG CHILDREN AND COMPUTERS

Computers are being increasingly integrated into early childhood programs. Over 25% of licensed preschools had microcomputers as early as 1984; it is predicted that virtually all will have such access sometime in the 1990s (Goodwin, Goodwin, & Garel, 1986). A similar ownership rate in homes is probable (Lieberman, 1985). There are still strong debates, however, about the wisdom of this trend. Are young children (here, from birth to 8 years) physically and cognitively ready to use computers? Will such use inhibit their socioemotional development? Can computers help build skills or develop problem-solving ability? Researchers have not answered these questions definitively. In just a few years since the publication of similar reviews (Barnes & Hill, 1983; Brady & Hill, 1984; Goodwin, Goodwin, & Garel, 1986; Lieberman, 1985), however, there has been a substantial increase in what we know about young children's use of computers. In contrast to approaches taken in other reviews (Roblyer, Castine, & King, 1988), we go beyond charting "average" effects in an attempt to understand factors accounting for variations in effects. Such understanding provides a basis for consultation regarding the effective implementation of computers in early childhood settings.[1]

*Now at the University of Connecticut.

[1]Computers have many valuable applications in school psychology, such as in assessment and diagnosis, program planning, therapeutic interventions, and professional development; however, consonant with the theme of this book, we focus on implementation in educational settings.

187

Are Computers Developmentally Appropriate?

Perhaps the first question we should ask about computers is this: Is their use developmentally appropriate for young children? An expressed concern is that children must reach the stage of concrete operations before they are ready to work with computers (Brady & Hill, 1984). Recent research, however, has found that preschoolers are more competent than has been thought and can, under certain conditions, exhibit thinking traditionally considered "concrete" (Gelman & Baillargeon, 1983). A related concern is that computer use demands symbolic competence. Much of the activity in which young children engage, however, is symbolic. They communicate with gestures and language, and they employ symbols in their play, song, and art (Sheingold, 1986). Thus, it appears that preschool children might benefit from using appropriate computer programs. In addition, they should be used in appropriate contexts (e.g., as books are used, with a loving teacher or parent).

But what is appropriate? Drawing shapes with Logo's "turtle" has been criticized: "What does it mean to children to command a perfect square but still not be able to draw it by themselves?" (Cuffaro, 1984, p. 561). Leaving aside that most adults cannot draw a "perfect" square either, what does the research say? It indicates that for some children, Logo drawing experience allows them to create pictures more elaborate than those that they can create by hand and suggests that they modify their conceptions and transfer components of this new conceptualization on to work with paper (Vaidya & Mckeeby, 1984). Such computer drawing is appropriate for children as young as 3 years, who show signs of developmental progression in the areas of drawing and geometry during such computer use (Alexander, 1983, in press).

Further, consider other criticisms of Logo mentioned in various critical essays (Cuffaro, 1984; Davy, 1984). Computers lack smells and sounds. Screens are two-dimensional. Logo shapes are uniform and allow but a few colors. Computer use constrains large-muscle movement. These statements have some validity. However, books seldom have sound or true movement. Drawing with crayons is two-dimensional. Building blocks limit the child basically to straight lines and preset curves and angles embodied in uniform, often colorless shapes. Puzzles restrict (most) large muscle movements. Yet books, crayons, blocks, and puzzles proliferate in early childhood classrooms, as they should.

Moreover, what is "concrete" to the child may have more to do with what is meaningful and manipulable than with its physical nature. Char (1989) compared a computer graphic felt board environment, in which children could freely construct "bean stick pictures" by selecting and arranging beans, sticks, and number symbols, to a real bean stick environment. The software environment actually offered equal, and sometimes greater control and flexibility to young children than actual bean sticks. It was found that both computer representations and real objects were worthwhile, but that one did not necessarily need to precede the other. In addition, computers enrich experience with regular manipulatives. In another study, third-grade students who used both manipulatives and software demonstrated a greater sophistication in classification and logical thinking, and showed more foresight and deliberation in classification, than did students who used only manipulatives (Olson, 1988).

Another line of criticism involves "rushing" children (Elkind, 1987). One response to such criticism is that computers are no more dangerous than books or pencils—all could be used to push a child to read or write too soon. Exacerbating the confusion are some critics' misconceptions about computer use; for example, that "to be used by young children, computers have to be converted into teaching machines presenting programmed learning" (Elkind, 1987, p. 8). As we see here, most of the promising uses of computers have nothing to do with programmed learning. In one study, only children using developmentally inappropriate drill and practice programs had significant losses in creativity (with scores decreasing by 50%). Children using developmentally appropriate software made significant gains in intelligence, nonverbal skills, structural knowledge, long-term memory, complex manual dexterity, and self-esteem (Haugland & Shade, in press). Watson, Nida, and Shade (1986) suggested that the dilemma best be handled by allowing children to select activities and to work with activities at their own level. We must also remember that we are just learning how to use computers. "Expectations are insightful when linked to a vision of what the child will someday understand, enjoy, or become. They are misguided when 'someday' fades impatiently into 'today.' The problem of 'hothousing' lies not in asking so much, or even too much of our children, but in asking it nonnegotiably too soon" (Fein, 1987, p. 228).

To a large degree, the veridicality of the criticisms rests on the assumption that computer activities will supplant "real" experiences (Cuffaro, 1984). But proponents do not advocate this type of use. In addition, detrimental effects from such supplantation would, realistically, involve more exposure than most educators could provide, or should allow. The arguments are missing the important issues. As one illustration, now that newer computers can show billions of colors, would the critics claim that they should replace 16-color crayon sets? Both old technologies (e.g., crayons, paint brushes) and new may be the most appropriate technology at a given time. The research reviewed here helps put the important issues in perspective. We begin by asking: How do children react to this new technological learning device?

YOUNG CHILDREN USING COMPUTERS

Young Children's Ability and Confidence in Operating Computers

Children approach computers with comfort and confidence, and appear to enjoy exploring this new medium (Binder & Ledger, 1985). Even preschoolers can work with minimal instruction and supervision, if they have adult support initially (Rosengren, Gross, Abrams, & Perlmutter, 1985; Shade, Nida, Lipinski, & Watson, 1986). However, adults play a significant role in successful computer use. Problem-solving programs demand more initial and continued support than simpler, practice programs (Genishi, 1988; Sivin, Lee, & Vollmer, 1985). For all types of programs, children are more attentive, more interested, and less frustrated when an adult is present (Binder & Ledger, 1985; Shade et al., 1986). Using the standard keyboard is not a problem for young children, and is often superior to other devices, such as a joystick. Indeed, typing appears to be a source of motivation and sense of competence for many (Borgh & Dickson, 1986b; Hungate & Heller, 1984; Kumpf, 1985; Lipinski, Nida, Shade, & Watson, 1986; Muller & Perlmutter, 1985; Swigger & Campbell, 1981).

In summary, even preschool children can enjoyably and successfully use and manage age-appropriate software requiring only one- or two-character keypresses. They can turn the computer on and off, remove and replace disks properly, follow instructions from a picture menu, use situational and visual cues in the aid of reading, and talk meaningfully about their computer activity (Hess & McGarvey, 1987; Watson, Chadwick, & Brinkley, 1986).

Preferences Relative to Other Educational Activities

A computer center may vary from being among the most popular free-time activity to being chosen slightly less than many other areas (King & Perrin, n.d.; Picard & Giuli, 1985). Physical setup, teacher interventions, and especially the computer programs (software), may cause such differences. For example, children prefer programs that are animated, problem-solving-oriented, and interactive—that give them a feeling of control over the computer (Lewis, 1981; Shade et al., 1986; Sherman, Divine, & Johnson, 1985; Sivin et al., 1985). In most studies, it appeared that 3- to 5-year-old children spend approximately the same amount of time playing in the computer center as drawing, talking, or playing in the block or art centers (Hoover & Austin, 1986; Picard & Giuli, 1985). This attraction outlives the novelty effect. However, play in other important centers, such as blocks, is not decreased by the presence of a computer. In one study, the only change was that some children's use of art centers diminished as they switched to using computers, but this involved performing art activities on the computers (Essa, 1987). In sum, the computer appears to be an interesting, but not overly engrossing, activity for young children (Lipinski et al., 1986).

Individual Differences

Do any characteristics distinguish preschoolers most interested in using computers? They tend to be older and exhibit significantly higher levels of cognitive maturity. They manifest higher levels of representational competence and vocabulary development, and display more organized and abstract forms of free play behavior. They do not differ from less interested peers in creativity, estimates of social maturity, or social-cognitive ability. Thus, there may be important cognitive underpinnings of computer involvement by preschoolers (Hoover & Austin, 1986; Johnson, 1985).

Although older children may be more interested in using computers, there is little evidence that computers should not be introduced to younger children. No major differences were found between the way computers were used by younger and older preschoolers (Beeson & Williams, 1985; Essa, 1987; Lewis, 1981), although 3-year-olds took longer to acclimate to the keyboard than 5-year-olds (Sivin et al., 1985). Some research suggests 3 years of age as an appropriate time for introducing a child to discovery-oriented software. However, even 2-year-olds might be introduced to simple, single-keystroke software, mainly for developing positive attitudes. The key is appropriately designed software (Shade & Watson, 1987).

If computers are seen as a general educational tool, perhaps no one is too young. Noting that handicapped infants are at high risk for learned helplessness, Brinker (1984) sought ways to use computers to help them exert control over their environment. Infants wore ribbons attached to switches. Their arm or leg movements sent different signals to a computer, which was programmed to turn on a tape recording of the mother's voice or music, show a picture, or activate a toy, with these consequences varying if habituation was detected. These activities built motivation to control such events and increased the infants' smiling and vocalizing.

Gender differences in computer use have been observed at all ages. A consistent finding is that as early as the later elementary school years, boys have more access to computers, own more computers, and use computers more frequently and with more control (Lieberman, 1985; Parker, 1984; Picard & Giuli, 1985). Is this imbalance present in early childhood? There are some similar signs. For example, a pair of studies found that although boys and girls 5 years or older used computers similarly, boys younger than 5 used the computer more than did girls of the same age (Beeson & Williams, 1985; Klinzing & Hall, 1985). In addition, two studies, one at the preschool and one at the primary level, have found that boys are more interested in creative problem-solving programs, whereas girls tend to stay within the dictates of established drill-and-practice programs (Shrock, Matthias, Anastasoff, Vensel, & Shaw, 1985; Swigger, Campbell, & Swigger, 1983). Other subtle differences are that girls exhibit greater overall computer competency, variety and detail in drawings, and degree of verbalization and that boys show greater ability on robot tasks (Jones, 1987). Other studies, however, have not revealed such differences (Sherman et al., 1985), and the vast majority report that girls and boys do not differ in the amount or type of computer use (Essa, 1987; Hess & McGarvey, 1987; Hoover & Austin, 1986; Johnson, 1985; King & Perrin, n.d.; Lipinski et al., 1986; Muller & Perlmutter, 1985; Shade et al., 1986; Sprigle & Schaefer, 1984; Swigger &

Campbell, 1981; Swigger et al., 1983). Considering the traditional heavy dominance of computer use by males, these researchers have recommended that the early years are the ideal time to introduce students to computers.

Special Populations

Computers hold promise for aiding the education of special populations through identification, program planning, and program implementation. Both as educational tools and as prosthetic devices, computers can provide sensory input; enhance mobility; develop cognitive, language, perceptual, and motor skills; and facilitate communication (Clements, 1985; Meyers, 1984; O'Connor & Schery, 1986). They can enhance sense of control, promote the understanding of cause–and–effect relationships, and provide a means of environmental control for both young children and older, severely-handicapped children (Brinker & Lewis, 1982). For the severely language-impaired or hearing-impaired student, the computer is an effective tool for improving speech production via dynamic visual displays of oral actions during speech or via speech synthesis (Bruno & Goodman, 1983; Fletcher, 1983).

Computers can contribute to the education of handicapped children at any age or level of functioning. The mildly handicapped should be able to use existing hardware and age-appropriate software without additions to the keyboard, merely using lower levels and slower pacing (Watson, Chadwick, & Brinkley, 1986). For the more severely handicapped, alterations are necessary. Modifications in hardware, such as switches as input devices, allow interaction with computers for the physically impaired. For the cognitively impaired, the developmental abilities of the child must be considered in choosing software (Clements, 1985; Porter, 1986). Like the nonhandicapped, these children choose computers frequently and prefer software that contains colorful graphics and animation and is user controlled. In one study with handicapped children, the need for teacher support was high initially but declined over time as students became more independent or relied on peers; low-functioning students (IQ below 65), however, required teacher assistance throughout (Fazio & Rieth, 1986).

With such teacher support, Computer Assisted Instruction (CAI) may even be more effective in providing basic skills instruction to special education students than to students in regular education, possibly due to the low-level content. In addition, CAI is perceived by students as less threatening than traditional classroom instruction (Swan, Guerrero, Mitrani, & Schoener, 1989). Other features of CAI that may make it especially suited for the handicapped include the systematic presentation of information in small increments, immediate feedback and positive reinforcement, consistent correction procedures, well-sequenced instruction, high frequency of student response, and the opportunity for extended remediation through branching (Watson, Chadwick, & Brinkley, 1986). In support of these claims, CAI has been used successfully to provide basic skills instruction to educationally disadvantaged school-aged children (Swan et al., 1989), to teach reading and writing skills to preschool and elementary-aged hearing-impaired children (Prinz, Nelson, & Stedt, 1982; Prinz & Nelson, 1985), and to improve the spelling skills of children with attention-deficit disorders (Fitzgerald, Fick, & Milich, 1986).

Concern exists, however, that special education teachers use computers predominantly for drill and practice and for rewarding desired behaviors (Christensen & Cosden, 1986). Alternatives are viable; special education students benefit from work with Logo or other discovery-oriented software (Hlawati, 1985; Lehrer & deBernard, 1987; Lehrer, Harckham, Archer, & Pruzek, 1986; Watson, Chadwick, & Brinkley, 1986; Weir, Russell, & Valente, 1982). In addition, computers can extend early childhood educational services to the home environment (Shade & Watson, 1985). Additional research relevant to educational applications is described in subsequent sections.

Another concern is exceptional children's inequitable access to computers. Such access is influenced by the locus of special education; computer programming and literacy skills are taught significantly less often in special education settings than in regular education settings. In the latter setting, handicapped and nonhandicapped children had equal access to such software (Christensen & Cosden, 1986).

Research on the applications of computers to early childhood special education has relied heavily on quasi-experimental designs such as case studies and pretest–postest one-group designs. Further research is needed to verify the initial evidence regarding the effectiveness of computers with this population (Fujiura & Johnson, 1986). It is no longer appropriate to ask if computers will have an effect on early childhood special education. Instead, we need to ask questions regarding the ways in which we can insure that the impact will be positive (Johnson, 1986). Behrmann (1984) suggests that the following questions be addressed when developing early childhood special education programs that incorporate computers: Can the computer provide a unique means of helping these children learn? Are software and hardware available for these purposes or can they be easily developed? Will such applications be cost effective relative to other methods?

SOCIOEMOTIONAL AND SOCIAL-COGNITIVE DEVELOPMENT

Do computers have potential benefits for children's socioemotional development? There has not always been agreement on this issue. Initially, the influx of computers into the school setting led to fears of social isolation (Barnes & Hill, 1983). On the other hand, there were claims that computers might serve as potential catalysts of social interaction (Papert, 1980). In response to these dissonant views, researchers have investigated several questions regarding the potential impact of computers on children's socioemotional development:

1. What is the nature of children's social interactions within educational computer environments? Do these differ from those in traditional educational settings?
2. How is social development affected by computer use? In addition, how are children's attitudes toward learning, intrinsic motivation, and sense of competence affected by computer use?
3. Do different computer environments differentially affect social and affective development?

In the following sections, these questions provide the framework for examining the potential influence of computers on socioemotional development of young children. Research findings are interpreted within the context of social and social-cognitive developmental theories. In addition, the influence of instructional and curricular variables are explored and interpreted within an ecological framework. These variables may be exogenous (as in the case of student–teacher or student–student interactions) or endogenous (i.e., features of the software) to the computer intervention.

Social Interactions

Taking a Vygotskian perspective, Emihovich and Miller (1988b) emphasized the importance of the social-interactional and the sociocultural context in which teaching and learning take place. In particular, they suggested that we examine the roles of "joint self-verbalization" and teacher mediation that occur during collaborative learning with the computer. From this perspective, children make sense of the learning events together, within a mutually constructed experience, and the teacher, through modeling of strategies, provides scaffolding to support the children's thinking until they can begin to practice the strategies independently. Such educational scaffolding supports children, lifting them so that they can perform tasks that they could not have performed alone, thus allowing them to build cognitive structures that they could not have built in isolation (Bruner, 1986; Vygotsky, 1978). For example, a teacher might perform just those components of a task that the children cannot perform; as children learn, the teacher encourages them to take over those components. Alternatively, peers might construct a solution cooperatively, each contributing to a solution that they could not initially have constructed by themselves. In either case, each child eventually becomes able to perform the task alone through internalization of the strategies and concepts that emerge from the intervention with teacher or peers—the interpsychological becomes the intrapsychological. An environment in which children work collaboratively and are free to introduce topics and initiate action, and in which the teacher plays a supportive or facilitative role, is one which is more likely to facilitate mediated learning (i.e., by providing scaffolding) and consequently internalization of higher-order regulatory (metacognitive) processes. This perspective provides a framework for the examination of social interactions that occur in educational computer environments and for the link of social to cognitive processes that is explored in a later section.

Children's Interactions in Computer Environments

The computer's presence in the preschool classroom has been shown to foster a positive climate characterized by praise and encouragement of peers (Klinzing & Hall, 1985). Four- and 5-year-olds from an inner-city, economically disadvantaged population asked others to join in, sought help from each other, and sought approval or acknowledgement from the teacher as they worked with computers (Bowman, 1985).

Children generally prefer social use of computers; that is, they prefer to work in dyads or triads rather than alone (Rosengren et al., 1985; Shade et al., 1986; Swigger et al., 1983; Swigger & Swigger, 1984). Even when working alone, young children consult their peers (Genishi, 1988; Genishi, McCollum, & Strand, 1985; Hungate & Heller, 1984). Several reports confirm that children spontaneously teach and help each other in computer environments (Borgh & Dickson, 1986b; Paris & Morris, 1985; Wright & Samaras, 1986). The results of at least one study suggest that children prefer asking peers rather than an adult for help (Lieberman, 1985).

Young children can be effective teachers and helpers with regard to the computer (Borgh & Dickson, 1986b; Wright & Samaras, 1986). Children as young as the age of 4 can successfully provide both verbal instruction and demonstration to peers (Paris & Morris, 1985). In one study, first graders engaged to a considerable degree in peer tutoring, often modeling their teacher's guided questioning approach (Kull, 1986). Receptivity from the partner may be important; in one study, attempts to teach peers were most successful when such assistance was requested (Paris & Morris, 1985).

Several studies have investigated the potential impact of the computer on the existing social ecology of the classroom. Findings from some studies suggest that the computer may enhance, rather than inhibit, existing patterns of social participation (Binder & Ledger, 1985; Rosengren et al., 1985; Swigger & Swigger, 1984). At the least, the amount of social interaction does not seem to change significantly following the introduction of the computer into a preschool classroom (Essa, 1987), and the specific nature of social interactions in the computer area of a preschool classroom resembles that of other areas (Klinzing & Hall, 1985; Lipinski et al., 1986). Furthermore, the computer does not seem to restrict the range of behaviors among preschoolers; both cooperative and independent play are encouraged (Klinzing & Hall, 1985).

The computer does not seem to disrupt existing friendship patterns in the preschool classroom and may even encourage new associations. Observations within a preschool classroom revealed that children tended to work with friends, although new bonds were formed among children with high interest in computer use and changes in sociometric status occurred as "experts" attained leadership status (Swigger & Swigger, 1984). Duration of the study was 3 weeks; thus, long-term effects on social structure remain to be examined.

In addition to fostering social interaction, computers may engender an advanced cognitive type of play among children. In one study, "games with rules" was the most frequently occurring type of play among preschoolers working at computers (Hoover & Austin, 1986). Similarly, Fein, Campbell, and Schwartz (1987) found that the dominant mode of cognitive activity was functional and constructive, and that functional play was higher on in-computer compared to out-computer days. Thus, already prevailing patterns of social participation and cognitive play were enhanced by the presence of computers.

Some studies have compared the extent to which computers may engender cooperative interactions and the specific nature of those interactions relative to other preschool activities. Observations of preschoolers revealed that they spent 63% of their time at the computer working with a peer, compared to only 7% when working with puzzles (Muller & Perlmutter, 1985). The prevailing form of social interaction at the computer was turn-taking, accounting for 70% of the interactions; another 20% of the interactions were characterized as instructing behaviors (explaining, 11%; showing, 9%). In contrast, while working with puzzles, the predominant interactive behavior was explaining (64%); children rarely initiated interactions with peers and engaged in no turn-taking.

Additional support for the facilitative effect of computers, compared to other preschool activities, is provided by Muhlstein and Croft (1986). The frequency of cooperative play at the computer was comparable to that exhibited during a fishing game (96% and 98%, respectively), but was much higher than that exhibited in other traditional preschool activities such as blocks (27%), play-dough (14%), and art (8%). The computer was the only activity that resulted in high levels of both language activity and cooperative play simultaneously.

Working with primary-grade students, Clements and Nastasi (1985) compared social interaction patterns during computer (Logo or drill CAI) and noncomputer (paper-and-pencil) activities. Children engaged in a greater amount of collaboration on the assigned task while working at a computer.

Computer-assisted writing activities also seem to engender cooperative learning among kindergarten through primary-grade children (Daiute, 1988; Hawisher, 1989; Heap, 1987). Children working with word processors engage in more peer collaboration, peer conferencing, and peer teaching than students working without the benefit of the computer (Cochran-Smith, Kahn, & Paris, 1988; Dickinson, 1986; Kurth, 1988). Whereas writing at the computer is characterized by frequent verbal interaction, paper–and–pencil writing activities are complete silently and privately (Dickinson, 1986).

Computer environments seem to engender verbalization and communication. In fact, children spend a great deal of time talking to others. Observing 5-year-olds, Hyson (1985) found that children working alone at a computer spoke more often to themselves or to observers than when watching television. In another study, about 95% of the verbalizations of kindergartners and first graders working at computers were task related and directed to each other or the teacher; in addition, these discussions were nonconflictual and nonargumenative (Genishi et al., 1985).

Thus, the computer seems to engender social interaction among children in preschool and primary grades. Conceivably, computers may only enhance those behaviors that are currently being fostered by the wider classroom environment (Fein et al., 1987). Behavioral changes and long-term developmental outcomes are not likely to have a simple relationship to the presence of a computer. In examining these relationships, one must give consideration to personal characteristics of the students (e.g., developmental level, previous experiences) as well as to ecological factors such as the level and nature of teacher participation and support, and characteristics of computer hardware and software.

An Ecological Perspective

Characteristics of the Learner.   From an ecological perspective, the attributes and needs of the student must be considered. Individual differences in children's developmental and ability levels, experiences, and personality may influence the nature and benefits of their interactions within computer environments.

Children's peer interactions at the computer vary with age and experience. Results from several studies suggest a developmental progression. The interactions of preschool-age children in one study were characterized by turn taking and peer teaching (Borgh & Dickson, 1986b). Kindergartners in another study engaged primarily in turn taking, with few episodes of collaboration, aggression, or assertiveness (Bergin, Ford, & Meyer-Gaub, 1986). Peer tutoring among these kindergartners did occur about once per minute, involving primarily verbal instruction or management of turn taking and transpiring in response to a partner's failure to respond or behave appropriately rather than as a planning strategy.

In contrast to the predominance of turn taking and peer teaching by younger children, the social interactions of older children are characterized by collaboration. For example, third and fourth graders working in pairs took a cooperative problem-solving approach to task completion and placed a strong emphasis on team work (Riel, 1985). Similarly, for first and third graders working in two different computer environments, the predominant mode of interaction was collaborative (Clements & Nastasi, 1985). These age variations might be best explained by developmental differences in social interaction skills such as perspective taking and communication. Although suggestive of a developmental trend, such results need further confirmation through cross-sectional or longitudinal research.

The quality of preschool children's interactions may also change as they become more familiar with their partners and the computer. The helping, assisting, and teaching behaviors among 4-year-olds in one study increased over a 4-week period, with a concomitant decrease in turn taking (Shade et al., 1986). This change reflects a shift from an egocentric to a peer-oriented focus. As children gain even more experience (e.g., 4 months), however, helping behaviors may decline (Bergin et al., 1986). In a similar vein, after seven sessions within a Logo environment, peer collaboration increased and teacher guidance decreased as 5-year-olds gained greater mastery and control over their learning (Emihovich & Miller, 1988c).

The pattern suggested by the results of these studies is an initial egocentric focus on turn taking, followed by a more peer-oriented emphasis on helping and instructing, and finally peer collaboration and independence from adult guidance. This pattern emerges both across developmental levels and with greater experience in some computer environments (e.g., Logo); this intriguing similarity deserves additional research attention.

Ability levels also deserve consideration. High-ability students are more likely to take a dominant role in group work at the computer (Bellows, 1987) and, when working with software that fosters competition, are more likely to engage in competitive interactions (Hativa, Swisa, & Lesgold, 1989). In contrast, low-ability students are less likely to contribute to cooperative computer activities (Kurth, 1988) and, in competitive situations, are more likely to be ridiculed by peers (Hativa et al., 1989).

Personality and motivational factors may also influence the nature of children's interactions. The less assertive child may be less likely to contribute to a cooperative computer activity (Kurth, 1988). In addition, the student with high levels of interest and engagement may be more likely to engage in peer collaboration and tutoring, but also more likely to try to control or dominate the computer (Bergin et al., 1986). It has been suggested that such inequity in participation might be overcome with homogeneous grouping and/or teacher assistance (Kurth, 1988). Informal observations by a number of researchers indicate that ecological factors may account for variations in children's behaviors in educational computer environments.

Instructional Influences.   The ecological factor that has most often been identified as influential involves the role of the teacher. When left to their own devices, young children may adopt desirable or undesirable patterns of interaction. For example, preschool children can work cooperatively at the computer with minimal supervision (Rosengren et al., 1985), generating their own rules regarding turn taking, sharing, and helping (Shade et al., 1986). However, without teacher direction or formal instruction, 5- to 7-year-old boys may adopt a turn taking, competitive approach similar to that used with videogames (Silvern, Countermine, & Williamson, 1988).

The mere presence or availability of the teacher may influence children's interactions. Peer collaboration can be facilitated by the teacher's inaccessibility (Genishi, 1988; Genishi et al., 1985); in a similar vein, peers may be less likely to give direct help or verbal instruction when the level of teacher intervention is high (Bergin et al., 1986). However, aggressive behavior initially exhibited by children (ages 3 to 5) as they "jockeyed" for positions at the computer also declined when teachers were present to provide instruction and assistance (Lipinski et al., 1986). Thus, an optimal level of teacher intervention might be one that inhibits inappropriate behaviors while not interfering with peer conferencing and peer instruction.

Furthermore, collaboration and peer teaching might be attributed to the teacher's differential encouragement of such behavior (Dickinson, 1986; Genishi, 1988; Genishi et al., 1985). Borgh and Dickson (1986b) attributed turn taking and peer teaching behaviors to the way in which the classroom teacher structured the educational environment: Teachers established a rule requiring that the children use computers in pairs, paired children who would likely work well together, and initially sat with children at the computer to encourage and support turn taking. Similarly, Bowman (1985) reported that the teacher facilitated social interaction by placing two chairs before the computer, devising rules regarding turn taking, and intervening to arbitrate disputes and provide technical assistance. Children reportedly learned to follow the rules and assume the roles defined by the teacher.

Other factors, such as the ratio of computers to children, may also influence social behaviors. Lipinski et al. (1986) found that only with a 1:22 ratio (and no teacher present) was there any aggressive behavior. With a ratio of 1:12, there was no such behavior. Thus, they suggest that a 1:10 ratio might ideally encourage computer use, cooperation, and equal access to girls and boys.

Teachers may alter their instructional styles for computer activities, for example, by providing more direction during computer activities compared to traditional preschool activities (Klinzing & Hall, 1985). Similarly, increased functional play by preschool children was associated with increased teacher involvement in such play when computers were present (Fein et al., 1987).

Furthermore, children's interactions with computers may be affected by instructional changes in other preschool activities. These effects may vary as a function of classroom and teacher. In the computer's presence, dramatic play decreased in one classroom and increased in the other, because only in the latter classroom were interesting changes being made in the dramatic play center (Fein et al., 1987).

Perhaps what is most critical is the match between the teacher's behavior and the needs of the students. In a study of word processing, Dickinson (1986) found that the teacher initially was uneasy with collaborative writing. The impetus to write collaboratively at the computer came from the children, who were accustomed to working collaboratively with Logo programming. The teacher finally worked to increase communication during writing; observing initial successes at collaborative writing at the computer, she encouraged its continuation. In a similar vein, others have reported decreases in teacher guidance concurrent with increases in peer tutoring and collaboration (Emihovich & Miller, 1988c; Riel, 1985). Thus, the teacher–student interaction is not unidirectional.

Curricular Influences.   Computer hardware and software may possess characteristics that alter the instructional environment and thus influence children's behavior. For example, access to the work of others through voice synthesis, the computer screen, and the printed copy may facilitate collaboration and helping on writing activities (Kurth, 1988). Genishi (1988) suggested that teachers choose software based on instructional goals. Thus, to encourage collaboration, one might choose software that fosters cooperative work and minimizes the need for teacher help.

In the studies that reported evidence of peer collaboration (Emihovich & Miller, 1988c; Riel, 1985), children worked with more open-ended, problem-solving oriented software (Logo and writing software). In contrast, a structured counting program elicited more "teaching" behaviors than did an open-ended graphics program (Borgh & Dickson, 1986b). Finally, turn-taking was elicited by CAI software (Bergin et al., 1986).

In particular, Logo and CAI environments may differentially influence the types of cooperative interaction. In a series of studies, children working with Logo were more likely to engage in self-directed work and to resolve conflicts successfully (Clements & Nastasi, 1985, 1988; Nastasi, Clements, & Battista, 1990). CAI may inhibit elaboration of responses. In one study, second graders working with CAI most frequently gave and received terminal responses and rarely gave explanations (Bellows, 1987). Furthermore, CAI may engender increases in competitive behavior and social comparison among students (Hativa et al., 1989). Features of the CAI environment believed to foster such behavior were the numbering of exercises by level of difficulty, screen feedback regarding success, and printed feedback regarding progress of the class. In this latter study, an attempt was made to foster individualized work, and thereby minimize competition, by placing computers in separate carrels. However, students still managed to view the work of others for the purpose of comparison (e.g., by looking over and around the partitions).

Concerns have also been raised about the potential negative effects of software with aggressive content. For example, videogames have been hypothesized to foster aggressive behaviors. In one study, the amount of aggressive behavior of 4- to 6-year-olds increased following participation in a videogame with aggressive content, although the absolute level of aggression did not vary from that exhibited following the viewing of an aggressive cartoon (Silvern & Williamson, 1987). Similarly, the amount of prosocial behavior decreased following the videogame, but did not vary from that exhibited following the cartoon. Other research suggests that competitive videogames do not necessarily foster aggressive behavior in young children (Silvern, Lang, & Williamson, 1987), but may reduce older children's generosity (Chambers & Ascione, 1985).

Finally, certain computer environments may facilitate the development of prosocial behaviors. A computer simulation of a Smurf playhouse attenuated the themes of territoriality and aggression that emerged with a real playhouse version of the Smurf environment (Forman, 1985, 1986a). This may be due to features of the computer; in the computer environment, the Smurf characters could literally share the same space and could even jump "through" one another. The "forced" shared space of the computer program also caused children to talk to each other more.

Computer environments, like any educational environment, may be structured to differentially encourage cooperation or competition. Such structuring may influence children's later attitudes and behavior. For example, primary-grade gifted students participating in competitive, but not cooperative, computer group activities evidenced a significant increase in preference for competition over cooperation (Kanevsky, 1985). Following participation in cooperative, competitive, or individualistic computer-game activity, 4- and 5-year-olds did not perform differently on tasks measuring cooperative behavior (Strein & Kachman, 1984). However, there were trends in the expected direction: Cooperative behavior following treatment was highest for those who participated in the cooperative condition and lowest for those in the competitive condition. In addition, children in the competitive condition showed decreases in cooperative behavior from pre- to post-treatment, whereas those in the cooperative condition showed increases in cooperative behavior.

In retrospect, the early concern that computers would stifle playful social interaction appears overstated. Children would either have to be forced or mesmerized into solitary use of computers for long periods. Actually, young children prefer social use of computers, and rarely work alone. The addition of a computer center does not seem to disrupt ongoing play activities, with many finding that social interaction is encouraged. People affect how computers are used more than computers affect people. Personal characteristics of the child such as age, ability level, and personality variables seem to be influential. In addition, ecological factors such as teacher–student interaction and types of software appear to be important determinants of the social effects of computers. It should be noted that most of the findings regarding the influence of ecological factors on children's interactions within computer environments are based on informal observation rather than systematic study. Whereas findings suggest the potential importance of instructional and curricular factors, further study of the connections between environmental events and child behaviors is needed.

Effectance Motivation

The construct of effectance, or competence, motivation (Harter, 1978) serves as a theoretical foundation for examining possible differential effects of computer environments on aspects of this construct—intrinsic motivation, attitudes toward learning, and perceived competence. Definitions and measurement of these constructs vary widely across studies and include behaviors such as sustained attention to task, independent self-directed work, planning and rule-making, persistence, and displays of pleasure at mastery. In some instances, the same behavior is utilized to define two different constructs. For example, sustained attention to task (time on task) might be interpreted as a manifestation of persistence (i.e., motivation) in one study, but indicative of interest (i.e., attitude toward the task) in another. In addition, measurement techniques vary widely and include direct observations (both systematic and narrative), self-reports, and teacher reports. Differences in definitions and techniques may account for inconsistencies in findings.

Harter's conceptualization of effectance motivation will be utilized as a means for reconciling the diversity of definitions and as a framework for synthesizing the findings. According to this view, effectance motivation is defined as the degree to which an individual desires to control or effect change in his or her environment (Harter, 1978). This motive can be expected to influence one's attitudes toward learning and attempts at problem solving or mastery. Successful attempts at effecting change, or solving problems, leads to the internalization of a self-reward system and development of a sense of competence that subsequently serves as a mediator of one's motivational orientation. Thus, one's motivation, attitudes toward learning, and sense of competence are interrelated. The extent to which computers provide opportunities for exploration and mastery will influence the extent to which they contribute to the enhancement of effectance motivation and perception of one's self as competent.

Attitudes

Young children typically display enthusiasm and positive affect in their interactions with computers (Corning & Halapin, 1989; Gélinas, 1986; Hyson & Morris, 1985; Wright & Samaras, 1986). High levels of curiosity and exploration are reported for preschoolers working individually at the computer (Hungate & Heller, 1984). In addition, cooperative work at the computer may further increase task enjoyment and engagement displayed during solitary work (Perlmutter, Behrend, Kuo, & Muller, 1986).

Children may prefer computers to other activities. Young children in one study reported greater liking for computer activities than for more traditional free-time activities such as playing, drawing, and talking (Picard & Giuli, 1985). Similarly, observations of 5-year-olds revealed that computer use produced far more active, positive, and emotionally varied facial expressions (including more smiling) and greater levels of concentration than did television watching (Hyson & Morris, 1985).

The use of computers as instructional tools may also enhance students' attitudes toward academic work. Based on a review of research, Hawisher (1989) concluded that writing with computers results in positive attitudes toward writing and word processing among students of all ages. In a study of third-grade Israeli children, Mevarech (1985) found that students receiving CAI mathematics instruction, compared to those receiving non-CAI instruction, exhibited less mathematics anxiety.

Furthermore, computers may foster more positive attitudes toward school in general. Educationally disadvantaged third-grade Israeli students who had participated in CAI mathematics instruction for 2 years, compared to those participating in traditional mathematics instruction, expressed greater satisfaction with school in general, a stronger commitment to schoolwork, and more favorable attitudes toward teachers (Mevarech & Rich, 1985).

Motivation

Learning within a computer environment may be intrinsically stimulating. Papert (1980), for example, has suggested that the Logo environment possesses intrinsically interesting phenomena and has a certain "holding power." Children's intrinsic motivation may be reflected in a number of behaviors, including sustained attention to task, engagement in self-directed activity, establishing of task parameters (engagement in rule-making and planning behaviors), persistence, and reports of a sense of control or mastery.

Children sustain attention for longer periods of time working on computers than on other curricular activities. Primary-grade students participating in a CAI remedial reading program were observed to be more task-oriented (spent more time "on task") and more reluctant to stop than those receiving traditional instruction (Silfen & Howes, 1984). Similarly, first and third graders were observed to be more task oriented in on-computer situations (either Logo or drill-and-practice CAI) than when working off-computer (Clements & Nastasi, 1985). Furthermore, second graders working with word processors tended to persist longer than students working without the benefit of the computer (Kurth, 1988).

All the evidence, however, is not favorable. Williams and Beeson (1986–1987) studied the "holding power" of the computer in contrast to that of more traditional preschool activities—puzzles and blocks. When given a choice, children ages 2 to 5 years spent more time working with puzzles and blocks than with computers. Because of wide individual differences in the time spent working on each of the activities, the authors cautioned against broad generalizations about the "holding power" of the computer.

It has been suggested that children's enthusiasm about computers reflects only a novelty effect. A decline in interest in computers among preschoolers following a 20-minute session was reported in one study; in addition, the computer rarely was chosen as the preferred activity over toys and books after three such sessions (Goodwin, Goodwin, Nansel, & Helm, 1986). These effects may be due in part to the environment: Children worked alone with software that offered minimal opportunity for exploration and creativity. In addition, preference was assessed through an interview procedure rather than observed engagement in the activities.

In contrast, several studies provide evidence that children's interest persists beyond initial exposure to the computer. Third graders who were encouraged to work together in three different problem-solving computer environments reported highly positive attitudes toward computer experiences after 8 months of instruction (Lehrer, Randle, & Sancilio, 1989). Similarly, primary-grade children working with Logo and CAI evinced high levels of on-task behavior (over 90% of the time) even after 3 months of instruction (Clements & Nastasi, 1985). Finally, the verbalizations of preschoolers working with Logo over 10 1-hour sessions were observed to be primarily task related; 93% of their statements were related to problem solving or other aspects of task execution (Strand, 1987). In the latter study, the level of engagement was high although the nature of the engagement varied from seemingly aimless exploration to purposeful activity. Thus, the measure used to assess interest may influence one's conclusions.

It is conceivable that any observed decline in interest may reflect a change in the nature of the child's behavior rather than a real decrease in interest. In one study, the high level of intense interest, or "exuberance," (e.g., child points, exclaims, jumps up and down) observed initially among kindergarten-age children tapered off after 2 months to an "ordinary" level of close attention (Bergin et al., 1986). Throughout the intervention, children were observed to be "on-task" 90% of the time, again suggesting only a change in the nature of "interest" behavior.

Children working with computers also exhibit an enhanced sense of control. Interviews with children as young as 4 years of age indicate a greater sense of control following educational computer experiences (Hyson & Morris, 1985). In fact, children of this age report that what they like most about working with the computer is the ability to exercise control over the machine (Shade et al., 1986). Observations of children within computer environments also reveal behaviors indicative of a sense of control. For example, children in one study engaged in more rule-making (planning) behavior and displayed more pleasure at successful problem solving while working with computers than on noncomputer tasks (Clements & Nastasi, 1985).

Such experiences with computers might foster the development of an internal locus of control (Wright & Samaras, 1986). Third-grade Israeli students receiving CAI mathematics instruction, compared to those receiving nonCAI instruction, were less likely to attribute success and failure to external factors; that is, they exhibited a more internal locus of control (Mevarech, 1985).

Perceived Competence

Although it appears that attitudes and motivation are enhanced by educational computer experiences, findings are equivocal with regard to effects on the individual's sense of competence. Research by Mevarech and Rich (1985) suggests that CAI may enhance the mathematics self-concept of educationally disadvantaged third-grade students. Emihovich and Miller (1988a), however, failed to find differences in the general self-concept of lower SES Black students who participated in either Logo and CAI compared to a no-treatment control group. Differences in findings may reflect the domain of competence that was the target of instruction. However, length of intervention, software, and culture also differed; the effects of these variables warrant further study.

Educational computer environments that encourage competition may engender negative self-images (Hativa et al., 1989). Israeli children in Grades 2 through 6 instructed in such an environment expressed negative feelings about themselves and about each other following failure. In addition, educationally disadvantaged students were more likely than educationally advantaged students to develop negative self-concepts as a result of being ridiculed by peers because of their poor performance.

An Ecological Perspective

Thus, although not always guaranteed, the use of computers may provide a learning environment that promotes high levels of motivation, discipline, independence, and perseverance. These effects have been attributed to certain characteristics inherent in computer environments. For example, Gélinas (1986) suggested that the developmental appropriateness of software contributed to the sense of ownership, whereas the rules inherent in the medium contributed to the self-discipline exhibited by kindergartners during computer work. Similarly, interest, concentration, and persistence were attributed to the playful aspect created by the use of games, the opportunities for decision making, provision of external feedback regarding success, successful experiences, and the presence of peers. Understanding the influence of such instructional and curricular factors may assist educators in creating effective computer environments.

Instructional Influences.   The mere presence or absence of the teacher may affect the nature of children's interactions related to enhancement of motivation and perceived competence. For example, when the teacher is unavailable, children as young as 4 years of age will generate their own rules (Shade et al., 1986). However, children's interest in and use of the computer may be enhanced by teacher presence (Shade et al., 1986). Thus, although opportunities to attempt tasks without adult direction may encourage self-directed activity, provision of such direction may help to facilitate interest. Similarly, in regard to task structuring, positive effects of CAI on locus of control may be further enhanced through individualization of instruction (Mevarech, 1985).

The nature of the instructional environment may also influence children's task control. The responses of 4-year-olds to interview questions revealed an increased sense of personal control over the computer following experience in an environment that encouraged independence and peer interaction (Hyson & Morris, 1985). Studies of children working with writing programs have yielded similar findings (Dickinson, 1986; Riel, 1985). First- and second-grade children verbalized more about planning during computer writing activities in which peer collaboration was emphasized than during traditional, paper-and-pencil writing activities (Dickinson, 1986). In another study in which peer collaboration was emphasized, students' attitudes toward writing improved as a result of computer-based writing experiences (Riel, 1985).

Emihovich and Miller (1988b) provided evidence of a reciprocal relationship in which observed changes in young children's (ages 4 to 6) initiation and elaboration during Logo tasks were consonant with changes in teacher–student interactions. As children took greater control of task formulation, teachers provided less prompting and instruction. The teacher's role changed from that of a model to that of an evaluator. These behavioral changes suggest that as children become more skilled at regulation of their own learning and perhaps at mediation of the learning of their partners, teachers provide less structure and guidance. The nature of the Emihovich and Miller study did not permit validation of causal direction. It is possible that children's behavior followed changes in the teacher's behavior (and not vice versa). That is, as the teacher became less active in the learning process, children began to take more responsibility for task formulation. In addition, the teacher's earlier modeling of task control may have provided a model for the students. Similarly, the teacher's modeling of enthusiasm and sense of efficacy may serve to increase young children's motivation and sense of competence (Genishi, 1988; Genishi et al., 1985). Gélinas (1986) suggested that the role of the teacher should be facilitative; that is, helping children to break problems down into manageable steps. Such modeling and proximal goal setting have been found to increase the self-efficacy of children within noncomputer learning environments (Schunk, 1984; Schunk & Hanson, 1985).

The initial structuring by the teacher may be necessary for early acquisition and practice of subordinate skills, but open-ended experiences and opportunities for exploration and self-generation of problems may be necessary for children to become independent problem solvers (Strand, 1987). And as children gain experience, they can take on the role of teacher. Thus, encouragement of peer collaboration and tutoring may facilitate greater independence and thus enhancement of motivation and sense of competence.

Curricular Influences.   The types of software and the nature of children's interactions with the computer might help to explain effects on effectance motivation. For example, a drawing program tended to elicit more indicators of engagement and planning than a face construction and counting program (Hyson,

1985). Open-ended programs elicited more wondering and hypothesizing (Borgh & Dickson, 1986b). Time-on-task, as well as mastery, were facilitated when the computer gave preschoolers global feedback on their progress through the overall task (Hungate & Heller, 1984). Four-year-olds who were aware of the connections between the action of keypressing and outcome on the screen worked for longer periods of time (Shade et al., 1986). This was especially true for those children who watched the screen as they pressed the keys rather than attending only in response to auditory cues from the computer. Finally, the responses of 4-year-olds to interview questions revealed an increased sense of personal control using problem-solving or graphic software (Hyson & Morris, 1985). Although not compared to other types of software, writing programs that promote collaborative work have been shown to foster student control of planning as well as positive attitudes toward learning among first and second graders (Dickinson, 1986; Riel, 1985).

Specific features of CAI programs are believed to foster competition and thereby account for negative self-evaluations (as well as peer evaluations); these include public screen feedback about individual success or failure and printed feedback about class progress (Hativa et al., 1989). Similarly, CAI programs with unequivocal answers elicited more verbalizations about correctness and winning among preschoolers than open-ended graphics programs (Borgh & Dickson, 1986b). In both studies, these conclusions were based on descriptive data. Nevertheless, these observations suggest that the nature of children's interactions, engendered by specific software features, may account for some of the observed effects of computer learning experiences on self-perception.

It has been suggested that Logo and CAI may enhance effectance motivation and perceived competence differentially (Nastasi, Clements, & Battista, 1990). Both environments embody characteristics that have been identified through research in noncomputer learning contexts as influential in the development of competence motivation and a sense of competence; namely, modeling, social feedback, and task structuring characterized by proximal goal setting and performance-contingent reward (Harter, 1978; Schunk, 1984; Schunk & Hanson, 1985). For example, both environments provide opportunities for the establishment of short-term goals. In Logo, goals are self-selected, whereas in CAI, goals are externally determined (e.g., in drill-and-practice) or more tightly constrained (e.g., in simulations or problem-solving CAI). In addition, children in both environments might benefit from collaboration with a partner who could provide feedback and a model of competence. Thus, enhancement of competence motivation and self-perception of competence might be expected in both computer environments.

There are, however, distinct features of the environments that may lead to differential enhancement of motivation and self-perception. One difference between the two environments concerns the provision of evaluative feedback. In CAI, the computer provides specific evaluative feedback; in Logo, such feedback is not provided. Thus, unless others (teacher, partner) in the environment provide such information, evaluation of success in Logo must be more internally determined. Consequently, children working with CAI may receive more frequent and consistent external feedback about performance, whereas children in Logo might engage more frequently in self-evaluation and self-reinforcement. Both environments may provide opportunities for enhancing effectance motivation and perceived competence, but through different paths. Logo, in contrast to CAI, might be expected to lead more directly to the development of a self-evaluative, self-reward system, because of the more self-directed nature of the environment.

Both Logo and CAI have been found to engender effectance motivation and positive attitudes toward learning among young children, with these effects transferring to regular classroom activities (Clements & Nastasi, 1985; Genishi et al., 1985; Lehrer et al., 1989; Mevarech & Rich, 1985; Silfen & Howes, 1984). In addition, elementary-grade children working with Logo exhibit more evidence of increased competence motivation, characterized by higher frequencies of rule making and pleasure at intellectual discovery, than those working in CAI drill-and-practice or problem-solving environments (Clements & Nastasi, 1985, 1988; Nastasi et al., 1990).

Further, Logo may foster independence among young problem solvers. For example, preschoolers working with Logo became more self-directed as learners, relying less on the teacher to answer their questions, as they gained experience (Miller & Emihovich, 1986). Similarly, other work suggests that primary-grade students are more likely to direct their own learning experiences when they work with Logo than with drill CAI (Clements & Nastasi, 1985). The benefit may be particularly important for younger children. In this same study, first but not third graders who had worked with CAI for 14 weeks were more likely to seek teacher assistance on off-computer tasks than were children who had worked with Logo. Results have not always favored Logo, however. One study comparing Logo and CAI failed to find differences in their effect on the attitudes of elementary-grade children (Barker, Merryman, & Bracken, 1988).

The specific content of the software and developmental level of the students should be considered. The results of one study revealed transfer in attitudes toward mathematics after children worked with computational software, but not after working with geometry-oriented Logo programming (Lehrer et al., 1989). Children may have connected only the former with their experiences with classroom mathematics. Clements and Nastasi (1985) reported that working with CAI drill (but not Logo) activities may foster dependency and boredom with paper-and-pencil tasks; this finding was evident for first- but not third-grade students. Children may have found the paper-and-pencil exercises lacking the motivational and feedback characteristics of the game-like CAI exercises.

Research provides conflicting evidence regarding the valence of self-evaluative statements by children working in Logo. In one study, the majority (86%) of the self-evaluative statements made by preschoolers working with Logo were positive (Strand, 1987). Other research failed to reveal differences in the frequency of self-evaluative statements exhibited by primary-grade children working in Logo and drill-and-practice CAI (Clements & Nastasi, 1985, 1988). Furthermore, elementary-grade children (Grades 4 and 6) working in Logo compared to those working with problem-solving CAI made fewer positive self-statements (Nastasi et al., 1990). The relative internal/external structuring of the Logo and CAI environments may account for the latter findings. That is, the externally structured CAI environment might be more likely to evoke positive self-appraisals of one's performance. Although the internally structured Logo environment does not provide this feedback, it does provide intrinsically interesting phenomena (Papert, 1980), which might be more likely to evoke feelings of pleasure or satisfaction with the product of one's efforts. In this same study, children working in Logo made more statements indicating pleasure at discovery than those working in CAI. The more frequent seeking of approval from the teacher by the students working in Logo, however, suggests the need for external feedback even within this environment (Harter, 1978; Nastasi et al., 1990).

Logo programming might be particularly effective for fostering a sense of control. Preschoolers working within Logo, for example, showed increases in their ability to take control of the learning situation after only 3 weeks of experience (Emihovich & Miller, 1988b). Similarly, third graders exhibited significant increases in internal locus of control following $4\frac{1}{2}$ months of Logo experience, compared to students receiving nonLogo computer experiences (Burns & Hagerman, 1989). Thus, Logo might serve to enhance mastery-oriented thinking in young children.

In summary, there is empirical support for Papert's (1980) belief in the holding power of the computer even for children as young as 3 years of age. Not all results have been positive, however. For example, the interest of one group of preschoolers declined (Goodwin, Goodwin, Nansel, & Helm, 1986). It may be significant that the experimental treatment was short, solitary, and inflexible. In comparison, other studies report that children verbalize considerable curiosity, interest, enthusiasm, and a sense of personal control after direct involvement with a computer (Hyson & Morris, 1985; Wright & Samaras, 1986). Thus, most, but not all, studies have reported increases in positive attitudes after computer use, especially when children work in groups, write on the computer, or program in Logo (Lieberman, 1985). This is promising, especially because the motivational advantages of good computer software—challenge, curiosity, control, and feedback—are compellingly consonant with the type of experiences desired for enhancing young children's intrinsic motivation and sense of competence.

Social-Cognitive Links

Social interactions within educational environments are important not only for the social benefits but also because such interaction is an essential component of cognitive development. Studies of cooperative learning in general suggest that achievement and cognitive growth are facilitated by children working together (Nastasi & Clements, 1991).

Collaborative Interactions Within Computer Environments

Interactions within educational computer environments may likewise facilitate young children's achievement and cognitive growth. Intensive observations of two mildly handicapped children revealed that they produced longer and structurally more complex stories on the computer while working together than either did when working alone (Goldman & Rueda, 1988). At the least, cooperative work does not appear to be harmful. Results of one study indicate that the use of computers in small groups is just as effective in enhancing second grader's learning of phonics as individual use (Smith, 1985).

The benefits of social interaction for learning may be restricted to children beyond the preschool years. In one study, 4-year-olds working in pairs showed greater enjoyment and attention to task, but not better achievement, than those working alone (Perlmutter et al., 1986). Five-year-olds, however, benefited both in achievement and social-emotional areas. The authors suggested that the combined social and cognitive demands of working together may overburden the capabilities of younger children and thus impede effective problem solving.

Nature of Collaborative Interactions

Peer collaboration may engender certain types of interactive behaviors that would in turn facilitate learning and cognitive growth. Social-cognitive theory suggests that cognitive growth is facilitated by peer interaction that requires coordination of actions or thoughts due to a conflict of centrations, or egocentric viewpoints (Perret-Clermont, 1980). Although conflicts of cognitive centrations within the individual also contribute to cognitive growth, research has indicated that such conflicts embedded in a social situation are more significant (Bearison, 1982; Doise & Mugny, 1979). Furthermore, reported learning outcomes from cooperative learning research have been attributed to the dissent or disagreement among group members about problem solving (Johnson, Brooker, Stutzman, Hultman, & Johnson, 1985; Johnson, Johnson, Pierson, & Lyons, 1985).

Research suggests that children working together in computer environments may be more likely to engage in cognitive conflict and metacognitive activity than those working alone. In one study, 5-, but not 4-, year-olds engaged in more conflict when paired than when not paired (even the latter group was free to interact with other students working in close proximity; Perlmutter et al., 1986). In addition, children at both age levels engaged in more metacognitive activity (goal setting and task management) when paired. In another study, the interactions of third graders working in dyads were characterized by cycles of disagreement and resolution, with the children typically resolving such conflicts before proceeding (Lehrer & Smith, 1986b). These dyads were more likely to engage in hierarchical (abstract) planning whereas those working individually engaged in nonhierarchical (opportunistic) planning. That is, problem solving within the cooperative context was characterized by preplanning on multiple levels (e.g., with decomposition of the problem into subproblems) and successive refinement of problem solution. In contrast, problem-solving behavior in the individual context was characterized by representation of the problem on a single level, backtracking, and abandonment of original plans.

Logo and CAI

Furthermore, certain computer environments may be more likely to facilitate cognitive growth than others. In particular, Logo programming seems to have greater higher-order cognitive benefit than various drill and problem-solving CAI environments (Battista & Clements, 1986; Clements, 1990). It has been suggested that these two types of environments may differentially engender social interactions that are responsible for cognitive growth, namely interactions that promote collaborative problem solving and cognitive conflict (Nastasi et al., 1990). When working with self-selected Logo projects, children engage in every step of problem solving. Especially in an environment that encourages collaboration and shared responsibility, children are likely to negotiate their problem definition and solution strategies so as to proceed successfully. Participants in such a coherent social problem-solving interaction each attempt to make sense of, or give meaning to, the other's actions, and continually modify their own goals in the process. If either their goals or their solutions diverge too much, their actions interfere with each other. Thus, children must continually validate their own problem-solving activity via comparison with their partners' activity, continually striving toward mutual agreement.

In contrast, children working in CAI environments may be more likely to maintain their own egocentric points of view. The computer structures the problem, the solution, and the interaction. Children working together may have different perspectives, and yet each may respond in turn to the computer's queries without reaching interpersonal agreement. In CAI, one child's response is not necessarily contingent upon, or even related to, the other child's. Therefore, whereas social interactions may show an increase in both environments, those focused on problem solving and conflict resolution may occur more frequently in Logo than in CAI environments.

Research suggests that Logo is more likely to engender collaborative problem solving. For example, first- and third-grade children working within Logo engaged in more cooperative rule-making behavior than those working with drill-and-practice CAI (Clements & Nastasi, 1985, 1988). In addition, peer-mediated problem solving during work with Logo has been found to be positively related to posttreatment achievement for both preschoolers and older students (Nastasi et al., 1990; Perlmutter et al., 1986). The Logo environment also may generate the collaborative use of higher-order cognitive processes by young children. Perlmutter et al. (1986) suggested that benefits of cooperative problem solving within Logo may be attributable to externalization of task structure and task management; that is, the children in their study engaged in relatively high levels of meta-task activity (goal setting and task structuring) but spent less time generating and implementing specific strategies. Similarly, preschoolers in another study exhibited an increased use of planning statements reflecting intended goals as a result of working collaboratively with Logo (Miller & Emihovich, 1986). These same students scored higher on a test of comprehension monitoring following a 3-week educational computer experience than their counterparts who had worked with CAI. Furthermore, primary-grade children working with Logo exhibited a higher frequency of behaviors indicative of executive-level processing (Clements & Nastasi, 1988). In particular, children in Logo were more likely to engage in those behaviors related to problem identification, planning, and monitoring of solution processes. Children working with drill CAI were more likely to engage in behaviors that involved responding to external feedback from the computer.

Finally, Logo environments engender conflict, and, more importantly, negotiation and resolution of that conflict (Clements & Nastasi, 1985, 1988; Nastasi et al., 1990). In earlier work (Clements & Nastasi, 1985, 1988), we observed first and third graders as they worked with Logo or drill CAI, following 14 weeks of experience in the respective environments. Although there was no evidence that children within the two settings exhibited different amounts of conflict, children working with Logo were more likely to resolve the conflicts that did arise. In addition, when compared to an off-computer task situation, children within both computer environments exhibited higher amounts of both conflictual behavior and successful conflict resolution (Clements & Nastasi, 1985). Thus, although both drill CAI and Logo were likely to engender disagreements, children working with Logo were more likely to reach a successful resolution.

A follow-up study with older students revealed a greater amount of conflict and conflict resolution in a Logo than a CAI problem-solving environment; importantly, these concerned conflict about ideas, not about social situations. Furthermore, critical for gains in higher-order thinking was the resolution of these idea-based conflicts (Nastasi et al., 1990). In a study of preschoolers, Perlmutter et al. (1986) found that conflict or disagreement was positively related to posttreatment achievement (knowledge of Logo), whereas congruence or harmonious interaction was negatively correlated with achievement. Thus, engagement in conflict and particularly in resolution of that conflict seems to facilitate learning and cognitive growth.

In summary, the admittedly small number of studies conducted to date suggest that collaborative interactions within computer environments have a facilitative effect on children's learning and cognitive growth. Furthermore, specific interactive behaviors may account for these gains; namely, engagement in rule-making or planning behaviors, and most importantly, engagement in cognitive conflict and its resolution. Finally, certain types of computer environments such as Logo programming may be more likely to engender these types of behaviors.

The teacher plays an important role in amplifying the benefits of Logo. Miller and Emihovich (Emihovich & Miller, 1988b; Miller & Emihovich, 1986) reported a change in the teacher's behavior that parallels a change in children's behavior as they work with Logo, reflecting a move from teacher-mediated to peer-mediated learning. The shift from teacher- to peer-mediated learning may be necessary for cognitive benefits to be seen. In fact, results of a study with preschoolers reveal that peer-mediated problem solving was positively correlated with posttreatment achievement, whereas teacher-mediated learning was negatively correlated with achievement (Perlmutter et al., 1986).

Teachers also need to be cognizant of the potential influence of group composition. Results of one study suggest that heterogeneous grouping may hinder learning for low-ability students (Kurth, 1988). Furthermore, these students did not necessarily benefit from working with other low-ability students unless the teacher provided guidance. Further information regarding group composition can be found in the literature on cooperative learning (Slavin et al., 1985).

In conclusion, an environment in which children work together and have greater freedom to introduce topics of learning and to initiate action, and in which the teacher plays a supportive role (i.e., through scaffolding), is one that is more likely to facilitate mediated learning and the consequent internalization of higher-order regulatory processes. Within such a sociocultural context, both student–student and teacher–student interactions are important. Further investigation of the connections between such interactions and documented cognitive gains within computer environments is needed. Such information will help us to design computer learning environments more effectively.

Final Words

In summary, application of computers in education may enhance social interactions, attitudes toward learning, intrinsic motivation, and children's sense of competence. In addition, collaborative interactions within computer environments are more likely to facilitate cognitive development. To realize this potential, research indicates that certain factors should be considered:

- Teachers make a difference. They can encourage and facilitate the social use of computers through establishment of rules, structuring of the setting and the task, and reinforcement of collaboration.
- Initially, children may need more support and guidance. Over time, however, self-directed and peer-mediated learning should be encouraged.

- Developmental limitations must be considered. For example, the limited perspective-taking abilities of young children may limit their ability to work collaboratively. In some cases, collaborative skills should be taught.
- Software should be chosen wisely. If you want to foster cooperation and effectance motivation, certain types of programs may more likely to achieve these goals (e.g., Logo or writing programs).
- Computer activities should be structured like other learning activities. An activity designed to engender cooperation, motivation, independence, and perseverance is likely to do so with and without a computer (of course, taking into consideration possible software effects).
- Cognitive growth is facilitated by adequate experience working independently of teacher guidance, with reliance on peer collaboration and peer mediation. Specific interactive behaviors that seem to be important in fostering cognitive growth include rule-making and planning, cognitive conflict, and resolution of that conflict.
- Some specific suggestions for the teacher in structuring computer environments are: provide mediation, decrease the amount of guidance as children become more independent and as peer collaboration and mediation increase, teach children strategies for effective conflict resolution, and teach children effective strategies for problem solving and use of higher-order processes.

COGNITION AND ACHIEVEMENT

Can computers "teach" young children? That is, do they enhance children's academic and cognitive development, especially in comparison to other types of instruction? Research results have been surprisingly comprehensive and illuminative regarding the use of computers for instruction in the language arts, mathematics, and higher-order thinking.

Language Arts

Language Development

Increases in social interaction and positive attitudes may help generate increased use of language. Preschoolers' language activity, measured as words spoken per minute, was almost twice as high at the computer as at any of the other activities such as playdough, blocks, art, or games (Muhlstein & Croft, 1986). Computer activity is slightly more effective than toy play in stimulating vocalizations in disabled preschoolers (McCormick, 1987).

Computer graphics is an especially generative environment. For example, children in a nursery setting tell longer and more structured stories following a computer graphics presentation than following a static presentation or no stimulus (Riding & Tite, 1985). Working within a language experience context, 3- and 4-year-old children verbalized (i.e., dictated) significantly more about their Logo computer pictures than about their hand-drawn works (Warash, 1984). Research with Logo also indicates that it engenders interaction and language rich with emotion, humor, and imagination (Genishi et al., 1985). Children were clearly and directly responsive to other children's requests for information.

Experience with Logo embedded in a narrative context has also been shown to enhance language-impaired preschool children's perceptual-language skills (Lehrer & deBernard, 1987) and increase first graders' scores on assessments of visual-motor development, vocabulary, and listening comprehension (Robinson, Gilley, & Uhlig, 1988; Robinson & Uhlig, 1988). Reports such as these help allay the fear that computers will de-emphasize play, fantasy, and the corresponding rich use of language. When children are in control, they create fantasy in computer programs beyond the producers' imaginations (Wright & Samaras, 1986).

Prereading and Reading Skills

Although not conclusive, research results concerning the effects of CAI on reading achievement are generally encouraging. As early as 1972, Atkinson and Fletcher taught kindergartners and first graders to read with computer programs emphasizing letter recognition and recall, sight words, spelling, phonics, and sentence and word meanings. After participating in 8 to 10 minutes of CAI per day for about $5\frac{1}{2}$ months, first-grade children gained 5.05 months over a control group, and maintained a 4.9-month gain for over a year (Atkinson & Fletcher, 1972).

Since then, it has been confirmed that about 10 minutes work with CAI per day significantly benefits primary-grade children's reading skill development (Piestrup, 1981; Ragosta, Holland, & Jamison, 1981; Watkins & Abram, 1985), especially for low achievers (Clements & Mcloughlin, 1986; Lavin & Sanders, 1983; Silfen & Howes, 1984; Teague, Wilson, & Teague, 1984). These studies, like much computer research, has not evaluated the cost effectiveness of their innovations.

Preschoolers can develop such reading readiness abilities as visual discrimination, letter naming, and beginning word recognition with computers (Lin, Vallone, & Lepper, 1985; Moxley & Barry, 1985; Smithy-Willis, Riley, & Smith, 1982; Swigger & Campbell, 1981). Such results, however, are not guaranteed. For example, computer presentation of sight words is not necessarily superior to flash-card presentation (Sudia, 1985). Also, three 20-minute sessions with simple readiness software failed to show an effect on preschoolers' prereading concepts in one study (Goodwin, Goodwin, Nansel, & Helm, 1986). In another study, however, placing computers and appropriate software in kindergartners' classrooms for several months significantly facilitated their acquisition of school readiness and reading readiness skills. When supplemented by concurrent computing activities outside of school (each child in one class also received a computer to use at home), academic gains were even greater (Hess & McGarvey, 1987).

Computers can make a special contribution to special needs children. After 6 weeks of reading instruction using a microcomputer, 3- to 6-year-old deaf children demonstrated a significant improvement in word recognition and identification (Prinz et al., 1982). Taking advantage of young children's cognitive readiness regardless of their primary mode of communication, the program allowed them to press a word (e.g., "flower") and see a picture of the object, the word, and a graphic representation of a manual sign.

Some critics despair of the emphasis on low-level reading skills; however, there is evidence of a causal relationship between decoding (including rapid word recognition) and comprehension in beginning readers (Lesgold, 1983; Perfetti, 1983). On this basis, computerized practice of information-processing components of reading can make an important contribution to reading success. Several developmental projects along these lines exist, and some have generated evidence supporting their efficacy (Lesgold, 1983; Perfetti, 1983; Roth & Beck, 1984). Grocke (1983) reported that both mildly handicapped and average children exposed to a sight word computer program that utilized speech made significantly greater gains in basic vocabulary recognition than a control group receiving regular instruction.

This type of drill software, however, takes an exclusively subskills perspective. In this view, reading is a linear, hierarchically ordered process that begins with the features of letters or words. In contrast, the holistic approach assumes that reading is a problem-solving process that begins in the mind with ideas about the nature of print and concepts about the world. Readers are seen as problem solvers, trying to discover what the author means as they build up their own meanings. Research is needed that uses holistically oriented software. For example, programs exist that ask students to test hypotheses or to act as the editor of a newspaper who, plagued by reporters who write passages with sentences that do not belong, must find and remove those sentences.

Finally, based on the view of readers as problem solvers, several researchers have engaged children in either skills- or problem-solving-oriented CAI. Although both groups made gains in reading achievement, the greatest gains were made by the children who worked with problem-solving CAI (Clements, 1987a; Norton & Resta, 1986). Similar results have been obtained for children as young as 5 years, where problem-solving computer activities were especially helpful for children who had initially low reading attainment (Riding & Powell, 1987). As a final example, Logo programming may have a diffuse and delayed effect on reading achievement. A longitudinal study reveals moderate to strong effects on reading vocabulary and comprehension in favor of children who experienced Logo in 1st grade (Clements, 1987c). These effects may be attributable not to direct practice during the treatment, but rather to an increase in comprehension monitoring skill, which was strongly affected by the Logo treatment. Similarly, substantial effects on language mechanics and spelling may be attributable to the development of strategies for processing detailed information more exhaustively and for detecting and correcting syntactic errors. Considering the range of instructional approaches and measures used, it is not surprising that effects in the reading/language arts area are some of the most variable in the field (Roblyer et al., 1988).

One program, Writing to Read, provides a link between reading and composition. Children work with computers, typewriters, and tape records in both drill-and-practice preparatory activities and story writing using a simplified phonetic alphabet. Most studies indicate that kindergartners and first graders learn to read and write better than those in control groups, with no evidence of deleterious effects on spelling (Murphy & Appel, 1984; Spillman, Hutchcraft, Olliff, Lutz, & Kray, 1986). Caution is warranted in interpreting these results. First, such gains may be due in large part to increased structured reading and writing time (Whitmer & Miller, 1987). Further, the program may not be as effective for below average children. Finally, critics have argued that the program de-emphasizes real communicative situations in favor of drill of a narrow range of skills out of context; utilizes a phonemic spelling system that may be based on an adult's logic of encoding words rather than on a children's development of strategies; and limits children's use of oral language to simple skills such as encoding words, repeating sounds, and reciting words (Piazza, 1988; Wallace, 1985). If valid, these criticisms imply gains on achievement tests, but to the detriment of other important aspects of literacy. Qualitative and quantitative research with this and similar programs is needed to test these alternate viewpoints.

Composition and Word Processing

Word Processing and Composition.   Why is writing, especially compared to speaking, so difficult for young children to learn? One reason is its tedium, another is its lack of power. Especially for young children, speech provides control. Writing is anemic in comparison. But certain computer environments provide young children with that control and thus imbue their writing with power. The written word can create animated pictures and stories that can be heard. Computers can also reduce the tedium of writing. Few studies have been conducted with the most innovative writing programs, but there is a significant research corpus on children's use of computers as word processors.

In general, these studies indicate that children using word processors write more, have fewer fine motor control problems, are less worried about making mistakes, and make fewer mechanical errors (Clements, 1987a; Daiute, 1988; Hawisher, 1989; Kurth, 1988; Phenix & Hannan, 1984; Roblyer et al., 1988). Findings regarding holistic ratings of quality are mixed, but generally positive (Bangert-Drowns, 1989; Hawisher, 1989).

Why do word processors help? Perhaps the main benefit of using word processors, especially for very young writers, is the provision of support (Clements, 1987a; Rosegrant, 1986). Such support, a form of scaffolding that involves the provision of physical tools, allows the child to use written language for its true purpose, communication. From the beginning, children can experiment with letters and words without being distracted by the fine motor aspects of handwriting. Thus, they both learn about composition in its entirety and build a sense of competence. In a word, young children can engage in creative writing that would be difficult if not impossible without computers.

Perhaps it is not surprising, then, that children who have the most difficulties in writing may benefit the most (Bangert-Drowns, 1989). Even those not yet capable of writing by hand are able to learn to use a keyboard to write and those reluctant to write with a pencil seem to enjoy writing with a word processor (Cochran-Smith et al., 1988).

Furthermore, word processors can support a constructive, process approach to composition. In an ethnographic study in kindergarten through fourth-grade classrooms using word processing, Cochran-Smith et al. (1988) found that children started first inventing spellings at the computer; interestingly, they produced only random letters with paper and pencil. In preschool and kindergarten children, word processing led to higher sensitivity to elements of text such as words and to elements of the writing process, such as thinking about the topic before writing about it. This awareness may have resulted from children's propensity to "play" with units of compositions (Lehrer, Levin, DeHart, & Comeaux, 1987).

At a more advanced level, it is logical to assume that word processors facilitate revision. Adding, deleting, changing, and moving text is simplified with computers. But do children take advantage of these features? Results are mixed, with some studies showing children revise more with word processors (correcting punctuation and spelling) and others failing to show differences (Bangert-Drowns, 1989; Clements, 1987a; Hawisher, 1989). Most of the latter studies did not measure revisions made on the computer before printed copy, and these may be the most significant. In addition, young children, more so than older children, are apparently more willing to take risks and then reread and revise (Cochran-Smith et al., 1988; Phenix & Hannan, 1984).

Young children derive satisfaction from being able to edit easily and produce clean, printed copies of their work. For this and other reasons, students have positive attitudes toward writing and word processing after working with computers (Bangert-Drowns, 1989; Hawisher, 1989; Lehrer et al., 1987). They gain confidence in their writing (Phenix & Hannan, 1984) and are motivated to write (Casey, 1984). Primary-grade students with learning difficulties evince a particularly striking change in their attitudes toward writing, especially in accepting editing as a fundamental component of the writing process. They write more and are more independent in that writing (Riel, 1985).

An ethnographic study in first- and second-grade classrooms provides specific examples (Dickinson, 1986). Paper-and-pencil work during writing time was nearly always done by children writing their own pieces and was accompanied by minimal talk about writing. Talk that did occur did not deal with planning, self-monitoring, and response to other children's work; one pair spent up to 30% of their time talking about penmanship while writing only 11 words, fewer than either normally produced working alone. In contrast, collaborative writing sessions at the computer included considerable talk conducive to planning, monitoring, and responding to what was being written. For example, children discussed spelling, punctuation, spacing, and text meaning and style. Revision was frequent, possibly because children are better at detecting errors in another child's writing than in their own. These corrections were striking in their frequency and sophistication.

The computer can serve as a tool to help foster collaboration and create a new social organization. It thus provides additional scaffolding to young writers due to its impact on the social life of the classroom—by providing support for cooperative learning. As we have seen earlier, social and cognitive benefits interact.

Talking Word Processors. Many age-appropriate word processors include speech synthesis; that is, the computer can pronounce what children type. Why? Speech provides an extra level of scaffolding for young writers (Borgh & Dickson, 1986a; Rosegrant, 1985). It increases the interactivity of the computer as a writing tool; children hear letter names and words as they write. Thus, "talking" word processors may help children build links between conversation and composition. They may take more risks and revise more frequently when they can hear what they have written. Finally, hearing their composition read may encourage them to take the perspective of their audience.

Research testing such hypotheses has a longer history than might be supposed. O.K. Moore's "talking typewriter" appeared over three decades ago. It was ahead of its technological time, but it was shown to significantly increase young children's scores on alphabet recognition and verbal ability tests (Israel, 1968). Beginning in 1967, young 3- to 6-year-old at-risk children were provided the Talking Typewriter's self-motivating computer-based program for an average of $2\frac{1}{2}$ years. Followed into the ninth grade, these children made incremental long-term gains in reading; that is, their achievement gains increased each year (Steg, Vaidya, & Hamdan, 1982).

More recent research with talking word processors shows that preschool to first-grade children were more able to express ideas, write simple sentences, and take risks in experimenting with their writing (Rosegrant, 1985, 1988). Such studies support and extend the research on word processors without speech. Others have directly compared word processing with and without speech in an attempt to delineate its specific effects.

In one such study, only voice-aided word processing acted as a scaffold for young children's writing by promoting the acquisition of several components of preschool literacy including symbol–sound and sound–symbol associations, the importance of vowels and the need to have distinctive boundaries (e.g., spaces) between words, reading of compositions, and metacognitive awareness of the purposes and processes of writing (Lehrer et al., 1987). Of what does such metacognitive awareness consist? Young writers need to develop an "inner voice" for constructing and editing text subvocally. Computerized speech can provide an external voice to read and re-read text during the composing and revising process. Research has demonstrated that children eventually read along with the speech synthesizer, adding intonations that complete the meaning, and ultimately become increasingly subvocal—an inner voice is developed. Children then simultaneously develop the ability to "hear" whether or not the text "sounds right" (Rosegrant, 1988).

Young writers do have the computer read their compositions—so much so, that children using talking word processors sometimes wrote shorter compositions than those using word processors without speech; both wrote more than paper-and-pencil groups (Kurth & Kurth, 1987). Later in the year, better readers listened to the computer less. Poor readers continued to use the synthesizer to read their stories. Thus, speech synthesis may be most important for beginning writers or less able readers (Kurth, 1988).

Does such computer-based reading affect children's invented spellings and editing? Although children using speech synthesis do invent spellings (Rosegrant, 1985, 1988), their final drafts include fewer invented spellings than do those of children not using synthesizers. Possibly the synthesizer could not pronounce the word correctly if spellings were not close to the phonetic pronunciation or to the preprogrammed spelling (Kurth, 1988; Kurth & Kurth, 1987).

In contrast, talking word processors increase the amount of editing children performed on their compositions, even compared to nontalking word processing (Borgh & Dickson, 1986a). Differences in the length or holistic quality, however, were not found (Borgh & Dickson, 1986a; Kurth, 1988; Kurth & Kurth, 1987; Lehrer et al., 1987). It may be that the spoken feedback specifically fostered an awareness of the need to edit.

Basic Skills.   All this emphasis on computers and compositions might raise a concern: Will there be a detrimental effect on basic skills? On the contrary, such an emphasis has the potential to improve basic skills such as spelling, punctuation, and grammar (Bangert-Drowns, 1989). Children using talking word processors improve significantly in their ability to name letters and sound out words (Rosegrant, 1985, 1988). Taking a different approach, kindergarten and first-grade children were encouraged to use invented spellings, writing stories with the aid of a program written in Logo. They developed both phonological spelling strategies similar to those that had been reported for children using pencil and paper and, simultaneously, developed visual spelling strategies earlier and in more detail than had been reported previously (Moxley & Joyce, 1990).

Typing and Keyboarding. Decades of research have consistently shown moderate but positive effects of using typewriters on syntax, spelling skills, reading comprehension, word identification, and vocabulary, and a greater potential effect on creative writing and motivation. No negative effects on handwriting ability were found. Young students (e.g., primary grades) can be expected to profit the most from typing, possibly due to a growth in word-recognition skills (Borthwick, 1987; Hoot, 1988).

Given the benefits derived from typing and word processing experience, questions regarding the teaching of keyboarding are sure to arise. Can young children use the standard adult keyboard? Can they learn to touch type? Is it worthwhile for them to do so? The answer to the first question is clear: Researchers consistently report that using the standard keyboard—even with only minimal instruction—is not a problem, even for very young children (Borgh & Dickson, 1986a; Hungate & Heller, 1984; Lipinski et al., 1986; Swigger & Campbell, 1981).

Can primary-grade children be taught touch typing? Although there are fewer investigations of this question, the answer appears to be "yes." Instruction can improve keyboarding skills in kindergarten through second-grade children, and these children are better prepared for later writing and Logo programming (Block, Simpson, & Reid, 1987; Britten, 1988). The answer to our final question—should they be instructed in keyboarding—is unfortunately not so clear. For example, goals such as high input rate and correct keyboarding style are suspect (Hoot, 1988). Furthermore, touch typing does not appear to result in greater benefits in language arts skills than the use of the "hunt and peck" method (Borthwick, 1987). Finally, young children seem to master word processing with little training (Kurth & Kurth, 1987). Thus, although typing and word processing are clearly beneficial activities, it is uncertain whether substantive direct instruction in keyboarding is worthwhile.

Special Populations. Computer technology can compensate for a wide range of disabilities. One early development, the Kurzweil Reading Machine, reads any written material aloud via a speech synthesizer. Braille material can also be printed if desired. (Clements, 1985, provides more information about computer prosthetics.)

Computers also can play a special role in supporting the writing and reading of special students, for example, facilitating writing, reading, and even verbalizations in nonvocal, severely physically impaired children (Meyers, 1984).

Deaf children as young as 3 to 5 years have improved their writing, reading, and general communication skills by composing with a special keyboard that included animation of color pictures and representations of signs from American Sign Language (Prinz, Pemberton, & Nelson, 1985). This represented a true communicative context for these children. Learning disabled students with a history of failure have been observed to write eagerly and continuously, though slowly (MacArthur & Shneiderman, 1986). Finally, computers have been used successfully in developing literacy among very young children—in this case, Spanish-speaking first-grade children—regardless of their initial ability to read and write (Brisk, 1985).

Disadvantages and Problems.   There are possible disadvantages of word processors as well. They can be expensive and complicated. The size of the screen limits the amount of text writers can see at one time, so text coherence may be affected negatively. For such reasons, some critics argue that word processors may have no effect or even a detrimental one. Although the research already reviewed tends to negate these arguments, the concerns cannot be summarily dismissed.

For example, we saw that learning disabled students may derive great benefits from word processing (MacArthur & Shneiderman, 1986). However, difficulties also arose that should not be overlooked. For instance, such students often use keys inefficiently (e.g., using the left arrow to move up one character at a time, or deleting several words to get back to a single minor mistake) and have misconceptions (e.g., initially inserting numerous spaces to make "room" for text to be added instead of just inserting the text).

Such difficulties are not unique to children with learning disabilities. All students may evince some conceptual problems, for example, equating keyboard-and-screen with pencil-and-paper (Cochran-Smith et al., 1988). They may believe one cannot insert words, or they may press "return" at the end of every line, not using the "wrap" feature of word processors.

Recommended, therefore, are "what-you-see-is-what-you-get" word processors and a logical structure for commands (MacArthur & Schneiderman, 1986). Teachers should provide instruction that gives students a clear conceptual model of the overall organization, as well as direct instruction and structured practice on points of difficulty such as saving and loading, insertion and deletion, and proper use of returns for paragraphs and blank lines.

Perhaps more important is the teaching and learning environment in which word processing is embedded. In one study, children with better typing skills wrote more, and those with poor typing skills wrote less (Wallace, 1985). Changes tended to be focused more on structural revisions such as spelling and punctuation rather than on the improvement of ideas. The conclusion of this researcher? Word processors will not have a major impact on children's writing without a corresponding change in the teacher's approach to composition to match the abilities of the learners.

Teachers create quite different environments for children to use word processing, attributable to assumptions teachers make about children, teaching, and learning. Assumptions have to do with whether learning is solitary and private or collaborative, whether the writing process is linear or recursive, and whether the teacher's role is the management of students or facilitation of their independence. Benefits are directly related to and derived from the environment established; word processing can enhance such an environment, but does not in and of itself establish it (Cochran-Smith et al., 1988).

Final Statements. Fortunately, the researchers and teachers in most recent projects are not only sensitive to the role instruction plays in combination with word processing, but also take care to create a setting in which the pedagogy is grounded in theory and research. There is also a movement away from mere revision to involving computers in the total composition process (Hawisher, 1989). This probably accounts for positive results of these studies. One must also remember factors that operated against successful use of word processing in most existing studies, such as short durations and small number of writing assignments. One group of researchers stated that if they had completed their evaluation after a couple of months, they would have concluded that none of the benefits occurred. Only after 1 full year and into the second year did the rich benefits emerge (Cochran-Smith et al., 1988).

Thus, it would seem that word processing can be successfully integrated into a process-oriented writing program as early as first grade, and that even younger students can use computers to explore written language. If used within the context of a theoretically based educational environment, computers can facilitate the development of a new view of writing, and a new social organization (cooperative learning) that supports young children's writing. Children plan, write, discuss, and revise more frequently in such environments. They use the computer as a language arts learning tool (Clements, 1987b).

Mathematics

CAI and Mathematics Achievement

Some reports suggest that the greatest gains in the use of CAI (usually drill and practice) have been in mathematics skills for primary-grade children (Lavin & Sanders, 1983; Niemiec & Walberg, 1984; Ragosta et al., 1981). Again, 10 minutes per day proved sufficient for significant gains; sessions of 20 minutes per day generated treatment effects about twice as large. Such results appear to be consistent across schools, years, and testing instruments and have been judged to be cost feasible (Ragosta et al., 1981). Providing computers every day for all students, however, demands substantial amounts of computer equipment.

Appropriate computer games may also be effective. Kraus (1981) reported that second graders with an average of 1 hour of interaction with a computer game over a 2-week period responded correctly to twice as many items on an addition facts speed test as did students in a control group.

Younger children also appear to benefit. Three-year-olds learned sorting from a computer task as easily as from a concrete doll task (Brinkley & Watson, 1987–1988). Reports of gains in such skills as counting have also been reported for kindergartners (Corning & Halapin, 1989; Hungate, 1982). Similarly, kindergartners in a computer group scored higher on numeral recognition tasks than those taught by a teacher (McCollister, Burts, Wright, & Hildreth, 1986). There was some indication, however, that instruction by a teacher was more effective for children just beginning to recognize numerals, but the opposite was true for more able children. This relates to the finding that children more interested in using computers had greater representational competence, and has implications for use of this type of program. Children should not work with such drill-and-practice programs until they understand the concepts; then, practice may be of real benefit. In a similar vein, CAI drill has been shown to positively influence total mathematics and computational skills more than other treatments, whereas concept application skills were improved more by regular mathematics curricula (McConnell, 1983). Thus, teachers must carefully match students and goals with appropriate treatments.

Special Needs and Individualization

Mathematics CAI appears especially effective in remedial situations and with students from schools serving lower socioeconomic populations (Corning & Halapin, 1989; Hotard & Cortez, 1983; Lavin & Sanders, 1983; McConnell, 1983; Ragosta et al., 1981). Both achievement and attitudes are positively affected (Mevarech & Rich, 1985).

CAI and individualized approaches may work particularly well together. For example, Mevarech (1985) found that CAI facilitated the acquisition of mathematics skills, alleviated mathematics anxiety, and reduced external locus of control in disadvantaged primary school children. Most interesting, however, is that CAI reduced external locus of control most in individualized rather than traditional settings. Conversely, CAI freed teachers to work on other aspects of learning, increasing the efficacy of the individualized approach. Thus, CAI and individualized approaches each ameliorated some of the problems associated with the other.

Such individualization ideally should encompass the entire educational environment, including the software. In one particular drill-and-practice CAI curriculum, it was found that above-average students progressed faster, even though they were working on more difficult problems (Hativa, 1988). The researchers found that lower-ability students were also hampered by numerous "child–machine" errors; that is, hardware and software difficulties such as switching digits, pressing wrong keys, and pressing keys too long. They had trouble determining the solution algorithm from the final answers presented briefly on the screen. In this case, such difficulties overpowered attempts at remediation. Thus, this system was not individualized for students, and those students most in need suffered for it.

Error Analysis

VanLehn and his colleagues have created a computer program, called Debuggy, which is able to diagnosis elementary students' errors in multidigit subtraction. Debuggy can explain the reason for the underlying error in students' subtraction processes, rather than simply identify the procedural mistake. Their theory holds that students' errors are of different types. Slips are careless, unintentional errors that we all experience. Bugs are systematic errors. Consider the following hypothetical student's work (VanLehn, 1981).

306	80	183	702	3005	34	251
−138	− 4	− 95	− 11	− 28	−14	− 47
78	76	88	591	1087	24	24

This student appears to have difficulty with renaming (or "borrowing"). Specifically, his errors can be precisely predicted if answers are computed using a procedure with a small modification of the correct procedure. This modification is called a "bug," as it is seen to be similar in some ways to a bug, or error, in a computer program which causes it to operate incorrectly. This student has the "Borrow-Across-Zero" bug. It modifies the correct subtraction procedure by skipping over the zero and borrowing from the next column. One can now attempt to predict exactly what the student would answer to new problems. A student may have more than one bug at a time. The student above answered the last two problems incorrectly, but another bug must be hypothesized to account for the error—in this case, the "$N - N = N$" bug. When the digits in a column are equal, the student writes the number, instead of zero, for the answer. Research has indicated that about a third of all students who have "buggy" subtraction procedures have more than one bug (VanLehn, 1981).

How do bugs arise? Their repair theory postulates that when students get stuck while executing an incomplete subtraction procedure, they are not likely to quit as a buggy computer program might. Rather, they will do a small amount of "patching" to get over the impasse. These local problem-solving strategies, called "repairs," may be as simple as skipping the operation or backing up and trying another path. For example, solving $504 - 286$, the student might think, "I can't subtract 6 from 4, so I'll borrow. But I can't take anything away from zero. So I'll go back and subtract 4 from 6 instead." Based on repair theory, the computer program Debuggy is as effective as expert human diagnosticians (VanLehn, 1981).

Using error analysis software can improve instruction. One third-grade teacher used computer-analyzed subtraction errors as a basis for error correction sessions (Drucker, Wilbur, & McBride, 1987). His class outperformed a class taught with a traditional approach. The latter apparently did not participate in error correction sessions, however, so the benefits cannot be attributed merely to use of the program.

Research with error analysis programs has uncovered additional instructionally relevant information. It appears that bugs are not stable; that is, they may appear throughout one test, but disappear on the next (VanLehn, 1981). This has implications for teachers—more practice at just this time may not be warranted, as students may commit to memory a newly invented bug. This is especially important in the primary grades, when multidigit subtraction is introduced. Additional research supports this conclusion. Children exposed to a drill-and-practice CAI program in mathematics outperformed control group children; however, a close look revealed that the former made the same type of errors (Alderman, Swinton, & Braswell, 1979). They merely omitted fewer items. Thus, they were more adept and efficient at answering questions without necessarily having a strong grasp of the concepts. This suggests that teachers ensure that students possess the prerequisite understandings necessary to work with the program correctly—practicing, in other words, procedures that are both correct and meaningful to them.

Error analysis is only one way of using the computer to study children's mathematical learning. For example, Newman and Berger (1984) used a microcomputer "dart" game to study how primary school students used counting to make numerical estimates. Results showed developmental differences in accuracy of estimation, fluency in counting, and sophistication of self-reported strategy use. Weir (1987) and Campbell (1987) have shown how the Logo computer language can be used as an "empirical window" into young children's thinking about number and measurement. (Logo and mathematics is the subject of a succeeding section.) Thus, the teacher can use interactions at the computer to better understand how children think about and learn mathematics and so individualize instruction. The school psychologist similarly has another means for performing curriculum-based assessment (i.e., assessment that focuses on how the child functions within the existing curriculum, aimed at better understanding the child's learning problems) as well as process-oriented assessment (i.e., looking at the processes vs. products of learning or thinking).

Geometric and Spatial Thinking

Given its graphics capabilities, the computer appears to have special potential for developing geometric and spatial thinking. Research supports this contention. Computer-based programs are as effective in teaching kindergartners about shapes as teacher-directed programs (von Stein, 1982), and more effective at teaching preschoolers relational concepts such as above–below and over–under than television (Brawer, cited in Lieberman, 1985). Even children as young as 3 years can use graphics editing programs and graphics-based computer learning games to gain spatial concepts (Piestrup, 1982).

Perhaps different approaches hold more promise. Working with preschoolers, Forman (1986b) found that certain graphics programs offer a new, dynamic way of drawing and exploring geometric concepts. For example, a "Boxes" function allows children to draw rectangles by stretching an electronic "rubber band." Using this stretching process may give children a different perspective on geometric figures. The "fill" function, which fills closed regions with color, prompts children to reflect on the topological features of closure as the consequence of actions, rather than merely a characteristic of static shapes. The power of such drawing tools lies in the possibility that children will internalize such functions, thus constructing new mental tools.

Logo provides a potentially more powerful and extensible tool. Piaget demonstrated that young children learn about geometric shapes not so much from their perception of objects as from the actions they perform on these objects. They must internalize their actions and abstract the corresponding geometric ideas. For example, children can walk a path and then program the Logo turtle to draw it on the screen. The programming helps children link their intuitive knowledge about moving and drawing to more explicit mathematical ideas. In constructing a series of commands to draw a rectangle, for example, they analyze the visual components and make conclusions about its properties. Such activity helps them develop a more sophisticated level of thinking (Clements & Battista, 1989, 1990; Lehren et al., 1989). Increased awareness of the properties of shapes and the meaning of angle and angle measure has been reported in several Logo studies with primary grade children (Clements & Battista, 1989; Hughes & Macleod, 1986).

Such benefits extend to geometric measurement. Logo provides an arena in which kindergarten and first-grade children use units of varying size, define and create their own units, maintain or predict unit size, and create length rather than "end point" representations, all without the distracting dexterity demands associated with measuring instruments. Logo-experienced children were better at estimating distances (particularly the longest distances), compensating for changes in unit size, and estimating the inverse relationship between the size of the unit and the number of units (Campbell, 1987). First graders use their own "standard units of measure" such as 44 or 66 (they said that they "wanted a big number and it's easiest to hit the same one twice") to make their drawings (Kull, 1986).

Logo and Mathematical Thinking

Does Logo also benefit other aspects of mathematics achievement? Across grades and types of applications of Logo, results are mixed and not particularly promising (Clements, 1986a; Robinson, Feldman, & Uhlig, 1987). Certain uses of Logo with young children, however, appear to facilitate the development of other mathematical competencies, from achieving basic number sense, to learning relationships between size of numbers and the length of a line drawn by the turtle, to engaging in high levels of mathematical discussion, although significant gains are not found on every ability (Bowman, 1985; Clements, 1987c; Hines, 1983; Hughes & Macleod, 1986; Perlman, 1976; Reimer, 1985; Robinson et al., 1988; Robinson & Uhlig, 1988). There appear to be no sex differences in such gains (Sprigle & Schaefer, 1984). Such benefits, however, may take time to evidence themselves. Akdag (1985) worked with kindergartners for a relatively short period of time. She failed to find treatment effects on mathematics readiness, although she did report gains by the Logo group on a geometry concept test. In addition, preschool children's conceptual difficulties with certain aspects of Logo (e.g., left and right, defining procedures) should not be underestimated. Certain specially designed Logo environments, however, can ameliorate these problems and enhance children's learning (Clements, 1983–1984; Clements & Gullo, 1984). In mastering Logo commands, children master the polar coordinate spatial system upon which the graphics version of Logo is based (Campbell, Fein, Scholnick, Frank, & Schwartz, 1986).

Logo does not provide efficient practice on arithmetic processes. However, it does provide a context in which there is a real need for these processes and in which children must clearly conceptualize which operation should be applied. For example, first-grade children determined the correct length for the bottom line of their drawing by adding the lengths of the three horizontal lines that they constructed at the top of the tower: $20 + 30 + 20 = 70$ (Clements, 1983–1984). Many students developed a new sense of arithmetic, numbers, and estimation within the context of their Logo work. Such experience has positively affected achievement test scores (Barker et al., 1988).

Other aspects of mathematical thinking may also be facilitated. First grader Ryan wanted to turn the turtle to point into his rectangle. He asked the teacher, "What's half of 90?" After she responded, he entered RT 45. "Oh, I went the wrong way." He paused, eyes on the screen. "Try LEFT 90," he said at last. This inverse operation produced exactly the desired effect (Kull, 1986).

In contrast to the pervasive tendency to use Logo and other problem-solving programs with higher SES children and drill with lower SES children, it has been found that Logo may provide a particularly beneficial environment for low SES Black children. These first-grade children outscored majority students on a standardized test of mathematics achievement following Logo experience (Emihovich & Miller, 1988a). These researchers claimed that Logo may have provided the children with a sense of mastery over their environment and first-hand experience in using metacognitive skills.

These studies indicate that if Logo is used thoughtfully, it can provide an additional evocative context for the young children's explorations of mathematical ideas. Teachers should never forgo concrete experiences, of course. Logo experiences are supplements and extensions, not replacements. Logo and real-world experiences differ, but both contribute to the child's development. In general, the opinion that children must reach a certain age or stage (e.g., concrete operations) before successfully using Logo appears invalid.

The question we have not answered is: What constitutes "thoughtful use" that can enrich early mathematical experiences? Such use demands that teachers structure and mediate Logo work to help children form correct, complete mathematical concepts, and help children build bridges between the Logo experience and their regular mathematics work (Clements, 1987c).

Creativity, Cognitive Development, and Problem Solving

Creativity

Several studies have documented an increase in creativity following Logo experience, although gains in some were moderate (Reimer, 1985; Vaidya & Mckeeby, 1984). Horton and Ryba (1986), reporting significant gains in creativity, noted that Logo students' graphic compositions were more fully developed in terms of completeness, originality, and drawing style. The first two of a series of studies assessed creativity with the Torrance Test of Creative Thinking—Figural (Clements, 1986b; Clements & Gullo, 1984). This type of assessment, shared by all previously discussed studies, leaves open the possibility that effects are limited to Logo-like graphic domains. However, in the third study, Logo increased young children's scores on both the Figural and Verbal portions, suggesting that general processes involved in creative thinking were enhanced. In sum, it appears that at least some components of creativity are amenable to development within Logo environments (Clements & Merriman, 1988; Roblyer et al., 1988).

Cognitive Development and Problem Solving

Only a few studies have examined the effect of computer experience on typical Piagetian cognitive development tasks. Whereas positive effects on seriation with primary grade students (Clements, 1986b) and conservation with preschoolers (Piel & Baller, 1986) have been documented, other reports show no such effects (Akdag, 1985; Howell, Scott, & Diamond, 1987).

Problem-solving computer activities create a high level of motivation, which seems to encourage children as young as kindergarten to make choices and decisions, alter their strategies based on feedback, and persist (Gélinas, 1986). This results in higher performance on tests of reasoning or critical thinking (Riding & Powell, 1986, 1987).

Again, computer problem-solving activities should supplement concrete activities, For example, 3- to 5-year-old children think more about process in a computer Smurf program and more about content in a three-dimensional doll house replica (Forman, 1986a). Children had to reflect more on the computer because choices must be more deliberate. Ideas for using miniature real objects seemed to flow from the physical manipulation of those objects, whereas ideas for use of the computer objects come full blown from premeditation, often announced to others. Thus, the computer may promote planfulness, possibly at the cost of an element of playfulness. Children had to be explicit about the "locations" to which they would move. The increased distance between their own action and the manipulation of the objects increased the need to reflect on their performance.

This distance is also important in watching a replay of their actions (in effect, a cartoon the children created that could be viewed repeatedly). Replay is powerful if the child thinks about the future when constructing the present action on the computer. In a sense, these children are both watching an action and watching themselves watching it later. Computers can present children with representations of their own past trials and errors. These representations can be observed and edited (Forman, 1985).

According to Forman (1986b), teachers who expect computer drawing tools:

> to help children draw more realistic pictures probably will be disappointed. Teachers who expect Paint and Play Workshop to generate emotionally rich stories probably will not be satisfied. On the other hand, teachers who see these media as new systems of cause and effect relations, logic relations, and spatial relations will make hundreds of interesting observations and will invent hundreds of games that children will find educational. (p. 73)

In summary, such computer environments present many unique opportunities for reflective problem solving (Forman, 1986b).

Logo's turtle graphics represents one widely studied computer environment. Many studies of Logo's effect on problem-solving performance have not been encouraging (Barker et al., 1988; Robinson et al., 1987), although a recent meta-analysis showed a substantial and homogeneous positive effect (Roblyer et al., 1988). Several studies reveal that Logo programming is an engaging activity to young children, fostering a high degree of problem-solving and other task-related behavior (Clements & Nastasi, 1988; Nastasi et al., 1990; Strand, 1987). The result is often increased problem-solving abilities in preschool to primary grade children (Degelman, Free, Scarlato, Blackburn, & Golden, 1986; Perlman, 1976), including special needs preschoolers (Lehrer et al., 1986).

One specific promising result is an increase in higher-order (metacognitive) abilities. Several studies have reported increases in both preschool and primary grade children's ability to monitor their comprehension and problem solving processes; that is, to "realize when you don't understand" (Clements, 1986b,

1990; Clements & Gullo, 1984; Lehrer & Randle, 1986; Miller & Emihovich, 1986). This may reflect the prevalence of "debugging" in Logo programming. Other abilities that may be positively affected include understanding the nature of a problem, representing that problem, and even "learning to learn" (Clements, 1990; Lehrer & Randle, 1986).

What is the difference between implementations that show quite positive effects and others that do not? A popular idea is that the degree of structure in the learning environment is the important difference, with advocates at each end. Actually, on a continuum from unguided discovery to total teacher telling, neither extreme appeared successful (Clements & Merriman, 1988). However, there was no discernable pattern in the middle of the continuum. Perhaps researchers are not being clear about what it is that is being structured. Successful teachers do structure students' experiences. Structure in this sense, however, is not equivalent to the use of lockstep teaching methods. It involves facilitating children's use and awareness of problem-solving processes. This kind of structure is also not equivalent to "control" of students. Several interventions tightly structured, or controlled, the students' minute-by-minute Logo activities to no avail—what they neglected to do was to structure the environment so as to encourage the use of higher-order thinking strategies. Often children were directed page-by-page through Logo programming worksheets, but were never encouraged to reflect on their activity. In addition, for young children who lack the knowledge base to perform even basic Logo tasks, structure and directive feedback on these elements are important. Once they attain these competencies, mediated experience with opened-ended problems is necessary for consolidation (Strand, 1987).

This leads to a second characteristic: A critical element in each successful intervention was the active role of the teacher encouraging, questioning, prompting, modeling, and, in general, mediating children's interaction with the computer. This scaffolding led children to reflect on their own thinking behaviors and bring problem-solving processes to an explicit level of awareness. For example, Lehrer and Smith (1986a) found that teacher mediation of Logo instruction was more effective in enhancing metacognitive skills and specific cognitive abilities than such instruction without the benefit of teacher scaffolding. Similarly, Clements (1990) described a Logo environment in which teachers used "homunculi"—cartoon characters to represent executive-level processes—to teach and encourage the use of higher-order cognitive processes. These students scored higher on a measure of executive-level processing following treatment than a control group working with creative problem-solving and writing software and without the benefit of the homunculi.

Logo does induce high quality instruction, even from fairly naive and inexperienced adults. However, "the importance of Logo is that it provides an unusually rich problem space within which children can confront important ideas; it does not guarantee that the confrontation will occur" (Fein, 1985, p. 22). These are probably valid conclusions for all types of problem-solving software.

Cognition and Achievement: Final Words

Meta-analyses reveal that young students make significant learning gains using CAI (Kulik, Kulik, & Bangert-Drowns, 1984; Lieberman, 1985; Niemiec & Walberg, 1984). This does not mean, however, that the use of any software under any conditions leads to such gains. The effectiveness depends critically on the quality of the software, the amount of time the software is used, and the way in which it is used. Not surprisingly, studies indicate that CAI can be effective if such critical features are considered, but that it will not be so if they are ignored.

We must also temper our optimism via the findings of comparative media research. Decades of precomputer research comparing the effects of different media on achievement show basically the same result: no significant difference (Clements, 1984). Although isolated studies have demonstrated increased learning upon the introduction of media, it is usually possible to attribute the results to a change of curriculum or teaching strategy. This may explain the positive results of many comparative studies of CAI (Clark, 1983).

What does this mean for the use of computers with young children? First, it should be recognized that there are other essential educational problems, including the cost, distribution, and efficiency of instruction. Research indicates that instructional computing may play a role in solving such problems, although cost effectiveness has not often been adequately considered. We should not lose sight of what we are comparing, and for what purpose we are comparing different media. In addition, there are certain things computers can do that cannot be duplicated in other situations (e.g., creating unique environments for developing higher-order thinking).

This may even be true for drill-and-practice CAI. For example, computers may be able to provide adaptive instruction to a degree almost impossible otherwise. One example is the technique of "increasing ratio review." In simple practice a missed item often is placed at the end of the list for additional practice (this is true of both traditional computer drills and typical noncomputer flashcard drills). Unfortunately, if the list is long, the student forgets the answer; if the list is short, the student is not assisted in remembering the item over longer time periods. Instead, in increasing ratio review, the computer inserts the missed item into the list at several places such as the 3rd, 7th, and 13th item to be presented to the student. This technique has been shown to increase students' achievement without increasing the total time they work on the task (Siegel & Misselt, 1984). It is unfortunate that present-day CAI (including that employed in the studies reviewed here) does not yet incorporate such techniques.

Computers are unique in more significant ways, such as providing experiences with talking word processors, Logo and combined Lego-Logo explorations, and beyond (simultaneously providing unique ways for teachers and researchers to learn more about children's thinking). Even though results are less consistently positive regarding these types of applications, recent recommendations for school reform (e.g., National Council of Teachers of Mathematics, 1988) demand that such uses be emphasized in comparison to drill approaches. Computers alone, however, will not lead to reform. Repeatedly, research indicates that benefits are contingent on a consonant teaching and learning context.

CONCLUSIONS

Despite early concerns and debates centering on it, the question "Should computers be used with young children?" is now vacuous. Computers will be a presence in young children's lives. In appropriate environments, children use computers confidently, successfully, and enthusiastically, and they can benefit from such use. The important questions are, "What are the specific benefits of computers for enhancing young children's development? What are appropriate environments; that is, how can computers best be used to realize this potential?"

Computers are typically considered as serving cognitive purposes. Research confirms that they do so, and effectively. Surprising, perhaps, are the reliable and substantive effects on socio-emotional development. Children generally prefer collaborative use of computers. Even when told to work alone, they consult and help each other. Computers enhance, rather than inhibit, existing patterns of social participation and interaction in early childhood classrooms by fostering greater social interaction and the development of new friendships. Sociometric status of children might even be improved through the development of computer skills. All of these results, but especially the latter ones, need further validation, in part due to the frequent reliance on anecdotal data.

Young children's motivation and attitudes toward learning are also enhanced through computer use. Not only are positive attitudes toward specific content areas engendered, but these effects are often generalized toward learning and school in general. Computer use also leads to a greater sense of control over learning and an increased sense of competence; these effects, of course, are difficult to separate from concomitant academic and cognitive gains.

In the cognitive sphere, appropriate use of computers is effective in facilitating young children's development of a variety of academic and cognitive abilities. Computer environments can strengthen expressive and receptive oral language, and prereading and reading skills. The most powerful uses, however, foster higher-level thinking and communication. Technological tools such as word processors amplify children's writing abilities, encouraging them to write and revise more, experiment with and reflect on their writing, and develop a sense of audience. Children who have the most difficulties in writing may benefit the most from such writing tools.

Some reports suggest that the greatest gains in the use of CAI across all ages and students and all subject areas have been in mathematics skills for primary-grade children. It appears especially effective in remedial situations and with students from schools serving lower socioeconomic populations. The skills developed tend to be low-level, however, and programs focusing on higher-level mathematical thinking have also proved efficacious for all children. For example, graphics environments such as drawing programs and Logo can build on young children's competence with and interest in manipulating spatial forms and thereby develop higher levels of geometric and wider logical-mathematical thinking. Finally, certain computer environments have the capability of evoking creative thinking, reflective problem solving, and use of executive-level cognitive processes.

Certain social benefits of computer use may mediate the frequently observed cognitive and academic benefits. Specifically, collaborative planning, and most importantly, cognitive conflict and its resolution during such collaboration are likely to facilitate cognitive development. Computers help foster such peer collaboration and create new social organizations in classrooms, providing additional scaffolding that supports young learners. Finally, computers have been shown to be effective with a wide variety of special populations.

These, then, are specific benefits of computer use. However, benefits are not guaranteed. Research indicates that the nature and extent of the impact of computer use on socioemotional and cognitive-academic development depends on a number of factors. These include specific characteristics of the child such as developmental, experiential, and personality differences, as well as environmental factors such as software and instructional strategies. Thus, the answer to the question of computer effects is a complex one. As we suggested earlier, this issue might be best addressed from an ecological perspective that considers the reciprocal nature of the student–environment relationship. This brings us to our next question—how to best use computers.

The answer to this question is remarkably consistent with regard to socioemotional and cognitive-academic benefits. As suggested earlier, the characteristics of the individual learner and the classroom ecology must be considered. This perspective implies sensitivity to individual differences among children with regard to cognitive, perceptual, motor, and language skills. Developmental limitations, however, should in no way imply limitations with regard to access (to computer hardware and also to higher-level software applications). In addition, research suggests that females and handicapped populations have inequitable access to computers but are just as likely to benefit from their use. Further, although the effectiveness of drill-and-practice CAI with special populations has been documented, higher-level programs are also valuable—in fact, we must be proactive in obtaining equal access to such applications for special education students. Therefore, computers have the potential to not only provide remediation, but also empower handicapped children to engage in many activities that they would not have been able to otherwise. In sum, early childhood may be an ideal time to introduce children to substantive computer use in order to avert such inequities.

Critical to effective use of computers within the classroom context is teacher participation and support. Optimally, the teacher's role should be that of a facilitator or mediator of children's learning. This implies that the teacher takes a supportive role, providing scaffolding consistent with the students' needs and abilities, type of software, and instructional goals. This scaffolding includes not only physical structuring of the environment, but also establishing standards for and supporting specific types of learning environments. For example, when using open-ended programs, considerable support may need to precede independent use. Additionally, the need for teacher guidance is likely to decrease as children begin to collaborate and as they develop more effective collaboration and problem-solving skills. Thus, the scaffolds provided by the teacher are likely to complement those provided by peers and software. Other important aspects of scaffolding include structuring and mediating computer work to help children form viable concepts and strategies, posing questions to help children reflect on these concepts and strategies, and "building bridges" to help children connect their computer and noncomputer experiences.

Finally, software and curriculum issues must be considered. Most importantly, computer activities should be matched with the instructional goals. Computers have the capability to reinforce lower-level skills or to engender the development of higher-level thinking. For example, one implication can be drawn from research on computers and young children's mathematical thinking: If you want a "safe" and relatively easy path, choose appropriate drill software and use it following the effective practices described previously; you will probably increase achievement. However, if you want to effect substantive change in the quality of young children's mathematical experiences, try Logo and other programs that demand significant mathematical thinking—but be ready to work hard at it (in the preschool, have a partner or aid who is also ready to work). This applies to other subject matter areas and other educational goals as well.

In their role as consultants, school psychologists can help teachers to utilize computers in enhancing children's development in both the social-emotional and academic-cognitive domains. In both domains, research indicates that computers are an efficacious tool—they have the potential for substantive educational benefit—but the realization of these benefits depends on personal and contextual factors. Specific suggestions regarding these factors have been provided. Despite early concerns, there is nothing to lose, and potentially rich benefits to acquire, through informed use of computers with young children.

ACKNOWLEDGMENTS

Time to prepare this material was partially provided by the National Science Foundation under Grant No. MDR-8651668. Any opinions, findings, and conclusions or recommendations expressed in this publication are those of the authors and do not necessarily reflect the views of the National Science Foundation.

REFERENCES

Akdag, F. S. (1985). *The effects of computer programming on young children's learning.* Unpublished doctoral dissertation, Ohio State University.

Alderman, D. L., Swinton, S. S., & Braswell, J. S. (1979). Assessing basic arithmetic skills and understanding across curricula: Computer-assisted instruction and compensatory education. *Journal of Children's Mathematical Behavior, 2,* 3–28.

Alexander, D. (1983). *Children's computer drawings.* Medford, MA: Tufts University. (ERIC Document Reproduction Service No. ED 238 562).

Alexander, D. (1984). Mathematical, geometric and spatial reasoning. In E. Pitcher, E. Feinburg, & D. Alexander (Eds.), *Helping young children learn.* (4th ed.). Columbus, OH: Charles E. Merrill.

Atkinson, R. C., & Fletcher, J. D. (1972). Teaching children to read with a computer. *The Reading Teacher, 25,* 319–327.

Bangert-Drowns, R. L. (1989, March). *Research on wordprocessing and writing instruction.* Paper presented at the meeting of the American Educational Research Association, San Francisco.

Barker, W. F., Merryman, J. D., & Bracken, J. (1988, April). *Microcomputers, math CAI, Logo, and mathematics education in elementary school: A pilot study.* Paper presented at the meeting of the American Educational Research Association, New Orleans.

Barnes, B. J., & Hill, S. (1983, May). Should young children work with microcomputers—Logo before Lego™? *The Computing Teacher,* pp. 11–14.

Battista, M. T., & Clements, D. H. (1986). The effects of Logo and CAI problem-solving environments on problem-solving abilities and mathematics achievement. *Computers in Human Behavior, 2,* 183–193.

Bearison, D. J. (1982). New directions in studies of social interaction and cognitive growth. In F. C. Serafica (Ed.), *Social-cognitive development in context* (pp. 199–221). New York: Guilford Press.

Beeson, B. S., & Williams, R. A. (1985). The effects of gender and age on preschool children's choice of the computer as a child-selected activity. *Journal of the American Society for Information Science, 36,* 339–341.

Behrmann, M. M. (1984). A brighter future for early learning through high tech. *The Pointer, 28*(2), 23–26.

Bellows, B. P. (1987, April). *What makes a team? The composition of small groups for C.A.I.* Paper presented at the meeting of the American Educational Research Association, Washington, DC.

Bergin, D., Ford, M. E., & Meyer-Gaub, B. (1986, April). *Social and motivational consequences of microcomputer use in kindergarten.* Paper presented at the meeting of the American Educational Research Association, San Francisco.

Binder, S., & Ledger, B. (1985). *Preschool computer project report.* Oakville, Ontario: Sheridan College.

Block, E. B., Simpson, D. L., & Reid, D. K. (1987). Teaching young children programming and word processing skills: The effects of three preparatory conditions. *Journal Educational Computing Research, 34,* 435–442.

Borgh, K., & Dickson, W. P. (1986a). *The effects on children's writing of adding speech synthesis to a word processor.* Unpublished manuscript, University of Wisconsin, Madison.

Borgh, K., & Dickson, W. P. (1986b). Two preschoolers sharing one microcomputer: Creating prosocial behavior with hardware and software. In P. F. Campbell & G. G. Fein (Eds.), *Young children and microcomputers* (pp. 37–44). Reston, VA: Reston Publishing.

Borthwick, A. G. (1987). *The effects of keyboarding/typewriting on the language arts skills of elementary school students: An integrative review.* Unpublished master's thesis, Kent State University.

Bowman, B. T. (1985, November). *Computers and young children.* Paper presented at the meeting of the National Association for the Education of Young Children, New Orleans.

Brady, E. H., & Hill, S. (1984, March). Research in review. Young children and microcomputers: Research issues and directions. *Young Children,* pp. 49–61.

Brinker, R. P. (1984). The microcomputer as perceptual tool: Searching for systematic learning strategies with handicapped infants. In R. E. Bennett & C. A. Maher (Eds.), *Microcomputers and exceptional children* (pp. 21–36). New York: Haworth Press.

Brinker, R. P., & Lewis, M. (1982). Making the world work with microcomputers: A learning prothesis for handicapped infants. *Exceptional Children, 49,* 163–170.

Brinkley, V. M., & Watson, J. A. (1987–1988). Effects of microworld training experience on sorting tasks by young children. *Journal of Educational Technology Systems, 16,* 349–364.

Brisk, M. E. (1985). Using the computer to develop literacy. *Equity and Choice, 1*(3), 25–32.

Britten, R. M. (1988, April). The effects of instruction on keyboarding skills in grade 2. *Educational Technology,* pp. 34–37.

Bruner, J. (1986). *Actual minds, possible worlds.* Cambridge, MA: Harvard University Press.

Bruno, J., & Goodman, J. (1983). Computer aided development of phonetic skills in non-vocal pre-reading children. *Journal of Special Education Technology, 6*(4), 39–45.

Burns, B., & Hagerman, A. (1989). Computer experience, self-concept and problem-solving: The effects of Logo on children's ideas of themselves as learners. *Journal of Educational Computing Research, 5,* 199–212.

Campbell, P. F. (1987). *Measuring distance: Children's use of number and unit. Final report submitted to the National Institute of Mental Health Under the ADAMHA Small Grant Award Program. Grant No. MSMA 1 R03 MH423435-01.* University of Maryland, College Park.

Campbell, P. F., Fein, G. G., Scholnick, E. K., Frank, R. E., & Schwartz, S. S. (1986). Initial mastery of the syntax and semantics of Logo positioning commands. *Journal of Educational Computing Research, 2,* 357–377.

Casey, J. M. (1984, March). *Beginning reading instruction: using the LEA approach with and without micro-computer intervention.* Paper presented at the meeting of the Western Regional Reading Conference of the International Reading Association, Reno, NV.

Chambers, J. H., & Ascione, F. R. (1985, April). *The effects of prosocial and aggressive videogames on children's donating and helping.* Paper presented at the meeting of the Society for Research in Child Development, Toronto.

Char, C. A. (1989, March). *Computer graphic feltboards: New software approaches for young children's mathematical exploration.* Paper presented at the meeting of the American Educational Research Association, San Francisco.

Christensen, C. A., & Cosden, M. A. (1986). The relationship between special education placement and instruction in computer literacy skills. *Journal of Educational Computing Research, 2,* 299–306.

Clark, R. E. (1983). Reconsidering research on learning from media. *Review of Educational Research, 53,* 445–459.

Clements, D. H. (1983–1984). Supporting young children's Logo programming. *The Computing Teacher, 11*(5), 24–30.

Clements, D. H. (1984, November). Implications of media research for the instructional application of computers with young children. *Educational Technology,* pp. 7–16.

Clements, D. H. (1985). *Computers in early and primary education.* Englewood Cliffs, NJ: Prentice-Hall.

Clements, D. H. (1986a, September). Early studies on Logo and mathematics. *Logo Exchange,* pp. 27–29.

Clements, D. H. (1986b). Effects of Logo and CAI environments on cognition and creativity. *Journal of Educational Psychology, 78,* 309–318.

Clements, D. H. (1987a). Computers and literacy. In J. L. Vacca, R. T. Vacca, & M. Gove (Eds.), *Reading and learning to read* (pp. 338–372). Boston: Little, Brown.

Clements, D. H. (1987b). Computers and young children: A review of the research. *Young Children, 43*(1), 34–44.

Clements, D. H. (1987c). Longitudinal study of the effects of Logo programming on cognitive abilities and achievement. *Journal of Educational Computing Research, 3*, 73–94.

Clements, D. H. (1990). Metacomponential development in a Logo programming environment. *Journal of Educational Psychology, 82*, 141–149.

Clements, D. H., & Battista, M. T. (1989). Learning of geometric concepts in a Logo environment. *Journal for Research in Mathematics Education, 20*, 450–467.

Clements, D. H., & Battista, M. T. (1990). The effects of Logo on children's conceptualizations of angle and polygons. *Journal for Research in Mathematics Education, 21*, 356–371.

Clements, D. H., & Gullo, D. F. (1984). Effects of computer programming on young children's cognition. *Journal of Educational Psychology, 76*, 1051–1058.

Clements, D. H., & Mcloughlin, C. S. (1986). Computer-aided instruction in word identification: How much is enough? *Educational and Psychological Research, 6*(3), 191–205.

Clements, D. H., & Merriman, S. L. (1988). Componential developments in Logo programming environments. In R. Mayer (Ed.), *Teaching and learning computer programming: Multiple research perspectives* (pp. 13–54). Hillsdale, NJ: Lawrence Erlbaum Associates.

Clements, D. H., & Nastasi, B. K. (1985). Effects of computer environments on social-emotional development: Logo and computer-assisted instruction. *Computers in the Schools, 2*(2–3), 11–31.

Clements, D. H., & Nastasi, B. K. (1988). Social and cognitive interactions in educational computer environments. *American Educational Research Journal, 25*, 87–106.

Cochran-Smith, M., Kahn, J., & Paris, C. L. (1988). When word processors come into the classroom. In J. L. Hoot & S. B. Silvern (Eds.), *Writing with computers in the early grades* (pp. 43–74). New York: Teachers College Press.

Corning, N., & Halapin, J. (1989, March). *Computer applications in an action-oriented kindergarten.* Paper presented at the meeting of the Connecticut Institute for Teaching and Learning Conference, Wallingfor, CT.

Cuffaro, H. K. (1984). Microcomputers in education: Why is earlier better? *Teachers College Record, 85*, 559–568.

Daiute, C. (1988). The early development of writing abilities: Two theoretical perspectives. In J. L. Hoot & S. B. Silvern (Eds.), *Writing with computers in the early grades* (pp. 10–22). New York: Teachers College Press.

Davy, J. (1984). Mindstorms in the lamplight. *Teachers College Record, 85*, 549–558.

Degelman, D., Free, J. U., Scarlato, M., Blackburn, J. M., & Golden, T. (1986). Concept learning in preschool children: Effects of a short-term Logo experience. *Journal of Educational Computing Research, 2*(2), 199–205.

Dickinson, D. K. (1986). Cooperation, collaboration, and a computer: Integrating a computer into a first–second grade writing program. *Research in the Teaching of English, 20*, 357–378.

Doise, W., & Mugny, G. (1979). Individual and collective conflicts of centrations in cognitive development. *European Journal of Social Psychology, 9*, 105–108.

Drucker, H., Wilbur, C., & McBride, S. (1987). Using a computer-based error analysis approach to improve basic subtraction skills in the third grade. *Journal of Educational Research, 80*, 363–365.

Elkind, D. (1987, May). The child yesterday, today, and tomorrow. *Young Children*, pp. 6–11.

Emihovich, C., & Miller, G. E. (1988a). Effects of Logo and CAI on black first graders' achievement, reflectivity, and self-esteem. *The Elementary School Journal, 88*, 473–487.

Emihovich, C., & Miller, G. E. (1988b). Learning Logo: The social context of cognition. *Journal of Curriculum Studies, 20*, 57–70.

Emihovich, C., & Miller, G. E. (1988c). Talking to the turtle: A discourse analysis of Logo instruction. *Discourse Processes, 11*, 183–201.

Essa, E. L. (1987). The effect of a computer on preschool children's activities. *Early Childhood Research Quarterly, 2*, 377–382.

Fazio, B. B., & Rieth, H. J. (1986). Characteristics of preschool handicapped children's microcomputer use during free-choice periods. *Journal of the Division for Early Childhood, 10*, 247–254.

Fein, G. G. (1985, April). *Logo instruction: A constructivist view.* Paper presented at the meeting of the American Educational Research Association, Chicago, IL.

Fein, G. G. (1987). Technologies for the young. *Early Childhood Research Quarterly, 2*, 227–243.

Fein, G. G., Campbell, P. F., & Schwartz, S. S. (1987). Microcomputers in the preschool: Effects on social participation and cognitive play. *Journal of Applied Developmental Psychology, 8*, 197–208.

Fitzgerald, G., Fick, L., & Milich, R. (1986). Computer-assisted instruction for students with attentional difficulties. *Journal of Learning Disabilities, 19*, 376–379.

Fletcher, S. G. (1983). Dynamic orometrics: A computer-based means of learning about and developing speech by deaf children. *American Annals of the Deaf, 128*, 525–534.

Forman, G. (1985, April). *The child's understanding of record and replay in computer animated graphics.* Paper presented at the meeting of the American Educational Research Association, Chicago, IL.

Forman, G. (1986a). Computer graphics as a medium for enhancing reflective thinking in young children. In J. Bishop, J. Lochhead, & D. N. Perkins (Eds.), *Thinking* (pp. 131–137). Hillsdale, NJ: Lawrence Erlbaum Associates.

Forman, G. (1986b). Observations of young children solving problems with computers and robots. *Journal of Research in Childhood Education, 1*, 60–74.

Fujiura, G., & Johnson, L. J. (1986). Methods of microcomputer research in early childhood special education. *Journal of the Division for Early Childhood, 10*, 264–269.

Gélinas, C. (1986). *Educational computer activities and problem solving at the kindergarten level.* Quebec City: Quebec Ministry of Education.

Gelman, R., & Baillargeon, R. (1983). A review of some Piagetian concepts. In P. H. Mussen (Ed.), *Handbook of child psychology* (pp. 167–230). New York: Wiley.

Genishi, C. (1988). Kindergartners and computers: A case study of six children. *The Elementary School Journal, 89*, 184–201.

Genishi, C., McCollum, P., & Strand, E. B. (1985). Research currents: The interactional richness of children's computer use. *Language Arts, 62*(5), 526–532.

Goldman, S. R., & Rueda, R. (1988). Developing writing skills in bilingual exceptional children. *Exceptional Children, 54*, 543–551.

Goodwin, L. D., Goodwin, W. L., & Garel, M. B. (1986). Use of microcomputers with preschoolers: A review of the literature. *Early Childhood Research Quarterly, 1*, 269–286.

Goodwin, L. D., Goodwin, W. L., Nansel, A., & Helm, C. P. (1986). Cognitive and affective effects of various types of microcomputer use by preschoolers. *American Educational Research Journal, 23*, 348–356.

Grocke, M. (1983). Computers in the classroom: How can they teach reading? *Australian Journal of Reading, 6*, 175–184.

Harter, S. (1978). Effectance motivation reconsidered: Toward a developmental model. *Human Development, 21*, 34–64.

Hativa, N. (1988). Computer-based drill and practice in arithmetic: Widening the gap between high- and low-achieving students. *American Educational Research Journal, 25*, 366–397.

Hativa, N., Swisa, S., & Lesgold, A. (1989, March). *Competition in individualized CAI.* Paper presented at the meeting of the American Educational Research Association, San Francisco.

Haugland, S. W., & Shade, D. D. (in press). The effect of developmentally appropriate software for preschool children's development. *Early Childhood Research Quarterly.*

Hawisher, G. E. (1989). Research and recommendations for computers and composition. In G. E. Hawisher & C. L. Selfe (Eds.), *Critical perspectives on computers and composition instruction* (pp. 44–69). New York: Teachers College Press.

Heap, J. L. (1987, April). *Organizational features of collaborative editing activities at a computer.*

Paper presented at the meeting of the American Educational Research Association, Washington, DC.

Hess, R., & McGarvey, L. (1987). School-relevant effects of educational uses of microcomputers in kindergarten classrooms and homes. *Journal of Educational Computer Research, 3,* 269–287.

Hines, S. N. (1983, July-August). Computer programming abilities of five-year-old children. *Educational Computer Magazine,* pp. 10–12.

Hlawati, B. (1985). *Effects of Logo and problem-solving CAI on the cognitive processes of gifted children.* Unpublished doctoral dissertation, Kent State University.

Hoot, J. L. (1988). Keyboarding in the writing process: Concerns and issues. In J. L. Hoot & S. B. Silvern (Eds.), *Writing with computers in the early grades* (pp. 181–195). New York: Teachers College Press.

Hoover, J., & Austin, A. M. (1986, April). *A comparison of traditional preschool and computer play from a social/cognitive perspective.* Paper presented at the meeting of the American Educational Research Association, San Francisco.

Horton, J., & Ryba, K. (19860. Assessing learning with Logo: A pilot study, *The Computing Teacher, 14*(1), 24–28.

Hotard, S. R., & Cortez, M. J. (1983). *Computer-assisted instruction as an enhancer of remediation.* Lafayette, LA: Lafayette Parish.

Howell, R. D., Scott, P. B., & Diamond, J. (1987). The effects of "instant" Logo computing language on the cognitive development of very young children. *Journal of Educational Computing Research, 3,* 249–260.

Hughes, M., & Macleod, H. (1986). Part II: Using Logo with very young children. In R. Lawler, B. D. Boulay, M. Hughes, & H. Macleod (Eds.), *Cognition and computers: Studies in learning* (pp. 179–219). Chichester, England: Ellis Horwood Limited.

Hungate, H. (1982, January). Computers in the kindergarten. *The Computing Teacher,* pp. 15–18.

Hungate, H., & Heller, J. I. (1984, April). *Preschool children and microcomputers.* Paper presented at the meeting of the American Educational Research Association, New Orleans.

Hyson, M. C. (1985). Emotions and the microcomputer: An exploratory study of young children's responses. *Computers in Human Behavior, 1,* 143–152.

Hyson, M. C., & Morris, S. K. (1985). 'Computers? I love them!': Young children's concepts and attitudes about computers. *Early Child Development and Care, 23,* 17–29.

Israel, B. L. (1968). *Responsive environment program: Brooklyn, N.Y.: Report of the first full year of operation. The Talking Typewriter.* Brooklyn, NY: Office of Economic Opportunity.

Johnson, D. W., Johnson, R. T., Pierson, W. T., & Lyons, V. (1985). Controversy versus concurrence seeking in multi-grade and single-grade learning groups. *Journal of Research in Science Teaching, 22,* 835–848.

Johnson, J. E. (1985). Characteristics of preschoolers interested in microcomputers. *Journal of Educational Research, 78,* 299–305.

Johnson, P. A. (1986). *Effects of computer-assisted instruction compared to teacher-directed instruction on comprehension of abstract concepts by the deaf* Unpublished doctoral dissertation, Northern Illinois University.

Johnson, R., Brooker, C., Stutzman, J., Hultman, D., & Johnson, D. W. (1985). The effects of controversy, concurrence seeking, and individualistic learning on achievement and attitude change. *Journal of Research in Science Teaching, 22,* 197–205.

Jones, E. E. (1987). *Sex differences in preschoolers' use of the computer?* Unpublished master's thesis. Medford, MA: Tufts University.

Kanevsky, L. (1985). Computer-basd math for gifted students: Comparison of cooperative and competitive strategies. *Journal for the Education of the Gifted, 8,* 239–255.

King, M., & Perrin, M. (n.d.). *An investigation of children's use of microcomputers in an early childhood program.* Unpublished manuscript. Ohio University, Athens.

Klinzing, D. G., & Hall, A. (1985, April). *A study of the behavior of children in a preschool equipped with computers.* Paper presented at the meeting of the American Educational Research Association, Chicago.

Kraus, W. H. (1981). Using a computer game to reinforce skills in addition basic facts in second grade. *Journal for Research in Mathematics Education, 12,* 152–155.

Kulik, C. C., Kulik, J., & Bangert-Drowns, R. L. (1984, April). *Effects of computer-based education of elementary school pupils.* Paper presented at the meeting of the American Educational Research Association, New Orleans, LA.

Kull, J. A. (1986). Learning and Logo. In P. F. Campbell & G. G. Fein (Eds.), *Young children and microcomputers* (pp. 103–130). Englewood Cliffs, NJ: Prentice-Hall.

Kumpf, G. H. (1985, April). *Utilizing microcomputer capabilities in the classroom: A look at word processing, graphics and electronic communication experiences in four case studies at third garde level.* Paper presented at the meeting of the American Educational Research Association, Chicago.

Kurth, R. J. (1988, April). *Process variables in writing instruction using word processing, word processing with voice synthesis, and no word processing.* Paper presented at the meeting of the American Educational Research Association, New Orleans.

Kurth, R. J., & Kurth, L. M. (1987, April). *A comparison of writing instruction using and word processing, word processing with voice synthesis, and no word processing in kindergarten and first grade.* Paper presented at the meeting of the American Educational Research Association, Washington, DC.

Lavin, R., & Sanders, J. (1983). *Longitudinal evaluation of the C/A/I Computer Assisted Instruction Title 1 Project: 1979-82.* Chelmsford, MA: Merrimack Education Center.

Lehrer, R., & deBernard, A. (1987). Language of learning and language of computing: The perceptual-language model. *Journal of Educational Psychology, 79,* 41–48.

Lehrer, R., Harckham, L. D., Archer, P., & Pruzek, R. M. (1986). Microcomputer-based instruction in special education. *Journal of Educational Computing Research, 2,* 337–355.

Lehrer, R., Levin, B. B., DeHart, P., & Comeaux, M. (1987). Voice-feedback as a scaffold for writing: A comparative study. *Journal of Educational Computing Research, 3,* 335–353.

Lehrer, R., & Randle, L. (1986). Problem solving, metacognition and composition: The effects of interactive software for first-grade children. *Journal of Educational Computing Research, 3,* 409–427.

Lehrer, R., Randle, L., & Sancilio, L. (1989). Learning pre-proof geometry with Logo. *Cognition and Instruction, 6,* 159–184.

Lehrer, R., & Smith, P. (1986a, April). *Logo learning: Is more better?* Paper presented at the meeting of the American Educational Research Association, San Francisco.

Lehrer, R., & Smith, P. C. (1986b, April). *Logo learning: Are two heads better than one?* Paper presented at the meeting of the American Educational Research Association, San Francisco.

Lesgold, A. M. (1983). A rationale for computer-based reading instruction. In A. C. Wilkinson (Ed.), *Classroom computers and cognitive science* (pp. 167–181). New York: Academic Press.

Lewis, C. (1981). A study of preschool children's use of computer programs. In D. Harris & L. Nelson-Heern (Eds.), *Proceedings of the National Educational Computing Conference* (pp. 272–274). Iowa City, IA: National Educational Computing Conference.

Lieberman, D. (1985). Research on children and microcomputers: A review of utilization and effects studies. In M. Chen & W. Paisley (Eds.), *Children and microcomputers: Research on the newest medium* (pp. 59–83). Beverly Hills: Sage.

Lin, S., Vallone, R. P., & Lepper, M. R. (1985, April). *Teaching early reading skills: Can computers help?* Paper presented at the meeting of the Western Psychological Association, San Jose, CA.

Lipinski, J. M., Nida, R. E., Shade, D. D., & Watson, J. A. (1986). The effects of microcomputers on young children: An examination of free-play choices, sex differences, and social interactions. *Journal of Educational Computing Research, 2,* 147–168.

MacArthur, C. A., & Shneiderman, B. (1986). Learning disabled students' difficulties in learning to use a word processor: Implications for instruction and software evaluation. *Journal of Learning Disabilities, 19,* 248–253.

McCollister, T. S., Burts, D. C., Wright, V. L., & Hildreth, G. J. (1986). Effects of computer-assisted instruction and teacher-assisted Instruction on arithmetic task achievement scores of kindergarten children. *Journal of Educational Research, 80,* 121–125.

McConnell, B. B. (1983). *Evaluation of computer instruction in math. Pasco School District. Final Report.* Pasco, WA: Pasco School District 1.

McCormick, L. (1987). Comparison of the effects of a microcomputer activity and toy play on social and communication behaviors of young children. *Journal of the Division for Early Childhood, 11,* 195–205.

Mevarech, Z. R. (1985). Computer-assisted instructional methods: A factorial study within mathematics disadvantaged classrooms. *Journal of Experimental Education, 54,* 22–27.

Mevarech, Z. R., & Rich, Y. (1985). Effects of computer-assisted mathematics instruction on disadvantaged pupil's cognitive and affective development. *Journal of Educational Research, 79,* 5–11.

Meyers, L. F. (1984). Unique contributions of microcomputers to language intervention with handicapped children. *Seminars in Speech and Language, 5,* 23–34.

Miller, G. E., & Emihovich, C. (1986). The effects of mediated programming instruction on preschool children's self-monitoring. *Journal of Educational Computing Research, 2*(3), 283–297.

Moxley, R. A., & Barry, P. A. (1985). Spelling with LEA on the microcomputer. *The Reading Teacher, 39,* 267–273.

Moxley, R. A., & Joyce, B. (1990). Early visual spelling on the microcomputer. *Journal of Computing in Childhood Education, 1*(3), 3–14.

Muhlstein, E. A., & Croft, D. J. (1986). *Using the microcomputer to enhance language experiences and the development of cooperative play among preschool children.* Cupertino, CA: De Anza College.

Muller, A. A., & Perlmutter, M. (1985). Preschool children's problem-solving interactions at computers and jigsaw puzzles. *Journal of Applied Developmental Psychology, 6,* 173–186.

Murphy, R. T., & Appel, L. R. (1984). *Evaluation of Writing to Read.* Princeton, NJ: Educational Testing Service.

Nastasi, B. K., & Clements, D. H. (1981). Research on cooperative learning: Implications for practice. *School Psychology Review, 20,* 110–131.

Nastasi, B. K., Clements, D. H., & Battista, M. T. (1990). Social-cognitive interactions, motivation, and cognitive growth in Logo programming and CAI problem-solving environments. *Journal of Educational Psychology, 82,* 150–158.

National Council of Teachers of Mathematics. (1988). *Curriculum and evaluation standards for school mathematics.* Reston, VA: Author.

Newman, R. S., & Berger, C. F. (1984). Children's numerical estimation: Flexibility in the use of counting. *Journal of Educational Psychology, 76,* 55–64.

Niemiec, R. P., & Walberg, H. J. (1984). Computers and achievement in the elementary schools. *Journal of Educational Computing Research, 1,* 435–440.

Norton, P., & Resta, V. (1986). Investigating the impact of computer instruction on elementary students' reading achievement. *Educational Technology, 26*(3), 35–41.

O'Connor, L., & Schery, T. K. (1986). A comparison of microcomputer-aided and traditional language therapy for developing communication skills in nonoral toddlers. *Journal of Speech and Hearing Disorders, 51,* 356–361.

Olson, J. K. (1988, August). *Microcomputers make manipulatives meaningful.* Paper presented at the meeting of the International Congress of Mathematics Education, Budapest, Hungary.

Papert, S. (1980). *Mindstorms: Children, computers, and powerful ideas.* New York: Basic Books.

Paris, C. L., & Morris, S. K. (1985, March). *The computer in the early childhood classroom: Peer helping and peer teaching.* Paper presented at the meeting of the Microworld for Young Children Conference, Cleege Park, MD.

Parker, J. (1984). *Some disturbing data: Sex differences in computer use.* Paper presented at the meeting of the National Educational Computing Conference, Dayton, OH.

Perfetti, C. A. (1983). Reading, vocabulary, and writing: Implications for computer-based instruction. In A. C. Wilkinson (Ed.), *Classroom computers and cognitive science* (pp. 145–163). New York: Academic Press.

Perlman, R. (1976). *Using computer technology to provide a creative learning environment for preschool children. AI Memo 360.* Cambridge, MA: MIT.

Perlmutter, M., Behrend, S., Kuo, F., & Muller, A. (1986). *Social influence on children's problem solving at a computer.* Unpublished manuscript, University of Michigan, Ann Arbor.

Perret-Clermont, A. (1980). *Social interaction and cognitive development in children.* New York: Academic Press.

Phenix, J., & Hannan, E. (1984). Word processing in the grade one classroom. *Language Arts, 61,* 804–812.

Piazza, C. L. (1988). Computer writing programs: Linking research and practice. In J. L. Hoot & S. B. Silvern (Eds.), *Writing with computers in the early grades* (pp. 196–218). New York: Teachers College Press.

Picard, A. J., & Guili, C. (1985). *Computers as a free-time activity in grades K-4: A two year study of attitudes and usage.* Unpublished manuscript, University of Hawaii, Honolulu.

Piel, J. A., & Baller, W. A. (1986). Effects of computer assistance on acquisition of Piagetian conceptualization among children of ages two to four. *AEDS Journal, 19,* 210–215.

Piestrup, A. M. (1981). *Preschool children use Apple II to test reading skills program.* Portola Valley, CA: Advanced Learning Technology.

Piestrup, A. M. (1982). *Young children use computer graphics.* Cambridge, MA: Harvard University, Graduate School of Design.

Porter, L. K. (1986). Designing picture-based software for the cognitively young. *Journal of the Division for Early Childhood, 10,* 231–239.

Prinz, P. M., & Nelson, K. E. (1985). "Alligator eats cookie": Acquisition of writing and reading skills by deaf children using the microcomputer. *Applied Psychologuistics, 6,* 283–306.

Prinz, P. M., Nelson, K. E., & Stedt, J. (1982). Early reading in young deaf children using microcomputer technology. *American Annals of the Deaf, 127,* 529–535.

Prinz, P. M., Pemberton, E., & Nelson, K. E. (1985). The ALPHA interactive microcomputer system for teaching reading, writing, and communication skills to hearing-impaired children. *American Annals of the Deaf, 130,* 444–461.

Ragosta, M., Holland, P., & Jamison, D. T. (1981). *Computer-assisted instruction and compensatory education: The ETS/LAUSD study.* Princeton, NJ: Educational Testing Service.

Reimer, G. (1985). Effects of a Logo computer programming experience on readiness for first grade, creativity, and self concept. "A pilot study in kindergarten." *AEDS Monitor, 23*(7–8), 8–12.

Riding, R., J., & Powell, S. D. (1986). The improvement of thinking skills in young children using computer activities: A replication and extension. *Educational Psychology, 6,* 179–183.

Riding, R., J., & Powell, S. D. (1987). The effect on reasoning, reading and number performance of computer-presented critical thinking activities in five-year-old children. *Educational Psychology, 7,* 55–65.

Riding, R., J., & Tite, H. C. (1985). The use of computer graphics to facilitate story telling in young children. *Educational Studies, 11,* 203–210.

Riel, M. (1985). The Computer Chronicles Newswire: A functional learning environment for acquiring literacy skills. *Journal of Educational Computing Research, 1,* 317–337.

Robinson, M. A., Feldman, P., & Uhlig, G. E. (1987). The effects of Logo in the elementary classroom: An analysis of selected recent dissertation research. *Education, 107,* 434–442.

Robinson, M. A., Gilley, W. F., & Uhlig, G. E. (1988). The effects of guided discovery Logo on SAT performance of first grade students. *Education, 109,* 226–230.

Robinson, M. A., & Uhlig, G. E. (1988). The effects of guided discovery Logo instruction on mathematical readiness and visual motor development in first grade students. *Journal of Human Behavior and Learning, 5,* 1–13.

Roblyer, M. D., Castine, W. H., & King, F. J. (1988). *Assessing the impact of computer-based instruction: A review of recent research.* New York: Haworth Press.

Rosegrant, T. J. (1985, April). *Using a microcomputer to assist children in their efforts to acquire beginning literacy.* Paper presented at the meeting of the American Educational Research Association, Chicago.

Rosegrant, T. J. (1986). Using the microcomputer as a scaffold for assisting beginning readers and writers. In J. Hoot (Ed.), *Computers in early childhood education: Issues and practices* (pp. 128–143). New York: Teachers College Press.

Rosegrant, T. J. (1988). Talking word processors for the early grades. In J. L. Hoot & S. B. Silvern (Eds.), *Writing with computers in the early grades* (pp. 143–159). New York: Teachers College Press.

Rosengren, K. S., Gross, D., Abrams, A. F., & Perlmutter, M. (1985, September). *An observational study of preschool children's computing activity.* Paper presented at the meeting of the "Perspectives on the Young Child and the Computer" conference, University of Texas at Austin, Austin.

Roth, S. F., & Beck, I. L. (1984, April). *Research and instructional issues related to the enhancement of children's decoding skills through a microcomputer program.* Paper presented at the meeting of the American Educational Research Association, New Orleans.

Schunk, D. H. (1984). Enhancing self-efficacy and achievement through rewards and goals: Motivational and information effects. *Journal of Educational Research, 78,* 29–34.

Schunk, D. H., & Hanson, A. R. (1985, April). *Influence of peer models on children's self-efficacy.* Paper presented at the meeting of the American Educational Research Association, Chicago.

Shade, D. D., Nida, R. E., Lipinski, J. M., & Watson, J. A. (1986). Microcomputers and preschoolers: Working together in a classroom setting. *Computers in the Schools, 3,* 53–61.

Shade, D. D., & Watson, J. A. (1985, April). *In mother's lap: The effect of microcomputers on mother teaching behavior and young children's classification skills.* Paper presented at the meeting of the Society for Research in Child Development, Toronto.

Shade, D. D., & Watson, J. A. (1987). Microworlds, mother teaching behavior, and concept formation in the very young child. *Early Child Development and Care, 28,* 97–113.

Sheingold, K. (1986). The microcomputer as a symbolic medium. In P. F. Campbell & G. G. Fein (Eds.), *Young children and microcomputers* (pp. 25–34). Reston, VA: Reston Publishing.

Sherman, J., Divine, K. P., & Johnson, B. (1985, May). An analysis of computer software preferences of preschool children. *Educational Technology,* pp. 39–41.

Schrock, S. A., Matthias, M., Anastasoff, J., Vensel, C., & Shaw, S. (1985, January). *Examining the effects of the microcomputer on a real world class: A naturalistic study.* Paper presented at the meeting of the Association for Educational Communications and Technology, Anaheim, CA.

Siegel, M. A., & Misselt, A. L. (1984). Adaptive feedback and review paradigm for computer-based drills. *Journal of Educational Psychology, 76,* 310–317.

Silfen, R., & Howes, A. C. (1984). A summer reading program with CAI: An evaluation. *Computers, Reading and Language Arts, 1*(4), 20–22.

Silvern, S. B., Countermine, T. A., & Williamson, P. A. (1988). Young children's interaction with a microcomputer. *Early Childhood Development and Care, 32,* 23–35.

Silvern, S. B., Lang, M. K., & Williamson, P. A. (1987). Social impact of video game play. In G. A. Fein (Ed.), *Playful meaning, meaningful play* (pp. 209–218). Champaign, IL: Human Kinetics Press.

Silvern, S. B., & Williamson, P. A. (1987). Aggression in young children and video game play. *Applied Developmental Psychology, 8,* 453–462.

Sivin, J. P., Lee, P. C., & Vollmer, A. M. (1985, April). *Introductory computer experiences with commercially-available software: Differences between three-year-olds and five-year-olds.* Paper presented at the meeting of the American Educational Research Association, Chicago, IL.

Slavin, R., Sharan, S., Kagan, S., Lazarowitz, R. H., Webb, C., & Schmuck, R. (1985). *Learning to cooperate, cooperating to learn.* New York: Plenum.

Smith, R. M. (1985). Effect of group size on computer learning in second grade students. *Dissertation Abstractions International, 46,* 72A. (University Microfilms No. DA8505588)

Smithy-Willis, D., Riley, M., & Smith, D. (1982, November/December). Visual discrimination and preschoolers. *Educational Computer Magazine,* pp. 19–20.

Spillman, C. V., Hutchcraft, G. R., Olliff, C., Lutz, J. P., & Kray, A. (1986, March). *Writing via reading software: An empirical study.* Paper presented at the meeting of the Southern Association on Children Under Six, Orlando, FL.

Sprigle, J. E., & Schaefer, L. (1984). Age, gender, and spatial knowledge influences on pre-schoolers' computer programming ability. *Early Child Development and Care, 14,* 243–250.

Steg, D. R., Vaidya, S., & Hamdan, P. F. (1982). Long term gains from early intervention through technology: An eleven year report. *Journal of Educational Technology Systems, 11,* 203–214.

Strand, E. B. (1987, April). *Observations of preschoolers' problem-solving experiences with Logo.* Paper presented at the meeting of the American Educational Research Association, Washington, DC.

Strein, W., & Kachman, W. (1984). Effects of computer games on young children's cooperative behavior: An exploratory study. *Journal of Research and Development in Education, 18,* 40–43.

Sudia, D. (1985). *The computer's effect on the learning of new words.* Unpublished master's thesis, Kean College of New Jersey.

Swan, K., Guerrero, F., Mitrani, M., & Schoener, J. (1989, March). *Honing in on the target: Who among the educationally disadvantaged benefits most from what CBI?* Paper presented at the meeting of the American Educational Research Association, San Francisco.

Swigger, K., & Campbell, J. (1981). Computers and the nursery school. In D. Harris & L. Nelson-Heern (Eds.), *Proceedings of the National Educational Computing Conference* (pp. 264–268). Iowa City, IA: National Educational Computing Conference.

Swigger, K. M., Campbell, J., & Swigger, B. K. (1983, January/February). Preschool children's preferences of different types of CAI programs. *Educational Computer Magazine,* pp. 38–40.

Swigger, K. M., & Swigger, B. K. (1984). Social patterns and computer use among preschool children. *AEDS Journal, 17,* 35–41.

Teague, G. V., Wilson, R. M., & Teague, M. G. (1984). Use of computer assisted instruction to improve spelling proficiency of low achieving first graders. *AEDS Journal, 17,* 30–35.

Vaidya, S., & Mckeeby, J. (1984, September). Computer turtle graphics: Do they affect children's thought processes? *Educational Technology,* pp. 46–47.

VanLehn, K. (1981). *Bugs are not enough: Empirical studies of bugs, impasses and repairs in procedural skills.* Palo Alto, CA: Xerox Palo Alto Research Center.

von Stein, J. H. (1982). An evaluation of the microcomputer as a facilitator of indirect learning for the kindergarten child. *Dissertation Abstractions International, 43,* 72A. (University Microfilms No. DA8214463).

Vygotsky, L. S. (1978). Internalization of higher psychological functions. In M. Cole, V. John-Steiner, S. Scribner, & E. Souberman (Eds.), *Mind in society* (pp. 52–57). Cambridge, MA: Harvard University Press.

Wallace, J. (1985). Write first, then read. *Educational Leadership, 42,* 20–24.

Warash, B. G. (1984, April). *Computer language experience approach.* Paper presented at the meeting of the National Council of Teachers of English Spring Conference, Columbus, OH.

Watkins, M. W., & Abram, S. (1985, April). Reading CAI with first grade students. *The Computing Teacher,* pp. 43–45.

Watson, J. A., Chadwick, S. S., & Brinkley, V. M. (1986). Special education technologies for young children: Present and future learning scenarios with related research literature. *Journal of the Division for Early Childhood, 10,* 197–208.

Watson, J. A., Nida, R. E., & Shade, D. D. (1986). Educational issues concerning young children and microcomputers: Lego with Logo? *Early Child Development and Care, 23,* 299–316.

Weir, S. (1987). *Cultivating minds: A Logo casebook.* New York: Harper & Row.

Weir, S., Russell, S. J., & Valente, J. A. (1982, September). Logo: An approach to educating disabled children. *BYTE,* pp. 342–360.

Whitmer, J. E., & Miller, M. (1987, October). *The effects of writing on reading abilities: A comparison of first grade writing programs with and without computer technology.* Paper presented at the meeting of the Annual Reading Conference, Greeley, CO.

Williams, R. A., & Beeson, B. S. (1986-1987). The "holding power" of the computers: A study of young children's computer time. *The Teacher Educator, 23*(3), 8–14.

Wright, J. L., & Samaras, A. S. (1986). Play worlds and microworlds. In P. F. Campbell & G. G. Fein (Eds.), *Young children and microcomputers* (pp. 73–86). Reston, VA: Reston Publishing.

Author Index

Italics denote reference pages.

A

Abbott, D., 100, *111*
Abery, B. 45. *47*
Abidim, R. R., 172, 173, *181*
Able-Boone, H., 102, *107*
Abram, S., 215, *245*
Abrams, A. F., 190, *244*
Abrams, P., 105, *110*
Adams, M. K., 98, *108*
Adcock, L., 23, 24, *53*
Adubato, S. A., 98, *108*
Afflect, G., 94, *108*
Ainsworth, M D. S., 4, *5,* 13, *46*
Akdag, F. S., 228, 229, *236*
Alderman, D. L., 226, *236*
Alexander, D., 188, *236*
Alexander, K., 168, 169, *182*
Allen, D. A., 94, 95, 96, *108*
Anastoff, J., 191, *244*
Anderson, K., 96, *108*
Anderson, R. B., 35, *52*
Andrews, S., 180, *182*
Antrobus, J., 129, *149*
Apolloni, T., 81, 82, *84*
Appel, L. R., 217, *242*
Archer, P., 193, *241*
Ascione, F. R., 201, *237*
Asher, S., 113, 114, 119, 121, 122, 124, 126, 127, 136, *142, 148*
Atkinson, R. C., 215, *236*
Austin, A. M., 190, 191, 196, *240*

B

Baer, D., 14, *46*
Bagnato, S. J., 43, *51,* 59, *84,* 106, *108*
Bailey, D. B., Jr., 38, 39, 41, 42, *46,* 52, 105, *108*
Bailey, D. J., 92, 93, 104, *108, 111*
Bailey, E. J., 69, 70, 74, *84*
Baillargeon, R., 188, *239*
Baker, B. L., 79, *84,* 98, *108*
Baker, J. A., 33, *51*
Bakeman, R., 116, *142*
Baldwin, V. L., 75, 78, *85*
Ball, R., 172, *184*
Baller, W. A., 229, *243*
Bandura, A., 16, *46*
Banet, B., 25, *48*
Bangert-Drowns, R. L., 218, 220, 232, *236, 241*
Barker, W. F., 208, 228, 230, *236*
Barnes, B. J., 187, 193, *236*
Barnett, D. W., 42 44, *46,* 60, *86*
Barnett, W. S., 32, 33, *46,* 59, 61, 63, 66, 68, *84, 86*
Barocas, R., 157, *185*
Barry, P. A., 215, *242*
Basham, R., 158, 162, *182*
Battista, M. T., 200, 207, 208, 209, 211, 212, 227, 230, *236, 238, 242*
Baudonniere, P. M., 116, 117, *142, 148*
Baumrind, D., 130, *142, 143*
Bearison, D. J., 210, *236*

247

Subject Index

DATE DUE

DEMCO 38-297